CHARLES S. PEIRCE
SELECTED WRITINGS

(VALUES IN A UNIVERSE OF CHANCE)

Edited,
with an Introduction
and Notes by
PHILIP P. WIENER

DOVER PUBLICATIONS, INC.
NEW YORK

Published in Canada by General Publishing Com-
pany, Ltd., 30 Lesmill Road, Don Mills, Toronto,
Ontario.
Published in the United Kingdom by Constable
and Company, Ltd., 10 Orange Street, London,
W.C. 2.

This Dover edition, first published in 1966, is an
unabridged and unaltered republication of the
work originally published by Doubleday & Company, Inc. in 1958. *Values in a Universe of Chance*
was the main title of the original edition of the
work, but here appears as a subtitle.

191
P378s

Library of Congress Catalog Card Number: 66-20418

Manufactured in the United States of America
Dover Publications, Inc.
180 Varick Street
New York, N. Y. 10014

Contents

Introduction   vii

Science, Materialism and Idealism

1. The Place of Our Age in the History of
   Civilization   3
2. Questions Concerning Certain Faculties
   Claimed for Man   15
3. Some Consequences of Four Incapacities   39
4. Critical Review of Berkeley's Idealism   73

Pragmaticism: A Philosophy of Science

5. The Fixation of Belief   91
6. How to Make Our Ideas Clear   113
7. Notes on Positivism   137
8. The Architecture of Theories   142
9. The Doctrine of Necessity   160
10. What Pragmatism Is   180
11. Issues of Pragmaticism   203

Lessons from the History of Scientific Thought

12. Lessons of the History of Science   227
13. Lowell Lectures on the History of Science
    (1892)   233
14. Kepler   250
15. Conclusion of the History of Science Lectures   257
16. The Nineteenth Century: Notes   261
17. The Century's Great Men in Science   265
18. Letters to Samuel P. Langley, and "Hume on
    Miracles and Laws of Nature"   275

Science and Education

19. Research and Teaching in Physics   325
20. Definition and Function of a University   331
21. Logic and a Liberal Education   336
22. Logic of Mathematics in Relation to Education   338

Science and Religion

23. Science and Immortality   345
    The Breakdown of the Mechanial Philosophy   348
    The Marriage of Religion and Science   350
    What Is Christian Faith?   353
    A Neglected Argument for the Reality of God   358
24. Letters to Lady Welby   380
    Bibliographical Note   433
    Index   435

Introduction

Two main purposes have guided the planning of the present collection of Peirce's writings: first, to introduce the general reader to the many sides of the most versatile, profound, and original philosopher that the United States has ever produced; second, to include unpublished and inaccessible material in which Peirce presented the cultural or humanistic aspects of science and philosophy and which have been neglected by students and editors of his work. Of course, it is hoped that the variety of specimens of Peirce's writings offered here will whet the reader's appetite for more, so that he will wish to look into the latest eight-volume Harvard University Press edition of Peirce's *Collected Papers*. But he should not be surprised to find some of our selections ("The Place of Our Age in the History of Civilization," the "Lowell Lectures on the History of Science," "Hume on the Laws of Nature," "Letter to President D. C. Gilman," and "Letters to Lady Welby") missing from the Harvard edition, since no edition of Peirce is complete. Since it is unlikely that there will ever be a complete edition of Peirce's scattered writings, fragments, letters, various drafts of a single essay, outlines of unfinished volumes, notes on earlier papers, U.S. Coast Survey Reports, translations, and reviews, the best guide for the further study of Peirce is the bibliography of his writings, arranged chronologically, by Arthur W. Burks, editor of the latest Harvard edition.

Because there is no full biography of Charles S. Peirce,

each topic has for the most part been arranged chronologically here, so that the reader may follow the development and turns of Peirce's thought and interests. Peirce was fascinated by so many complex and difficult subjects that towards the end of his life he compared himself to "a mere table of contents, so abstract, a very snarl of twine." He hoped that some day an interested scholar would bring his writings together in some orderly way so that their general philosophical message could be preserved.

The gist of that message lies in Peirce's profound sense of the fallibility and yet supreme value of honest, persevering inquiry by individual minds sharing a common desire to learn and a common faith that an indefinite community of such investigators must sooner or later discover the truth and the reality corresponding to it. He joins a high idealism of the inner world of values to his "Common-Sense Realism," or belief in an independent world of external things with qualities existing pretty nearly as we ordinarily experience them or instinctively react to them. If water quenches our thirst and washes our bodies clean, then water really has these properties, and anything else that produces the same effects has a valid claim to be considered or called "water." No vain world of "mere" appearances or obscure realm of "things in themselves," such as we find in theories of "Being as such" in the history of "ontology" from Plato to the existentialists in our own day, plays an effective role in our learning or conduct, and hence, on Peirce's pragmatic rule, most metaphysics of the ontological sort is "moonshine or gibberish," of no significance for science or ordinary common-sense knowledge.

Those who decry the narrow practicalism and materialistic commercialism of American life and thought, and ignorantly identify opportunism with "pragmatism," can find no better refutation of their misconception than Peirce's writings. His disinterested quest for a truly humane synthesis of common sense, science, philosophy, and religion appears in his earliest public pronouncements and persists in his last writings. Despite his many technical contributions to mathematics, logic, physics, astronomy, and psychology, his chief contribution and importance as a thinker may well turn out to be his logic and ethics of science in relation to civilization and education. Students of American culture will find a rich vein in Peirce's reflections on the nineteenth century and its great men. Like his contemporaries Gibbs and Veblen, Peirce was too far ahead of his times to be appreciated in his own lifetime.

Charles S. Peirce is not an easy philosopher to read or to understand for several reasons. First, he wrote for a motley variety of readers, ranging from scientific specialists and technical philosophers to the lay audience of his public lectures, without sugar-coating his encyclopedic erudition or abandoning his ideals of logical rigor and philosophic integrity. Second, he was an original and independent investigator concerned primarily with research and pioneering in exact sciences and philosophy rather than with ladling out pleasing or consoling generalities acceptable to the respectable conformist. Third, he found it necessary to invent new technical terms—often derived from Greek roots, e.g., tychism, agapism, synechism for defining his key ideas of chance, love, and logic—and thus employed a vocabulary remote from both ordinary and scientific discourse. Finally, he had a steadfast faith in the power of truth to liberate men from moral confusion *provided* they were willing to inquire arduously and subordinate private interests to publicly verifiable knowledge. Tragically enough, he was to become a solitary thinker exploring ideas beyond the range of most of his contemporaries. Yet Peirce's philosophic vision is able to play an increasing role in shaping our philosophical attitudes to the central problem of our culture, namely, the humanizing of the sciences and their increasing role in dealing with the moral and educational phases of our industrial age.

This problem of humanizing sciences is not a new one, but it appears in different guise with each great burst of scientific advance. Among the Greeks who gave us our first lessons in mathematics, theoretical physics, biology, medicine, psychology, and social sciences as well as in history, rhetoric, drama, poetry, music, painting, architecture, and sculpture—there appeared the great classical systems of philosophy, the synoptic visions of the leading ideas that unite the mind of man to nature: Thales, Pythagoras, Parmenides, Heraclitus, Democritus, Socrates, Plato, Aristotle, the Sophists, the Stoics and Epicureans, the Cynics and Skeptics, the Neoplatonic mystics. A similar galaxy of giant stars marks the aftermath of the Renaissance in the seventeenth century, called by Whitehead "the century of genius": Bacon, Hobbes, Boyle, Newton, Locke, Descartes, Fermat, Pascal, Malebranche, Spinoza, Leibniz, Leuwenhoek, Grotius, Suarez, and others. The latter part of the nineteenth century witnessed a third powerful growth of mathematics, logic, physics, biology, and psychology in the works of Boole, Frege, Weierstrass, Dedekind, Cantor, Klein, Liouville, Poincaré, Maxwell, Gibbs, Mendeleef, Wallace, Darwin, Huxley, Freud, and others who with a similar impetus due to their scientific training were able to modify traditional philosophic thinking in harmony with the new scientific discoveries.

Among these scientifically bent philosophers in the United States was a group at Harvard in the 1870s (Chauncey Wright, Charles S. Peirce, William James, O. W. Holmes, Jr., F. E. Abbot, St. John Green, John Fiske) who met informally to discuss the controversies provoked by the rise of the sciences and "positivism," the name given by Auguste Comte to the view that the sciences alone provide reliable knowledge and progress. Such a scientific philosophy, positivists claimed, was inevitably bound to displace the older "theological" and "metaphysical" stages of thought which featured man's animistic and scholastic ways of thinking in the past. Darwin's theory of natural selection with his scientific account of the descent of man from the primates was the burning focus of the controversy over positivism because the advance of the sciences seemed to threaten the traditional religious basis of morals and civilization. In Europe the leading positivists (after Auguste Comte and his followers) were Ernst Mach, the great Viennese physicist, Herbert Spencer, the British evolutionary sociologist, Pierre Duhem, the French Catholic physical chemist and historian of science, Poincaré, the mathematician, Karl Pearson, the statistician, and many others who urged the extension of scientific methods to all human experience, although some hesitated and some refused to include moral and social issues under this extended scientific point of view.

Charles S. Peirce made it his life work to analyze, as thoroughly as any single mind could, the basic logic and structure of the sciences before committing himself to a philosophical world view or ethical conclusions about the human uses of science.

It is from this standpoint—the meaning of scientific thought in its bearings on human conduct—that pragmatism may best be viewed as the philosophical contribution of American thought to the urgent problem of humanizing the sciences; that is, creating the attitudes among scientists and the public that will converge on mankind's common problems: bigotry, ignorance, poverty, war, disease. William James is better known popularly and internationally than Charles Peirce because James wrote with more emotional appeal and literary skill in expressing his sensitivity to the common man's mental, moral, and religious problems; Peirce approached philosophy with the rarer and more technical instruments of exact logic, mathematical analysis, and the history of science and philosophy. Although James credited Peirce with the first formulation of pragmatism as a doctrine of meaning and method of inquiry, Peirce was more analytical and more precise than James, and finally labeled his own logical formulation *pragmaticism* in order to distinguish it from the psychological version of James's *pragmatism*.

One reason that Peirce insulated himself from the psychological approach of James and the idealists (from Berkeley to Hegel) was that he condemned the subjectivism that tinged all such philosophies. The relativizing of all knowledge and reduction of all meaning to sensations or ideas leaves us with the particular things of experience and uniformities or laws as final fixtures of reality. This relegates the universal traits of existence and general principles of logic, science, and ethics to the passing figments of the mind.

That the spontaneous variety and regularities of external nature are continuous with the life of the mind is the objective basis of Peirce's realism as opposed to the nominalistic view that the characters of objects when known are only names for our ideas or opinions about them. The *meaning* of any conception, like the hardness of diamonds, is to be found in the total conceivable consequences which the *object* of our conception has on our conduct, e.g., we can use the general property of a diamond's hardness in drilling through most rocks. But the *truth* which we learn by observing whether our present and future experience conforms to the predicted behavior of the diamond reveals a reality which is independent of anybody's opinion or idea of hardness. Thus Peirce distinguishes more clearly and sharply than James between the subjective meaning of our beliefs and the objective properties of what our beliefs imply concerning objects and events which we are compelled to recognize logically as independent of our thoughts and labels.

Peirce devoted much of his logical powers to the analysis of signs in everyday and scientific language, so that much of contemporary semantics is a continuation of Peirce's theories. His penetrating discussions of icons, indices, and symbols are still very useful in dealing with the problems of the theory of knowledge and meaning.

In the field of symbolic logic he stands with Boole, Frege, and Schröder as the forerunner of the calculus of propositions, classes, and relations, and showed how symbolic logic could be used to investigate the foundations of mathematics. He rejected the view that probability was merely the measure of our ignorance by showing that the degree of belief varies with evidence derived from previous experience of the frequency or infrequency of classes of events; for example, because infant mortality has been higher than the death rate among other age groups, it is more probable that a newborn baby will die in the first year than that he will die in the next twenty years. Insurance companies also base their premium rates on frequency-tables of life expectation at different ages, based on past tables of death rates which enable one to predict for large numbers of people in various age groups the probabilities of living another ten or twenty years, etc. Now, the idea

that a scientific estimate of the likelihood of events of a
certain kind is possible when we are dealing with large
numbers of individuals encouraged Peirce to find in the
idea of chance a common denominator for the logic of the
physical, biological, and social sciences. This still left the
individual particle, living creature, and human being partly
undetermined as to the ultimate laws of its behavior because these very laws were conceived by Peirce to be probability averages of the net or resultant effect of a large number of causes. Similar considerations in the physics of gases
had led Maxwell and Gibbs to a statistical form of laws
of thermodynamics, and it was the transition from their
views to modern quanta mechanics that Peirce was witness
to. Sensing the importance of the fundamental changes that
were taking place in physics, he contributed his share to
the quest for a new logical framework for scientific theory,
and to the breakdown of the mechanistic view of nature.

Peirce's views of logic, purpose, and free will in a universe of chance *and* law contrast sharply with the mechanistic fatalism of a Schopenhauer and the *fin de siècle*
pessimism of a Hardy, Ibsen, Mark Twain, or Shaw. His
philosophy also aimed at disillusioning the overoptimistic
believers in mechanical evolutionary progress.

Bergson's *Creative Evolution* and his appeal to an *anti-
scientiste* intuition, F. H. Bradley's relapse into immediate
experience, and Husserl's idealistic plunge into a bottom-
less analysis of the contents of a universal mind left Peirce
with his old conviction that philosophy was falling back
into the impasse of anti-intellectual nominalism and subjectivism. Whether today's existentialism and other revivals of
anti-intellectualism are not vindications of Peirce's philosophical criticisms we leave as a suggestion to the reader.

There is enough variety and depth in the selections we
have made from the scattered writings of Peirce to introduce the reader to the stimulating ways of thinking of a
philosopher who was so thoroughly a master of exact science and so well versed in the history of scientific and philosophic thought.

Three different ways of looking at the world are linked

by Peirce to three types of mind: the businessman's, the artist's, and the scientist's. The first looks at things, and unfortunately often at people, as means for making money. The artist looks at the qualities he perceives in objects or persons as occasions or materials for creating works of beauty. The scientist is impressed by the mysterious course of nature and restlessly desires to unravel and exhibit its wondrous patterns. Taking for granted that his countrymen needed no special urge to continue their commercial life, Peirce stressed the esthetic and moral values of the evolution of science, and of disinterested pursuits such as he had himself experienced as a physicist, mathematician, astronomer, historian, and philosopher.

Unlike most professional philosophers—"seminary minds" Peirce called the bookishly trained products of the graduate school seminars—Peirce was a "laboratory mind" who did not regard a question or solution significant unless it could be brought to the test of some observations or experiments such as we find in the research practices and techniques of scientists and analysts. Peirce was early initiated by his father, the great Harvard mathematician Benjamin Peirce, into the fascinating problems and methods of mathematics, physics, and astronomy. After graduating from Harvard in 1859 and taking a master's degree in chemistry, he was employed as a physicist and astronomer in the United States Coast and Geodetic Survey for thirty years, making many scientific visits abroad. He attained international recognition as an astronomer, based on his pendulum experiments for measuring g (gravitational acceleration) and *Photometric Researches*, the only book of his published in his lifetime. He had collaborated with his father in articles for the mathematical journals, and continued on his own to contribute articles on the improvement of traditional logic along the mathematical lines so fruitfully employed by George Boole, Augustus De Morgan, and William Stanley Jevons. His own logic of relations marks a great advance toward modern logic and the calculus of probabilities.

His only teaching position was that of an instructor in Logic (1879–84) at the Johns Hopkins University, the first graduate school in the United States. Its first president, Daniel C. Gilman, had assembled such distinguished minds as Cayley, Sylvester, Lord Kelvin, and Rowland among the scientists, and George Sylvester Morris, G. Stanley Hall, and William James (as an occasional lecturer, since Harvard would not let him go) among the philosophers; John Dewey, Josiah Royce, and Thorstein Veblen were among the first to obtain the Ph.D. in philosophy at Johns Hopkins while Peirce was teaching logic. Dewey tells us that he did not appreciate Peirce's work in logic until twenty years later.

At the Johns Hopkins University, Peirce did not attract large numbers of students as did G. Stanley Hall in his course on the new psychology or George S. Morris on the consolations of Hegelian idealism. He also ran into personal difficulties with Sylvester, the British visiting professor of mathematics, over a question of priority of discovery of an abstract theory (nonions). In any case, after five years (1879–84) of lecturing on Logic to no more than a dozen students in any of his courses, Peirce was not reappointed and never resumed a teaching position in any college. Perhaps his irregular habits, divorcing a New England woman (Melusina Fay) of a clerical family and marrying a French girl (Juliette Tourtalai), and an irascible way of expressing his moral indignation (on behalf of the radical Unitarian "scientific theist" Francis E. Abbot against Royce's condemnation) all led to his becoming *persona non grata* in academic circles, especially at Harvard; there President Eliot refused to listen to William James's pleas for Peirce and declared him off the reservation after a bitter correspondence between Peirce and the trustees, when Peirce asked that Royce be reprimanded for his scathing condemnation of Abbot. Royce later apologized to Peirce, and was deeply affected by the news of Abbot's suicide.

From 1900 to his death in 1914 from a cancer that had afflicted him for two years, Peirce lived with his French wife in extreme poverty; there was no money even for a decent burial. His widow sold all his manuscripts to Harvard University for $500. It was not until 1931 that the first of six volumes of Peirce's *Collected Papers*, edited by

Charles Hartshorne and Paul Weiss, was published by Harvard University Press; only in 1958 are the seventh and eighth volumes, edited by Arthur W. Burks, expected. Enough writings remain to fill several more volumes.

Although he had been honored by membership in the National Academy of Sciences, Peirce had to eke out a living by doing much hack work for philosophical dictionaries, the *Century Dictionary*, the Smithsonian Institution, reviews for the *Nation*, the *North American Review*, and popular journals so that he could go on to compose the systematic development of his philosophy that would serve as a guide to the scientific and moral problems of mankind. The critical and speculative articles which he wrote for the *Journal of Speculative Philosophy* in 1868, before he was thirty, already reveal a daring and profound philosophical grasp of the main problems and logical power to deal with them. Three years later (1871) he showed his dialectical skill in writing for the *North American Review* a masterly critique of Berkeley's nominalism, defending a form of scholastic realism in which general principles, laws or habits, universal qualities and relations are imbedded in individual realities. He ended his review with a plea for more disinterested scientific and speculative thought against the narrow practicalism of those who saw only commercial and technological uses for science. A nation or people that failed to see that truth and justice were living realities, as objectively real as the hardness of diamonds or laws of the physical world, was doomed to live in confusion.

The long warfare between science and religion seemed to Peirce to be logically unnecessary, and his "musements" on the reality of God are highly suggestive, no matter how unconvincing they may appear to the skeptical, or to the dogmatically committed mind.

Even those who disagree with Peirce's speculations do not hesitate to grant that he is still one of the most powerfully stimulating and suggestive philosophers of our troubled age.

The formidable list of American and European philosophers markedly influenced by Peirce's seminal thought includes among others William James, Josiah Royce, John

Dewey, George H. Mead, C. I. Lewis, H. M. Sheffer, Morris R. Cohen, Ernest Nagel, Norbert Wiener, F. P. Ramsey, R. B. Braithwaite, Hans Reichenbach, Ernst Schröder, Jürgen von Kempski, and the editors and commentators of Peirce. Peirce's technical, scientific, and logical contributions have already been absorbed in the fast-moving current of research.

The present collection aims not only to acquaint the general reader with the elementary ideas in the logic of science to which Peirce devoted most of his life of inquiry, but to show a side of his thought usually neglected by technical philosophers, namely, his historical, humanistic interests. These pertain to his early concern with the linguistic, cultural, and evolutionary phases of thought; they appear in his study of the place of science in a Christian civilization, the impact of the history of science on philosophy, the analysis and classification of signs and their role in scientific, ethical, and esthetic thought. Much of what passes as novel in recent discussions of semantics and "the wisdom enshrined in common-sense language" seems like old hat when we read some of Peirce's penetrating remarks on the various functions of signs.

Most important of all for understanding the man and the deep humanistic undercurrent of even his abstruse speculations and technical researches is Peirce's view of higher education. A college or university should be a community of scholars devoted to study and to enlarging the sphere of knowledge so that teaching may spread the desire to learn how things really are, instead of aiming at increasing the prospects of financial or social success for its graduates.

Nearly a generation after Peirce's death at the age of seventy-five, which terminated all his plans for finishing his many inquiries and cherished projects, scholars throughout the world first began to appreciate the fact that the United States had produced a great philosopher of the stature and encyclopedic sweep of a Leibniz. Why such a mind should have been allowed to die in abject poverty and seclusion is partly explained by the failure of American university officials like President Eliot either to forgive Peirce's refusal

to conform or to encourage the unique originality and depth
of his thinking. Philosophy and learning in America were in
the nineteenth century still tied to the training of respectable ministers and lawyers, so that iconoclasts like Whitman,
Veblen, or Peirce struggled in vain to receive social recognition or support. Yet the rapid growth of the sciences,
technology, and industry was shaping the course of people's
lives more powerfully than genteel academic traditions in
America. The cultural reconstruction needed in our universities, law courts, government, and other social institutions
cried out for scholars, writers, artists, scientists, reformers,
and philosophers who could think experimentally and
bravely of the future. Peirce's pragmatic philosophy of inquiry was a plea for disinterested pursuit of truth and justice which he proclaimed as "two of the greatest powers
on earth." Hence, the long warfare between science and a
truly philosophical religion seemed unnecessary to Peirce,
convinced as he was of the reality of a living, growing God,
a conception that surely influenced his friend William
James. The last writings of Peirce, like his first, deal with
religious philosophy and the power of signs.

Peirce approved of Lady Welby's dicta that "language
is only the extreme form of expression" and that "life itself
may be considered (should be recognized) as *Expression*."
He inquired of Lady Welby what method she had for analyzing signs in her proposed *Encyclopaedia Britannica* article on "Significs," for Peirce urged, the study of Methods
is "about what Morals comes to: If you have considered
well your methods I shall certainly get some good, some
practical applications to my own doings [in the analysis of
signs] from what you tell me, while in any case it is not
likely to be altogether profitless for you to set down for the
benefit of another what you so often ruminate upon for
yourself, since one generally gains some new *aperçu* in
putting one's personal meditations into shape for communication."

Peirce's meditations on logic as rooted in the social principle, and on the role of signs in ethical deliberation, are
likely to be profitable for some generations to come, which

will continue to be confronted with the complex scientific and technological changes that threaten to alienate men from one another and from themselves when our common humanity and self-control are abandoned by greedy manipulators and shortsighted users of our sciences.

The social and ethical idealism which motivated Peirce's pragmatic method is evident in his emphasis on the collective character of all advances in civilization, including not only science but the daily labors of mankind, even when the ideal is not consciously pursued as a social good. In order to dissociate his own version of pragmatism from individualistic and materialistic opportunism, Peirce added the following idealistic note, in 1893, which he was planning to incorporate in a book, *Search for a Method:*

"To say that man accomplishes nothing but that to which his endeavors are directed would be a cruel condemnation of the great bulk of mankind and their families. But, without directly striving for it, they perform all that civilization requires, and bring forth another generation to advance history another step. Their fruit is, therefore, collective; it is the achievement of the whole people. What is it, then, that the whole people is about, what is this civilization that is the outcome of history, but is never completed? We cannot expect to attain a complete conception of it; but we can see that it is a gradual process, that it involves a realization of ideas in man's consciousness and in his works, and that it takes place by virtue of man's capacity for learning, and by experience continually pouring upon him ideas that he has not yet acquired. We may say that it is the process whereby man with all his miserable littlenesses, becomes gradually more and more imbued with the spirit of God, in which Nature and History are rife. We are also told to believe in a world to come; but the idea is itself too vague to contribute much to the perspicuity of ordinary ideas. It is a common observation that those who dwell continually upon their expectations are apt to become oblivious to the requirements of their actual station. The great principle of logic is self-surrender, which does not mean that the self is to lie low for the sake of an ultimate triumph. It may turn out so, but that must not be the governing purpose.

"When we come to the great principle of continuity and see how all is fluid and every point directly partakes the being of every other, it will appear that individualism and falsity are one and the same. Meantime, we know that man is not whole as long as he is single, that he is essentially a possible member of society. Especially, one man's experience is nothing if it stands alone. If he sees what others cannot, we call it hallucination. It is not 'my' experience but 'our' experience that has to be thought of; and this 'us' has indefinite possibilities.

"Neither must we understand the practical in any low and sordid sense. Individual action is a means and not our end. Individual pleasure is not our end; we are all putting our shoulders to the wheel for an end that none of us can catch more than a glimpse at—that which the generations are working out. But we can see that the development of embodied ideas is what it will consist in.—1893."

Though close to Hegel's Absolute Idea unfolding itself in history, Peirce's idealism differs from Hegel's in important ways: it disclaims ultimate knowledge of the final purpose of civilization; it denies absolute certainty to any metaphysics of history; it prefers the tentative self-corrective method of science to the absolute pretensions of dialectics; it does not identify the absolute goal of history with the aims of any ruler; it values the individual above the state.

Thirteen years later Peirce went back to these notes on his first pragmatic essays and wrote: "I did not mean to say that acts, which are more strictly singular than anything, could constitute the purport, or adequate proper interpretations of any symbol. I compared action to the finale of the symphony of thought, belief being a demicadence. Nobody conceives that the few bars at the end of a musical movement are the purpose of the movement. They may be called its upshot. But the figure would not bear detailed application . . . Pragmaticism makes thought ultimately apply to action exclusively—to conceived action. It makes thinking consist in the living inferential metaboly of symbols whose purport lies in conditional general resolutions to act. As for the ultimate purpose of thought which must be the ultimate purpose of everything, it is beyond human comprehension; but according to the stage of approach which my thought has made of it—with aid from many persons among whom I may mention Royce (in the *World and the Individual*), Schiller (in his *Riddles of the Sphinx*) as well, by the way, as the famous poet Friedrich Schiller (in his *Aesthetische Briefe*), Henry James the Elder (in his *Substance and Shadow* and in his conversations), together with Swedenborg himself—it is by the indefinite replication of self-control upon self-control that the *vir* [man] is begotten, and by action, through thought, he grows an esthetic ideal, not for the behoof of his own poor noddle merely, but as the share which God permits him to have in the work of creation. This ideal, by modifying the rules of self-control modifies action, and so experience too —both the man's own and that of others. . . ."

Peirce's doctrine of fallibilism reminds us that while we seek ideals leading in our moral development to firmer satisfaction with a described ideal, and in that sense true or real, we must not be too sure of our choice: "Just as it is not the self-righteous man who brings multitudes to a sense of sin, but the man who is most deeply conscious that he is himself a sinner, and it is only by a sense of sin that man can escape its thraldom; so it is not the man who thinks he knows it all that can bring other men to feel their need of learning, and it is only a deep sense that one is miserably ignorant that can spur one on in the toilsome path of learning."

Parts of the following selected writings have been omitted (as indicated by dots) whenever a passage is repetitious, out of date, or of very minor relevance. All bracketed parts are the editor's insertions. All footnotes other than Peirce's are indicated as "Editor's note."

Thanks are due to Dr. Irwin C. Lieb, editor of *Peirce's Letters to Lady Welby*, and to Mr. Reverdy Whitlock, publisher of these valuable letters, for their very kind permission to reproduce those portions of the letters and Dr. Lieb's editorial notes included here. The Philosophy Department of Harvard University has permitted me to publish for the first time some of Peirce's Lectures on the History of Science and other notes.

I am deeply grateful to Mr. Jason Epstein and his Anchor Books staff for their very competent editing and friendly cooperation.

1839: September 10. Tuesday. Born.

1840: Christened.

1841: Made a visit to Salem which I distinctly remember.

1842: July 31. Went to church for the first time.

1843: Attended a marriage.

1844: Fell violently in love with Miss W[are] and commenced my education.

1845: Moved into new house on Quincy St.

1846: Stopped going to Ma'am Sessions and began to go to Miss Ware's—a very pleasant school where I learnt much and fell violently in love with another Miss W whom for distinction's sake I shall designate Miss W'.

1847: Began to be most seriously and hopelessly in love. Sought to drown my care by taking up the subject of chemistry—an antidote which long experience enables me to recommend as sovereign.

1848: Went to dwell in town with my uncle C. H. Mills and went to school to the Rev. T. H. Sullivan, where I received my first lessons in elocution.

1849: In consequence of playing truant and laving in the frog-pond, was taken ill. On my recovery, I was recalled to Cambridge and admitted a member of the Cambridge High School.

1850: Wrote a "History of Chemistry."

1851: Established a printing-press.

1852: Joined a debating society.

1853: Set up for a fast man and became a bad school boy.

1854: Left the High School with honor after having been turned out several times. Worked at Mathematics for about six months and then joined Mr. Dixwell's school in town.

1855: Graduated at Dixwell's and entered College.
Read Schiller's Aesthetic Letters [*Aesthetische Briefe*] & began the study of Kant.

1856: *Sophomore*. Gave up the idea of being a fast man and undertook the pursuit of pleasure.

1857: *Junior*. Gave up the pursuit of pleasure and undertook to enjoy life.

1858: *Senior*. Gave up enjoying life and exclaimed "Vanity of vanities!"

Science, Materialism
and Idealism

1. The Place of Our Age
in the History of Civilization

[The progress of civilization depends on the freedom achieved through scientific thought as well as through political and religious emancipation from tyranny and superstition. Such is the large thesis of Peirce's Oration in his first public appearance as a philosopher, at the age of twenty-four, a year after receiving the degree of M.A. *summa cum laude* in Chemistry. Our scientific age of reason was ushered in by the great discoveries in mathematics and physical sciences of the seventeenth century. The steam engine and other inventions that have so materially benefited mankind were made possible by the ever-restless spirit of free inquiry. The continuity of modern science with the intellectual progress made by the transmission of ancient Greek and medieval thought to our age, so rhetorically expressed here by the young Peirce, was the leitmotif of his philosophy of science and civilization in all his later writings on the subject. Earlier in the nineteenth century Hegel had sought to establish historical continuity within a rigid absolutistic idealism. Peirce prefers the more experimental approach to history by pointing to the "methodical skepticism" of science and the growth of individual freedom from political and religious absolutism based on power and superstition. Granting that the "materialistic tendency of our age" is one-sided and shortsighted in forgetting the impermanence of material things and the deeper spiritual values of liberty, Peirce also suggests that idealism can receive support from the mastery of material things through the progress of physical sciences. Only the union of the material uses of science with the spiritual goals of a religious humanitarianism can approximate the "majestic symphony" played by the sciences in their rendition of the cosmos. "Materialism without idealism is blind, idealism without materialism is void."]

(Extracts from an Oration Delivered at the Reunion of the Cambridge High School Association Thursday Evening, November 12, 1863)[1]

Ladies and Gentlemen of the High School Association: In attempting to address you, I feel keenly the disadvantage of never having made any matter of general interest a special study. I am, therefore, forced to select a topic on which I have scarcely a right to an original opinion—certainly not to urge my opinion as entitled to much credit. I beg you, then, to regard whatever I say on "The Place of Our Age in the History of Civilization" as such a suggestion as might be put forth in conversation, and nothing more.

By *our age* I mean the seventeenth, eighteenth, and nineteenth centuries. There are those who, dazzled by the steam engine and the telegraph, regard the nineteenth century as something *sui generis*. But this, I think, is doing injustice to ourselves.

Bring Bacon or Newton here, and display to him the wonders our century has to show, and he will tell you, "All this is remarkable and deeply interesting, but it is not surprising. I knew," he will say, "that all this or something very like it must come at this time, for it is nothing more than the certain consequence of the principles laid down by me and my contemporaries for your guidance." Either of them will say this. But now let us turn from the Century to the Age (reckoning from the settlement of Jamestown).

---

[1] *Cambridge Chronicle*, a Weekly (Sat., Nov. 21, 1863), Vol. XVIII, No. 47, p. 1.

Let us bring the sublimest intellect that ever shone before, and what would Dante say? Let him trace the rise of constitutional government, see a down-trodden people steadily bend a haughty dynasty to obedience, give it laws and bring it to trial and execution, and finally reduce it to a convenient cipher; let him see the most enthralled people under the sun blow their rulers into a thousand pieces and establish such a terror that "all the kings of the earth, and the great men and the rich men and the chief captains and the mighty men and every bondman and every freeman hide themselves in the dens and in the rocks of the mountains"; let him see the human mind try its religion in a blazing fire, expose the falsity of its history, the impossibility of its miracles, the humanity of its revelations, until the very "heavens depart as a scroll when it is rolled together"; and then let him see the restless boundary of man's power extending over the outward world, see him dashing through time, conversing through immense distances, doing violence to the lightning, and living in such a fire of activity as less salamandrine generations could not have endured; and he who viewed Hell without dismay would fall to the earth quailing before the terrific might of intellect which God has scattered broadcast over this whole age.

This century's doings taken apart are mere jugglery—clever feats—but this age is that in which "the sun becomes black as sack-cloth of hair, and the moon becomes as blood, and the stars of heaven fall unto the earth even as a fig-tree casteth her untimely figs, when she is shaken of a mighty wind."

I equally disagree with those who think we are living in the age of the Reformation. I do so on the ground that there was nothing rationalistic in the tendency of that age. In our time, if we wish to found a new government, religion, or art, we begin at first principles, consider the philosophy of our object and follow it out. But the Reformation, as its name implies, was an attempt to suppress abuses in existing institutions without doing away with the institutions themselves. In religion, they reformed the church, but still they had a church. In our times, new denominations cast aside the church, at least. In politics, they resisted the growing power of royalty, but only in favor of the ancient system. Even their great inventions, gun-powder, printing, and the compass were not the results of original research but were heard of in old books. The discovery of America, itself, was suggested by a study of the ancient geographers. The passion for antiquity was intense, inconceivable to us, except by remembering that the age which had preceded them, that of the Crusades, was far more magnificent than theirs, and that the Greeks were both in mind and manners most evidently their superiors.

Then there was another great difference between them and us: their attempts at emancipating the human mind either from mistake or insufficiency were always failures; their republics were swept away, the power of royalty was more firmly established than ever, their noblest arts perished, and the churches which they had set up gave no more room for freedom of thought than mother Rome herself. There was a stifled cry for liberty—a blind groping for the light, backward instead of onward.

The Reformation was a struggle for humanity to regain its rightful master; in our day the aim is absolute liberty. . . . But who will say that these are primary tendencies of the age? They are rather reactions against the extravagancies of the times. From the moment when the ball of human progress received its first impetus from the mighty hands of Descartes, of Bacon, and of Galileo, we hear, as the very sound of the stroke, the decisive protest against any authority, however venerable, against any arbiter of truth except our own reason. Descartes is the father of modern metaphysics, and you know it was he who introduced the term "philosophic doubt"; he, first, declaring that a man should begin every investigation entirely without doubt; and he followed a completely independent train of thought, as though, before him, nobody had ever thought anything correctly. Bacon, also, respects no philosophers except certain Greeks [e.g., Democritus] *whose works are lost;* Aristotle he scouts at, and maintains that there has been no science before his time and that nothing has ever been discovered except by accident.

The human mind having been emancipated by these

great skeptics, works of great originality were speedily produced, so that the same century saw the productions of Hobbes, Cudworth, Malebranche, Spinoza, Locke, Leibniz, and Newton. The effect of these works was stupendous. Every question that the human mind had to ask seemed at once answered, and that too by works of such greatness of thought and power of logic that the attention of every reasoning mind was engrossed by them. Their vastness, indeed, was overwhelming; so complete were they, so true, so profound, that at first they seemed to check originality. In the first half of the eighteenth century scarcely anything new seems to have been produced [in philosophy].

At last, however, the ball of progress was struck again. And by whom? By another, more powerful doubter, the immortal Hume. In his day, the philosophical world was divided between the doctrines of Leibniz and Locke, the former of whom maintained the existence of innate ideas while the latter rejected them. Hume, accepting the latter doctrine, which was prevalent in England, asked, "How do we know that every change has a cause?" He demonstrated by invincible logic that upon Locke's system it was impossible to prove this, and that it ought not to be admitted as a principle at all. Of course, the doctrine of a first cause and the very idea of miracles vanish with the notion of causality.

Immanuel Kant was reposing in a firm belief in the metaphysics of Leibniz, as theologized by Wolff, when he first read the book of Hume. How many scholastics, nay how many theologians of our own day, would have done otherwise than say, "Behold the fruit of our opponent's system of philosophy!" This mean, degraded spirit, which is eager to answer an opponent and still remain the slave of error, was far from being Kant's. He set about asking his own philosophy the question that Hume had asked of Locke's. "We say that this and the other are innate ideas," he said, "but how do we know that our innate ideas are true?"

The book [Kant's *Critique of Pure Reason*] in which he embodied the discussion of this question is, perhaps, the greatest work of the human intellect. All later philosophies are to be classified according to the ideas contained in it, for it is all the direct result of this production. And in these later philosophies, whether we consider their profundity or their number, our age ranges far above all others put together. This wonderful fecundity of thought, I say, is the direct result of Kant's *Kritik;* and it is to be explained by the fact that Kant presented a more insoluble doubt than all the rest, and one which has not been answered to this day, for while he showed that our innate ideas of space, time, quantity, reality, cause, possibility, and so on are true, he found himself utterly unable to do this respecting the ideas of Immortality, Freedom, and God. Accordingly, all metaphysicians since his time have been endeavoring to remove this difficulty, but not altogether with success.

Hegel's system seemed, at first, satisfactory, but its further development resulted in Strauss' *Life of Jesus,* against which the human soul, the datum upon which he proceeded, itself cried out; the sense of mankind, which he had elevated into a God, itself repudiated the claim. We thus see, however, that all the progress we have made in philosophy, that is, all that has been made since the Greeks, is the result of that methodical skepticism which is the first element of human freedom.

I need not repeat the political history of the last 250 years to prove the predominance of the spirit of liberty in that sphere. You will find an ever-increasing irreverence toward rulers, from the days of Hampden to ours, when some of the more advanced spirits look forward to the time when there shall be no government. If then, all the glory of our age has sprung from a spirit of Skepticism and Irreverence, it is easy to say where its faults are to be found.

Modern progress, having been detached from its ancient mother by the Dark Ages, that fearful parturition, has since now lived a self-sustaining life. Its growth, its outline, its strength are all its own; influenced to some degree by its parent, but only through an exterior medium. The only cord which ever bound them, and which belonged to either, is Christianity. . . .[2]

2 Peirce outlines six stages in the growth of civilization: first, the Rise of Christianity; second, the Barbarian Migrations; third, establishment of the modern Nations; fourth, the Cru-

Modern times, modern breadth of thought, and modern freedom from ecclesiastical superstition followed the Crusades, in place of the mediæval narrowness and fondness for ignorance which had preceded them. The great idea which emerged was that the church is a great and good thing, but that it should not be allowed to override all the other means and appliances of civilization.

We have now come down to the age of the Reformation, the character of which I need not sketch. It seems to me apparent that all this civilization is the work of Christianity. . . .

Christianity is not a doctrine, or a possible law; it is an actual law—a kingdom. And a kingdom over what? "All things shall be put under his feet." What then does it not include? Do you assert that liberty is of any value? "His service is perfect freedom." We are accustomed to say that these phrases are hyperbolical. But that is an unwarrantable assumption—a mere subterfuge to reconcile the statement with the fact. The Jews were given to understand, by every token that language or the miraculous course of history could convey, that they were to be taken care of and saved as a nation. I say that no human being however spiritually minded could have read those Jewish prophecies and have got any other idea from *them* than that the Messiah these promised them was a Prince, seated upon the throne of his fathers, conducting the affairs of the nation, and leading them on to national glory as much as to individual immortality. When the promise was extended to the Gentiles, it meant the same thing for them. If, therefore, we are Christians, it seems to me we must believe that Christ is now directing the course of history and presiding over the destinies of kings, and that there is no branch of the public weal which does not come within the bounds of his realm. And civilization is nothing but Christianity on the grand scale.

. . . Now let us see if Christianity, the plot of history, does not follow determinate laws in its development, so that

___

sades; fifth, the Reformation; sixth, the Age of Reason, each lasting about 325 years.—Editor's note.

from a consideration of them we can gather where we are and whither we are tending.

Religion ought not to be regarded either as a subjective or an objective phenomenon. That is to say, it is neither something within us nor yet altogether without us—but bears a third relation to us, namely, that of existing in our communion with another being. Nevertheless, religion may be revealed in either of three ways—by an inward self-development, or by seeing it about us, or by a personal communication from the Most High. An example of revealed religion in the first way is natural religion. A man looks upon nature, sees its sublimity and beauty, and his spirit gradually rises to the idea of a God. He does not see the Divinity, nor does nature prove to him the existence of that Being, but it does excite his mind and his imagination until the idea becomes rooted in his heart. In the same way, the continual change and movement in nature suggest the idea of omnipresence. And finally, by the events in his own life, he becomes persuaded of the relation of that Being with his own soul. Such a religion, where all is hinted at, nought revealed, is natural religion. Of much the same character is the religion of the Jews. Though they had miracles, so it appeared did the Egyptians and Canaanites, so that these miracles did not *prove* their religion. Nowhere did they actually see, for that is not possible except to an already developed spiritual insight, the intimate union of man with God. Their wonderful history led them to believe it, and their prophets told them of it; but all this only amounted to suggestion. And by these suggestions it was impressed.

. . . In order to understand the history of Christianity or civilization, we must seek to know the successive conditions of the development of religion in man. . . .

The most striking tendency of our age is our materialistic tendency. We see it in the development of the material arts and the material sciences; in the desire to see all our theories, philosophical or moral, exemplified in the material world, and the tendency to value the system only for the practice. This tendency often seems to be opposed to another great movement of our age, the idealistic movement.

The idealist regards abstractions as having a real existence. Hence, he places as much value on them as on things. Moreover, by his wide and deep study of the human mind he has proved that the knowledge of things can only be attained by the knowledge of ideas. This truth is very distasteful to the materialist. His object being the ideas contained in things, there is nothing that he would more carefully eradicate than any admixture of ideas from our own minds; so that it seems to him like overturning natural science altogether to tell him that all truth is attained by such an admixture. He thinks at least that nothing more than common sense should be admitted from the mind. This amounts to admitting the loose ideas of the untrained intellect into his science, but to refuse admission to such as have been exercised, strengthened, and developed. He retorts that the conjunction of speculation with science has constantly led to error. Be it so; but then it is only by means of idealism that truth is possible in science. Human learning must fail somewhere. Materialism fails on the side of incompleteness. Idealism always presents a systematic totality, but it must always have some vagueness and thus lead to error. Materialism is destitute of a philosophy. Thus it is necessarily one-sided. It misunderstands its relations to idealism; it misunderstands the nature of its own logic.

But if materialism without idealism is blind, idealism without materialism is void.

Look through the wonderful philosophies of this age and you will find in every one of them evidences that their novel conceptions have been to a very large extent suggested by physical sciences. In one point of view indeed, pure *a priori* reasoning is a misnomer; it is as much as to say analysis with nothing to analyze. Analysis of what? I ask. Of those ideas which no man is without. Of common sense. But why *common* sense? Metaphysics stands in need of all the phases of thought of that uncommon sense which results from the physical sciences in order to comprehend perfectly the conceptions of the mind. So much so that I think that a due recognition of the obligations of the idealists to natural science will show that even their claims will receive a just award if we interpret the greatness of our age according to this materialistic tendency.

See, too, what truth and what peculiarly Christian truth there is in this tendency. . . . It is the assertion that man was not made to turn his eye inward, was not made for himself alone, but for the sake of what he should do in the outward world. And I will now ask how Christianity will appear if we look upon it from a materialistic point of view? . . . There will be no German refining away of Christ into a class or into self. It will be inclined to slight the subtleties of dogmas and look upon dogmas in a common-sense way. True religion, it will think, consists in more than a mere dogma, in visiting the fatherless and the widows and in keeping ourselves unspotted from the world. It will say that Christianity reaches beyond even that, reaches beyond the good conscience, beyond the individual life; must transfuse itself through all human law—through the social organization, the nation, the relationships of the peoples and the races. It will demand that not only where man's determinate action goes on, but even where he is the mere tool of providence and in the realm of inanimate nature, Christ's kingdom shall be seen.

Our age is brilliant, and apparently confident of its own eternity. But is it never to end, as the Greek merged in the Roman? The human mind cannot go on eon after eon with the same characteristics, for such monotony is too poor for it. Is our age never to end? Are we then to go on forever toying with electricity and steam, whether in the laboratory or in business, and never *use* these means in the broad field of humanity and social destiny? I seem, perhaps, to sneer at what you respect. And I confess we have utilized a little surplus energy in the business of philanthropy on our triumphant road to wooing things. . . .

"Things are in the saddle, and ride mankind."

The fulcrum has yet to be found that shall enable the lever of love to move the world. Is our age never to end? As man cannot do two things at once, so mankind cannot do two things at once. Now Lord Bacon, our great master, has said that the *end* of science is the glory of God, and the use of man. If, then, this is so, action is higher than reason, for it is its purpose; and to say that it is not is the essence of selfishness and atheism. So then our age shall end; and, indeed, the question is not so much why should it not, as why should it continue? What sufficient nature is there for man, a being in whom the natural impulse is— first, to sensation, then reasoning, then imagination, then desire, then action—to stop at reasoning, as he has been doing for the last 250 years? It is unnatural, and cannot last. Man must go on to use these powers and energies that have been given him, in order that he may impress nature with his own intellect, converse and not merely listen.

First, there was the egotistical age when man arbitrarily imagined perfection, now is the idistical stage when he observes it. Hereafter must be the more tuisical stage when he shall be in communion with her.

When the conclusion of our age comes, and skepticism and materialism have done their perfect work, we shall have a far greater faith than ever before. For then man will see God's wisdom and mercy, not only in every event of his own life, but in that of the gorilla, the lion, the fish, the polyp, the tree, the crystal, the grain of dust, the atom. He will see that each one of these has an inward existence of its own, for which God loves it, and that He has given to it a nature of endless perfectibility. He will see the folly of saying that nature was created for his use. He will see that God has no other creation than his children. So the poet in our days—and the true poet is the true prophet— personifies everything, not rhetorically but in his own feeling. He tells us that he feels an affinity for nature, and loves the stone or the drop of water. But the time is coming when there shall be no more poetry, for that which was poetically divined shall be scientifically known. It is true that the progress of science may die away, but then its essence will have been extracted. This cessation itself will give us time to see that cosmos, that esthetic view of science which Humboldt prematurely conceived. Physics will have made us familiar with the body of all things, and the unity of the body of all; natural history will have shown us the soul of all things in their infinite and amiable idiosyncrasies.

Philosophy will have taught us that it is this *all* which constitutes the church. Ah! what a heavenly harmony will be that when all the sciences, one as viol, another as flute, another as trumpet, shall peal forth in that majestic symphony of which the noble organ of astronomy forever sounds the theme.

2. Questions Concerning Certain
Faculties Claimed for Man[1]

[The *Journal of Speculative Philosophy* was founded in 1867 by W. T. Harris, leader of the St. Louis School of German Idealism which succeeded and partly fused with the Concord School of Emerson and the Transcendentalists. Although he was sympathetic to the high spiritual aims of these romantic idealists, Peirce found their logic and understanding of the sciences so weak as to lead to an unnecessary and sterile separation of philosophic from scientific thought, of so-called pure reason from experimental reasoning, of *a priori* knowledge from empirical thinking by use of signs. The main desideratum was the grounding of logic in existential relations, in the representation of external fact, and this could be done by a proper theory of the function of signs rather than by juggling concepts dialectically, or by falling back on self-evident intuitions.

I

Question 1 is directed against the alleged faculty of recognizing intuitively what premises must be taken as absolute starting points, independently of previous knowledge. Peirce doubts that we have any sure means of knowing

[1] *Journal of Speculative Philosophy*, Vol. 2, pp. 103–114 (1868). "Premiss" is Peirce's preferred spelling of "premise" in this essay and elsewhere.—Editor's note.

whether we have such an *a priori* faculty of knowledge independent of previous experience or reasoning from signs. For example, the medieval acceptance of Aristotle's treatises as authority for our knowledge of nature did not prevent disputes about which of his premises (for example, that the world had no beginning) had to be taken as true. The same fate awaits our reliance on the "indubitable" claims of all our introspective or internal authority, Peirce concludes from an astute analysis of historical and psychological evidence.

Questions 2, 3, and 4 show why we have to doubt the necessity of supposing an intuitive knowledge of our own states of mind, since there is always some reasoning from external facts in any introspection. This reasoning may be unexpressed; for example, "this is a table" is not merely given immediately by inspection but entails "this has certain features common to objects called tables" from which "this is a table" follows.

Every thought is a sign, and we cannot think without the use of signs, verbal or gestural. Signs stand for something to somebody. Hence, every thought must address itself to something other than the immediate thought itself, as signs normally do not refer to themselves, although, of course, signs can and do refer to other signs. A dispute whether a given object is a table may lead to a discussion of either the external properties and uses of the object or to a dictionary definition of "table." Thus, Peirce suggests an objective way of considering thought as functioning in relation to external fact and through signs.

In Question 6, Peirce agrees with the Hegelians against Kant and Spencer that there is no sense to "things-in-themselves" absolutely unknowable, for we always know something, no matter how slight, about the unknown, say, as the cause of our sensations or thoughts or as the object of our inquiries.

The final conclusion, in Question 7, is that all knowing is *continuous* with previous knowledge in an endless process of reasoning and learning from signs.

II

As a consequence of the essential continuity of thought with previous knowledge of external facts, we must reject Descartes' method of universal doubt and appeal to self-evidence. Modern science accepts no proposition as self-evident but rests on the consensus of the community of scientific investigators as to what premises one may adopt for the sake of inquiry. Self-evident truths are thus replaced by *hypotheses* and inferences of two sorts: *deductive inference,* where our ideas are simply unfolded or explicated, and *inductive inference,* where our previous knowledge is admittedly incomplete, but amplified.

When the historian reconstructs past events or when the cryptographer guesses on the basis of frequency-tables what letter a certain mark in a cypher represents, use is made of the method of establishing *hypotheses* based on previous knowledge; for example, the hypothesis that a certain mark stands for the letter *e* rests on the general truth that that letter recurs more frequently than any other letter in English texts. This general truth is known by *inductive inference* from the observation of a large sample of English texts even though nobody has made a complete examination of all English writings. If we know also that the writer of the message knew only English, we easily *deduce* that the message to be deciphered is in English. Deduction is not always so easy, as we know from the use made of ingenious deductive inference in mathematics and logic. Some sets of postulates are more "fruitful" or "powerful" than others in enabling the mathematician or logician to derive an extensive and sometimes "surprising" set of theorems in an unfamiliar abstract domain of relationships far from self-evident in their implications. An axiom-set is justified not by being intuitively self-evident but by yielding unsuspected results. Peirce, trained in modern mathematical methods, was therefore able to enter the lists of professional philosophers in these articles in the *Journal of Speculative Philosophy* by laying down the gauntlet to traditional loose ways of thinking.

Three categories emerged from Peirce's treatment of

thoughts as signs: (1) the function of *representation* of objects, imagined or real; (2) the *relation* of the applicability of one thought to another; (3) the material *quality* or "feeling"—the aesthetic character of thought. These are distinguishable but inseparable features of all signs that enter into the life of all inquiry. Forty years later, in his letters to Lady Welby (see Selection 24), Peirce was still elaborating the role of signs.]

QUESTION 1. *Whether by the simple contemplation of a cognition, independently of any previous knowledge and without reasoning from signs, we are enabled rightly to judge whether that cognition has been determined by a previous cognition or whether it refers immediately to its object.*

Throughout this paper, the term *intuition* will be taken as signifying a cognition not determined by a previous cognition of the same object, and therefore so determined by something out of the consciousness.[2] Let me request the reader to note this. *Intuition* here will be nearly the same as "premiss not itself a conclusion"; the only difference being that premisses and conclusions are judgments, whereas an intuition may, as far as its definition states, be

[2] The word *intuitus* first occurs as a technical term in St. Anselm's *Monologium*. He wished to distinguish between our knowledge of God and our knowledge of finite things (and in the next world, of God, also); and thinking of the saying of St. Paul, *Videmus nunc per speculum in aenigmate: tunc autem facie ad faciem*, he called the former *speculation* and the latter *intuition*. This use of "speculation" did not take root, because that word already had another exact and widely different meaning. In the Middle Ages the term "intuitive cognition" had two principal senses; first, as opposed to abstractive cognition, it meant the knowledge of the present as present, and this is its meaning in Anselm; but second, as no intuitive cognition was allowed to be determined by a previous cognition, it came to be used as the opposite of discursive cognition (see Scotus, *In sentent.*, lib. 2, dist. 3, qu. 9), and this is nearly the sense in which I employ it. This is also nearly the sense in which Kant uses it, the former distinction being expressed by his *sensuous* and *non-sensuous*. . . . An enumeration of six meanings of intuition may be found in Hamilton's *Reid*, p. 759.

any kind of cognition whatever. But just as a conclusion (good or bad) is determined in the mind of the reasoner by its premiss, so cognitions not judgments may be determined by previous cognitions; and a cognition not so determined, and therefore determined directly by the transcendental object, is to be termed an *intuition*. . . .

There is no evidence that we have this faculty, except that we seem to *feel* that we have it. But the weight of that testimony depends entirely on our being supposed to have the power of distinguishing in this feeling whether the feeling be the result of education, old associations, etc., or whether it is an intuitive cognition; or, in other words, it depends on presupposing the very matter testified to. Is this feeling infallible? And is this judgment concerning it infallible, and so on, *ad infinitum?* Supposing that a man really could shut himself up in such a faith, he would be, of course, impervious to the truth, "evidence-proof."

But let us compare the theory with the historic facts. The power of intuitively distinguishing intuitions from other cognitions has not prevented men from disputing very warmly as to which cognitions are intuitive. In the Middle Ages reason and external authority were regarded as two co-ordinate sources of knowledge, just as reason and the authority of intuition are now; only the happy device of considering the enunciations of authority to be essentially indemonstrable had not yet been hit upon. All authorities were not considered as infallible, any more than all reasons; but when Berengarius said that the authoritativeness of any particular authority must rest upon reason, the proposition was scouted as opinionated, impious, and absurd. Thus, the credibility of authority was regarded by men of that time simply as an ultimate premiss, as a cognition not determined by a previous cognition of the same object, or, in our terms, as an intuition. It is strange that they should have thought so, if, as the theory now under discussion supposes, by merely contemplating the credibility of the authority, as a Fakir does his God, they could have seen that it was not an ultimate premiss! Now, what if our *internal* authority should meet the same fate, in the history of opinions, as that external authority has met? Can that be

said to be absolutely certain which many sane, well-in-
formed, and thoughtful men already doubt?[3]

Every lawyer knows how difficult it is for witnesses to
distinguish between what they have seen and what they
have inferred. This is particularly noticeable in the case of
a person who is describing the performances of a spiritual
medium or of a professed juggler. The difficulty is so great
that the juggler himself is often astonished at the discrepancy between the actual facts and the statement of an intelligent witness who has not understood the trick. A part
of the very complicated trick of the Chinese rings consists
in taking two solid rings linked together, talking about them
as though they were separate—taking it for granted, as it
were—then pretending to put them together, and handing
them immediately to the spectator that he may see that
they are solid. The art of this consists in raising, at first, the
strong suspicion that one is broken. I have seen McAlister
do this with such success that a person sitting close to him,
with all his faculties straining to detect the illusion, would
have been ready to swear that he saw the rings put together, and, perhaps, if the juggler had not professedly
practised deception, would have considered a doubt of it
as a doubt of his own veracity. This certainly seems to
show that it is not always very easy to distinguish between
a premiss and a conclusion, that we have no infallible power
of doing so, and that in fact our only security in difficult
cases is in some signs from which we can infer that a given
fact must have been seen or must have been inferred. In
trying to give an account of a dream, every accurate person
must often have felt that it was a hopeless undertaking to

[3] The most striking characteristic of medieval reasoning, in
general, is the perpetual resort to authority. . . . Abelard
(*Ouvrages*, p. 179) thinks it worth while to cite Boëthius, when
he says that space has three dimensions, and when he says that
an individual cannot be in two places at once. . . . The authority is the final court of appeal. . . . Recognized authorities
were certainly sometimes disputed in the twelfth century; their
mutual contradictions insured that; and the authority of philosophers was regarded as inferior to that of theologians. Still,
it would be impossible to find a passage where the authority
of Aristotle is directly denied upon any logical question. . . .

attempt to disentangle waking interpretations and fillings out from the fragmentary images of the dream itself.

The mention of dreams suggests another argument. A dream, as far as its own content goes, is exactly like an actual experience. It is mistaken for one. And yet all the world believes that dreams are determined, according to the laws of the association of ideas, etc., by previous cognitions. If it be said that the faculty of intuitively recognizing intuitions is asleep, I reply that this is a mere supposition, without other support. Besides, even when we wake up, we do not find that the dream differed from reality, except by certain *marks,* darkness and fragmentariness. Not unfrequently a dream is so vivid that the memory of it is mistaken for the memory of an actual occurrence.

A child has, as far as we know, all the perceptive powers of a man. Yet question him a little as to *how* he knows what he does. In many cases, he will tell you that he never learned his mother tongue; he always knew it, or he knew it as soon as he came to have sense. It appears, then, that *he* does not possess the faculty of distinguishing, by simple contemplation, between an intuition and a cognition determined by others.

There can be no doubt that before the publication of Berkeley's book on Vision [*An Essay Towards a New Theory of Vision,* 1709], it had generally been believed that the third dimension of space was immediately intuited, although, at present, nearly all admit that it is known by inference. We had been *contemplating* the object since the very creation of man, but this discovery was not made until we began to *reason* about it.

Does the reader know of the blind spot on the retina? Take a number of this journal, turn over the cover so as to expose the white paper, lay it sideways upon the table before which you must sit, and put two cents upon it, one near the left-hand edge, and the other to the right. Put your left hand over your left eye, and with the right eye look *steadily* at the left-hand cent. Then, with your right hand, move the right-hand cent (which is now plainly seen) *towards* the left hand. When it comes to a place near the middle of the page it will disappear—you cannot see it without turning your eye. Bring it nearer to the other cent, or carry it further away, and it will reappear; but at that particular spot it cannot be seen. Thus it appears that there is a blind spot nearly in the middle of the retina; and this is confirmed by anatomy. It follows that the space we immediately see (when one eye is closed) is not, as we had imagined, a continuous oval, but is a ring, the filling up of which must be the work of the intellect. What more striking example could be desired of the impossibility of distinguishing intellectual results from intuitional data by mere contemplation?

A man can distinguish different textures of cloth by feeling; but not immediately, for he requires to move his fingers over the cloth, which shows that he is obliged to compare the sensations of one instant with those of another.

The pitch of a tone depends upon the rapidity of the succession of the vibrations which reach the ear. Each of those vibrations produces an impulse upon the ear. Let a single such impulse be made upon the ear, and we know, experimentally, that it is perceived. There is, therefore, good reason to believe that each of the impulses forming a tone is perceived. Nor is there any reason to the contrary. So that this is the only admissible supposition. Therefore, the pitch of a tone depends upon the rapidity with which certain impressions are successively conveyed to the mind. These impressions must exist previously to any tone; hence, the sensation of pitch is determined by previous cognitions. Nevertheless, this would never have been discovered by the mere contemplation of that feeling.

A similar argument may be urged in reference to the perception of two dimensions of space. This appears to be an immediate intuition. But if we were to *see* immediately an extended surface, our retinas must be spread out in an extended surface. Instead of that, the retina consists of innumerable needles pointing towards the light, and whose distances from one another are decidedly greater than the *minimum visibile*. Suppose each of those nerve-points conveys the sensation of a little colored surface. Still, what we immediately see must even then be, not a continuous surface, but a collection of spots. Who could discover this by mere intuition? But all the analogies of the nervous system are against the supposition that the excitation of a single nerve can produce an idea as complicated as that of a space, however small. If the excitation of no one of these nerve points can immediately convey the impression of space, the excitation of all cannot do so. For the excitation of each produces some impression (according to the analogies of the nervous system), hence, the sum of these impressions is a necessary condition of any perception produced by the excitation of all; or, in other terms, a perception produced by the excitation of all is determined by the mental impressions produced by the excitation of every one. This argument is confirmed by the fact that the existence of the perception of space can be fully accounted for by the action of faculties known to exist, without supposing it to be an immediate impression. For this purpose, we must bear in mind the following facts of physio-psychology: (1) The excitation of a nerve does not of itself inform us where the extremity of it is situated. If, by a surgical operation, certain nerves are displaced, our sensations from those nerves do not inform us of the displacement. (2) A single sensation does not inform us how many nerves or nerve-points are excited. (3) We can distinguish between the impressions produced by the excitations of different nerve-points. (4) The differences of impressions produced by different excitations of similar nerve-points are similar. Let a momentary image be made upon the retina. By No. 2, the impression thereby produced will be indistinguishable from what might be produced by the excitation of some conceivable single nerve. It is not conceivable that the momentary excitation of a single nerve should give the sensation of space. Therefore, the momentary excitation of all the nerve-points of the retina cannot, immediately or mediately, produce the sensation of space. The same argument would apply to any unchanging image on the retina. Suppose, however, that the image moves over the retina. Then the peculiar excitation which at one instant affects one nerve-point, at a later instant will affect another. These will convey impressions which are very similar by 4, and yet which are distinguishable by 3. Hence, the conditions for the recognition of a relation between these impressions are present. There being, however, a very great number of nerve-points affected by a very great number of successive excitations, the relations of the resulting impressions will be almost inconceivably complicated. Now, it is a known law of mind that when phenomena of an extreme complexity are presented, which yet would be reduced to *order* or mediate simplicity by the application of a certain conception, that conception sooner or later arises in application to those phenomena. In the case under consideration, the conception of extension would reduce the phenomena to unity, and, therefore, its genesis is fully accounted for. It remains only to explain why the previous cognitions which determine it are not more clearly apprehended. For this explanation, I shall refer to a paper upon a new list of categories, Section 5,[4] merely adding that just as we are able to recognize our friends by certain appearances, although we cannot possibly say what those appearances are and are quite unconscious of any process of reasoning, so in any case when the reasoning is easy and natural to us, however complex may be the premisses, they sink into insignificance and oblivion proportionately to the satisfactoriness of the theory based upon them. This theory of space is confirmed by the circumstance that an exactly similar theory is imperatively demanded by the facts in reference to time. That the course of time should be immediately felt is obviously impossible. For, in that case, there must be an element of this feeling at each instant. But in an instant there is no duration and hence no immediate feeling of duration. Hence, no one of these elementary feelings is an immediate feeling of duration; and, hence, the sum of all is not. On the other hand, the impressions of any moment are very complicated—containing all the images (or the elements of the images) of sense and memory, which complexity is reducible to mediate simplicity by means of the conception of time.[5]

[4] *Proceedings of the American Academy,* May 14, 1867.
[5] The above theory of space and time does not conflict with that of Kant so much as it appears to do. They are in fact the solutions of different questions. Kant, it is true, makes space and

We have, therefore, a variety of facts, all of which are most readily explained on the supposition that we have no intuitive faculty of distinguishing intuitive from mediate cognitions. Some arbitrary hypothesis may otherwise explain any one of these facts; this is the only theory which brings them to support one another. Moreover, no facts require the supposition of the faculty in question. Whoever has studied the nature of proof will see, then, that there are here very strong reasons for disbelieving the existence of this faculty. These will become still stronger when the consequences of rejecting it have, in this paper and in a following one, been more fully traced out.

QUESTION 2. *Whether we have an intuitive self-consciousness.*

Self-consciousness, as the term is here used, is to be distinguished both from consciousness generally, from the in-

---

time intuitions, or rather forms of intuition, but it is not essential to his theory that intuition should mean more than "individual representation." The apprehension of space and time results, according to him, from a mental *process*—the "Synthesis der Apprehension in der Anschauung." (See *Kritik d. reinen Vernunft.* ed. 1781, pp. 98 *et seq.*) My theory is merely an account of this synthesis.

The gist of Kant's Transcendental Æsthetic is contained in two principles. First, that universal and necessary propositions are not given in experience. Second, that universal and necessary facts are determined by the conditions of experience in general. By a universal proposition is meant merely, one which asserts something of *all* of a sphere—not necessarily one which all men believe. By a necessary proposition is meant one which asserts what it does, not merely of the actual condition of things, but of every possible state of things; it is not meant that the proposition is one which we cannot help believing. Experience, in Kant's first principle, cannot be used for a product of the objective understanding, but must be taken for the first impressions of sense with consciousness conjoined and worked up by the imagination into images, together with all which is logically deducible therefrom. In this sense, it may be admitted that universal and necessary propositions are not given in experience. But, in that case, neither are any inductive conclusions which might be drawn from experience, given in it. In fact, it is the peculiar function of induction to produce universal and neces-

ternal sense, and from pure apperception. Any cognition is a consciousness of the object as represented; by self-consciousness is meant a knowledge of ourselves. Not a mere feeling of subjective conditions of consciousness, but of our personal selves. Pure apperception is the self-assertion of THE *ego;* the self-consciousness here meant is the recognition of my *private* self. I know that *I* (not merely *the* I) exist. The question is, how do I know it; by a special intuitive faculty, or is it determined by previous cognitions?

Now, it is not self-evident that we have such an intuitive faculty, for it has just been shown that we have no intuitive power of distinguishing an intuition from a cognition determined by others. Therefore, the existence or non-existence of this power is to be determined upon evidence, and the question is whether self-consciousness can be explained by

---

sary propositions. Kant points out, indeed, that the universality and necessity of scientific inductions are but the analogues of philosophic universality and necessity; and this is true, in so far as it is never allowable to accept a scientific conclusion without a certain indefinite drawback. But this is owing to the insufficiency in the number of the instances; and whenever instances may be had in as large numbers as we please, *ad infinitum,* a truly universal and necessary proposition is inferable. As for Kant's second principle, that the truth of universal and necessary propositions is dependent upon the conditions of the general experience, it is no more nor less than the principle of Induction. I go to a fair and draw from the "grab-bag" twelve packages. Upon opening them, I find that every one contains a red ball. Here is a universal fact. It depends, then, on the condition of the experience. What is the condition of the experience? It is solely that the balls are the contents of packages drawn from that bag, that is, the only thing which determined the experience was the drawing from the bag. I infer, then, according to the principle of Kant, that what is drawn from the bag will contain a red ball. This is induction. Apply induction not to any limited experience but to all human experience and you have the Kantian philosophy, so far as it is correctly developed.

Kant's successors, however, have not been content with his doctrine. Nor ought they to have been. For, there is this third principle: "Absolutely universal propositions must be analytic." For whatever is absolutely universal is devoid of all content or determination, for all determination is by negation. The problem, therefore, is not how universal propositions can be synthetical, but how universal propositions appearing to be synthetical can be evolved by thought alone from the purely indeterminate.

the action of known faculties under conditions known to exist, or whether it is necessary to suppose an unknown cause for this cognition, and, in the latter case, whether an intuitive faculty of self-consciousness is the most probable cause which can be supposed.

It is first to be observed that there is no known self-consciousness to be accounted for in extremely young children. It has already been pointed out by Kant[6] that the late use of the very common word "I" with children indicates an imperfect self-consciousness in them, and that, therefore, so far as it is admissible for us to draw any conclusion in regard to the mental state of those who are still younger, it must be against the existence of any self-consciousness in them.

On the other hand, children manifest powers of thought much earlier. Indeed, it is almost impossible to assign a period at which children do not already exhibit decided intellectual activity in directions in which thought is indispensable to their well-being. The complicated trigonometry of vision, and the delicate adjustments of co-ordinated movement, are plainly mastered very early. There is no reason to question a similar degree of thought in reference to themselves.

A very young child may always be observed to watch its own body with great attention. There is every reason why this should be so, for from the child's point of view this body is the most important thing in the universe. Only what it touches has any actual and present feeling; only what it faces has any actual color; only what is on its tongue has any actual taste.

No one questions that, when a sound is heard by a child, he thinks, not of himself as hearing, but of the bell or other object as sounding. How when he wills to move a table? Does he then think of himself as desiring, or only of the table as fit to be moved? That he has the latter thought is beyond question; that he has the former must, until the existence of an intuitive self-consciousness is proved, remain an arbitrary and baseless supposition. There is no good rea-

6 *Werke*, vii. (2), 11.

son for thinking that he is less ignorant of his own peculiar condition than the angry adult who denies that he is in a passion.

The child, however, must soon discover by observation that things which are thus fit to be changed are apt actually to undergo this change, after a contact with that peculiarly important body called Willy or Johnny. This consideration makes this body still more important and central, since it establishes a connection between the fitness of a thing to be changed and a tendency in this body to touch it before it is changed.

The child learns to understand the language; that is to say, a connection between certain sounds and certain facts becomes established in his mind. He has previously noticed the connection between these sounds and the motions of the lips of bodies somewhat similar to the central one, and has tried the experiment of putting his hand on those lips and has found the sound in that case to be smothered. He thus connects that language with bodies somewhat similar to the central one. By efforts, so unenergetic that they should be called rather instinctive, perhaps, than tentative, he learns to produce those sounds. So he begins to converse.

It must be about this time that he begins to find that what these people about him say is the very best evidence of fact. So much so, that testimony is even a stronger mark of fact than *the facts themselves,* or rather than what must now be thought of as the *appearances* themselves. (I may remark, by the way, that this remains so through life; testimony will convince a man that he himself is mad.) A child hears it said that the stove is hot. But it is not, he says; and, indeed, that central body is not touching it, and only what that touches is hot or cold. But he touches it, and finds the testimony confirmed in a striking way. Thus, he becomes aware of ignorance, and it is necessary to suppose a *self* in which this ignorance can inhere. So testimony gives the first dawning of self-consciousness.

But, further, although usually appearances are either only confirmed or merely supplemented by testimony, yet there is a certain remarkable class of appearances which are continually contradicted by testimony. These are those predicates which *we* know to be emotional, but which *he* distinguishes by their connection with the movements of that central person, himself (that the table wants moving, etc.). These judgments are generally denied by others. Moreover, he has reason to think that others, also, have such judgments which are quite denied by all the rest. Thus, he adds to the conception of appearance as the actualization of fact, the conception of it as something *private* and valid only for one body. In short, *error* appears, and it can be explained only by supposing a *self* which is fallible.

Ignorance and error are all that distinguish our private selves from the absolute *ego* of pure apperception.

Now, the theory which, for the sake of perspicuity, has thus been stated in a specific form, may be summed up as follows: At the age at which we know children to be self-conscious, we know that they have been made aware of ignorance and error; and we know them to possess at that age powers of understanding sufficient to enable them to infer from ignorance and error their own existence. Thus we find that known faculties, acting under conditions known to exist, would rise to self-consciousness. The only essential defect in this account of the matter is that, while we know that children exercise *as much* understanding as is here supposed, we do not know that they exercise it in precisely this way. Still the supposition that they do so is infinitely more supported by facts than the supposition of a wholly peculiar faculty of the mind.

The only argument worth noticing for the existence of an intuitive self-consciousness is this: We are more certain of our own existence than of any other fact; a premiss cannot determine a conclusion to be more certain than it is itself; hence, our own existence cannot have been inferred from any other fact. The first premiss must be admitted, but the second premiss is founded on an exploded theory of logic. A conclusion cannot be more certain than that some one of the facts which support it is true, but it may easily be more certain than any one of those facts. Let us suppose, for example, that a dozen witnesses testify to an occurrence. Then my belief in that occurrence rests on the belief that each of those men is generally to be believed upon oath. Yet the fact testified to is made more certain than that any one of those men is generally to be believed. In the same way, to the developed mind of man, his own existence is supported by *every other fact,* and is, therefore, incomparably more certain than any one of these facts. But it cannot be said to be more certain than that there is another fact, since there is no doubt perceptible in either case.

It is to be concluded, then, that there is no necessity of supposing an intuitive self-consciousness, since self-consciousness may easily be the result of inference.

QUESTION 3. *Whether we have an intuitive power of distinguishing between the subjective elements of different kinds of cognitions.*

Every cognition involves something represented, or that of which we are conscious, and some action or passion of the self whereby it becomes represented. The former shall be termed the objective, the latter the subjective, element of the cognition. The cognition itself is an intuition of its objective element, which may therefore be called, also, the immediate object. The subjective element is not necessarily immediately known, but it is possible that such an intuition of the subjective element of a cognition of its character, whether that of dreaming, imagining, conceiving, believing, etc., should accompany every cognition. The question is whether this is so.

It would appear, at first sight, that there is an overwhelming array of evidence in favor of the existence of such a power. The difference between seeing a color and imagining it is immense. There is a vast difference between the most vivid dream and reality. And if we had no intuitive power of distinguishing between what we believe and what we merely conceive, we never, it would seem, could in any way distinguish them; since if we did so by reasoning, the question would arise whether the argument itself was believed or conceived, and this must be answered before the conclusion could have any force. And thus there would be a *regressus ad infinitum.* Besides, if we do not know that we believe, then, from the nature of the case, we do not believe.

But be it noted that we do not intuitively know the existence of this faculty. For it is an intuitive one, and we cannot intuitively know that a cognition is intuitive. The question is, therefore, whether it is necessary to suppose the existence of this faculty, or whether then the facts can be explained without this supposition.

In the first place, then, the difference between what is imagined or dreamed and what is actually experienced is no argument in favor of the existence of such a faculty. For it is not questioned that there are distinctions in what is present to the mind, but the question is, whether independently of any such distinctions in the immediate *objects* of consciousness, we have any immediate power of distinguishing different modes of consciousness. Now, the very fact of the immense difference in the immediate objects of sense and imagination, sufficiently accounts for our distinguishing those faculties; and instead of being an argument in favor of the existence of an intuitive power of distinguishing the subjective elements of consciousness, it is a powerful reply to any such argument, so far as the distinction of sense and imagination is concerned.

Passing to the distinction of belief and conception, we meet the statement that the knowledge of belief is essential to its existence. Now, we can unquestionably distinguish a belief from a conception, in most cases, by means of a peculiar feeling of conviction; and it is a mere question of words whether we define belief as that judgment which is accompanied by this feeling, or as that judgment from which a man will act. We may conveniently call the former *sensational*, the latter *active*, belief. That neither of these necessarily involves the other will surely be admitted without any recital of facts. Taking belief in the sensational sense, the intuitive power of reorganizing it will amount simply to the capacity for the sensation which accompanies the judgment. This sensation, like any other, is an object of consciousness; and therefore the capacity for it implies no intuitive recognition of subjective elements of consciousness. If belief is taken in the active sense, it may be discovered by the observation of external facts and by inference from the sensation of conviction which usually accompanies it.

Thus, the arguments in favor of this peculiar power of consciousness disappear, and the presumption is again against such a hypothesis. Moreover, as the immediate objects of any two faculties must be admitted to be different, the facts do not render such a supposition in any degree necessary.

QUESTION 4. *Whether we have any power of introspection, or whether our whole knowledge of the internal world is derived from the observation of external facts.*

It is not intended here to assume the reality of the external world. Only, there is a certain set of facts which are ordinarily regarded as external, while others are regarded as internal. The question is whether the latter are known otherwise than by inference from the former. By introspection, I mean a direct perception of the internal world, but not necessarily a perception of it *as* internal. Nor do I mean to limit the signification of the word to intuition, but would extend it to any knowledge of the internal world not derived from external observation.

There is one sense in which any perception has an internal object, namely, that every sensation is partly determined by internal conditions. Thus, the sensation of redness is as it is, owing to the constitution of the mind; and in this sense it is a sensation of something internal. Hence, we may derive a knowledge of the mind from a consideration of this sensation, but that knowledge would, in fact, be an inference from redness as a predicate of something external. On the other hand, there are certain other feelings—the emotions, for example—which appear to arise in the first place, not as predicates at all, and to be referable to the mind alone. It would seem, then, that by means of these, a knowledge of the mind may be obtained, which is not inferred from any character of outward things. The question is whether this is really so.

Although introspection is not necessarily intuitive, it is

not self-evident that we possess this capacity; for we have no intuitive faculty of distinguishing different subjective modes of consciousness. The power, if it exists, must be known by the circumstance that the facts cannot be explained without it.

In reference to the above argument from the emotions, it must be admitted that if a man is angry, his anger implies, in general, no determinate and constant character in its object. But, on the other hand, it can hardly be questioned that there is some relative character in the outward thing which makes him angry, and a little reflection will serve to show that his anger consists in his saying to himself, "this thing is vile, abominable, etc.," and that it is rather a mark of returning reason to say, "I am angry." In the same way any emotion is a predication concerning some object, and the chief difference between this and an objective intellectual judgment is that while the latter is relative to human nature or to mind in general, the former is relative to the particular circumstances and disposition of a particular man at a particular time. What is here said of emotions in general is true in particular of the sense of beauty and of the moral sense. Good and bad are feelings which first arise as predicates, and therefore are either predicates of the not-I, or are determined by previous cognitions (there being no intuitive power of distinguishing subjective elements of consciousness).

It remains, then, only to inquire whether it is necessary to suppose a particular power of introspection for the sake of accounting for the sense of willing. Now, volition, as distinguished from desire, is nothing but the power of concentrating the attention, of abstracting. Hence, the knowledge of the power of abstracting may be inferred from abstract objects, just as the knowledge of the power of seeing is inferred from colored objects.

It appears, therefore, that there is no reason for supposing a power of introspection; and, consequently, the only way of investigating a psychological question is by inference from external facts.

QUESTION 5. *Whether we can think without signs.*

This is a familiar question, but there is, to this day, no better argument in the affirmative than that thought must precede every sign. This assumes the impossibility of an infinite series. But Achilles, as a fact, will overtake the tortoise. *How* this happens is a question not necessary to be answered at present, as long as it certainly does happen.

If we seek the light of external facts, the only cases of thought which we can find are of thought in signs. Plainly, no other thought can be evidenced by external facts. But we have seen that only by external facts can thought be known at all. The only thought, then, which can possibly be cognized is thought in signs. But thought which cannot be cognized does not exist. All thought, therefore, must necessarily be in signs.

A man says to himself, "Aristotle is a man; *therefore,* he is fallible." Has he not, then, thought what he has not said to himself, that all men are fallible? The answer is that he has done so, so far as this is said in his *therefore.* According to this, our question does not relate to *fact,* but is a mere asking for distinctness of thought.

From the proposition that every thought is a sign, it follows that every thought must address itself to some other, must determine some other, since that is the essence of a sign. This, after all, is but another form of the familiar axiom that in intuition, i.e., in the immediate present, there is no thought, or, that all which is reflected upon has past. *Hinc loquor inde est.* That, since any thought, there must have been a thought has its analogue in the fact that, since any past time, there must have been an infinite series of times. To say, therefore, that thought cannot happen in an instant, but requires a time, is but another way of saying that every thought must be interpreted in another, or that all thought is in signs.

QUESTION 6. *Whether a sign can have any meaning, if by its definition it is the sign of something absolutely incognizable.*

It would seem that it can, and that universal and hypothetical propositions are instances of it. Thus, the universal proposition, "all ruminants are cloven-hoofed," speaks of a possible infinity of animals, and no matter how many ruminants may have been examined, the possibility must remain that there are others which have not been examined. In the case of a hypothetical proposition, the same thing is still more manifest; for such a proposition speaks not merely of the actual state of things, but of every possible state of things, all of which are not knowable, inasmuch as only one can so much as exist.

On the other hand, all our conceptions are obtained by abstractions and combinations of cognitions first occurring in judgments of experience. Accordingly, there can be no conception of the absolutely incognizable, since nothing of that sort occurs in experience. But the meaning of a term is the conception which it conveys. Hence, a term can have no such meaning.

If it be said that the incognizable is a concept compounded of the concept *not* and *cognizable,* it may be replied that *not* is a mere syncategorematic term and not a concept by itself.

If I think "white," I will not go so far as Berkeley and say that I think of a person seeing, but I will say that what I think is of the nature of a cognition, and so of anything else which can be experienced. Consequently, the highest concept which can be reached by abstractions from judgments of experience—and therefore, the highest concept which can be reached at all—is the concept of something of the nature of a cognition. *Not,* then, or *what is other than,* if a concept, is a concept of the cognizable. Hence, not-cognizable, if a concept, is a concept of the form "A, not-A," and is, at least, self-contradictory. Thus, ignorance and error can only be conceived as correlative to a real knowledge and truth, which latter are of the nature of cognitions. Over against any cognition, there is an unknown but knowable reality; but over against all possible cognition, there is only the self-contradictory. In short, *cognizability* (in its widest sense) and *being* are not merely metaphysically the same, but are synonymous terms.

To the argument from universal and hypothetical propositions, the reply is that though their truth cannot be cognized with absolute certainty, it may be probably known by induction.

QUESTION 7.   *Whether there is any cognition not determined by a previous cognition.*

It would seem that there is or has been; for since we are in possession of cognitions, which are all determined by previous ones, and these by cognitions earlier still, there must have been a *first* in this series or else our state of cognition at any time is completely determined, according to logical laws, by our state at any previous time. But there are many facts against the last supposition, and therefore in favor of intuitive cognitions.

On the other hand, since it is impossible to know intuitively that a given cognition is not determined by a previous one, the only way in which this can be known is by hypothetic inference from observed facts. But to adduce the cognition by which a given cognition has been determined is to explain the determinations of that cognition. And it is the only way of explaining them. For something entirely out of consciousness which may be supposed to determine it can, as such, only be known and only adduced in the determinate cognition in question. So that to suppose that a cognition is determined solely by something absolutely external is to suppose its determinations incapable of explanation. Now, this is a hypothesis which is warranted under no circumstances, inasmuch as the only possible justification for a hypothesis is that it explains the facts, and to say that they are explained and at the same time to suppose them inexplicable is self-contradictory.

If it be objected that the peculiar character of *red* is not determined by any previous cognition, I reply that that character is not a character of red as a cognition; for if there be a man to whom red things look as blue ones do to me and vice versa, that man's eyes teach him the same facts that they would if he were like me.

Moreover, we know of no power by which an intuition

could be known. For, as the cognition is beginning, and therefore in a state of change, at only the first instant would it be intuition. And, therefore, the apprehension of it must take place in no time and be an event occupying no time.[7] Besides, all the cognitive faculties we know of are relative, and consequently their products are relations. But the cognition of a relation is determined by previous cognitions. No cognition not determined by a previous cognition, then, can be known. It does not exist, then, first, because it is absolutely incognizable, and second, because a cognition only exists so far as it is known.

The reply to the argument that there must be a first is as follows: In retracing our way from conclusions to premisses, or from determined cognitions to those which determine them, we finally reach, in all cases, a point beyond which the consciousness in the determined cognition is more lively than in the cognition which determines it. We have a less lively consciousness in the cognition which determines our cognition of the third dimension than in the latter cognition itself; a less lively consciousness in the cognition which determines our cognition of a continuous surface (without a blind spot) than in this latter cognition itself; and a less lively consciousness of the impressions which determine the sensation of tone than of that sensation itself. Indeed, when we get near enough to the external this is the universal rule. Now let any horizontal line represent a cognition, and let the length of the line serve to measure (so to speak) the liveliness of consciousness in that cognition. A point, having no length, will, on this principle, represent an object quite out of consciousness. Let one horizontal line below another represent a cognition which determines the cognition represented by that other and which has the same object as the latter. Let the finite distance between two such lines represent that they are two different cognitions. With this aid to thinking, let us see whether "there must be a first." Suppose an inverted triangle ∇ to be gradually dipped into water. At any date or

---

[7] This argument, however, only covers a part of the question. It does not go to show that there is no cognition undetermined except by another like it.

instant, the surface of the water makes a horizontal line across that triangle. This line represents a cognition. At a subsequent date, there is a sectional line so made, higher upon the triangle. This represents another cognition of the same object determined by the former, and having a livelier consciousness. The apex of the triangle represents the object external to the mind which determines both these cognitions. The state of the triangle before it reaches the water represents a state of cognition which contains nothing which determines these subsequent cognitions. To say, then, that if there be a state of cognition by which all subsequent cognitions of a certain object are not determined, there must subsequently be some cognition of that object not determined by previous cognitions of the same object, is to say that when that triangle is dipped into the water there must be a sectional line made by the surface of the water lower than which no surface line had been made in that way. But draw the horizontal line where you will, as many horizontal lines as you please can be assigned at finite distances below it and below one another. For any such section is at some distance above the apex, otherwise it is not a line. Let this distance be a. Then there have been similar sections at the distances $\frac{1}{2}a$, $\frac{1}{4}a$, $\frac{1}{8}a$, $1/16a$, above the apex, and so on as far as you please. So that it is not true that there must be a first. Explicate the logical difficulties of this paradox (they are identical with those of the Achilles) in whatever way you may. I am content with the result as long as your principles are fully applied to the particular case of cognitions determining one another. Deny motion, if it seems proper to do so; only then deny the process of determination of one cognition by another. Say that instants and lines are fictions; only say, also, that states of cognition and judgments are fictions. The point here insisted on is not this or that logical solution of the difficulty, but merely that cognition arises by a *process* of beginning, as any other change comes to pass.

In a subsequent paper, I shall trace the consequences of these principles, in reference to the questions of reality, of individuality, and of the validity of the laws of logic.

3. Some Consequences of Four Incapacities[1]

Descartes is the father of modern philosophy, and the spirit of Cartesianism—that which principally distinguishes it from the scholasticism which it displaced—may be compendiously stated as follows:

1. It teaches that philosophy must begin with universal doubt; whereas scholasticism had never questioned fundamentals.

2. It teaches that the ultimate test of certainty is to be found in the individual consciousness; whereas scholasticism had rested on the testimony of sages and of the Catholic Church.

3. The multiform argumentation of the Middle Ages is replaced by a single thread of inference depending often upon inconspicuous premises.

4. Scholasticism had its mysteries of faith, but undertook to explain all created things. But there are many facts which Cartesianism not only does not explain but renders absolutely inexplicable, unless to say that "God makes them so" is to be regarded as an explanation.

In some, or all of these respects, most modern philosophers have been, in effect, Cartesians. Now without wishing to return to scholasticism, it seems to me that modern science and modern logic require us to stand upon a very different platform from this.

[1] *Journal of Speculative Philosophy*, Vol. 2, pp. 140–157 (1868).

1. We cannot begin with complete doubt. We must begin with all the prejudices which we actually have when we enter upon the study of philosophy. These prejudices are not to be dispelled by a maxim, for they are things which it does not occur to us *can* be questioned. Hence this initial skepticism will be a mere self-deception, and not real doubt; and no one who follows the Cartesian method will ever be satisfied until he has formally recovered all those beliefs which in form he has given up. It is, therefore, as useless a preliminary as going to the North Pole would be in order to get to Constantinople by coming down regularly upon a meridian. A person may, it is true, in the course of his studies, find reason to doubt what he began by believing; but in that case he doubts because he has a positive reason for it, and not on account of the Cartesian maxim. Let us not pretend to doubt in philosophy what we do not doubt in our hearts.

2. The same formalism appears in the Cartesian criterion, which amounts to this: "Whatever I am clearly convinced of, is true." If I were really convinced, I should have done with reasoning and should require no test of certainty. But thus to make single individuals absolute judges of truth is most pernicious. The result is that metaphysicians will all agree that metaphysics has reached a pitch of certainty far beyond that of the physical sciences—only they can agree upon nothing else. In sciences in which men come to agreement, when a theory has been broached it is considered to be on probation until this agreement is reached. After it is reached, the question of certainty becomes an idle one, because there is no one left who doubts it. We individually cannot reasonably hope to attain the ultimate philosophy which we pursue; we can only seek it, therefore, for the *community* of philosophers. Hence, if disciplined and candid minds carefully examine a theory and refuse to accept it, this ought to create doubts in the mind of the author of the theory himself.

3. Philosophy ought to imitate the successful sciences in its methods, so far as to proceed only from tangible premisses which can be subjected to careful scrutiny, and to trust rather to the multitude and variety of its arguments than

to the conclusiveness of any one. Its reasoning should not form a chain which is no stronger than its weakest link, but a cable whose fibers may be ever so slender, provided they are sufficiently numerous and intimately connected.

4. Every unidealistic philosophy supposes some absolutely inexplicable, unanalyzable ultimate; in short, something resulting from mediation itself not susceptible of mediation. Now that anything *is* thus inexplicable can only be known by reasoning from signs. But the only justification of an inference from signs is that the conclusion explains the fact. To suppose the fact absolutely inexplicable is not to explain it, and hence this supposition is never allowable.

In the last number of this journal will be found a piece entitled "Questions concerning certain Faculties claimed for Man" [Paper No. I], which has been written in this spirit of opposition to Cartesianism. That criticism of certain faculties resulted in four denials, which for convenience may here be repeated:

1. We have no power of Introspection, but all knowledge of the internal world is derived by hypothetical reasoning from our knowledge of external facts.

2. We have no power of Intuition, but every cognition is determined logically by previous cognitions.

3. We have no power of thinking without signs.

4. We have no conception of the absolutely incognizable.

These propositions cannot be regarded as certain; and, in order to bring them to a further test, it is now proposed to trace them out to their consequences. We may first consider the first alone; then trace the consequences of the first and second; then see what else will result from assuming the third also; and, finally, add the fourth to our hypothetical premises.

In accepting the first proposition, we must put aside all prejudices derived from a philosophy which bases our knowledge of the external world on our self-consciousness. We can admit no statement concerning what passes within us except as a hypothesis necessary to explain what takes place in what we commonly call the external world. Moreover when we have upon such grounds assumed one faculty or mode of action of the mind, we cannot, of course, adopt any other hypothesis for the purpose of explaining any fact which can be explained by our first supposition, but must carry the latter as far as it will go. In other words, we must, as far as we can do so without additional hypotheses, reduce all kinds of mental action to one general type.

The class of modifications of consciousness with which we must commence our inquiry must be one whose existence is indubitable, and whose laws are best known, and, therefore (since this knowledge comes from the outside), which most closely follows external facts; that is, it must be some kind of cognition. Here we may hypothetically admit the second proposition of the former paper, according to which there is no absolutely first cognition of any object, but cognition arises by a continuous process. We must begin, then, with a *process* of cognition, and with that process whose laws are best understood and most closely follow external facts. This is no other than the process of valid inference, which proceeds from its premiss, A, to its conclusion, B, only if, as a matter of fact, such a proposition as B is always or usually true when such a proposition as A is true. It is a consequence, then, of the first two principles whose results we are to trace out, that we must, as far as we can, without any other supposition than that the mind reasons, reduce all mental action to the formula of valid reasoning.

But does the mind in fact go through the syllogistic process? It is certainly very doubtful whether a conclusion—as something existing in the mind independently, like an image—suddenly displaces two premises existing in the mind in a similar way. But it is a matter of constant experience that, if a man is made to believe in the premises, in the sense that he will act from them and will say that they are true, under favorable conditions he will also be ready to act from the conclusion and to say that that is true. Something, therefore, takes place within the organism which is equivalent to the syllogistic process.

A valid inference is either *complete* or *incomplete*. An incomplete inference is one whose validity depends upon some matter of fact not contained in the premisses. This implied fact might have been stated as a premiss, and its relation to the conclusion is the same whether it is explicitly posited or not, since it is at least virtually taken for granted; so that every valid incomplete argument is virtually complete. Complete arguments are divided into *simple* and *complex*. A complex argument is one which from three or more premisses concludes what might have been concluded by successive steps in reasonings each of which is simple. Thus, a complex inference comes to the same thing in the end as a succession of simple inferences.

A complete, simple, and valid argument, or syllogism, is either *apodictic* or *probable*. An apodictic or deductive syllogism is one whose validity depends unconditionally upon the relation of the fact inferred to the facts posited in the premisses. A syllogism whose validity should depend not merely upon its premisses, but upon the existence of some other knowledge, would be impossible; for either this other knowledge would be posited, in which case it would be a part of the premisses, or it would be implicitly assumed, in which case the inference would be incomplete. But a syllogism whose validity depends partly upon the *non-existence* of some other knowledge is a *probable* syllogism.

A few examples will render this plain. The two following arguments are apodictic or deductive:

1. No series of days of which the first and last are different days of the week exceeds by one a multiple of seven days; now the first and last days of any leap-year are different days of the week, and therefore no leap-year consists of a number of days one greater than a multiple of seven.

2. Among the vowels there are no double letters; but one of the double letters (w) is compounded of two vowels; hence, a letter compounded of two vowels is not necessarily itself a vowel.

In both these cases, it is plain that as long as the premisses are true, however other facts may be, the conclusions will be true. On the other hand, suppose that we reason as follows: "A certain man had the Asiatic cholera. He was in a state of collapse, livid, quite cold, and without perceptible pulse. He was bled copiously. During the process he came out of collapse, and the next morning was well enough to be about. Therefore, bleeding tends to cure the cholera." This is a fair probable inference, provided that the premisses represent our whole knowledge of the matter. But if we knew, for example, that recoveries from cholera were apt to be sudden, and that the physician who had reported this case had known of a hundred other trials of the remedy without communicating the result, then the inference would lose all its validity.

The absence of knowledge which is essential to the validity of any probable argument relates to some question which is determined by the argument itself. This question, like every other, is whether certain objects have certain characters. Hence, the absence of knowledge is either whether besides the objects which, according to the premisses, possess certain characters, any other objects possess them; or, whether besides the characters which, according to the premisses, belong to certain objects, any other characters not necessarily involved in these belong to the same objects. In the former case, the reasoning proceeds as though all the objects which have certain characters were known, and this is *induction;* in the latter case, the inference proceeds as though all the characters requisite to the determination of a certain object or class were known, and this is *hypothesis*. This distinction, also, may be made more plain by examples.

Suppose we count the number of occurrences of the different letters in a certain English book, which we may call A. Of course, every new letter which we add to our count will alter the relative number of occurrences of the different letters; but as we proceed with our counting, this change will be less and less. Suppose that we find that as we increase the number of letters counted, the relative number of *e*'s approaches nearly 11¼ per cent of the whole, that of the *t*'s 8½ per cent, that of the *a*'s 8 per cent, that of the *s*'s 7½ per cent, etc. Suppose we repeat the same observations with half a dozen other English writings (which we may designate as B, C, D, E, F, G) with the like result. Then we may infer that in every English writing of some length, the different letters occur with nearly those relative frequencies.

Now this argument depends for its validity upon our *not* knowing the proportion of letters in any English writing besides A, B, C, D, E, F, and G. For if we know it in respect to H, and it is not nearly the same as in the others, our conclusion is destroyed at once; if it is the same, then the legitimate inference is from A, B, C, D, E, F, G, and H, and not from the first seven alone. This, therefore, is an *induction*.

Suppose, next, that a piece of writing in cipher is presented to us, without the key. Suppose we find that it contains something less than 26 characters, one of which occurs about 11 per cent of all the times, another 8½ per cent, another 8 per cent, and another 7½ per cent. Suppose that when we substitute for these *e, t, a,* and *s,* respectively, we are able to see how single letters may be substituted for each of the other characters so as to make sense in English, provided, however, that we allow the spelling to be wrong in some cases. If the writing is of any considerable length, we may infer with great probability that this is the meaning of the cipher.

The validity of this argument depends upon there being no other known characters of the writing in cipher which would have any weight in the matter; for if there are—if we know, for example, whether or not there is any other solution of it—this must be allowed its effect in supporting or weakening the conclusion. This, then, is *hypothesis*.

All valid reasoning is either deductive, inductive, or hypothetic; or else it combines two or more of these characters. Deduction is pretty well treated in most logical textbooks; but it will be necessary to say a few words about induction and hypothesis in order to render what follows more intelligible.

Induction may be defined as an argument which proceeds upon the assumption that all the members of a class or aggregate have all the characters which are common to all those members of this class concerning which it is known, whether they have these characters or not; or, in other words, which assumes that that is true of a whole collection which is true of a number of instances taken from it at random. This might be called statistical argument. In the long run, it must generally afford pretty correct conclusions from true premisses. If we have a bag of beans partly black and partly white, by counting the relative proportions of the two colors in several different handfuls, we can approximate more or less to the relative proportions in the whole bag, since a sufficient number of handfuls would constitute all the beans in the bag. The central characteristic and key to induction is that by taking the conclusion so reached as major premiss of a syllogism, and the proposition stating that such and such objects are taken from the class in question as the minor premiss, the other premiss of the induction will follow from them deductively. Thus, in the above example we concluded that all books in English have about 11¼ per cent of their letters *e*'s. From that as major premiss, together with the proposition that A, B, C, D, E, F, and G are books in English, it follows deductively that A, B, C, D, E, F, and G have about 11¼ per cent of their letters *e*'s. Accordingly, induction has been defined by Aristotle as the inference of the major premiss of a syllogism from its minor premiss and conclusion. The function of an induction is to substitute for a series of many subjects a single one which embraces them and an indefinite number of others. Thus it is a species of "reduction of the manifold to unity."

Hypothesis may be defined as an argument which proceeds upon the assumption that a character which is known necessarily to involve a certain number of others, may be probably predicated of any object which has all the characters which this character is known to involve. Just as induction may be regarded as the inference of the major premiss of a syllogism, so hypothesis may be regarded as the inference of the minor premiss, from the other two propositions. Thus, the example taken above consists of two such inferences of the minor premisses of the following syllogisms:

    1.   Every English writing of some length in which such and such characters denote *e*, *t*, *a*, and *s* has about 11¼

per cent of the first sort of marks, 8½ of the second, 8 of the third, and 7½ of the fourth.

This secret writing is an English writing of some length, in which such and such characters denote *e, t, a,* and *s,* respectively:

∴ This secret writing has about 11¼ per cent of its characters of the first kind, 8½ of the second, 8 of the third, and 7½ of the fourth.

2. A passage written with such an alphabet makes sense when such and such letters are severally substituted for such and such characters.

This secret writing is written with such an alphabet.

∴ This secret writing makes sense when such and such substitutions are made.

The function of hypothesis is to substitute for a great series of predicates forming no unity in themselves, a single one (or small number) which involves them all, together (perhaps) with an indefinite number of others. It is, therefore, also a reduction of a manifold to unity.[2] Every de-

---

[2] Several persons versed in logic have objected that I have here quite misapplied the term *hypothesis,* and that what I so designate is an argument from *analogy.* It is a sufficient reply to say that the example of the cipher has been given as an apt illustration of hypothesis by Descartes (Rule 10 *Œuvres choisies:* Paris, 1865, page 334), by Leibniz (*Nouv. Ess.,* lib. 4, ch. 12, § 13, Ed. Erdmann, p. 383 *b*), and (as I learn from D. Stewart: *Works,* Vol. 3, pp. 305, *et seq.*) by Gravesande, Boscovich, Hartley, and G. L. Le Sage. The term Hypothesis has been used in the following senses: (1) For the theme or proposition forming the subject of discourse. (2) For an assumption. Aristotle divides *theses* or propositions adopted without any reason into definitions and hypotheses. The latter are propositions stating the existence of something. Thus the geometer says, "Let there be a triangle." (3) For a condition in a general sense. We are said to seek other things than happiness *éx hypothéseos,* conditionally. The best republic is the ideally perfect, the second the best on earth, the third the best *éx hypothéseos,* under the circumstances. Freedom is the *hypóthesis* or condition of democracy. (4) For the antecedent of a hypothetical proposition. (5) For an oratorical question which assumes facts. (6) In the *Synopsis* of Psellus, for the reference of a subject to the things it denotes. (7) Most commonly in modern times, for the conclusion of an argument from consequence and consequent to antecedent. This is my use of the

ductive syllogism may be put into the form

If A, then B;

But A:

∴ B.

And as the minor premiss in this form appears as antecedent or reason of a hypothetical proposition, hypothetic inference may be called reasoning from consequent to antecedent.

The argument from analogy, which a popular writer [John Stuart Mill] upon logic calls reasoning from particulars to particulars, derives its validity from its combining the characters of induction and hypothesis, being analyzable either into a deduction or an induction, or a deduction and a hypothesis.

But though inference is thus of three essentially different species, it also belongs to one genus. We have seen that no conclusion can be legitimately derived which could not have been reached by successions of arguments having two premises each, and implying no fact not asserted.

Either of these premises is a proposition asserting that certain objects have certain characters. Every term of such a proposition stands either for certain objects or for certain characters. The conclusion may be regarded as a proposition substituted in place of either premiss, the substitution being justified by the fact stated in the other premiss. The conclusion is accordingly derived from either premiss by substituting either a new subject for the subject of the premiss, or a new predicate for the predicate of the premiss, or by both substitutions. Now the substitution of one term for another can be justified only so far as the term substituted represents only what is represented in the term replaced. If, therefore, the conclusion be denoted by the formula,

S is P;

and this conclusion be derived, by a change of subject, from a premiss which may on this account be expressed by the formula,

term. (8) For such a conclusion when too weak to be a theory accepted into the body of a science. . . . [Peirce cites a few authorities to support the seventh use.]

M is P,

then the other premiss must assert that whatever thing is represented by S is represented by M, or that

Every S is an M;

while, if the conclusion, S is P, is derived from either premiss by a change of predicate, that premiss may be written

S is M;

and the other premiss must assert that whatever characters are implied in P are implied in M, or that

Whatever is M is P.

In either case, therefore, the syllogism must be capable of expression in the form,

S is M; M is P:
∴ S is P.

Finally, if the conclusion differs from either of its premisses, both in subject and predicate, the form of statement of conclusion and premiss may be so altered that they shall have a common term. This can always be done, for if P is the premiss and C the conclusion, they may be stated thus:

The state of things represented in P is real, and

The state of things represented in C is real.

In this case the other premiss must in some form virtually assert that every state of things such as is represented by C is the state of things represented in P.

All valid reasoning, therefore, is of one general form; and in seeking to reduce all mental action to the formulas of valid inference, we seek to reduce it to one single type.

An apparent obstacle to the reduction of all mental action to the type of valid inferences is the existence of fallacious reasoning. Every argument implies the truth of a general principle of inferential procedure (whether involving some matter of fact concerning the subject of argument, or merely a maxim relating to a system of signs), according to which it is a valid argument. If this principle is false, the argument is a fallacy; but neither a valid argument from false premisses, nor an exceedingly weak, but not altogether illegitimate, induction or hypothesis, however its force may be over-estimated, however false its conclusion, is a fallacy.

Now words, taken just as they stand, if in the form of an argument, thereby do imply whatever fact may be neces-

sary to make the argument conclusive; so that to the formal
logician, who has to do only with the meaning of the words
according to the proper principles of interpretation, and not
with the intention of the speaker as guessed at from other
indications, the only fallacies should be such as are simply
absurd and contradictory, either because their conclusions
are absolutely inconsistent with their premises, or because
they connect propositions by a species of illative conjunction, by which they cannot under any circumstances be
validly connected.

But to the psychologist an argument is valid only if the
premises from which the mental conclusion is derived
would be sufficient, if true, to justify it, either by themselves, or by the aid of other propositions which had previously been held for true. But it is easy to show that all
inferences made by man, which are not valid in this sense,
belong to four classes, viz.: (1) those whose premises are
false; (2) those which have some little force, though only
a little; (3) those which result from confusion of one proposition with another; (4) those which result from the indis-
tinct apprehension, wrong application, or falsity, of a rule
of inference. For, if a man were to commit a fallacy not of
either of these classes, he would, from true premises conceived with perfect distinctness, without being led astray
by any prejudice or other judgment serving as a rule of
inference, draw a conclusion which had really not the least
relevancy. If this could happen, calm consideration and
care could be of little use in thinking, for caution only serves
to insure our taking all the facts into account, and to make
those which we do take account of, distinct; nor can cool-
ness do anything more than to enable us to be cautious,
and also to prevent our being affected by a passion in in-
ferring that to be true which we wish were true, or which
we fear may be true, or in following some other wrong rule
of inference. But experience shows that the calm and careful consideration of the same distinctly conceived premises
(including prejudices) will insure the pronouncement of
the same judgment by all men. Now if a fallacy belongs to
the first of these four classes and its premises are false, it
is to be presumed that the procedure of the mind from

these premisses to the conclusion is either correct, or errs in one of the other three ways; for it cannot be supposed that the mere falsity of the premisses should affect the procedure of reason when that falsity is not known to reason. If the fallacy belongs to the second class and has some force, however little, it is a legitimate probable argument, and belongs to the type of valid inference. If it is of the third class and results from the confusion of one proposition with another, this confusion must be owing to a resemblance between the two propositions; that is to say, the person reasoning, seeing that one proposition has some of the characters which belong to the other, concludes that it has all the essential characters of the other, and is equivalent to it. Now this is a hypothetic inference, which though it may be weak, and though its conclusion happens to be false, belongs to the type of valid inferences; and, therefore, as the *nodus* of the fallacy lies in this confusion, the procedure of the mind in these fallacies of the third class conforms to the formula of valid inference. If the fallacy belongs to the fourth class, it either results from wrongly applying or misapprehending a rule of inference, and so is a fallacy of confusion, or it results from adopting a wrong rule of inference. In this latter case, this rule is in fact taken as a premiss, and therefore the false conclusion is owing merely to the falsity of a premiss. In every fallacy, therefore, possible to the mind of man, the procedure of the mind conforms to the formula of valid inference.

The third principle whose consequences we have to deduce is, that, whenever we think, we have present to the consciousness some feeling, image, conception, or other representation, which serves as a sign. But it follows from our own existence (which is proved by the occurrence of ignorance and error) that everything which is present to us is a phenomenal manifestation of ourselves. This does not prevent its being a phenomenon of something without us, just as a rainbow is at once a manifestation both of the sun and of the rain. When we think, then, we ourselves, as we are at that moment, appear as a sign. Now a sign has, as such, three references: first, it is a sign *to* some thought which interprets it; second, it is a sign *for* some object to which in that thought it is equivalent; third, it is a sign, *in* some respect or quality, which brings it into connection with its object. Let us ask what the three correlates are to which a thought-sign refers.

(1) When we think, to what thought does that thought-sign which is ourself address itself? It may, through the medium of outward expression, which it reaches perhaps only after considerable internal development, come to address itself to thought of another person. But whether this happens or not, it is always interpreted by a subsequent thought of our own. If, after any thought, the current of ideas flows on freely, it follows the law of mental association. In that case, each former thought suggests something to the thought which follows it, i.e., is the sign of something to this latter. Our train of thought may, it is true, be interrupted. But we must remember that, in addition to the principal element of thought at any moment, there are a hundred things in our mind to which but a small fraction of attention or consciousness is conceded. It does not, therefore, follow, because a new constituent of thought gets the uppermost that the train of thought which it displaces is broken off altogether. On the contrary, from our second principle, that there is no intuition or cognition not determined by previous cognitions, it follows that the striking in of a new experience is never an instantaneous affair, but is an *event* occupying time, and coming to pass by a continuous process. Its prominence in consciousness, therefore, must probably be the consummation of a growing process; and if so, there is no sufficient cause for the thought which had been the leading one just before, to cease abruptly and instantaneously. But if a train of thought ceases by gradually dying out, it freely follows its own law of association as long as it lasts, and there is no moment at which there is a thought belonging to this series, subsequently to which there is not a thought which interprets or repeats it. There is no exception, therefore, to the law that every thought-sign is translated or interpreted in a subsequent one, unless it be that all thought comes to an abrupt and final end in death.

(2) The next question is: For what does the thought-sign stand—what does it name—what is its *suppositum?* The outward thing, undoubtedly, when a real outward thing is thought of. But still, as the thought is determined by a previous thought of the same object, it only refers to the thing through denoting this previous thought. Let us suppose, for example, that Toussaint is thought of, and first thought of as a *negro,* but not distinctly as a man. If this distinctness is afterwards added, it is through the thought that a *negro* is a *man;* that is to say, the subsequent thought, *man,* refers to the outward thing by being predicated of that previous thought, *negro,* which has been had of that thing. If we afterwards think of Toussaint as a general, then we think that this negro, this man, was a general. And so in every case the subsequent thought denotes what was thought in the previous thought.

(3) The thought-sign stands for its object in the respect which is thought; that is to say, this respect is the immediate object of consciousness in the thought, or, in other words, it is the thought itself, or at least what the thought is thought to be in the subsequent thought to which it is a sign.

We must now consider two other properties of signs which are of great importance in the theory of cognition. Since a sign is not identical with the thing signified, but differs from the latter in some respects, it must plainly have some characters which belong to it in itself, and have nothing to do with its representative function. These I call the *material* qualities of the sign. As examples of such qualities, take in the word "man," its consisting of three letters—in a picture, its being flat and without relief. In the second place, a sign must be capable of being connected (not in the reason but really) with another sign of the same object, or with the object itself. Thus, words would be of no value at all unless they could be connected into sentences by means of a real copula which joins signs of the same thing. The usefulness of some signs—as a weathercock, a tally, etc.—consists wholly in their being really connected with the very things they signify. In the case of a picture such a connection is not evident, but it exists in the power of association which connects the picture with the brain-sign which labels it. This real, physical connection of a sign with its object, either immediately or by its connection with another sign, I call the *pure demonstrative application* of the sign. Now the representative function of a sign lies neither in its material quality nor in its pure demonstrative application; because it is something which the sign is, not in itself or in a real relation to its object, but which it is *to a thought,* while both of the characters just defined belong to the sign independently of its addressing any thought. And yet if I take all the things which have certain qualities and physically connect them with another series of things, each to each, they become fit to be signs. If they are not regarded as such, they are not actually signs, but they are so in the same sense, for example, in which an unseen flower can be said to be *red,* this being also a term relative to a mental affection.

Consider a state of mind which is a conception. It is a conception by virtue of having a *meaning,* a logical comprehension; and if it is applicable to any object, it is because that object has the characters contained in the comprehension of this conception. Now the logical comprehension of a thought is usually said to consist of the thoughts contained in it; but thoughts are events, acts of the mind. Two thoughts are two events separated in time, and one cannot literally be contained in the other. It may be said that all thoughts exactly similar are regarded as one; and that to say that one thought contains another means that it contains one exactly similar to that other. But how can two thoughts be similar? Two objects can only be *regarded* as similar if they are compared and brought together in the mind. Thoughts have no existence except in the mind; only as they are regarded do they exist. Hence, two thoughts cannot *be* similar unless they are brought together in the mind. But, as to their existence, two thoughts are separated by an interval of time. We are too apt to imagine that we can frame a thought similar to a past thought, by matching it with the latter, as though this past thought were still present to us. But it is plain that the knowledge that one thought is similar to or in any way truly representative of another cannot be derived from immediate perception, but must be an hypothesis (unquestionably fully justifiable by facts), and that therefore the formation of such a representing thought must be dependent upon a real effective force behind consciousness, and not merely upon a mental comparison. What we must mean, therefore, by saying that one concept is contained in another is that we normally represent one to be in the other; that is, that we form a particular kind of judgment,[3] of which the subject signifies one concept and the predicate the other.

No thought in itself, then, no feeling in itself, contains any others, but is absolutely simple and unanalyzable; and to say that it is composed of other thoughts and feelings is like saying that a movement upon a straight line is composed of the two movements of which it is the resultant; that is to say, it is a metaphor, or fiction, parallel to the truth. Every thought, however artificial and complex, is, so far as it is immediately present, a mere sensation without parts, and therefore, in itself, without similarity to any other, but incomparable with any other and absolutely *sui generis*.[4] Whatever is wholly incomparable with anything else is wholly inexplicable, because explanation consists in bringing things under general laws or under natural classes. Hence every thought, in so far as it is a feeling of a peculiar sort, is simply an ultimate, inexplicable fact. Yet this does not conflict with my postulate that that fact should be allowed to stand as inexplicable; for, on the one hand, we never can think, "This is present to me," since, before we have time to make the reflection, the sensation is past, and, on the other hand, when once past, we can never bring back the quality of the feeling as it was *in and for itself*, or

[3] A judgment concerning a minimum of information, for the theory of which see my paper on Comprehension and Extension [*Proceedings of the American Academy of Arts and Sciences*, Vol. 7 (Nov. 13, 1867), pp. 416–32].

[4] Observe that I say *in itself*. I am not so wild as to deny that my sensation of red today is like my sensation of red yesterday. I only say that the similarity can *consist* only in the physiological force behind consciousness—which leads me to say, I recognize this feeling the same as the former one, and so does not consist in a community of sensation.

know what it was like *in itself*, or even discover the existence of this quality except by a corollary from our general theory of ourselves, and then not in its idiosyncrasy, but only as something present. But, as something present, feelings are all alike and require no explanation, since they contain only what is universal. So that nothing which we can truly predicate of feelings is left inexplicable, but only something which we cannot reflectively know. So that we do not fall into the contradiction of making the Mediate immediable. Finally, no present actual thought (which is a mere feeling) has any meaning, any intellectual value; for this lies not in what is actually thought, but in what this thought may be connected with in representation by subsequent thoughts; so that the meaning of a thought is altogether something virtual. It may be objected that if no thought has any meaning, all thought is without meaning. But this is a fallacy similar to saying that, if in no one of the successive spaces which a body fills there is room for motion, there is no room for motion throughout the whole. At no one instant in my state of mind is there cognition or representation, but in the relation of my states of mind at different instants there is.[5] In short, the Immediate (and therefore in itself unsusceptible of mediation—the Unanalyzable, the Inexplicable, the Unintellectual) runs in a continuous stream through our lives; it is the sum total of consciousness, whose mediation, which is the continuity of it, is brought about by a real effective force behind consciousness.

Thus, we have in thought three elements: first, the representative function which makes it a *representation;* second, the pure denotative application, or real connection, which brings one thought into *relation* with another; and third, the material quality, or how it feels, which gives thought its *quality*.

That a sensation is not necessarily an intuition, or first impression of sense, is very evident in the case of the sense of beauty; and has been shown [above], in the case of

[5] Accordingly, just as we say that a body is in motion, and not that motion is in a body, we ought to say that we are in thought and not that thoughts are in us.

sound. When the sensation beautiful is determined by previous cognitions, it always arises as a predicate; that is, we think that something is beautiful. Whenever a sensation thus arises in consequence of others, induction shows that those others are more or less complicated. Thus, the sensation of a particular kind of sound arises in consequence of impressions upon the various nerves of the ear being combined in a particular way, and following one another with a certain rapidity. A sensation of color depends upon impressions upon the eye following one another in a regular manner, and with a certain rapidity. The sensation of beauty arises upon a manifold of other impressions. And this will be found to hold good in all cases. Secondly, all these sensations are in themselves simple, or more so than the sensations which give rise to them. Accordingly, a sensation is a simple predicate taken in place of a complex predicate; in other words, it fulfills the function of an hypothesis. But the general principle that everything to which such and such a sensation belongs, has such and such a complicated series of predicates, is not one determined by reason (as we have seen), but is of an arbitrary nature. Hence, the class of hypothetic inferences which the arising of a sensation resembles is that of reasoning from definition to definitum, in which the major premiss is of an arbitrary nature. Only in this mode of reasoning, this premiss is determined by the conventions of language, and expresses the occasion upon which a word is to be used; and in the formation of a sensation, it is determined by the constitution of our nature, and expresses the occasions upon which sensation, or a natural mental sign, arises. Thus, the sensation, so far as it represents something, is determined, according to a logical law, by previous cognitions; that is to say, these cognitions determine that there shall be a sensation. But so far as the sensation is a mere feeling of a particular sort, it is determined only by an inexplicable, occult power; and so far, it is not a representation, but only the material quality of a representation. For just as in reasoning from definition to definitum, it is indifferent to the logician how the defined word shall sound, or how many letters it shall contain, so in the case of this constitutional word, it is not determined by an inward law how it shall feel in itself. A feeling, therefore, as a feeling, is merely the *material quality* of a mental sign.

But there is no feeling which is not also a representation, a predicate of something determined logically by the feelings which precede it. For if there are any such feelings not predicates, they are the emotions. Now every emotion has a subject. If a man is angry, he is saying to himself that this or that is vile and outrageous. If he is in joy, he is saying "this is delicious." If he is wondering, he is saying "this is strange." In short, whenever a man feels, he is thinking of *something*. Even those passions which have no definite object—as melancholy—only come to consciousness through tingeing the *objects of thought*. That which makes us look upon the emotions more as affections of self than other cognitions, is that we have found them more dependent upon our accidental situation at the moment than other cognitions; but that is only to say that they are cognitions too narrow to be useful. The emotions, as a little observation will show, arise when our attention is strongly drawn to complex and inconceivable circumstances. Fear arises when we cannot predict our fate; joy, in the case of certain indescribable and peculiarly complex sensations. If there are some indications that something greatly for my interest, and which I have anticipated would happen, may not happen; and if, after weighing probabilities, and inventing safeguards, and straining for further information, I find myself unable to come to any fixed conclusion in reference to the future, in the place of that intellectual hypothetic inference which I seek, the feeling of *anxiety* arises. When something happens for which I cannot account, I *wonder*. When I endeavor to realize to myself what I never can do, a pleasure in the future, I *hope*. "I do not understand you" is the phrase of an angry man. The indescribable, the ineffable, the incomprehensible, commonly excite emotion; but nothing is so chilling as a scientific explanation. Thus an emotion is always a simple predicate substituted by an operation of the mind for a highly complicated predicate. Now if we consider that a very complex predicate demands explanation by means of an hypothesis, that that hypothesis must be a simpler predicate substituted for that complex one; and that when we have an emotion, an hypothesis, strictly speaking, is hardly possible—the analogy of the parts played by emotion and hypothesis is very striking. There is, it is true, this difference between an emotion and an intellectual hypothesis, that we have reason to say in the case of the latter, that to whatever the simple hypothetic predicate can be applied, of that the complex predicate is true; whereas, in the case of an emotion this is a proposition for which no reason can be given, but which is determined merely by our emotional constitution. But this corresponds precisely to the difference between hypothesis and reasoning from definition to definitum, and thus it would appear that emotion is nothing but sensation. There appears to be a difference, however, between emotion and sensation, and I would state it as follows:

There is some reason to think that, corresponding to every feeling within us, some motion takes place in our bodies. This property of the thought-sign, since it has no rational dependence upon the meaning of the sign, may be compared with what I have called the material quality of the sign; but it differs from the latter inasmuch as it is not essentially necessary that it should be felt in order that there should be any thought-sign. In the case of a sensation, the manifold of impressions which precede and determine it are not of a kind, the bodily motion corresponding to which comes from any large ganglion or from the brain, and probably for this reason the sensation produces no great commotion in the bodily organism; and the sensation itself is not a thought which has a very strong influence upon the current of thought except by virtue of the information it may serve to afford. An emotion, on the other hand, comes much later in the development of thought—I mean, further from the first beginning of the cognition of its object—and the thoughts which determine it already have motions corresponding to them in the brain, or the chief ganglion; consequently, it produces large movements in the body, and independently of its representative value, strongly affects the current of thought. The animal motions to which I allude are, in the first place and obviously, blushing, blenching, staring, smiling, scowling, pouting, laughing, weeping, sobbing, wriggling, flinching, trembling, being petrified, sighing, sniffing, shrugging, groaning, heartsinking, trepidation, swelling of the heart, etc., etc. To these may, perhaps, be added, in the second place, other more complicated actions, which nevertheless spring from a direct impulse and not from deliberation.

That which distinguishes both sensations proper and emotions from the feeling of a thought is that in the case of the two former the material quality is made prominent, because the thought has no relation of reason to the thoughts which determine it, which exists in the last case and detracts from the attention given to the mere feeling. By there being no relation of reason to the determining thoughts, I mean that there is nothing in the content of the thought which explains why it should arise only on occasion of these determining thoughts. If there is such a relation of reason, if the thought is essentially limited in its application to these objects, then the thought comprehends a thought other than itself; in other words, it is then a complex thought. An incomplex thought can, therefore, be nothing but a sensation or emotion, having no rational character. This is very different from the ordinary doctrine, according to which the very highest and most metaphysical conceptions are absolutely simple. I shall be asked how such a conception of a *being* is to be analyzed, or whether I can ever define *one, two,* and *three,* without a diallelon. Now I shall admit at once that neither of these conceptions can be separated into two others higher than itself; and in that sense, therefore, I fully admit that certain very metaphysical and eminently intellectual notions are absolutely simple. But though these concepts cannot be defined by genus and difference, there is another way in which they can be defined. All determination is by negation; we can first recognize any character only by putting an object which possesses it into comparison with an object which possesses it not. A conception, therefore, which was quite universal in every respect would be unrecognizable and impossible. We do not obtain the conception of Being, in the sense implied in the copula, by observing that all the things which we can think of have something in common, for there is no such thing to be observed. We get it by reflecting upon signs—words or thoughts; we observe that different predicates may be attached to the same subject, and that each makes some conception applicable to the subject; then we imagine that a subject has something true of it merely because a predicate (no matter what) is attached to it—and that we call Being. The conception of being is, therefore, a conception about a sign—a thought, or word; and since it is not applicable to every sign, it is not primarily universal, although it is so in its mediate application to things. Being, therefore, may be defined; it may be defined, for example, as that which is common to the objects included in any class, and to the objects not included in the same class. But it is nothing new to say that metaphysical conceptions are primarily and at bottom thoughts about words, or thoughts about thoughts; it is the doctrine both of Aristotle (whose categories are parts of speech) and of Kant (whose categories are the characters of different kinds of propositions).

Sensation and the power of abstraction or attention may be regarded as, in one sense, the sole constituents of all thought. Having considered the former, let us now attempt some analysis of the latter. By the force of attention, an emphasis is put upon one of the objective elements of consciousness. This emphasis is, therefore, not itself an object of immediate consciousness; and in this respect it differs entirely from a feeling. Therefore, since the emphasis, nevertheless, consists in some effect upon consciousness, and so can exist only so far as it affects our knowledge; and since an act cannot be supposed to determine that which precedes it in time, this act can consist only in the capacity which the cognition emphasized has for producing an effect upon memory, or otherwise influencing subsequent thought. This is confirmed by the fact that attention is a matter of continuous quantity; for continuous quantity, so far as we know it, reduces itself in the last analysis to time. Accordingly, we find that attention does, in fact, produce a very great effect upon subsequent thought. In the first place, it strongly affects memory, a thought being remembered for a longer time the greater the attention originally paid to it.

In the second place, the greater the attention, the closer the connection and the more accurate the logical sequence of thought. In the third place, by attention a thought may be recovered which has been forgotten. From these facts, we gather that attention is the power by which thought at one time is connected with and made to relate to thought at another time; or, to apply the conception of thought as a sign, that it is the *pure demonstrative application* of a thought-sign.

Attention is roused when the same phenomenon presents itself repeatedly on different occasions, or the same predicate in different subjects. We see that A has a certain character, that B has the same, C has the same; and this excites our attention, so that we say, *"These* have this character." Thus attention is an act of induction; but it is an induction which does not increase our knowledge, because our "these" covers nothing but the instances experienced. It is, in short, an argument from enumeration.

Attention produces effects upon the nervous system. These effects are habits, or nervous associations. A habit arises when, having had the sensation of performing a certain act, *m,* on several occasions *a, b, c,* we come to do it upon every occurrence of the general event, *l,* of which *a, b,* and *c* are special cases. That is to say, by the cognition that

Every case of *a, b,* or *c,* is a case of *m,* is determined the cognition that

Every case of *l* is a case of *m.*

Thus the formation of a habit is an induction, and is therefore necessarily connected with attention or abstraction. Voluntary actions result from the sensations produced by habits, as instinctive actions result from our original nature.

We have thus seen that every sort of modification of consciousness—Attention, Sensation, and Understanding—is an inference. But the objection may be made that inference deals only with general terms, and that an image, or absolutely singular representation, cannot therefore be inferred.

"Singular" and "individual" are equivocal terms. A singular may mean that which can be but in one place at one time. In this sense it is not opposed to general. *The sun* is a singular in this sense, but, as is explained in every good treatise on logic, it is a general term. I may have a very general conception of Hermolaus Barbarus, but still I conceive him only as able to be in one place at one time. When an image is said to be singular, it is meant that it is absolutely determinate in all respects. Every possible character, or the negative thereof, must be true of such an image. In the words of [Berkeley] the most eminent expounder of the doctrine, the image of a man "must be either of a white, or a black, or a tawny; a straight or a crooked; a tall, or a low, or a middle-sized man." It must be of a man with his mouth open or his mouth shut, whose hair is precisely of such and such a shade, and whose figure has precisely such and such proportions. No statement of Locke has been so scouted by all friends of images as his denial that the "idea" of a triangle must be either of an obtuse-angled, right-angled, or acute-angled triangle. In fact, the image of a triangle must be of one, each of whose angles is of a certain number of degrees, minutes, and seconds.

This being so, it is apparent that no man has a *true* image of the road to his office, or of any other real thing. Indeed he has no image of it at all unless he can not only recognize it, but imagine it (truly or falsely) in all its infinite details. This being the case, it becomes very doubtful whether we ever have any such thing as an image in our imagination. Please, reader, to look at a bright red book, or other brightly colored object, and then to shut your eyes and say whether you *see* that color, whether brightly or faintly—whether, indeed, there is anything like sight there. Hume and the other followers of Berkeley maintain that there is no difference between the sight and the memory of the red book except in "their different degrees of force and vivacity." "The colors which the memory employs," says Hume, "are faint and dull compared with those in which our original perceptions are clothed." If this were a correct statement of the difference, we should remember the book as being less red than it is; whereas, in fact, we remember the color with very great precision for a few moments (please to test this point, reader), although we do not see anything like it. We carry away absolutely nothing of the

color except the *consciousness that we could recognize it.*
As a further proof of this, I will request the reader to try
a little experiment. Let him call up, if he can, the image of
a horse—not of one which he has ever seen, but of an imaginary one—and before reading further let him by contemplation fix the image in his memory . . . [sic]. Has the
reader done as requested? For I protest that it is not fair
play to read further without doing so. Now, the reader
can say in general of what color that horse was, whether
grey, bay, or black. But he probably cannot say *precisely*
of what shade it was. He cannot state this as exactly as he
could just after having *seen* such a horse. But why, if he
had an image in his mind which no more had the general
color than it had the particular shade, has the latter vanished so instantaneously from his memory while the former
still remains? It may be replied that we always forget the
details before we do the more general characters; but that
this answer is insufficient is, I think, shown by the extreme
disproportion between the length of time that the exact
shade of something looked at is remembered as compared
with that instantaneous oblivion to the exact shade of the
thing imagined, and the but slightly superior vividness of
the memory of the thing seen as compared with the memory of the thing imagined.

The nominalists, I suspect, confound together thinking a
triangle without thinking that it is either equilateral, isosceles, or scalene, and thinking a triangle without thinking
whether it is equilateral, isosceles, or scalene.

It is important to remember that we have no intuitive
power of distinguishing between one subjective mode of
cognition and another; and hence often think that something is presented to us as a picture, while it is really constructed from slight data by the understanding. This is the
case with dreams, as is shown by the frequent impossibility
of giving an intelligible account of one without adding
something which we feel was not in the dream itself. Many
dreams, of which the waking memory makes elaborate and
consistent stories, must probably have been in fact mere
jumbles of these feelings of the ability to recognize this and
that which I have just alluded to.

I will now go so far as to say that we have no images even in actual perception. It will be sufficient to prove this in the case of vision; for if no picture is seen when we look at an object, it will not be claimed that hearing, touch, and the other senses are superior to sight in this respect. That the picture is not painted on the nerves of the retina is absolutely certain, if, as physiologists inform us, these nerves are needle-points pointing to the light and at distances considerably greater than the *minimum visibile*. The same thing is shown by our not being able to perceive that there is a large blind spot near the middle of the retina. If, then, we have a picture before us when we see, it is one constructed by the mind at the suggestion of previous sensations. Supposing these sensations to be signs, the understanding by reasoning from them could attain all the knowledge of outward things which we derive from sight, while the sensations are quite inadequate to forming an image or representation absolutely determinate. If we have such an image or picture, we must have in our minds a representation of a surface which is only a part of every surface we see, and we must see that each part, however small, has such and such a color. If we look from some distance at a speckled surface, it seems as if we did not see whether it were speckled or not; but if we have an image before us, it must appear to us either as speckled or as not speckled. Again, the eye by education comes to distinguish minute differences of color; but if we see only absolutely determinate images, we must, no less before our eyes are trained than afterwards, see each color as particularly such and such a shade. Thus to suppose that we have an image before us when we see is not only a hypothesis which explains nothing whatever, but is one which actually creates difficulties which require new hypotheses in order to explain them away.

One of these difficulties arises from the fact that the details are less easily distinguished than, and forgotten before, the general circumstances. Upon this theory, the general features exist in the details: the details are, in fact, the whole picture. It seems, then, very strange that that which exists only secondarily in the picture should make more impression than the picture itself. It is true that in an old painting the details are not easily made out; but this is because we know that the blackness is the result of time, and is no part of the picture itself. There is no difficulty in making out the details of the picture as it looks at present; the only difficulty is in guessing what it used to be. But if we have a picture on the retina, the minutest details are there as much as, nay, more than, the general outline and significancy of it. Yet that which must actually be seen, it is extremely difficult to recognize; while that which is only abstracted from what is seen is very obvious.

But the conclusive argument against our having any images, or absolutely determinate representations in perception, is that in that case we have the materials in each such representation for an infinite amount of conscious cognition, which we yet never become aware of. Now there is no meaning in saying that we have something in our minds which never has the least effect on what we are conscious of knowing. The most that can be said is that when we see, we are put in a condition in which we are able to get a very large and perhaps indefinitely great amount of knowledge of the visible qualities of objects.

Moreover, that perceptions are not absolutely determinate and singular is obvious from the fact that each sense is an abstracting mechanism. Sight by itself informs us only of colors and forms. No one can pretend that the images of sight are determinate in reference to taste. They are, therefore, so far general that they are neither sweet nor nonsweet, bitter nor non-bitter, having savor nor insipid.

The next question is whether we have any general conceptions except in judgments. In perception, where we know a thing as existing, it is plain that there is a judgment that the thing exists, since a mere general concept of a thing is in no case a cognition of it as existing. It has usually been said, however, that we can call up any concept without making any judgment; but it seems that in this case we only arbitrarily suppose ourselves to have an experience. In order to conceive the number 7, I suppose, that is, I arbitrarily make the hypothesis or judgment, that there are certain points before my eyes, and I judge that these are seven. This seems to be the most simple and rational view of the matter, and I may add that it is the one which has been adopted by the best logicians. If this be the case, what goes by the name of the association of images is in reality an association of judgments. The association of ideas is said to proceed according to three principles—those of resemblance, of contiguity, and of causality. But it would be equally true to say that signs denote what they do on the three principles of resemblance, contiguity, and causality. There can be no question that anything *is* a sign of whatever is associated with it by resemblance, by contiguity, or by causality: nor can there be any doubt that any sign recalls the thing signified. So, then, the association of ideas consists in this, that a judgment occasions another judgment, of which it is the sign. Now this is nothing less nor more than inference.

Everything in which we take the least interest creates in us its own particular emotion, however slight this may be. This emotion is a sign and a predicate of the thing. Now, when a thing resembling this thing is presented to us, a similar emotion arises; hence, we immediately infer that the latter is like the former. A formal logician of the old school may say that in logic no term can enter into the conclusion which had not been contained in the premisses, and that therefore the suggestion of something new must be essentially different from inference. But I reply that that rule of logic applies only to those arguments which are technically called completed. We can and do reason—

Elias was a man;
∴ He was mortal.

And this argument is just as valid as the full syllogism, although it is so only because the major premiss of the latter happens to be true. If to pass from the judgment "Elias was a man" to the judgment "Elias was mortal," without actually saying to one's self that "All men are mortal," is not inference, then the term "inference" is used in so restricted a sense that inferences hardly occur outside of a logic-book.

What is here said of association by resemblance is true of all association. All association is by signs. Everything has

its subjective or emotional qualities, which are attributed
either absolutely or relatively, or by conventional imputation to anything which is a sign of it. And so we reason,

> The sign is such and such;
> ∴ The sign is that thing.

This conclusion receiving, however, a modification, owing
to other considerations, so as to become—
The sign is almost (is representative of) that thing.

We come now to the consideration of the last of the four
principles whose consequences we were to trace; namely,
that the absolutely incognizable is absolutely inconceivable.
That upon Cartesian principles the very realities of things
can never be known in the least, most competent persons
must long ago have been convinced. Hence the breaking forth of idealism, which is essentially anti-Cartesian,
in every direction, whether among empiricists (Berkeley,
Hume), or among noologists (Hegel, Fichte). The principle now brought under discussion is directly idealistic; for,
since the meaning of a word is the conception it conveys,
the absolutely incognizable has no meaning because no conception attaches to it. It is, therefore, a meaningless word;
and, consequently, whatever is meant by any term as "the
real" is cognizable in some degree, and so is of the nature
of a cognition, in the objective sense of that term.

At any moment we are in possession of certain information, that is, of cognitions which have been logically derived by induction and hypothesis from previous cognitions
which are less general, less distinct, and of which we have
a less lively consciousness. These in their turn have been
derived from others still less general, less distinct, and less
vivid; and so on back to the ideal[6] first, which is quite
singular, and quite out of consciousness. This ideal first is
the particular thing-in-itself. It does not exist *as such*. That
is, there is no thing which is in-itself in the sense of not
being relative to the mind, though things which are relative

---

[6] By an ideal, I mean the limit which the possible cannot
attain.

to the mind doubtless are, apart from that relation. The cognitions which thus reach us by this infinite series of inductions and hypotheses (which though infinite *a parte ante logice*, is yet as one continuous process not without a beginning *in time*) are of two kinds, the true and the untrue, or cognitions whose objects are *real* and those whose objects are *unreal*. And what do we mean by the real? It is a conception which we must first have had when we discovered that there was an unreal, an illusion; that is, when we first corrected ourselves. Now the distinction for which alone this fact logically called was between an *ens* relative to private inward determinations, to the negations belonging to idiosyncrasy, and an *ens* such as would stand in the long run. The real, then, is that which, sooner or later, information and reasoning would finally result in, and which is therefore independent of the vagaries of me and you. Thus, the very origin of the conception of reality shows that this conception essentially involves the notion of a COMMUNITY, without definite limits, and capable of a definite increase of knowledge. And so those two series of cognition—the real and the unreal—consist of those which, at a time sufficiently future, the community will always continue to reaffirm; and of those which, under the same conditions, will ever after be denied. Now, a proposition whose falsity can never be discovered, and the error of which therefore is absolutely incognizable, contains, upon our principle, absolutely no error. Consequently, that which is thought in these cognitions is the real, as it really is. There is nothing, then, to prevent our knowing outward things as they really are, and it is most likely that we do thus know them in numberless cases, although we can never be absolutely certain of doing so in any special case.

But it follows that since no cognition of ours is absolutely determinate, generals must have a real existence. Now this scholastic realism is usually set down as a belief in metaphysical fictions. But, in fact, a realist is simply one who knows no more recondite reality than that which is represented in a true representation. Since, therefore, the word "man" is true of something, that which "man" means is real. The nominalist must admit that man is truly applicable to something; but he believes that there is beneath this a thing in itself, an incognizable reality. His is the metaphysical figment. Modern nominalists are mostly superficial men, who do not know, as the more thorough Roscellinus and Ockham did, that a reality which has no representation is one which has no relation and no quality. The great argument for nominalism is that there is no man unless there is some particular man. That, however, does not affect the realism of Scotus; for although there is no man of whom all further determination can be denied, yet there is a man, abstraction being made of all further determination. There is a real difference between man irrespective of what the other determinations may be, and man with this or that particular series of determinations, although undoubtedly this difference is only relative to the mind and not *in re*. Such is the position of Scotus. Ockham's great objection is, there can be no real distinction which is not *in re*, in the thing-in-itself; but this begs the question, for it is itself based only on the notion that reality is something independent of representative relation.

Such being the nature of reality in general, in what does the reality of the mind consist? We have seen that the content of consciousness, the entire phenomenal manifestation of mind, is a sign resulting from inference. Upon our principle, therefore, that the absolutely incognizable does not exist, so that the phenomenal manifestation of a substance is the substance, we must conclude that the mind is a sign developing according to the laws of inference. What distinguishes a man from a word? There is a distinction, doubtless. The material qualities, the forces which constitute the pure denotative application, and the meaning of the human sign, are all exceedingly complicated in comparison with those of the word. But these differences are only relative. What other is there? It may be said that man is conscious, while a word is not. But consciousness is a very vague term. It may mean that emotion which accompanies the reflection that we have animal life. This is a consciousness which is dimmed when animal life is at its ebb in old age, or sleep, but which is not dimmed when the spiritual life is at its ebb; which is the more lively the better *animal* a man is, but which is not so, the better *man* he is. We do not attribute this sensation to words, because we have reason to believe that it is dependent upon the possession of an animal body. But this consciousness, being a mere sensation, is only a part of the *material quality* of the man-sign. Again, consciousness is sometimes used to signify the *I think*, or unity in thought; but the unity is nothing but consistency, or the recognition of it. Consistency belongs to every sign, so far as it is a sign; and therefore every sign, since it signifies primarily that it is a sign, signifies its own consistency. The man-sign acquires information, and comes to mean more than he did before. But so do words. Does not electricity mean more now than it did in the days of Franklin? Man makes the word, and the word means nothing which the man has not made it mean, and that only to some man. But since man can think only by means of words or other external symbols, these might turn round and say: "You mean nothing which we have not taught you, and then only so far as you address some word as the interpretant of your thought." In fact, therefore, men and words reciprocally educate each other; each increase of a man's information involves, and is involved by, a corresponding increase of a word's information.

Without fatiguing the reader by stretching this parallelism too far, it is sufficient to say that there is no element whatever of man's consciousness which has not something corresponding to it in the word; and the reason is obvious. It is that the word or sign which man uses *is* the man himself. For, as the fact that every thought is a sign, taken in conjunction with the fact that life is a train of thought, proves that man is a sign; so, that every thought is an *external* sign proves that man is an external sign. That is to say, the man and the external sign are identical, in the same sense in which the words *homo* and *man* are identical. Thus my language is the sum total of myself; for the man is the thought.

It is hard for man to understand this, because he persists in identifying himself with his will, his power over the animal organism, with brute force. Now the organism is only an instrument of thought. But the identity of a man consists in the *consistency* of what he does and thinks, and consistency is the intellectual character of a thing, that is, is its expressing something.

Finally, as what anything really is, is what it may finally come to be known to be in the ideal state of complete information, so that reality depends on the ultimate decision of the community; so thought is what it is only by virtue of its addressing a future thought which is in its value as thought identical with it, though more developed. In this way, the existence of thought now depends on what is to be hereafter; so that it has only a potential existence, dependent on the future thought of the community.

The individual man, since his separate existence is manifested only by ignorance and error, so far as he is anything apart from his fellows, and from what he and they are to be, is only a negation. This is man,

> ". . . proud man,
> Most ignorant of what he's most assured,
> His glassy essence."[7]

[7] Cf. Peirce's essay "Man's Glassy Essence," *The Monist* (Oct. 1892), which attempted a molecular theory of protoplasm and a solution to the mind-body problem.—Editor's note.

4. Critical Review of Berkeley's Idealism[1]

[The following review of Fraser's edition of Berkeley's works is the most important early philosophical statement of Peirce's own "realism," as a "highly practical and common-sense position," which led him to his pragmatic formulations of truth and reality. Berkeley's idealism is traced to its medieval antecedents in the nominalism of William of Ockham, who had reduced general truths and realities to signs or thoughts; Berkeley reduced the material world to sensations or "ideas," and the laws of nature to uniform successions of ideas. The historical continuity in British philosophy from the fourteenth-century nominalists to Bacon, Hobbes, Locke, Berkeley, and Hume is representative of the British nation's mental development and cultural preference for concrete, practical (in the sense of immediately tangible) realities. The main point of Peirce's criticism of Berkeley is directed to the subjectivist assumption that ideas exist only in the mind. Peirce, following the medieval Duns Scotus, who placed universal ideas in individual things, argues that general ideas are signs which are both mental (insofar as they require a consensus of minds) and objective (insofar as they refer to realities independent of man's opinions). The realist must not regard "in the mind" and "outside the mind" as incompatible modes of existence, for the mind is not a container with an inside and outside.

[1] From the *North American Review*, Vol. 93 (Oct. 1871), pp. 449–472.

But whatever ideas the community of minds (in the future as well as in the present) finds itself constrained to accept and agree upon, after continued observation and reflection, will constitute "the truth." And "reality" will consist of the objects, qualities, or events to which true ideas direct the minds of men.]

The Works of GEORGE BERKELEY, D.D., *formerly Bishop of Cloyne: including many of his Writings hitherto unpublished.* With Prefaces, Annotations, his Life and Letters, and an Account of his Philosophy. By ALEXANDER CAMPBELL FRASER, M.A., Professor of Logic and Metaphysics in the University of Edinburgh. In Four Volumes. Oxford: At the Clarendon Press. 8vo. 1871.

. . . Berkeley's metaphysical theories have at first sight an air of paradox and levity very unbecoming to a bishop. He denies the existence of matter, our ability to see distance, and the possibility of forming the simplest general conception; while he admits the existence of Platonic ideas; and argues the whole with a cleverness which every reader admits, but which few are convinced by. His disciples seem to think the present moment a favorable one for obtaining for their philosophy a more patient hearing than it has yet got. It is true that we of this day are skeptical and not given to metaphysics, but so, say they, was the generation which Berkeley addressed and for which his style was chosen; while it is hoped that the spirit of calm and thorough inquiry which is now, for once, almost the fashion, will save the theory from the perverse misrepresentations which formerly assailed it, and lead to a fair examination of the arguments which, in the minds of his sectators, put the truth of it beyond all doubt. But above all it is anticipated that the Berkeleyan treatment of that question of the validity of human knowledge and of the inductive process of science, which is now so much studied, is such as to command the attention of scientific men to the idealistic system. To us these hopes seem vain. The truth is that the minds from whom the spirit of the age emanates have now no interest in the only problems that metaphysics ever pretended to solve. The abstract acknowledgment of God, Freedom, and Immortality, apart from those other religious beliefs (which cannot possibly rest on metaphysical grounds) which alone may animate this, is now seen to have no practical consequence whatever. The world is getting to think of these creatures of metaphysics, as Aristotle of the Platonic ideas: *teretísmata gar esti, kai ei estin, ouden pros ton logon* [for the Ideas are extravagant, and if they are, they are not needed by reason]. The question of the grounds of the validity of induction has, it is true, excited an interest, and may continue to do so (though the argument is now become too difficult for popular apprehension); but whatever interest it has had has been due to a hope that the solution of it would afford the basis for sure and useful maxims concerning the logic of induction —a hope which would be destroyed so soon as it were shown that the question was a purely metaphysical one. This is the prevalent feeling among advanced minds. It may not be just, but it exists. And its existence is an effectual bar (if there were no other) to the general acceptance of Berkeley's system. The few who do now care for metaphysics are not of that bold order of minds who delight to hold a position so unsheltered by the prejudices of common sense as that of the good bishop.

As a matter of history, however, philosophy must always be interesting. It is the best representative of the mental development of each age. It is so even of ours, if we think what really is our philosophy. Metaphysical history is one of the chief branches of history, and ought to be expounded side by side with the history of society, of government, and of war; for in its relations with these we trace the significance of events for the human mind. The history of philosophy in the British Isles is a subject possessing more unity and entirety within itself than has usually been recognized in it. The influence of Descartes was never so great in England as that of traditional conceptions, and we can trace a continuity between modern and mediæval thought there, which is wanting in the history of France, and still more, if possible, in that of Germany.

From very early times, it has been the chief intellectual characteristic of the English to wish to effect everything by the plainest and directest means, without unnecessary contrivance. In war, for example, they rely more than any other people in Europe upon sheer hardihood, and rather despise military science. The main peculiarities of their system of law arise from the fact that every evil has been rectified as it became intolerable, without any thoroughgoing measure. The bill for legalizing marriage with a deceased wife's sister is yearly pressed because it supplies a remedy for an inconvenience actually felt; but nobody has proposed a bill to legalize marriage with a deceased husband's brother. In philosophy, this national tendency appears as a strong preference for the simplest theories, and a resistance to any complication of the theory as long as there is the least possibility that the facts can be explained in the simpler way. And, accordingly, British philosophers have always desired to weed out of philosophy all conceptions which could not be made perfectly definite and easily intelligible, and have shown strong nominalistic tendencies since the time of Edward I, or even earlier. Berkeley is an admirable illustration of this national character, as well as of that strange union of nominalism with Platonism, which has repeatedly appeared in history, and has been such a stumbling-block to the historians of philosophy.

The mediæval metaphysic is so entirely forgotten, and has so close a historic connection with modern English philosophy, and so much bearing upon the truth of Berkeley's doctrine, that we may perhaps be pardoned a few pages on the nature of the celebrated controversy concerning universals. And first let us set down a few dates. It was at the very end of the eleventh century that the dispute concerning nominalism and realism, which had existed in a vague way before, began to attain extraordinary proportions. During the twelfth century it was the matter of most interest to logicians, when William of Champeaux, Abélard, John of Salisbury, Gilbert de la Porrée, and many others, defended as many different opinions. But there was no historic connection between this controversy and those of scholasticism proper, the scholasticism of Aquinas, Scotus, and Ockham. For about the end of the twelfth century a great revolution of thought took place in Europe. What the influences were which produced it requires new historical researches to say. No doubt, it was partly due to the Crusades. But a great awakening of intelligence did take place at that time. It requires, it is true, some examination to distinguish this particular movement from a general awakening which had begun a century earlier, and had been growing stronger ever since. But now there was an accelerated impulse. Commerce was attaining new importance, and was inventing some of her chief conveniences and safeguards. Law, which had hitherto been utterly barbaric, began to be a profession. The civil law was adopted in Europe, the canon law was digested; the common law took some form. The Church, under Innocent III, was assuming the sublime functions of a moderator over kings. And those orders of mendicant friars were established, two of which did so much for the development of the scholastic philosophy.

Art felt the spirit of a new age, and there could hardly be a greater change than from the highly ornate round-arched architecture of the twelfth century to the comparatively simple Gothic of the thirteenth. Indeed, if anyone wishes to know what a scholastic commentary is like, and what the tone of thought in it is, he has only to contemplate a Gothic cathedral. The first quality of either is a religious devotion, truly heroic. One feels that the men who did these works did really believe in religion as we believe in nothing. We cannot easily understand how Thomas Aquinas can speculate so much on the nature of angels, and whether ten thousand of them could dance on a needle's point. But it was simply because he held them for real. If they are real, why are they not more interesting than the bewildering varieties of insects which naturalists study; or why should the orbits of double stars attract more attention than spiritual intelligences? It will be said that we have no means of knowing anything about them. But that is on a par with censuring the schoolmen for referring questions to the authority of the Bible and of the Church. If they really believed in their religion, as they did, what bet-

ter could they do? And if they found in these authorities
testimony concerning angels, how could they avoid admitting it? Indeed, objections of this sort only make it appear still more clearly how much those were the ages of
faith. And if the spirit was not altogether admirable, it is
only because faith itself has its faults as a foundation for
the intellectual character. The men of that time did fully
believe and did think that, for the sake of giving themselves
up absolutely to their great task of building or of writing,
it was well worth while to resign all the joys of life. Think
of the spirit in which Duns Scotus must have worked, who
wrote his thirteen volumes in folio, in a style as condensed
as the most condensed parts of Aristotle, before the age of
thirty-four. Nothing is more striking in either of the great
intellectual products of that age, than the complete absence of self-conceit on the part of the artist or philosopher.
That anything of value can be added to his sacred and
catholic work by its having the smack of individuality about
it, is what he has never conceived. His work is not designed
to embody *his* ideas, but the universal truth; there will not
be one thing in it however minute, for which you will not
find that he has his authority; and whatever originality
emerges is of that inborn kind which so saturates a man
that he cannot himself perceive it. The individual feels his
own worthlessness in comparison with his task, and does
not dare to introduce his vanity into the doing of it. Then
there is no machine-work, no unthinking repetition about
the thing. Every part is worked out for itself as a separate
problem, no matter how analogous it may be in general to
another part. And no matter how small and hidden a detail may be, it has been conscientiously studied, as though
it were intended for the eye of God. Allied to this character is a detestation of antithesis or the studied balancing of
one thing against another, and of a too geometrical group-
ing—a hatred of posing which is as much a moral trait as
the others. Finally, there is nothing in which the scholastic
philosophy and the Gothic architecture resemble one another more than in the gradually increasing sense of immensity which impresses the mind of the student as he
learns to appreciate the real dimensions and cost of each.

It is very unfortunate that the thirteenth, fourteenth, and fifteenth centuries should, under the name of Middle Ages, be confounded with others, which they are in every respect as unlike as the Renaissance is from modern times. In the history of logic, the break between the twelfth and thirteenth centuries is so great that only one author of the former age is ever quoted in the latter. If this is to be attributed to the fuller acquaintance with the works of Aristotle, to what, we would ask, is this profounder study itself to be attributed, since it is now known that the knowledge of those works was not imported from the Arabs? The thirteenth century was realistic, but the question concerning universals was not as much agitated as several others. Until about the end of the century, scholasticism was somewhat vague, immature, and unconscious of its own power. Its greatest glory was in the first half of the fourteenth century. Then Duns Scotus,[1] a Briton (for whether Scotch, Irish, or English is disputed), first stated the realistic position consistently, and developed it with great fullness and applied it to all the different questions which depend upon it. His theory of "formalities" was the subtlest, except perhaps Hegel's logic, ever broached, and he was separated from nominalism only by the division of a hair. It is not therefore surprising that the nominalistic position was soon adopted by several writers, especially by the celebrated William of Ockham, who took the lead of this party by the thoroughgoing and masterly way in which he treated the theory and combined it with a then rather recent but now forgotten addition to the doctrine of logical terms. With Ockham, who died in 1347, scholasticism may be said to have culminated. After him the scholastic philosophy showed a tendency to separate itself from the religious element which alone could dignify it, and sunk first into extreme formalism and fancifulness, and then into the merited contempt of all men; just as the Gothic architecture had a very similar fate, at about the same time, and for much the same reasons.

The current explanations of the realist-nominalist con-

[1] Died 1308.

troversy are equally false and unintelligible. They are said to be derived ultimately from Bayle's Dictionary; at any rate, they are not based on a study of the authors. "Few, very few, for a hundred years past," says Hallam, with truth, "have broken the repose of the immense works of the schoolmen." Yet it is perfectly possible so to state the matter that no one shall fail to comprehend what the question was, and how there might be two opinions about it.

Are universals real? We have only to stop and consider a moment what was meant by the word *real,* when the whole issue soon becomes apparent. Objects are divided into figments, dreams, etc., on the one hand, and realities on the other. The former are those which exist only inasmuch as you or I or some man imagines them; the latter are those which have an existence independent of your mind or mine or that of any number of persons. The real is that which is not whatever we happen to think it, but is unaffected by what we may think of it. The question, therefore, is whether *man, horse,* and other names of natural classes, correspond with anything which all men, or all horses, really have in common, independent of our thought, or whether these classes are constituted simply by a likeness in the way in which our minds are affected by individual objects which have in themselves no resemblance or relationship whatsoever. Now that this is a real question which different minds will naturally answer in opposite ways, becomes clear when we think that there are two widely separated points of view, from which *reality,* as just defined, may be regarded. Where is the real, the thing independent of how we think it, to be found? There must be such a thing, for we find our opinions constrained; there is something, therefore, which influences our thoughts, and is not created by them. We have, it is true, nothing immediately present to us but thoughts. Those thoughts, however, have been caused by sensations, and those sensations are constrained by something out of the mind. This thing out of the mind, which directly influences sensation, and through sensation thought, because it *is* out of the mind, is independent of how we think it, and is, in short, the real. Here is one view of reality, a very familiar one. And from this point of view it is clear that the nominalistic answer must be given to the question concerning universals. For, while from this stand-point it may be admitted to be true as a rough statement that one man is like another, the exact sense being that the realities external to the mind produce sensations which may be embraced under one conception, yet it can by no means be admitted that the two real men have really anything in common, for to say that they are both men is only to say that the one mental term or thought-sign "man" stands indifferently for either of the sensible objects caused by the two external realities; so that not even the two sensations have in themselves anything in common, and far less is it to be inferred that the external realities have. This conception of reality is so familiar that it is unnecessary to dwell upon it; but the other, or realist conception, if less familiar, is even more natural and obvious. All human thought and opinion contains an arbitrary, accidental element, dependent on the limitations in circumstances, power, and bent of the individual; an element of error, in short. But human opinion universally tends in the long run to a definite form, which is the truth. Let any human being have enough information and exert enough thought upon any question, and the result will be that he will arrive at a certain definite conclusion, which is the same that any other mind will reach under sufficiently favorable circumstances. Suppose two men, one deaf, the other blind. One hears a man declare he means to kill another, hears the report of the pistol, and hears the victim cry; the other sees the murder done. Their sensations are affected in the highest degree with their individual peculiarities. The first information that their sensations will give them, their first inferences, will be more nearly alike, but still different; the one having, for example, the idea of a man shouting, the other of a man with a threatening aspect; but their final conclusions, the thought the remotest from sense, will be identical and free from the one-sidedness of their idiosyncrasies. There is, then, to every question a true answer, a final conclusion, to which the opinion of every man is constantly gravitating. He may for a time recede from it, but give him more experience and time for consideration, and he will finally approach it. The individual may not live to reach the truth; there is a residuum of error in every individual's opinions. No matter; it remains that there is a definite opinion to which the mind of man is, on the whole and in the long run, tending. On many questions the final agreement is already reached, on all it will be reached if time enough is given. The arbitrary will or other individual peculiarities of a sufficiently large number of minds may postpone the general agreement in that opinion indefinitely; but it cannot affect what the character of that opinion shall be when it is reached. This final opinion, then, is independent, not indeed of thought in general, but of all that is arbitrary and individual in thought; is quite independent of how you, or I, or any number of men think.

Everything, therefore, which will be thought to exist in the final opinion is real, and nothing else. What is the POWER of external things, to affect the senses? To say that people sleep after taking opium because it has a soporific *power,* is that to say anything in the world but that people sleep after taking opium because they sleep after taking opium? To assert the existence of a power or potency, is it to assert the existence of anything actual? Or to say that a thing has a potential existence, is it to say that it has an actual existence? In other words, is the present existence of a power anything in the world but a regularity in future events relating to a certain thing regarded as an element which is to be taken account of beforehand, in the conception of that thing? If not, to assert that there are external things which can be known only as exerting a power on our sense, is nothing different from asserting that there is a general *drift* in the history of human thought which will lead it to one general agreement, one catholic consent. And any truth more perfect than this destined conclusion, any reality more absolute than what is thought in it, is a fiction of metaphysics. It is obvious how this way of thinking harmonizes with a belief in an infallible Church, and how much more natural it would be in the Middle Ages than in Protestant or positivist times.

This theory of reality is instantly fatal to the idea of a thing in itself—a thing existing independent of all relation to the mind's conception of it. Yet it would by no means forbid, but rather encourage, us to regard the appearances of sense as only signs of the realities. Only, the realities which they represent would not be the unknowable cause of sensation, but *noumena,* or intelligible conceptions which are the last products of the mental action which is set in motion by sensation. The matter of sensation is altogether accidental; precisely the same information, practically, being capable of communication through different senses. And the catholic consent which constitutes the truth is by no means to be limited to men in this earthly life or to the human race, but extends to the whole communion of minds to which we belong, including some probably whose senses are very different from ours, so that in that consent no predication of a sensible quality can enter, except as an admission that so certain sorts of senses are affected. This theory is also highly favorable to a belief in external realities. It will, to be sure, deny that there is any reality which is absolutely incognizable in itself, so that it cannot be taken into the mind. But observing that "the external" means simply that which is independent of what phenomenon is immediately present, that is, of how we may think or feel; just as "the real" means that which is independent of how we may think or feel *about it;* it must be granted that there are many objects of true science which are external, because there are many objects of thought which, if they are independent of that thinking whereby they are thought (that is, if they are real), are indisputably independent of all *other* thoughts and feelings.

It is plain that this view of reality is inevitably realistic, because general conceptions enter into all judgments, and therefore into true opinions. Consequently a thing in the general is as real as in the concrete. It is perfectly true that all white things have whiteness in them, for that is only saying, in another form of words, that all white things are white; but since it is true that real things possess whiteness, whiteness is real. It is a real which only exists by virtue of an act of thought knowing it, but that thought is not an arbitrary or accidental one dependent on any idiosyncrasies, but one which will hold in the final opinion.

This theory involves a phenomenalism. But it is the phenomenalism of Kant, and not that of Hume. Indeed, what Kant called his Copernican step was precisely the passage from the nominalistic to the realistic view of reality. It was the essence of his philosophy to regard the real object as determined by the mind. That was nothing else than to consider every conception and intuition which enters necessarily into the experience of an object, and which is not transitory and accidental, as having objective validity. In short, it was to regard the reality as the normal product of mental action, and not as the incognizable cause of it.

This realistic theory is thus a highly practical and common-sense position. Wherever universal agreement prevails, the realist will not be the one to disturb the general belief by idle and fictitious doubts. For according to him it is a consensus or common confession which constitutes reality. What he wants, therefore, is to see questions put to rest. And if a general belief, which is perfectly stable and immovable, can in any way be produced, though it be by the fagot and the rack, to talk of any error in such belief is utterly absurd. The realist will hold that the very same objects which are immediately present in our minds in experience really exist just as they are experienced out of the mind; that is, he will maintain a doctrine of immediate perception. He will not, therefore, sunder existence out of the mind and being in the mind as two wholly improportionable modes. When a thing is in such relation to the individual mind that that mind cognizes it, it is in the mind; and its being so in the mind will not in the least diminish its external existence. For he does not think of the mind as a receptacle, which if a thing is in, it ceases to be out of. To make a distinction between the true conception of a thing and the thing itself, he will say, only to regard one and the same thing from two different points of view; for the immediate object of thought in a true judgment *is* the reality. The realist will, therefore, believe in the objectivity of all necessary conceptions, space, time, relation, cause, and the like. . . .

We ought to say one word about Berkeley's theory of

vision. It was undoubtedly an extraordinary piece of reasoning, and might have served for the basis of the modern
science. Historically it has not had that fortune, because the
modern science has been chiefly created in Germany,
where Berkeley is little known and greatly misunderstood.
We may fairly say that Berkeley taught the English some
of the most essential principles of that hypothesis of sight
which is now getting to prevail, more than a century before
they were known to the rest of the world. This is much; but
what is claimed by some of his advocates is astounding. One
writer says that Berkeley's theory has been accepted by the
leaders of all schools of thought! Professor Fraser admits
that it has attracted no attention in Germany, but thinks the
German mind too *a priori* to like Berkeley's reasoning. But
Helmholtz, who has done more than any other man to bring
the empiricist theory into favor, says: "Our knowledge of
the phenomena of vision is not so complete as to allow only
one theory and exclude every other. It seems to me that
the choice which different *savants* make between different
theories of vision has thus far been governed more by their
metaphysical inclinations than by any constraining power
which the facts have had." The best authorities, however,
prefer the empiricist hypothesis; the fundamental proposition of which, as it is of Berkeley's, is that the sensations
which we have in seeing are signs of the relations of things
whose interpretation has to be discovered inductively. In
the enumeration of the signs and of their uses, Berkeley
shows considerable power in that sort of investigation,
though there is naturally no very close resemblance between his and the modern accounts of the matter. There is
no modern physiologist who would not think that Berkeley
had greatly exaggerated the part that the muscular sense
plays in vision.

Berkeley's theory of vision was an important step in the
development of the associationalist psychology. He thought
all our conceptions of body and of space were simply re-
productions in the imagination of sensations of touch (including the muscular sense). This, if it were true, would be
a most surprising case of mental chemistry, that is of a sensation being felt and yet so mixed with others that we can-

not by an act of simple attention recognize it. Doubtless this theory had its influence in the production of Hartley's system.

Hume's phenomenalism and Hartley's associationalism were put forth almost contemporaneously about 1750. They contain the fundamental positions of the current English "positivism." From 1750 down to 1830—eighty years—nothing of particular importance was added to the nominalistic doctrine. At the beginning of this period Hume's was toning down his earlier radicalism, and Smith's theory of Moral Sentiments appeared. Later came Priestley's materialism, but there was nothing new in that; and just at the end of the period, Brown's *Lectures on the Human Mind*. The great body of the philosophy of those eighty years is of the Scotch common-sense school. It is a weak sort of realistic reaction, for which there is no adequate explanation within the sphere of the history of philosophy. It would be curious to inquire whether anything in the history of society could account for it. In 1829 appeared James Mill's *Analysis of the Human Mind*, a really great nominalistic book again. This was followed by Stuart Mill's *Logic* in 1843. Since then, the school has produced nothing of the first importance; and it will very likely lose its distinctive character now for a time, by being merged in an empiricism of a less metaphysical and more working kind. Already in Stuart Mill the nominalism is less salient than in the classical writers, though it is quite unmistakable.

Thus we see how large a part of the metaphysical ideas of today have come to us by inheritance from very early times, Berkeley being one of the intellectual ancestors whose labors did as much as anyone's to enhance the value of the bequest. The realistic philosophy of the last century has now lost all its popularity, except with the most conservative minds. And science as well as philosophy is nominalistic. The doctrine of the correlation of forces, the discoveries of Helmholtz, and the hypotheses of Liebig and of Darwin, have all that character of explaining familiar phenomena apparently of a peculiar kind by extending the operation of simple mechanical principles, which belongs to nominalism. Or if the nominalistic character of these doctrines themselves cannot be detected, it will at least be admitted that they are observed to carry along with them those daughters of nominalism—sensationalism, phenomenalism, individualism, and materialism. That physical science is necessarily connected with doctrines of a debasing moral tendency will be believed by few. But if we hold that such an effect will not be produced by these doctrines on a mind which really understands them, we are accepting this belief, not on experience, which is rather against it, but on the strength of our general faith that what is really true it is good to believe and evil to reject. On the other hand, it is allowable to suppose that science has no essential affinity with the philosophical views with which it seems to be every year more associated. History cannot be held to exclude this supposition; and science as it exists is certainly much less nominalistic than the nominalists think it should be. Whewell represents it quite as well as Mill. Yet a man who enters into the scientific thought of the day and has not materialistic tendencies is getting to be an impossibility. So long as there is a dispute between nominalism and realism, so long as the position we hold on the question is not determined by any proof *indisputable,* but is more or less a matter of inclination, a man as he gradually comes to feel the profound hostility of the two tendencies will, if he is not less than man, become engaged with one or other and can no more obey both than he can serve God and Mammon. If the two impulses are neutralized within him, the result simply is that he is left without any great intellectual motive. There is, indeed, no reason to suppose the logical question is in its own nature unsusceptible of solution. But that path out of the difficulty lies through the thorniest mazes of a science as dry as mathematics. Now there is a demand for mathematics; it helps to build bridges and drive engines, and therefore it becomes somebody's business to study it severely. But to have a philosophy is a matter of luxury; the only use of that is to make us feel comfortable and easy. It is a study for leisure hours; and we want it supplied in an elegant, an agreeable, an interesting form. The law of natural selection, which is the precise analogue in another realm of the law of supply and demand, has the most im-

mediate effect in fostering the other faculties of the understanding, for the men of mental power succeed in the
struggle for life; but the faculty of philosophizing, except
in the literary way, is not called for; and therefore a difficult
question cannot be expected to reach solution until it takes
some practical form. If anybody should have the good luck
to find out the solution, nobody else would take the trouble
to understand it. But though the question of realism and
nominalism has its roots in the technicalities of logic, its
branches reach about our life. The question whether the
genus homo has any existence except as individuals, is the
question whether there is anything of any more dignity,
worth, and importance than individual happiness, individual aspirations, and individual life. Whether men really
have anything in common, so that the *community* is to be
considered as an end in itself, and if so, what the relative
value of the two factors is, is the most fundamental practical question in regard to every public institution the
constitution of which we have it in our power to influence.

Pragmaticism: A Philosophy of Science

5. The Fixation of Belief[1]

[This and the next essay ("How To Make Our Ideas Clear") were the first two of six papers written by Peirce for the *Popular Science Monthly* as "Illustrations of the Logic of Science" (1877–78). They were his first popular philosophical articles, but they did not earn for him any notable prominence as an American philosopher until twenty years later when "the potent pen of Professor (William) James brought their chief thesis to the attention of the philosophic world (in his Berkeley address, 'Philosophical Conceptions and Practical Results') . . . The doctrine of this pair of chapters had already for some years been known among friends of the writer (Peirce) by the name he had proposed for it, which was 'Pragmatism.'"

The term "fixation of belief" refers to the ways of arriving at ideas that settle down in the minds of a people as habits, customs, traditions, "folkways" of thought, ranging from personal tenacity to fashions in metaphysics. They influence conduct insofar as a belief is "that upon which a man is prepared to act," so defined by the British psychologist and philosopher Bain and his American disciple Nicholas St.

[1] The original essay appeared in the November 1877 issue of the *Popular Science Monthly*, Vol. 12, pp. 1–15. Peirce kept coming back to it in his Notes on Pragmatism, in his *Search for a Method* (1893), and *Grand Logic*, which he never completed. Some of his later revisions and comments on it are added here to the footnotes he originally had in the 1877 article.—Editor's note.

John Green, "the grandfather of pragmatism," according to Peirce. "Common sense" is replete with such modes of thinking which Peirce calls tenacity, authority, and the *a priori* method, before the logic of scientific thinking can be applied to it, as it should be if we are to rid ourselves of some of the narrow prejudices, dogmas, and bad metaphysics with which "common sense" is deeply imbued. Tenacity is illustrated today in the belief in white man supremacy. Authority has its practical uses in military, governmental, and church organizations in stabilizing a community against willful disobedience, but as a method of arriving at general truths in exploring the unknown, it is too inflexible. The *a priori* method, practiced by rationalists like Plato and Descartes, is often no more than a rationalization of what is pleasing to the system-building, rationalizing mind of the introspective philosopher, impervious to fresh evidence. The only way out of the incorrigible tendencies of tenacity, authority, and *a priori* speculation—which may have their good purposes in building character, social institutions, and new perspectives, but are unreliable as modes of inquiry for settling conflicts or doubts—is the "self-corrective," scientific method whose experimental results are always subject to revision by future evidence. The historical or evolutionary approach of Peirce makes it clear that scientific logic is a very late arrival in a civilization that has been and still is largely shaped by the other methods that form the crusted cake of custom. Hence, the first essay is as much the psychology and sociology of science as it is a defense of the virtues of the logic of science.]

I

Few persons care to study logic, because everybody conceives himself to be proficient enough in the art of reasoning already. But I observe that this satisfaction is limited to one's own ratiocination, and does not extend to that of other men.

We come to the full possession of our power of drawing inferences the last of all our faculties, for it is not so much a natural gift as a long and difficult art. The history of its

practice would make a grand subject for a book. The mediæval schoolman, following the Romans, made logic the
earliest of a boy's studies after grammar, as being very easy.
So it was as they understood it. Its fundamental principle,
according to them, was that all knowledge rests on either
authority or reason; but that whatever is deduced by reason
depends ultimately on a premise derived from authority.
Accordingly, as soon as a boy was perfect in the syllogistic
procedure, his intellectual kit of tools was held to be
complete.

To Roger Bacon, that remarkable mind who in the middle of the thirteenth century was almost a scientific man,
the schoolmen's conception of reasoning appeared only an
obstacle to truth. He saw that experience alone teaches anything—a proposition which to us seems easy to understand,
because a distinct conception of experience has been
handed down to us from former generations; which to him
also seemed perfectly clear, because its difficulties had not
yet unfolded themselves. Of all kinds of experience, the best,
he thought, was interior illumination, which teaches many
things about nature which the external senses could never
discover, such as the transubstantiation of bread.

Four centuries later, the more celebrated Bacon, in the
first book of his *Novum Organum,* gave his clear account
of experience as something which must be opened to verification and re-examination. But, superior as Lord Bacon's
conception is to earlier notions, a modern reader who is not
in awe of his grandiloquence is chiefly struck by the inadequacy of his view of scientific procedure. That we have
only to make some crude experiments, to draw up briefs of
the results in certain blank forms, to go through these by
rule, checking off everything disproved and setting down
the alternatives, and that thus in a few years physical science would be finished up—what an idea! "He wrote on science like a Lord Chancellor,"[2] indeed, as Harvey, a genuine
man of science, said.

The early scientists, Copernicus, Tycho Brahe, Kepler,
Galileo, Harvey, and Gilbert, had methods more like those

[2] Cf. J. Aubrey's *Brief Lives* (Oxford, ed. 1898), I, 299.

of their modern brethren. Kepler undertook to draw a curve through the places of Mars;[3] and his greatest service to science was in impressing on men's minds that this was the thing to be done if they wished to improve astronomy; that they were not to content themselves with inquiring whether one system of epicycles was better than another but that they were to sit down by the figures and find out what the curve, in truth, was. He accomplished this by his incomparable energy and courage, blundering along in the most inconceivable way (to us), from one irrational hypothesis to another, until, after trying twenty-two of these, he fell, by the mere exhaustion of his invention, upon the orbit which a mind well furnished with the weapons of modern logic would have tried almost at the outset.

In the same way, every work of science great enough to be remembered for a few generations affords some exemplification of the defective state of the art of reasoning of the time when it was written; and each chief step in science has been a lesson in logic. It was so when Lavoisier and his contemporaries took up the study of Chemistry. The old chemist's maxim had been *Lege, lege, lege, labora, ora, et relege.* Lavoisier's method was not to read and pray, not to dream that some long and complicated chemical process would have a certain effect, to put it into practice with dull patience, after its inevitable failure to dream that with some modification it would have another result, and to end by publishing the last dream as a fact: his way was to carry his mind into his laboratory, and to make of his alembics and cucurbits instruments of thought, giving a new conception of reasoning as something which was to be done with one's eyes open, by manipulating real things instead of words and fancies.

The Darwinian controversy is, in large part, a question of logic. Mr. Darwin proposed to apply the statistical

[3] Not quite so, but as nearly as can be told in a few words. [Peirce noted, in 1893, that Kepler's work on Mars "is the most marvellous piece of inductive reasoning I have been able to find." See his Lowell Lecture of 1892 on "Kepler", Selection 14, pp. 250–6, below.]

method to biology.[4] The same thing has been done in a widely different branch of science, the theory of gases. Though unable to say what the movement of any particular molecule of gas would be on a certain hypothesis regarding the constitution of this class of bodies, Clausius and Maxwell were yet able, by the application of the doctrine of probabilities, to predict that in the long run such and such a proportion of the molecules would, under given circumstances, acquire such and such velocities; that there would take place, every second, such and such a number of collisions, etc.; and from these propositions they were able to deduce certain properties of gases, especially in regard to their heat-relations. In like manner, Darwin, while unable to say what the operation of variation and natural selection in every individual case will be, demonstrates that in the long run they will adapt animals to their circumstances. Whether or not existing animal forms are due to such action, or what position the theory ought to take, forms the subject of a discussion in which questions of fact and questions of logic are curiously interlaced.

II

The object of reasoning is to find out, from the consideration of what we already know, something else which we do not know. Consequently, reasoning is good if it be such[5] as to give a true conclusion from true premises, and not otherwise. Thus, the question of validity is purely one of fact and not of thinking. A being the premises and B being the conclusion, the question is, whether these facts are really so related that if A is B is. If so, the inference is valid; if not, not. It is not in the least the question whether, when the premises are accepted by the mind, we feel an impulse to accept the conclusion also. It is true that we do generally reason correctly by nature. But that is an accident; the true

[4] "We now know what was authoritatively denied when I first suggested it, that he took a hint from Malthus' book on population."—Peirce's added note, 1903.

[5] "I.e., be denominated by such a habit as generally to give" —inserted by Peirce in 1903.

conclusion would remain true if we had no impulse to accept it; and the false one would remain false, though we could not resist the tendency to believe in it.

We are, doubtless, in the main logical animals, but we are not perfectly so. Most of us, for example, are naturally more sanguine and hopeful than logic would justify. We seem to be so constituted that in the absence of any facts to go upon we are happy and self-satisfied; so that the effect of experience is continually to counteract our hopes and aspirations. Yet a lifetime of the application of this corrective does not usually eradicate our sanguine disposition. Where hope is unchecked by any experience, it is likely that our optimism is extravagant. Logicality in regard to practical matters is the most useful quality an animal can possess, and might, therefore, result from the action of natural selection; but outside of these it is probably of more advantage to the animal to have his mind filled with pleasing and encouraging visions, independently of their truth; and thus, upon unpractical subjects, natural selection might occasion a fallacious tendency of thought.[6]

That which determines us, from given premises, to draw one inference rather than another is some habit of mind, whether it be constitutional or acquired. The habit is good or otherwise, according as it produces true conclusions from true premises or not; and an inference is regarded as valid or not, without reference to the truth or falsity of its conclusion specially, but according as the habit which determines it is such as to produce true conclusions in general or not. The particular habit of mind which governs this or that inference may be formulated in a proposition whose truth depends on the validity of the inferences which the habit determines; and such a formula is called a *guiding principle* of inference. Suppose, for example, that we observe that a rotating disk of copper quickly comes to rest when placed between the poles of a magnet, and we infer that this will happen with every disk of copper. The guid-

---

[6] "Let us not, however, be cocksure that natural selection is the only factor of evolution." In this note of 1903, Peirce suggests that science itself, "the force of very sound reasoning," is also a factor in the evolution of the world.

ing principle is that what is true of one piece of copper is true of another. Such a guiding principle with regard to copper would be much safer than with regard to many other substances—brass, for example.

A book might be written to signalize all the most important of these guiding principles of reasoning. It would probably be, we must confess, of no service to a person whose thought is directed wholly to practical subjects, and whose activity moves along thoroughly beaten paths. The problems which present themselves to such a mind are matters of routine which he has learned once for all to handle in learning his business. But let a man venture into an unfamiliar field, or where his results are not continually checked by experience, and all history shows that the most masculine intellect will ofttimes lose his orientation and waste his efforts in directions which bring him no nearer to his goal, or even carry him entirely astray. He is like a ship on the open sea, with no one on board who understands the rules of navigation. And in such a case some general study of the guiding principles of reasoning would be sure to be found useful.

The subject could hardly be treated, however, without being first limited; since almost any fact may serve as a guiding principle. But it so happens that there exists a division among facts, such that in one class are all those which are absolutely essential as guiding principles, while in the other are all those which have any other interest as objects of research. This division is between those which are necessarily taken for granted in asking whether a certain conclusion follows from certain premises, and those which are not implied in that question. A moment's thought will show that a variety of facts are already assumed when the logical question is first asked. It is implied, for instance, that there are such states of mind as doubt and belief—that a passage from one to the other is possible, the object of thought remaining the same, and that this transition is subject to some rules which all minds are alike bound by. As these are facts which we must already know before we can have any clear conception of reasoning at all, it cannot be supposed to be any longer of much interest to inquire into their truth or falsity. On the other hand, it is easy to believe that those rules of reasoning which are deduced from the very idea of the process are the ones which are the most essential; and, indeed, that so long as it conforms to these it will, at least, not lead to false conclusions from true premises. In point of fact, the importance of what may be deduced from the assumptions involved in the logical question turns out to be greater than might be supposed, and this for reasons which it is difficult to exhibit at the outset. The only one which I shall here mention is that conceptions which are really products of logical reflections, without being readily seen to be so, mingle with our ordinary thoughts, and are frequently the causes of great confusion. This is the case, for example, with the conception of quality. A quality as such is never an object of observation. We can see that a thing is blue or green, but the quality of being blue and the quality of being green are not things which we see; they are products of logical reflections. The truth is that common sense, or thought as it first emerges above the level of the narrowly practical, is deeply inbued with that bad logical quality to which the epithet *metaphysical* is commonly applied; and nothing can clear it up but a severe course of logic.

III

We generally know when we wish to ask a question and when we wish to pronounce a judgment, for there is a dissimilarity between the sensation of doubting and that of believing.

But this is not all which distinguishes doubt from belief. There is a practical difference. Our beliefs guide our desires and shape our actions. The Assassins, or followers of the Old Man of the Mountain, used to rush into death at his least command, because they believed that obedience to him would insure everlasting felicity. Had they doubted this, they would not have acted as they did. So it is with every belief, according to its degree. The feeling of believing is a more or less sure indication of there being established in our nature some habit which will determine our actions. Doubt never has such an effect.

Nor must we overlook a third point of difference. Doubt is an uneasy and dissatisfied state from which we struggle to free ourselves and pass into the state of belief;[7] while the latter is a calm and satisfactory state which we do not wish to avoid, or to change to a belief in anything else.[8] On the contrary, we cling tenaciously, not merely to believing, but to believing just what we do believe.

Thus, both doubt and belief have positive effects upon us, though very different ones. Belief does not make us act at once, but puts us into such a condition that we shall behave in a certain way, when the occasion arises. Doubt has not the least effect of this sort, but stimulates us to action until it is destroyed. This reminds us of the irritation of a nerve and the reflex action produced thereby; while for the analogue of belief, in the nervous system, we must look to what are called nervous associations—for example, to that habit of the nerves in consequence of which the smell of a peach will make the mouth water.

IV

The irritation of doubt causes a struggle to attain a state of belief.[9] I shall term this struggle *inquiry*, though it

[7] "In this, it [doubt] is like any other stimulus. It is true that just as man may, for the sake of the pleasures of the table, like to be hungry and take means to make themselves so, although hunger always involves a desire to fill the stomach, so for the sake of the pleasures of inquiry, men may like to seek out doubts. Yet for all that, doubt essentially involves a struggle to escape it." Peirce's note of 1903.

[8] I am not speaking of secondary effects occasionally produced by the interference of other impulses.

[9] "Doubt, however, is not usually hesitancy about what is to be done then and there. It is anticipated hesitancy about what I shall do hereafter, or a feigned hesitancy about a fictitious state of things. It is the power of making believe we hesitate, together with the pregnant fact that the decision upon the make-believe dilemma goes toward forming a bona fide habit that will be operative in a real emergency." Peirce's note of 1893.

must be admitted that this is sometimes not a very apt designation.

The irritation of doubt is the only immediate motive for the struggle to attain belief. It is certainly best for us that our beliefs should be such as may truly guide our actions so as to satisfy our desires; and this reflection will make us reject any belief which does not seem to have been so formed as to insure this result. But it will only do so by creating a doubt in the place of that belief. With the doubt, therefore, the struggle begins, and with the cessation of doubt it ends. Hence, the sole object of inquiry is the settlement of opinion. We may fancy that this is not enough for us, and that we seek not merely an opinion, but a true opinion. But put this fancy to the test, and it proves groundless; for as soon as a firm belief is reached we are entirely satisfied, whether the belief be false or true. And it is clear that nothing out of the sphere of our knowledge can be our object, for nothing which does not affect the mind can be a motive for a mental effort. The most that can be maintained is that we seek for a belief that we shall *think* to be true. But we think each one of our beliefs to be true, and, indeed, it is mere tautology to say so.[10]

That the settlement of opinion is the sole end of inquiry is a very important proposition. It sweeps away, at once, various vague and erroneous conceptions of proof. A few of these may be noticed here.

1. Some philosophers have imagined that to start an inquiry it was only necessary to utter or question or set it down on paper, and have even recommended us to begin our studies with questioning everything! But the mere putting of a proposition into the interrogative form does not stimulate the mind to any struggle after belief. There must be a real and living doubt, and without all this, discussion is idle.

10 "For truth is neither more nor less than that character of a proposition which consists in this, that belief in the proposition would, with sufficient experience and reflection, lead us to such conduct as would tend to satisfy the desires we should then have. To say that truth means more than this is to say that it has no meaning at all." Peirce's note of 1903.

2. It is a very common idea that a demonstration must rest on some ultimate and absolutely indubitable propositions. These, according to one school, are first principles of a general nature; according to another, are first sensations. But, in point of fact, an inquiry, to have that completely satisfactory result called demonstration, has only to start with propositions perfectly free from all actual doubt. If the premises are not in fact doubted at all, they cannot be more satisfactory than they are.[11]

3. Some people seem to love to argue a point after all the world is fully convinced of it. But no further advance can be made. When doubt ceases, mental action on the subject comes to an end; and, if it did go on, it would be without a purpose, except that of self-criticism.

V

If the settlement of opinion is the sole object of inquiry, and if belief is of the nature of a habit, why should we not attain the desired end, by taking any answer to a question, which we may fancy, and constantly reiterating it to ourselves, dwelling on all which may conduce to that belief, and learning to turn with contempt and hatred from anything which might disturb it? This simple and direct method is really pursued by many men. I remember once being entreated not to read a certain newspaper lest it might change my opinion upon free-trade. "Lest I might be entrapped by its fallacies and misstatements" was the form of expression. "You are not," my friend said, "a special student of political economy. You might, therefore, easily be deceived by fallacious arguments upon the subject. You

[11] "Doubts about them [the premises] may spring up later; but we can find no propositions which are not subject to this contingency." This note, of 1893, indicates Peirce's view of the probability and fallibility of any particular assertion about reality, without denying that some common-sense assertions about reality must be taken as certain even while questioning the others. For example, I may doubt that I see a bent stick in the water without doubting that it seems bent. Thus Peirce called himself a "critical common-sensist" and "fallibilist."—Editor's note.

might, then, if you read this paper, be led to believe in protection. But you admit that free-trade is the true doctrine; and you do not wish to believe what is not true." I have often known this system to be deliberately adopted. Still oftener, the instinctive dislike of an undecided state of mind, exaggerated into a vague dread of doubt, makes men cling spasmodically to the views they already take. The man feels that if he only holds to his belief without wavering, it will be entirely satisfactory. Nor can it be denied that a steady and immovable faith yields great peace of mind. It may, indeed, give rise to inconveniences, as if a man should resolutely continue to believe that fire would not burn him, or that he would be eternally damned if he received his *ingesta* otherwise than through a stomach-pump. But then the man who adopts this method will not allow that its inconveniences are greater than its advantages. He will say, "I hold steadfastly to the truth and the truth is always wholesome." And in many cases it may very well be that the pleasure he derives from his calm faith overbalances any inconveniences resulting from its deceptive character. Thus, if it be true that death is annihilation, then the man who believes that he will certainly go straight to heaven when he dies, provided he have fulfilled certain simple observances in this life, has a cheap pleasure which will not be followed by the least disappointment. A similar consideration seems to have weight with many persons in religious topics, for we frequently hear it said, "Oh, I could not believe so-and-so, because I should be wretched if I did." When an ostrich buries its head in the sand as danger approaches, it very likely takes the happiest course. It hides the danger, and then calmly says there is no danger; and, if it feels perfectly sure there is none, why should it raise its head to see? A man may go through life, systematically keeping out of view all that might cause a change in his opinions, and if he only succeeds—basing his method, as he does, on two fundamental psychological laws—I do not see what can be said against his doing so. It would be an egotistical impertinence to object that his procedure is irrational, for that only amounts to saying that his method of settling belief is not ours. He does not propose to himself to be rational, and indeed, will often talk with scorn of man's weak and illusive reason. So let him think as he pleases.

But this method of fixing belief, which may be called the method of tenacity, will be unable to hold its ground in practice. The social impulse is against it. The man who adopts it will find that other men think differently from him, and it will be apt to occur to him in some saner moment that their opinions are quite as good as his own, and this will shake his confidence in his belief. This conception, that another man's thought or sentiment may be equivalent to one's own, is a distinctly new step, and a highly important one. It arises from an impulse too strong in man to be suppressed, without danger of destroying the human species. Unless we make ourselves hermits, we shall necessarily influence each other's opinions; so that the problem becomes how to fix belief, not in the individual merely, but in the community.

Let the will of the state act, then, instead of that of the individual. Let an institution be created which shall have for its object to keep correct doctrines before the attention of the people, to reiterate them perpetually, and to teach them to the young; having at the same time power to prevent contrary doctrines from being taught, advocated, or expressed. Let all possible causes of a change of mind be removed from men's apprehensions. Let them be kept ignorant, lest they should learn of some reason to think otherwise than they do. Let their passions be enlisted, so that they may regard private and unusual opinions with hatred and horror. Then, let all men who reject the established belief be terrified into silence. Let the people turn out and tar-and-feather such men, or let inquisitions be made into the manner of thinking of suspected persons, and, when they are found guilty of forbidden beliefs, let them be subjected to some signal punishment. When complete agreement could not otherwise be reached, a general massacre of all who have not thought in a certain way has proved a very effective means of settling opinion in a country. If the power to do this be wanting, let a list of opinions be drawn up, to which no man of the least independence of thought can assent, and let the faithful be required to accept all these propositions, in order to segregate them as radically as possible from the influence of the rest of the world.

This method has, from the earliest times, been one of the chief means of upholding correct theological and political doctrines, and of preserving their universal or catholic character. In Rome, especially, it has been practiced from the days of Numa Pompilius to those of Pius Nonus. This is the most perfect example in history; but wherever there is a priesthood—and no religion has been without one—this method has been more or less made use of. Wherever there is aristocracy, or a guild, or any association of a class of men whose interests depend or are supposed to depend on certain propositions, there will be inevitably found some traces of this natural product of social feeling. Cruelties always accompany this system; and when it is consistently carried out, they become atrocities of the most horrible kind in the eyes of any rational man. Nor should this occasion surprise, for the officer of a society does not feel justified in surrendering the interests of that society for the sake of mercy, as he might his own private interests. It is natural, therefore, that sympathy and fellowship should thus produce a most ruthless power.

In judging this method of fixing belief, which may be called the method of authority, we must, in the first place, allow its immeasurable mental and moral superiority to the method of tenacity. Its success is proportionally greater; and in fact it has over and over again worked the most majestic results. The mere structures of stone which it has caused to be put together—in Siam, for example, in Egypt, and in Europe—have many of them a sublimity hardly more than rivaled by the greatest works of nature. And, except the geological epochs, there are no periods of time so vast as those which are measured by some of these organized faiths. If we scrutinize the matter closely, we shall find that there has not been one of their creeds which has remained always the same; yet the change is so slow as to be imperceptible during one person's life, so that individual belief remains sensibly fixed. For the mass of mankind, then, there is perhaps no better method than this. If it is

their highest impulse to be intellectual slaves, then slaves
they ought to remain.

But no institution can undertake to regulate opinions
upon every subject. Only the most important ones can be
attended to, and on the rest men's minds must be left to the
action of natural causes. This imperfection will be no source
of weakness so long as men are in such a state of culture
that one opinion does not influence another—that is, so long
as they cannot put two and two together. But in the most
priest-ridden states some individuals will be found who are
raised above that condition. These men possess a wider sort
of social feeling; they see that men in other countries and
in other ages have held to very different doctrines from
those which they themselves have been brought up to believe; and they cannot help seeing that it is the mere accident of their having been taught as they have, and of their
having been surrounded with the manners and associations
they have, that has caused them to believe as they do and
not far differently. And their candor cannot resist the reflection that there is no reason to rate their own views at a
higher value than those of other nations and other centuries; and this gives rise to doubts in their minds.

They will further perceive that such doubts as these must
exist in their minds with reference to every belief which
seems to be determined by the caprice either of themselves
or of those who originated the popular opinions. The willful
adherence to a belief, and the arbitrary forcing of it upon
others, must, therefore, both be given up and a new method
of settling opinions must be adopted, which shall not only
produce an impulse to believe, but shall also decide what
proposition it is which is to be believed. Let the action of
natural preferences be unimpeded, then, and under their
influence let men conversing together and regarding matters in different lights, gradually develop beliefs in harmony with natural causes. This method resembles that by
which conceptions of art have been brought to maturity.
The most perfect example of it is to be found in the history
of metaphysical philosophy. Systems of this sort have not
usually rested upon observed facts, at least not in any great
degree. They have been chiefly adopted because their fun-

damental propositions seemed "agreeable to reason." This is an apt expression; it does not mean that which agrees with experience, but that which we find ourselves inclined to believe. Plato, for example, finds it agreeable to reason that the distances of the celestial spheres from one another should be proportional to the different lengths of strings which produce harmonious chords. Many philosophers have been led to their main conclusions by considerations like this; but this is the lowest and least developed form which the method takes, for it is clear that another man might find Kepler's [earlier] theory, that the celestial spheres are proportional to the inscribed and circumscribed spheres of the different regular solids, more agreeable to *his* reason. But the shock of opinions will soon lead men to rest on preferences of a far more universal nature. Take, for example, the doctrine that man only acts selfishly—that is, from the consideration that acting in one way will afford him more pleasure than acting in another. This rests on no fact in the world, but it has had a wide acceptance as being the only reasonable theory.

This method is far more intellectual and respectable from the point of view of reason than either of the others which we have noticed.[12] But its failure has been the most manifest. It makes of inquiry something similar to the development of taste; but taste, unfortunately, is always more or less a matter of fashion, and accordingly, metaphysicians have never come to any fixed agreement, but the pendulum has swung backward and forward between a more material and a more spiritual philosophy, from the earliest times to the latest. And so from this, which has been called the *a priori* method, we are driven, in Lord Bacon's phrase, to a true induction. We have examined into this *a priori* method as something which promised to deliver our opinions from their accidental and capricious element. But development,

12 "Indeed, as long as no better method can be applied, it [the *a priori* method] ought to be followed, since it is then the expression of instinct which must be the ultimate cause of belief in all cases."—Peirce's note of 1910. Compare F. H. Bradley's view that metaphysics consists in finding bad reasons for what we believe on instinct, but the giving of such reasons is itself an instinct.—Editor's note.

while it is a process which eliminates the effect of some casual circumstances, only magnifies that of others. This method, therefore, does not differ in a very essential way from that of authority. The government may not have lifted its finger to influence my convictions; I may have been left outwardly quite free to choose, we will say, between monogamy and polygamy, and appealing to my conscience only, I may have concluded that the latter practice is in itself licentious. But when I come to see that the chief obstacle to the spread of Christianity among a people of as high culture as the Hindoos has been a conviction of the immorality of our way of treating women, I cannot help seeing that, though governments do not interfere, sentiments in their development will be very greatly determined by accidental causes. Now, there are some people, among whom I must suppose that my reader is to be found, who, when they see that any belief of theirs is determined by any circumstance extraneous to the facts, will from that moment not merely admit in words that that belief is doubtful, but will experience a real doubt of it, so that it ceases in some degree at least to be a belief.

To satisfy our doubts, therefore, it is necessary that a method should be found by which our beliefs may be caused by nothing human, but by some external permanency—by something upon which our thinking has no effect. Some mystics imagine that they have such a method in a private inspiration from on high. But that is only a form of the method of tenacity, in which the conception of truth as something public is not yet developed. Our external permanency would not be external, in our sense, if it was restricted in its influence to one individual. It must be something which affects, or might affect, every man. And, though these affections are necessarily as various as are individual conditions, yet the method must be such that the ultimate conclusion of every man shall be the same, or would be the same if inquiry were sufficiently persisted in. Such is the method of science. Its fundamental hypothesis, restated in more familiar language, is this: There are real things, whose characters are entirely independent of our opinions about them; those realities affect our senses according to regular laws, and, though our sensations are as different as our relations to the objects, yet, by taking advantage of the laws of perception, we can ascertain by reasoning how things really are, and any man, if he have sufficient experience and reason enough about it, will be led to the one true conclusion. The new conception here involved is that of reality. It may be asked how I know that there are any realities. If this hypothesis is the sole support of my method of inquiry, my method of inquiry must not be used to support my hypothesis. The reply is this: (1) If investigation cannot be regarded as proving that there are real things, it at least does not lead to a contrary conclusion; but the method and the conception on which it is based remain ever in harmony. No doubts of the method, therefore, necessarily arise from its practice, as is the case with all the others. (2) The feeling which gives rise to any method of fixing belief is a dissatisfaction at two repugnant propositions. But here already is a vague concession that there is some *one* thing to which a proposition should conform. Nobody, therefore, can really doubt that there are realities, or, if he did, doubt would not be a source of dissatisfaction. The hypothesis, therefore, is one which every mind admits. So that the social impulse does not cause men to doubt it. (3) Everybody uses the scientific method about a great many things, and only ceases to use it when he does not know how to apply it. (4) Experience of the method has not led us to doubt it, but, on the contrary, scientific investigation has had the most wonderful triumphs in the way of settling opinion. These afford the explanation of my not doubting the method or the hypothesis which it supposes; and not having any doubt, nor believing that anybody else whom I could influence has, it would be the merest babble for me to say more about it. If there be anybody with a living doubt upon the subject, let him consider it.

To describe the method of scientific investigation is the object of this series of papers. At present I have only room to notice some points of contrast between it and other methods of fixing belief.

This is the only one of the four methods which presents

any distinction of a right and a wrong way. If I adopt the method of tenacity and shut myself out from all influences, whatever I think necessary to doing this is necessary according to that method. So with the method of authority: the state may try to put down heresy by means which, from a scientific point of view, seems very ill-calculated to accomplish its purposes; but the only test *on that method* is what the state thinks, so that it cannot pursue the method wrongly. So with the *a priori* method. The very essence of it is to think as one is inclined to think. All metaphysicians will be sure to do that, however they may be inclined to judge each other to be perversely wrong. The Hegelian system recognizes every natural tendency of thought as logical, although it is certain to be abolished by counter-tendencies. Hegel thinks there is a regular system in the succession of these tendencies, in consequence of which, after drifting one way and the other for a long time, opinion will at last go right. And it is true that metaphysicians get the right ideas at last; Hegel's system of Nature represents tolerably the science of his day; and one may be sure that whatever scientific investigation has put out of doubt will presently receive *a priori* demonstration on the part of the metaphysicians. But with the scientific method the case is different. I may start with known and observed facts to proceed to the unknown; and yet the rules which I follow in doing so may not be such as investigation would approve. The test of whether I am truly following the method is not an immediate appeal to my feelings and purposes, but, on the contrary, itself involves the application of the method. Hence it is that bad reasoning as well as good reasoning is possible; and this fact is the foundation of the practical side of logic.

It is not to be supposed that the first three methods of settling opinion present no advantage whatever over the scientific method. On the contrary, each has some peculiar convenience of its own. The *a priori* method is distinguished for its comfortable conclusions. It is the nature of the process to adopt whatever belief we are inclined to, and there are certain flatteries to one's vanities which we all believe by nature, until we are awakened from our pleasing dream by rough facts. The method of authority will always govern the mass of mankind; and those who wield the various forms of organized force in the state will never be convinced that dangerous reasoning ought not to be suppressed in some way. If liberty of speech is to be untrammeled from the grosser forms of constraint, then uniformity of opinion will be secured by a moral terrorism to which the respectability of society will give its thorough approval. Following the method of authority is the path of peace. Certain non-conformities are permitted; certain others (considered unsafe) are forbidden. These are different in different countries and in different ages; but, wherever you are let it be known that you seriously hold a tabooed belief, and you may be perfectly sure of being treated with a cruelty no less brutal but more refined than hunting you like a wolf. Thus, the greatest intellectual benefactors of mankind have never dared, and dare not now, to utter the whole of their thought; and thus a shade of *prima facie* doubt is cast upon every proposition which is considered essential to the security of society. Singularly enough, the persecution does not all come from without; but a man torments himself and is oftentimes most distressed at finding himself believing propositions which he has been brought up to regard with aversion. The peaceful and sympathetic man will, therefore, find it hard to resist the temptation to submit his opinions to authority. But most of all I admire the method of tenacity for its strength, simplicity, and directness. Men who pursue it are distinguished for their decision of character, which becomes very easy with such a mental rule. They do not waste time in trying to make up their minds to what they want, but, fastening like lightning upon whatever alternative comes first, they hold to it to the end, whatever happens, without an instant's irresolution. This is one of the splendid qualities which generally accompany brilliant, unlasting success. It is impossible not to envy the man who can dismiss reason, although we know how it must turn out at last.

Such are the advantages which the other methods of settling opinions have over scientific investigation. A man should consider well of them; and then he should consider that, after all, he wishes his opinions to coincide with the fact, and that there is no reason why the results of those first three methods should do so. To bring about this effect is the prerogative of the method of science. Upon such considerations he has to make his choice—a choice which is far more than the adoption of any intellectual opinion, which is one of the ruling decisions of his life, to which when once made he is bound to adhere. The force of habit will sometimes cause a man to hold on to old beliefs after he is in a condition to see that they have no sound basis. But reflection upon the state of the case will overcome these habits, and he ought to allow reflection full weight. People sometimes shrink from doing this, having an idea that beliefs are wholesome which they cannot help feeling rest on nothing. But let such persons suppose an analogous though different case from their own. Let them ask themselves what they would say to a reformed Mussulman who should hesitate to give up his old notions in regard to the relations of the sexes; or to a reformed Catholic who should still shrink from the Bible. Would they not say that these persons ought to consider the matter fully, and clearly understand the new doctrine, and then ought to embrace it in its entirety? But, above all, let it be considered that what is more wholesome than any particular belief is integrity of belief; and that to avoid looking into the support of any belief from a fear that it may turn out rotten is quite as immoral as it is disadvantageous. The person who confesses that there is such a thing as truth, which is distinguished from falsehood simply by this, that if acted on it should, on full consideration, carry us to the point we aim at and not astray, and then, though convinced of this, dares not know the truth and seeks to avoid it, is in a sorry state of mind, indeed.

Yes, the other methods do have their merits: a clear logical conscience does cost something—just as any virtue, just as all that we cherish, costs us dear. But, we should not desire it to be otherwise. The genius of a man's logical method should be loved and reverenced as his bride, whom he has chosen from all the world. He need not condemn the others; on the contrary, he may honor them deeply, and in doing so he only honors her the more. But she is the one that he has chosen, and he knows that he was right in making that choice. And having made it, he will work and fight for her, and will not complain that there are blows to take, hoping that there may be as many and as hard to give, and will strive to be the worthy knight and champion of her from the blaze of whose splendors he draws his inspiration and his courage.

6.   How to Make Our Ideas Clear[1]

[This second paper was originally written in French for the *Revue Philosophique* in 1877, and appeared with a translation of the first paper in Volumes 6 and 7 (December 1878 and January 1879) of that French periodical. Perhaps no earlier and clearer presentation of the "operationalist" theory of meaning can be found in American philosophy, and no bolder claim to improve upon Descartes' method of *a priori* appeal to self-evidence and Leibniz's method of abstract definition. These first two levels of clarity are limited by the fact that what is evident to one mind may not be so to another, and by the fact that "nothing new can ever be learned by analyzing definitions." Peirce's third and highest level of clarification appears in his maxim that the whole meaning of any idea is to be found in considering what effects that "might conceivably have practical bearings, we conceive the object of our conception to have." This operational and pragmatic maxim renders meaningless any notion that there is something more to the meaning of electricity than the sum total of its possible effects on observable objects like magnetized wires or ionized substances or a shocked animal. Any hypothesis about electricity is meaningful to the extent that it specifies what we must do to observe certain effects predesignated by the hypothesis. So also, a personality, dead or alive, has his meaning preserved in his effects on other living persons and in

[1] *Popular Science Monthly* (Jan. 1878), pp. 286–302.

the changes he has wrought in his environment. Consider Emerson's notion that an institution is the shadow of a great man, and Peirce's theory can be seen to have its illustrations in the human as well as in the physical domain from which he draws his illustrations (hardness, force, reality). "Truth" means that opinion which investigators are bound to come to in the long run, and the object of their convergent opinion would be the meaning of "reality."]

I

Whoever has looked into a modern treatise on logic of the common sort, will doubtless remember the two distinctions between *clear* and *obscure* conceptions, and between *distinct* and *confused* conceptions. They have lain in the books now for nigh two centuries, unimproved and unmodified, and are generally reckoned by logicians as among the gems of their doctrine.

A clear idea is defined as one which is so apprehended that it will be recognized wherever it is met with, and so that no other will be mistaken for it. If it fails of this clearness, it is said to be obscure.

This is rather a neat bit of philosophical terminology; yet, since it is clearness that they were defining, I wish the logicians had made their definition a little more plain. Never to fail to recognize an idea, and under no circumstances to mistake another for it, let it come in how recondite a form it may, would indeed imply such prodigious force and clearness of intellect as is seldom met with in this world. On the other hand, merely to have such an acquaintance with the idea as to have become familiar with it, and to have lost all hesitancy in recognizing it in ordinary cases, hardly seems to deserve the name of clearness of apprehension, since after all it only amounts to a subjective feeling of mastery which may be entirely mistaken. I take it, however, that when the logicians speak of "clearness," they mean nothing more than such a familiarity with an idea, since they regard the quality as but a small merit, which needs to be supplemented by another, which they call *distinctness*.

A distinct idea is defined as one which contains nothing which is not clear. This is technical language; by the *contents* of an idea logicians understand whatever is contained in its definition. So that an idea is *distinctly* apprehended, according to them, when we can give a precise definition of it, in abstract terms. Here the professional logicians leave the subject; and I would not have troubled the reader with what they have to say if it were not such a striking example of how they have been slumbering through ages of intellectual activity, listlessly disregarding the enginery of modern thought, and never dreaming of applying its lessons to the improvement of logic. It is easy to show that the doctrine that familiar use and abstract distinctness make the perfection of apprehension, has its only true place in philosophies which have long been extinct; and it is now time to formulate the method of attaining to a more perfect clearness of thought, such as we see and admire in the thinkers of our own time.

When Descartes set about the reconstruction of philosophy, his first step was to (theoretically) permit skepticism and to discard the practice of the schoolmen of looking to authority as the ultimate source of truth. That done, he sought a more natural fountain of true principles, and professed to find it in the human mind; thus passing, in the directest way, from the method of authority to that of apriority, as described in my first paper. Self-consciousness was to furnish us with our fundamental truths, and to decide what was agreeable to reason. But since, evidently, not all ideas are true, he was led to note, as the first condition of infallibility, that they must be clear. The distinction between an idea *seeming* clear and really being so, never occurred to him. Trusting to introspection, as he did, even for a knowledge of external things, why should he question its testimony in respect to the contents of our own minds? But then, I suppose, seeing men, who seemed to be quite clear and positive, holding opposite opinions upon fundamental principles, he was further led to say that clearness of ideas is not sufficient, but that they need also to be distinct, i.e., to have nothing unclear about them. What he probably

meant by this (for he did not explain himself with precision) was that they must sustain the test of dialectical examination; that they must not only seem clear at the outset,
but that discussion must never be able to bring to light
points of obscurity connected with them.

Such was the distinction of Descartes, and one sees that
it was precisely on the level of his philosophy. It was somewhat developed by Leibniz. This great and singular genius
was as remarkable for what he failed to see as for what
he saw. That a piece of mechanism could not do work perpetually without being fed with power in some form, was
a thing perfectly apparent to him; yet he did not understand that the machinery of the mind can only transform
knowledge, but never originate it, unless it be fed with facts
of observation. He thus missed the most essential point of
the Cartesian philosophy, which is, that to accept propositions which seem perfectly evident to us is a thing which,
whether it be logical or illogical, we cannot help doing. Instead of regarding the matter in this way, he sought to reduce the first principles of science to formulas which cannot
be denied without self-contradiction, and was apparently
unaware of the great difference between his position and
that of Descartes.[2] So he reverted to the old formalities of
logic, and, above all, abstract definitions played a great part
in his philosophy. It was quite natural, therefore, that on
observing that the method of Descartes labored under the
difficulty that we may seem to ourselves to have clear apprehensions of ideas which in truth are very hazy, no better
remedy occurred to him than to require an abstract definition of every important term. Accordingly, in adopting the
distinction of *clear* and *distinct* notions, he described the
latter quality as the clear apprehension of everything contained in the definition; and the books have ever since

[2] He was, however, above all, one of the minds that grow;
while at first he was an extreme nominalist, like Hobbes, and
dabbled in the nonsensical and impotent *Ars Magna* of Ray-
mond Lully, he subsequently embraced the law of continuity
and other doctrines opposed to nominalism. I speak here of his
early views.—1903.

copied his words. There is no danger that his chimerical scheme will ever again be overvalued. Nothing new can ever be learned by analyzing definitions. Nevertheless, our existing beliefs can be set in order by this process, and order is an essential element of intellectual economy, as of every other. It may be acknowledged, therefore, that the books are right in making familiarity with a notion the first step toward clearness of apprehension, and the defining of it the second. But in omitting all mention of any higher perspicuity of thought, they simply mirror a philosophy which was exploded a hundred years ago. That much-admired "ornament of logic"—the doctrine of clearness and distinctness—may be pretty enough, but it is high time to relegate to our cabinet of curiosities the antique *bijou*, and to wear about us something better adapted to modern uses.

The very first lesson that we have a right to demand that logic shall teach us is how to make our ideas clear; and a most important one it is, depreciated only by minds who stand in need of it. To know what we think, to be masters of our own meaning, will make a solid foundation for great and weighty thought. It is most easily learned by those whose ideas are meagre and restricted; and far happier they than such as wallow helplessly in a rich mud of conceptions. A nation, it is true, may, in the course of generations, overcome the disadvantage of an excessive wealth of language and its natural concomitant, a vast, unfathomable deep of ideas. We may see it in history, slowly perfecting its literary forms, sloughing at length its metaphysics, and, by virtue of the untirable patience which is often a compensation, attaining great excellence in every branch of mental acquirement. The page of history is not yet unrolled which is to tell us whether such a people will or will not in the long run prevail over one whose ideas (like the words of their language) are few, but which possesses a wonderful mastery over those which it has. For an individual, however, there can be no question that a few clear ideas are worth more than many confused ones. A young man would hardly be persuaded to sacrifice the greater part of his thoughts to save the rest; and the muddled head

is the least apt to see the necessity of such a sacrifice. Him
we can usually only commiserate, as a person with a con-
genital defect. Time will help him, but intellectual maturity
with regard to clearness comes rather late, an unfortunate
arrangement of nature, inasmuch as clearness is of less use
to a man settled in life, whose errors have in great measure
had their effect, than it would be to one whose path lies
before him. It is terrible to see how a single unclear idea,
a single formula without meaning, lurking in a young man's
head, will sometimes act like an obstruction of inert matter
in an artery, hindering the nutrition of the brain, and condemning its victim to pine away in the fullness of his intellectual vigor and in the midst of intellectual plenty. Many
a man has cherished for years as his hobby some vague
shadow of an idea, too meaningless to be positively false;
he has, nevertheless, passionately loved it, has made it his
companion by day and by night, and has given to it his
strength and his life, leaving all other occupations for its
sake, and in short has lived with it and for it, until it has
become, as it were, flesh of his flesh and bone of his bone;
and then he has waked up some bright morning to find it
gone, clean vanished away like the beautiful Melusina of
the fable, and the essence of his life gone with it. I have
myself known such a man; and who can tell how many
histories of circle-squarers, metaphysicians, astrologers, and
what not, may not be told in the old German story?

II

The principles set forth in the first of these papers lead,
at once, to a method of reaching a clearness of thought of
a far higher grade than the "distinctness" of the logicians.
We have there found that the action of thought is excited
by the irritation of doubt, and ceases when belief is attained; so that the production of belief is the sole function
of thought. All these words, however, are too strong for my
purpose. It is as if I had described the phenomena as they
appear under a mental microscope. Doubt and Belief, as
the words are commonly employed, relate to religious or

other grave discussions. But here I use them to designate the starting of any question, no matter how small or how great, and the resolution of it. If, for instance, in a horse-car, I pull out my purse and find a five-cent nickel and five coppers, I decide, while my hand is going to the purse, in which way I will pay my fare. To call such a question Doubt, and my decision Belief, is certainly to use words very disproportionate to the occasion. To speak of such a doubt as causing an irritation which needs to be appeased, suggests a temper which is uncomfortable to the verge of insanity. Yet, looking at the matter minutely, it must be admitted that, if there is the least hesitation as to whether I shall pay the five coppers or the nickel (as there will be sure to be, unless I act from some previously contracted habit in the matter), though irritation is too strong a word, yet I am excited to such small mental activity as may be necessary to deciding how I shall act. Most frequently doubts arise from some indecision, however momentary, in our action. Sometimes it is not so. I have, for example, to wait in a railway-station, and to pass the time I read the advertisements on the walls, I compare the advantages of different trains and different routes which I never expect to take, merely fancying myself to be in a state of hesitancy, because I am bored with having nothing to trouble me. Feigned hesitancy, whether feigned for mere amusement or with a lofty purpose, plays a great part in the production of scientific inquiry. However the doubt may originate, it stimulates the mind to an activity which may be slight or energetic, calm or turbulent. Images pass rapidly through consciousness, one incessantly melting into another, until at last, when all is over—it may be in a fraction of a second, in an hour, or after long years—we find ourselves decided as to how we should act under such circumstances as those which occasioned our hesitation. In other words, we have attained belief.

In this process we observe two sorts of elements of consciousness, the distinction between which may best be made clear by means of an illustration. In a piece of music there are the separate notes, and there is the air. A single tone may be prolonged for an hour or a day, and it exists as perfectly in each second of that time as in the whole taken together; so that, as long as it is sounding, it might be present to a sense from which everything in the past was as completely absent as the future itself. But it is different with the air, the performance of which occupies a certain time, during the portions of which only portions of it are played. It consists in an orderliness in the succession of sounds which strike the ear at different times; and to perceive it there must be some continuity of consciousness which makes the events of a lapse of time present to us. We certainly only perceive the air by hearing the separate notes; yet we cannot be said to directly hear it, for we hear only what is present at the instant, and an orderliness of succession cannot exist in an instant. These two sorts of objects, what we are *immediately* conscious of and what we are *mediately* conscious of, are found in all consciousness. Some elements (the sensations) are completely present at every instant so long as they last, while others (like thought) are actions having beginning, middle, and end, and consist in a congruence in the succession of sensations which flow through the mind. They cannot be immediately present to us, but must cover some portion of the past or future. Thought is a thread of melody running through the succession of our sensations.

We may add that just as a piece of music may be written in parts, each part having its own air, so various systems of relationship of succession subsist together between the same sensations. These different systems are distinguished by having different motives, ideas, or functions. Thought is only one such system; for its sole motive, idea, and function is to produce belief, and whatever does not concern that purpose belongs to some other system of relations. The action of thinking may incidentally have other results. It may serve to amuse us, for example, and among *dilettanti* it is not rare to find those who have so perverted thought to the purposes of pleasure that it seems to vex them to think that the questions upon which they delight to exercise it may ever get finally settled; and a positive discovery which takes a favorite subject out of the arena of literary debate is met with ill-concealed dislike. This disposition is the very debauchery of thought. But the soul and meaning of thought, abstracted from the other elements which accompany it, though it may be voluntarily thwarted, can never be made to direct itself toward anything but the production of belief. Thought in action has for its only possible motive the attainment of thought at rest; and whatever does not refer to belief is no part of the thought itself.

And what, then, is belief? It is the demi-cadence which closes a musical phrase in the symphony of our intellectual life. We have seen that it has just three properties: first, it is something that we are aware of; second, it appeases the irritation of doubt; and, third, it involves the establishment in our nature of a rule of action, or, say for short, a *habit*. As it appeases the irritation of doubt, which is the motive for thinking, thought relaxes, and comes to rest for a moment when belief is reached. But, since belief is a rule for action, the application of which involves further doubt and further thought, at the same time that it is a stopping-place, it is also a new starting-place for thought. That is why I have permitted myself to call it thought at rest, although thought is essentially an action. The *final* upshot of thinking is the exercise of volition, and of this thought no longer forms a part; but belief is only a stadium of mental action, an effect upon our nature due to thought, which will influence future thinking.

The essence of belief is the establishment of a habit, and different beliefs are distinguished by the different modes of action to which they give rise. If beliefs do not differ in this respect, if they appease the same doubt by producing the same rule of action, then no mere differences in the manner of consciousness of them can make them different beliefs, any more than playing a tune in different keys is playing different tunes. Imaginary distinctions are often drawn between beliefs which differ only in their mode of expression—the wrangling which ensues is real enough, however. To believe that any objects are arranged among themselves as in Fig. 1, and to believe that they are arranged as in Fig. 2, are one and the same belief; yet it is

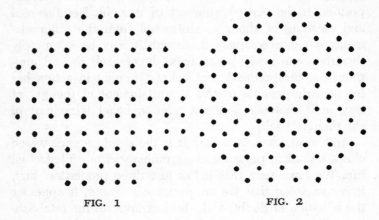

FIG. 1   FIG. 2

conceivable that a man should assert one proposition and deny the other. Such false distinctions do as much harm as the confusion of beliefs really different, and are among the pitfalls of which we ought constantly to beware, especially when we are upon metaphysical ground. One singular deception of this sort, which often occurs, is to mistake the sensation produced by our own unclearness of thought for a character of the object we are thinking. Instead of perceiving that the obscurity is purely subjective, we fancy that we contemplate a quality of the object which is essentially mysterious; and if our conception be afterward presented to us in a clear form we do not recognize it as the same, owing to the absence of the feeling of unintelligibility. So long as this deception lasts, it obviously puts an impassable barrier in the way of perspicuous thinking; so that it equally interests the opponents of rational thought to perpetuate it, and its adherents to guard against it.

Another such deception is to mistake a mere difference in the grammatical construction of two words for a distinction between the ideas they express. In this pedantic age, when the general mob of writers attend so much more to words than to things, this error is common enough. When I just said that thought is an *action*, and that it consists in a *relation*, although a person performs an action but not a relation, which can only be the result of an action, yet there was no inconsistency in what I said, but only a grammatical vagueness.

From all these sophisms we shall be perfectly safe so long as we reflect that the whole function of thought is to produce habits of action; and that whatever there is connected with a thought, but irrelevant to its purpose, is an accretion to it, but no part of it. If there be a unity among our sensations which has no reference to how we shall act on a given occasion, as when we listen to a piece of music, why, we do not call that thinking. To develop its meaning, we have, therefore, simply to determine what habits it produces, for what a thing means is simply what habits it involves. Now, the identity of a habit depends on how it might lead us to act, not merely under such circumstances as are likely to arise, but under such as might possibly occur, no matter how improbable they may be. What the habit is depends on *when* and *how* it causes us to act. As for the *when*, every stimulus to action is derived from perception; as for the *how*, every purpose of action is to produce some sensible result. Thus, we come down to what is tangible and practical as the root of every real distinction of thought, no matter how subtle it may be; and there is no distinction of meaning so fine as to consist in anything but a possible difference of practice.

To see what this principle leads to, consider in the light of it such a doctrine as that of transubstantiation. The Protestant churches generally hold that the elements of the sacrament are flesh and blood only in a tropical sense; they nourish our souls as meat and the juice of it would our bodies. But the Catholics maintain that they are literally just that, meat and blood; although they possess all the sensible qualities of wafer-cakes and diluted wine. But we can have no conception of wine except what may enter into a belief, either—

1. That this, that, or the other, is wine; or,
2. That wine possesses certain properties.

Such beliefs are nothing but self-notifications that we should, upon occasion, act in regard to such things as we believe to be wine according to the qualities which we believe wine to possess. The occasion of such action would be some sensible perception, the motive of it to produce some sensible result. Thus our action has exclusive reference to what affects the senses, our habit has the same bearing as our action, our belief the same as our habit, our conception the same as our belief; and we can consequently mean nothing by wine but what has certain effects, direct or indirect, upon our senses; and to talk of something as having all the sensible characters of wine, yet being in reality blood, is senseless jargon. Now, it is not my object to pursue the theological question; and having used it as a logical example I drop it, without caring to anticipate the theologian's reply. I only desire to point out how impossible it is that we should have an idea in our minds which relates to anything but conceived sensible effects of things. Our idea of anything *is* our idea of its sensible effects; and if we fancy that we have any other we deceive ourselves, and mistake a mere sensation accompanying the thought for a part of the thought itself. It is absurd to say that thought has any meaning unrelated to its only function. It is foolish for Catholics and Protestants to fancy themselves in disagreement about the elements of the sacrament, if they agree in regard to all their sensible effects, here or hereafter.

It appears, then, that the rule for attaining the third grade of clearness of apprehension is as follows: consider what effects, which might conceivably have practical bearings, we conceive the object of our conception to have. Then, our conception of these effects is the whole of our conception of the object.

III

Let us illustrate this rule by some examples; and, to begin with the simplest one possible, let us ask what we mean by calling a thing *hard*. Evidently that it will not be scratched by many other substances. The whole conception of this quality, as of every other, lies in its conceived effects. There is absolutely no difference between a hard thing and a soft thing so long as they are not brought to the test. Suppose, then, that a diamond could be crystallized in the midst of a cushion of soft cotton, and should remain there until it was finally burned up. Would it be false to say that that diamond was soft? This seems a foolish question, and would be so, in fact, except in the realm of logic. There such questions are often of the greatest utility as serving to bring logical principles into sharper relief than real discussions ever could. In studying logic we must not put them aside with hasty answers, but must consider them with attentive care, in order to make out the principles involved. We may, in the present case, modify our question, and ask what prevents us from saying that all hard bodies remain perfectly soft until they are touched, when their hardness increases with the pressure until they are scratched. Reflection will show that the reply is this: there would be no *falsity* in such modes of speech. They would involve a modification of our present usage of speech with regard to the words "hard" and "soft," but not of their meanings. For they represent no fact to be different from what it is; only they involve arrangements of facts which would be exceedingly maladroit. This leads us to remark that the question of what would occur under circumstances which do not actually arise is not a question of fact, but only of the most perspicuous arrangement of them. For example, the question of free-will and fate in its simplest form, stripped of verbiage, is something like this: I have done something of which I am ashamed; could I, by an effort of the will, have resisted the temptation, and done otherwise? The philosophical reply is that this is not a question of fact, but only of the [possible] arrangement of facts. Arranging them so as to exhibit what is particularly pertinent to my question—namely, that I ought to blame myself for having done wrong—it is perfectly true to say that, if I had willed to do otherwise than I did, I should have done otherwise. On the other hand, arranging the facts so as to exhibit another important consideration, it is equally true that when a temptation has once been allowed to work, it will, if it has a certain force, produce its effect, let me struggle how I may. There is no objection to a contradiction in what would result from a false supposition. The *reductio ad absurdum* consists in showing that contradictory results would follow from a hypothesis which is consequently judged to be false. Many questions are involved in the free-will discussion, and I am far from desiring to say that both sides are equally right. On the contrary, I am of opinion that one side [determinism] denies important facts, and that the other does not. But what I do say is that the above single question was the origin of the whole doubt; that, had it not been for this question, the controversy would never have arisen; and that this question is perfectly solved in the manner which I have indicated.

Let us next seek a clear idea of Weight. This is another very easy case. To say that a body is heavy means simply that, in the absence of opposing force, it will fall. This (neglecting certain specifications of how it will fall, etc., which exist in the mind of the physicist who uses the word) is evidently the whole conception of weight. It is a fair question whether some particular facts may not *account* for gravity; but what we mean by the force itself is completely involved in its effects.

This leads us to undertake an account of the idea of Force in general. This is the great conception which, developed in the early part of the seventeenth century from the rude idea of a cause, and, constantly improved upon since, has shown us how to explain all the changes of motion which bodies experience, and how to think about all physical phenomena; which has given birth to modern science, and changed the face of the globe; and which, aside from its more special uses, has played a principal part in directing the course of modern thought, and in furthering modern social development. It is, therefore, worth some pains to comprehend it. According to our rule, we must begin by asking what is the immediate use of thinking about force; and the answer is that we thus account for changes of motion. If bodies were left to themselves, without the intervention of forces, every motion would continue unchanged both in velocity and in direction. Furthermore, change of motion never takes place abruptly; if its direction is changed, it is always through a curve without angles; if its velocity alters, it is by degrees. The gradual changes which are constantly taking place are conceived by geometers to be compounded together according to the rules of the parallelogram of forces. If the reader does not already know what this is, he will find it, I hope, to his advantage to endeavor to follow the following explanation; but if mathematics are insupportable to him, pray let him skip three paragraphs rather than that we should part company here.

A *path* is a line whose beginning and end are distinguished. Two paths are considered to be equivalent, which, beginning at the same point, lead to the same point. Thus the two paths, *A B C D E* and *A F G H E* (Fig. 3), are equivalent. Paths which do *not* begin at the same point are considered to be equivalent, provided that, on moving either of them without turning it, but keeping it always parallel to its original position, [so that] when its beginning coincides with that of the other path, the ends also coincide. Paths are considered as geometrically added together, when one begins where the other ends; thus the path *A E* is conceived to be a sum of *A B*, *B C*, *C D*, and *D E*. In the parallelogram of Fig. 4 the diagonal *A C* is the sum of *A B* and *B C*; or, since *A D* is geometrically equivalent to *B C*, *A C* is the geometrical sum of *A B* and *A D*.

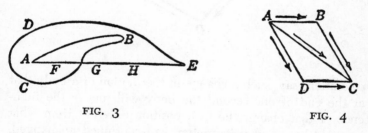

FIG. 3   FIG. 4

All this is purely conventional. It simply amounts to this: that we choose to call paths having the relations I have described equal or added. But, though it is a convention, it is a convention with a good reason. The rule for geometrical addition may be applied not only to paths, but to any other things which can be represented by paths. Now, as a path is determined by the varying direction and distance of the point which moves over it from the starting-point, it follows that anything which from its beginning to its end is determined by a varying direction and a varying magnitude is capable of being represented by a line. Accordingly, *velocities* may be represented by lines, for they have only directions and rates. The same thing is true of *accelerations,* or changes of velocities. This is evident enough in the case of velocities; and it becomes evident for accelerations if we consider that precisely what velocities are to positions—namely, states of change of them—that accelerations are to velocities.

The so-called "parallelogram of forces" is simply a rule for compounding accelerations. The rule is, to represent the accelerations by paths, and then to geometrically add the paths. The geometers, however, not only use the "parallelogram of forces" to compound different accelerations, but also to resolve one acceleration into a sum of several. Let *A B* (Fig. 5) be the path which represents a certain ac-

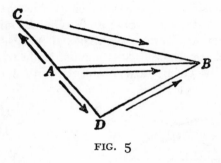

FIG. 5

celeration—say, such a change in the motion of a body that at the end of one second the body will, under the influence of that change, be in a position different from what it would have had if its motion had continued unchanged, such that a path equivalent to *A B* would lead from the latter position to the former. This acceleration may be considered as the sum of the accelerations represented by *A C* and *C B*. It may also be considered as the sum of the very different accelerations represented by *A D* and *D B*, where *A D* is almost the opposite of *A C*. And it is clear that there is an immense variety of ways in which *A B* might be resolved into the sum of two accelerations.

After this tedious explanation, which I hope, in view of the extraordinary interest of the conception of force, may not have exhausted the reader's patience, we are prepared at last to state the grand fact which this conception embodies. This fact is that if the actual changes of motion which the different particles of bodies experience are each resolved in its appropriate way, each component acceleration is precisely such as is prescribed by a certain law of Nature, according to which bodies in the relative positions which the bodies in question actually have at the moment,[3] always receive certain accelerations, which, being compounded by geometrical addition, give the acceleration which the body actually experiences.

This is the only fact which the idea of force represents, and whoever will take the trouble clearly to apprehend what this fact is perfectly comprehends what force is. Whether we ought to say that a force *is* an acceleration, or that it *causes* an acceleration, is a mere question of propriety of language, which has no more to do with our real meaning than the difference between the French idiom "*Il fait froid*" and its English equivalent "*It is cold.*" Yet it is surprising to see how this simple affair has muddled men's minds. In how many profound treatises is not force spoken of as a "mysterious entity," which seems to be only a way of confessing that the author despairs of ever getting a clear notion of what the word means! In a recent, admired work on *Analytic Mechanics* [by Kirchhoff] it is stated that we understand precisely the effect of force, but what force itself is we do not understand! This is simply a self-contradiction. The idea which the word "force" excites in our minds has no other function than to affect our actions, and these actions can have no reference to force otherwise than through its effects. Consequently, if we know what the effects of force are, we are acquainted with every fact which is implied in saying that a force exists, and there is nothing more to know. The truth is, there is some vague notion afloat that a question may mean something which the mind cannot conceive; and when some hair-splitting philosophers have been confronted with the absurdity of such a view, they have invented an empty distinction between positive

[3] Possibly the velocities also have to be taken into account.

and negative conceptions, in the attempt to give their non-idea a form not obviously nonsensical. The nullity of it is sufficiently plain from the considerations given a few pages back; and, apart from those considerations, the quibbling character of the distinction must have struck every mind accustomed to real thinking.

IV

Let us now approach the subject of logic, and consider a conception which particularly concerns it, that of *reality*. Taking clearness in the sense of familiarity, no idea could be clearer than this. Every child uses it with perfect confidence, never dreaming that he does not understand it. As for clearness in its second grade, however, it would probably puzzle most men, even among those of a reflective turn of mind, to give an abstract definition of the real. Yet such a definition may perhaps be reached by considering the points of difference between reality and its opposite, fiction. A figment is a product of somebody's imagination; it has such characters as his thought impresses upon it. That those characters are independent of how you or I think is an external reality. There are, however, phenomena within our own minds, dependent upon our thought, which are at the same time real in the sense that we really think them. But though their characters depend on how we think, they do not depend on what we think those characters to be. Thus, a dream has a real existence as a mental phenomenon, if somebody has really dreamt it; that he dreamt so and so, does not depend on what anybody thinks was dreamt, but is completely independent of all opinion on the subject. On the other hand, considering, not the fact of dreaming, but the thing dreamt, it retains its peculiarities by virtue of no other fact than that it was dreamt to possess them. Thus we may define the real as that whose characters are independent of what anybody may think them to be.

But, however satisfactory such a definition may be found, it would be a great mistake to suppose that it makes the idea of reality perfectly clear. Here, then, let us apply our rules. According to them, reality, like every other quality, consists in the peculiar, sensible effects which things partaking of it produce. The only effect which real things have is to cause belief, for all the sensations which they excite emerge into consciousness in the form of beliefs. The question, therefore, is, how is true belief (or belief in the real) distinguished from false belief (or belief in fiction). Now, as we have seen in the former paper, the ideas of truth and falsehood, in their full development, appertain exclusively to the scientific method of settling opinion. A person who arbitrarily chooses the propositions which he will adopt can use the word truth only to emphasize the expression of his determination to hold on to his choice. Of course, the method of tenacity never prevailed exclusively; reason is too natural to men for that. But in the literature of the Dark Ages we find some fine examples of it. When Scotus Erigena is commenting upon a poetical passage in which hellebore is spoken of as having caused the death of Socrates, he does not hesitate to inform the inquiring reader that Helleborus and Socrates were two eminent Greek philosophers, and that the latter having been overcome in argument by the former took the matter to heart and died of it! What sort of an idea of truth could a man have who could adopt and teach, without the qualification of a "perhaps," an opinion taken so entirely at random? The real spirit of Socrates, who I hope would have been delighted to have been "overcome in argument," because he would have learned something by it, is in curious contrast with the naïve idea of the glossist, for whom (as for the "born missionary" of today) discussion would seem to have been simply a struggle. When philosophy began to awake from its long slumber, and before theology completely dominated it, the practice seems to have been for each professor to seize upon any philosophical position he found unoccupied and which seemed a strong one, to intrench himself in it, and to sally forth from time to time to give battle to the others. Thus, even the scanty records we possess of those disputes enable us to make out a dozen or more opinions held by different teachers at one time concerning the question of nominalism and realism.

Read the opening part of the *Historia Calamitatum* of Abélard, who was certainly as philosophical as any of his contemporaries, and see the spirit of combat which it breathes. For him, the truth is simply his particular stronghold. When the method of authority prevailed, the truth meant little more than the Catholic faith. All the efforts of the scholastic doctors are directed toward harmonizing their faith in Aristotle and their faith in the Church, and one may search their ponderous folios through without finding an argument which goes any further. It is noticeable that where different faiths flourish side by side, renegades are looked upon with contempt even by the party whose belief they adopt; so completely has the idea of loyalty replaced that of truth-seeking. Since the time of Descartes, the defect in the conception of truth has been less apparent. Still, it will sometimes strike a scientific man that the philosophers have been less intent on finding out what the facts are than on inquiring what belief is most in harmony with their system. It is hard to convince a follower of the *a priori* method by adducing facts; but show him that an opinion he is defending is inconsistent with what he has laid down elsewhere, and he will be very apt to retract it. These minds do not seem to believe that disputation is ever to cease; they seem to think that the opinion which is natural for one man is not so for another, and that belief will, consequently, never be settled. In contenting themselves with fixing their own opinions by a method which would lead another man to a different result, they betray their feeble hold of the conception of what truth is.

On the other hand, all the followers of science are fully persuaded that the processes of investigation, if only pushed far enough, will give one certain solution to each question to which they can be applied. One man may investigate the velocity of light by studying the transits of Venus and the aberration of the stars; another by the oppositions of Mars and the eclipses of Jupiter's satellites; a third by the method of Fizeau; a fourth by that of Foucault; a fifth by the motions of the curves of Lissajous; a sixth, a seventh, an eighth, and a ninth, may follow the different methods of comparing the measures of statical and dynamical electricity. They may at first obtain different results, but, as each perfects his method and his processes, the results will move steadily together toward a destined center. So with all scientific research. Different minds may set out with the most antagonistic views, but the progress of investigation carries them by a force outside of themselves to one and the same conclusion. This activity of thought by which we are carried, not where we wish, but to a foreordained goal, is like the operation of destiny. No modification of the point of view taken, no selection of other facts for study, no natural bent of mind even, can enable a man to escape the predestinate opinion. This great law is embodied in the conception of truth and reality. The opinion which is fated[4] to be ultimately agreed to by all who investigate is what we mean by the truth, and the object represented in this opinion is the real. That is the way I would explain reality.

But it may be said that this view is directly opposed to the abstract definition which we have given of reality, inasmuch as it makes the characters of the real depend on what is ultimately thought about them. But the answer to this is that, on the one hand, reality is independent, not necessarily of thought in general, but only of what you or I or any finite number of men may think about it; and that, on the other hand, though the object of the final opinion depends on what that opinion is, yet what that opinion is does not depend on what you or I or any man thinks. Our perversity and that of others may indefinitely postpone the settlement of opinion; it might even conceivably cause an arbitrary proposition to be universally accepted as long as the human race should last. Yet even that would not change the nature of the belief, which alone could be the result of investigation carried sufficiently far; and if, after the extinction of our race, another should arise with faculties and disposition for investigation, that true opinion must be the one which

---

[4] Fate means merely that which is sure to come true, and can nohow be avoided. It is a superstition to suppose that a certain sort of events are ever fated, and it is another to suppose that the word "fate" can never be freed from its superstitious taint. We are all fated to die.

they would ultimately come to. "Truth crushed to earth shall rise again," and the opinion which would finally result from investigation does not depend on how anybody may actually think. But the reality of that which is real does[5] depend on the real fact that investigation is destined to lead, at last, if continued long enough, to a belief in it.

But I may be asked what I have to say to all the minute facts of history, forgotten never to be recovered, to the lost books of the ancients, to the buried secrets.

> "Full many a gem of purest ray serene
>   The dark, unfathomed caves of ocean bear;
> Full many a flower is born to blush unseen,
>   And waste its sweetness on the desert air."

Do these things not really exist because they are hopelessly beyond the reach of our knowledge? And then, after the universe is dead (according to the prediction of some scientists), and all life has ceased forever, will not the shock of atoms continue though there will be no mind to know it? To this I reply that, though in no possible state of knowledge can any number be great enough to express the relation between the amount of what rests unknown to the amount of the known, yet it is unphilosophical to suppose that, with regard to any given question (which has any clear meaning), investigation would not bring forth a solution of it, if it were carried far enough. Who would have said, a few years ago, that we could ever know of what substances stars are made whose light may have been longer in reaching us than the human race has existed? Who can be sure of what we shall not know in a few hundred years? Who can guess what would be the result of continuing the pursuit of science for ten thousand years, with the activity of the last hundred? And if it were to go on for a million, or a billion, or any number of years you please, how is it possible to say that there is any question which might not ultimately be solved?

5 In the French version, of which this essay is a translation, "does not depend" (*ne dépend pas*); cf. *Revue Philosophique*, "Comment rendre nos idées claires" (Jan. 1879), p. 56.—Editor's note.

But it may be objected, "Why make so much of these remote considerations, especially when it is your principle that only practical distinctions have a meaning?" Well, I must confess that it makes very little difference whether we say that a stone on the bottom of the ocean, in complete darkness, is brilliant or not—that is to say, that it *probably* makes no difference, remembering always that that stone *may* be fished up tomorrow. But that there are gems at the bottom of the sea, flowers in the untraveled desert, etc., are propositions which, like that about a diamond being hard when it is not pressed, concern much more the arrangement of our language than they do the meaning of our ideas.

It seems to me, however, that we have, by the application of our rule, reached so clear an apprehension of what we mean by reality, and of the fact which the idea rests on, that we should not, perhaps, be making a pretension so presumptuous as it would be singular, if we were to offer a metaphysical theory of existence for universal acceptance among those who employ the scientific method of fixing belief. However, as metaphysics is a subject much more curious than useful, the knowledge of which, like that of a sunken reef, serves chiefly to enable us to keep clear of it, I will not trouble the reader with any more Ontology at this moment.[6] I have already been led much further into that path than I should have desired; and I have given the reader such a dose of mathematics, psychology, and all that is most abstruse, that I fear he may already have left me, and that what I am now writing is for the compositor and proofreader exclusively. I trusted to the importance of the subject. There is no royal road to logic, and really valuable ideas can only be had at the price of close attention. But I know that in the matter of ideas the public prefer the cheap and nasty; and in my next paper I am going to return to the easily intelligible, and not wander from it again. The reader who has been at the pains of wading through this paper shall be rewarded in the next one by seeing how beautifully what has been developed in this

[6] The French version ends here.—Editor's note.

tedious way can be applied to the ascertainment of the rules of scientific reasoning.

We have, hitherto, not crossed the threshold of scientific logic. It is certainly important to know how to make our ideas clear, but they may be ever so clear without being true. How to make them so, we have next to study. How to give birth to those vital and procreative ideas which multiply into a thousand forms and diffuse themselves everywhere, advancing civilization and making the dignity of man, is an art not yet reduced to rules, but of the secret of which the history of science affords some hints.[7]

[7] In a later article of 1905 (see Selection 11, below, pp. 203f) Peirce criticized and modified his view of possibility, stated above, so that it would *not* be a merely verbal question whether a diamond formed in a bed of cotton-wool and consumed there, without ever having been pressed upon, were really hard. —Editor's note.

7. Notes on Positivism

[This undated manuscript at Widener Library is 18 pages long, and was evidently intended as an article critical of Comte's positivism and its followers, e.g., Karl Pearson. Its content is summarized by the following nine section-topics and the excerpts here given. Positivism tries to replace metaphysics and theology by scientific method and empirically verifiable statements.]

§ 1. Statement of the doctrine by which Positivism is distinguished from all other philosophies.

§ 2. That this doctrine has a favorable influence upon scientific investigation, and that the Positivists have been clever *savants*.

§ 3. That this doctrine is fatal to religion, and that the religious side of Positivism is its weakness.

§ 4. That it is possible and usual for scientific men to occupy another position equally advantageous in reference to scientific research and not so destructive of religious faith.

§ 5. Of Positivism as held by unphilosophic and unscientific persons, not owing to severe thought but to the influence of the "spirit of the age."

§ 6. That the fundamental position of Positivism is false.

§ 7. The true doctrine and its consequences.

§ 7½. Of some doctrines allied to Positivism.

§ 8. In what sense Positivism has deeply influenced the age and in what sense it has not.

§ 9. Conclusion.

The positivistic philosophy has now become the fashion. The first disciples of the positive philosophy (I do not speak of its doctors) were men interested in carrying the research of what ordinary people call "causes" into realms which had hitherto been trodden only by the foot of the metaphysician or the classifier. Without allowing all its rules for this kind of investigation, we may admit that it has been of real service to those men and through them to the world. Its scientific side is its strength. But now that it has become the fashion, it has been taken up by persons who have neither the stern masculinity proper for positive philosophers nor any business with physical sciences. By these persons it is regarded in its practical and especially its religious aspect. This is decidedly its weak side.

These modern disciples . . . prefer to discard all religious belief altogether . . . by persuading themselves that theism could offer no rational consolation to its believers, even if it could be rationally accepted. Herein they show the secret influence of the capital principle of theism, namely, that whatever is, is best. Only by a covert faith in this could they commit the absurdity of maintaining that God, Freedom, and Immortality would be evils.

Now the pleasantness or unpleasantness of consequences is no argument for or against a speculative opinion. But a man fights the battle of life better under the stimulus of hope. . . .

Instead of arguing from the historical effects of skepticism and theism, we prefer to begin with this undoubted fact: All men and all animals love life. . . .

The objects of this passion are firstly and primarily ourselves, in a less strong degree our friends, then our blood, then our country, then our race, and finally, it is still a deep and lively emotion even in its reference to intellect in general. . . . This love extends beyond the grave: even atheists provide for those who come after. . . . Nay, Hume was anxious for his own good reputation among succeeding generations. The *love of life* is more than the love of sensuous life: it is also a love of rational life. . . .

Now some Positivists—whom I should certainly adduce as instances of sneaking skeptics—endeavor to conceal the bearing of their doctrine upon religion. They seek to represent that it merely defines the possibility of arriving at scientific certainty with regard to such matters and not the possibility of reading highly probable conclusions. But this is a miserable falsification. *The doctrine that it implies that knowing a thing to be probable is not knowledge* is not only unsound in itself, it is so also on positivist principles, and is distinctly recognized as being so by the Positivists themselves. A Positivist to be consequent should hold that all religious belief is superstition, and that all superstitions which do not come into conflict with any scientifically known fact are on one level of credibility. . . .

It is true that one of the most eminent American metaphysicians is of opinion that religion might be based on positive philosophy as Comte defines it. . . . But this goes contrary to the positivistic restriction of observability on any theory . . . regarding belief in immortality, that there always should be intellect in the universe, that there should not come a time when it all dies out forever. . . .

[Positivism assumes:] Life upon the globe is a phase, quite accidental, tending as far as we know to no permanent end, of no sort of use, except in producing a pleasant titillation now and then on the nerves of this or that wayfarer on this weary and purposeless journey—which like a treadmill starts nowhere and goes nowhere, and whose machinery produces nothing at all. There is no good in life but its occasional pleasures; these are mostly delusive, and as like as not will soon utterly pass away.

Let us now turn to theism. The capital principle of this is that nature is absolutely conformed to an end; or in other words, that there is a reason in the nature of things. Now from what has been said before it follows that so far as we attain true culture, so far will the sum of all our impulses come to the love of reason as it necessarily is, and therefore so far as we are as we ought to be, so far are we perfectly gratified by what according to the nature of things takes place; which is another way of saying that whatever is, is best. Now this is . . . the very sum, quintessence, and acme of consolation.

I know very well that a great many theists are nearer pessimists than optimists, but they are unsound and inconsistent. To say, however, that whatever is, is best is not to deny the existence of evil, but only to maintain that if any event is bad in one way it more than counterbalances for it by being good in another or higher way.

Differences of opinion among metaphysicians have been growing less and less from one century to another owing to a gradual clearing up of conceptions. . . . Every great branch of science has once been in the state in which metaphysics is now, that is, when fundamental conceptions were vague and consequently its doctrines utterly unsettled; and there is no reason whatever to despair of metaphysics eventually becoming a real science like the rest; but at present that is not the case.

What is reality? Suppose we say it is that which is independently of our belief and which could be properly inferred (by the most thorough discussion) from the sum of all impressions of sense whatever. If that is what the Positivist means by reality (and since he does not tell us we must guess for ourselves), then he ought to be not a skeptic but an atheist, for that which we cannot possibly be in a state to infer is not then a reality at all. And, indeed, *I should be glad to know what the Positivist does mean by an existence which cannot possibly be known.*

. . . Positivism is only a particular species of metaphysics open to all the uncertainty of metaphysics, and its conclusions are for that reason of not enough weight to disturb any practical belief.

. . . I should define the end of a theory as to carry one thread of consciousness through different states of consciousness. Now all theories have this in common. They are inferences of the unobserved from the observed—of the *present* in experience to the *future* in experience. Now who does not see that the future is not observable except when the present is not, so that we either reason to conclusions which are absolutely unobservable or from facts which are absolutely unobservable. This is the conclusive objection to Positivism. . . .

Can *time* be observed to flow?

All science depends upon the record of the past, and a record other than that in the memory is plainly something which cannot be verified by direct observation.

. . . Verification is the watchword of Positivism. But it is easy to see that a proposition is no more verifiable by direct observation for being such as we can suppose (by a recognized falsification) to be observed unless it is also such as really can be observed. This maxim, therefore, must refer to really possible observations, not such as are supposably possible, for the proof they give leads to that or nothing.

. . . It is not a question capable of being decided by direct observation, what is and what is not direct observation. The logical rule, therefore, which is the whole basis of Positivism appears to me to be entirely false.

8.   The Architecture of Theories[1]

[In order to show how radically the progress of modern
science affects the philosophy of nature or our over-all view
of the world, Peirce wrote a series of five articles for a
journal called *The Monist,* edited by Paul Carus and devoted to the unity of science. This first article outlines the
main elements of Peirce's own philosophy of science. Instead of the "simple" axioms of Euclid, the classical guide
to physical space, Peirce refers to the new conceptions of
projective and non-Euclidean geometries which offer a
greater and richer variety of perspectives. Instead of accepting the billiard-ball image of physical change, Peirce
expresses "serious doubt whether the fundamental laws of
mechanics hold good for single atoms." This is a remarkable
anticipation of recent developments in physical theory in
which quantum mechanics gives us a statistical type of law.
For example, Heisenberg's principle of indeterminacy holds
for the average behavior of trillions of particles, but each
individual particle eludes our instruments of measurement.
Peirce noted, as a physicist, that the more precise our measurements were, the greater was the number of small deviations from any regularity fixed too rigidly by a law. Since
not all of these minute deviations are attributable to imperfect instruments or errors of observation, Peirce argues
that there is an element of spontaneous variation or minute
swerving from absolute conformity to law. Now this sort of

[1] *The Monist* (Jan. 1891), pp. 161–176.

spontaneous chance variation was assumed by Darwin in his epoch-making theory of natural selection in biology. Peirce tries to generalize the idea of chance variation so that it operates in both the physical and living worlds, and thus explain some of their nonmechanical features of feeling, growth, and thought.

Chance is only one of the three main features or categories of the universe; the other two are Reaction and Law. Reaction is the mark of brute existence. It is illustrated in the elimination of organisms or mutations unadapted to environmental changes, more simply by the usual fact that a "real" wall is not as penetrable as an imaginary one. Newton's law of action and reaction also illustrates Peirce's category of "Secondness," his general name for the hard resistance offered by existing circumstances. Law is the third category ("Thirdness") of Peirce's philosophy. It evolves from the generalizing tendencies or habits of feeling which crystallize into natural uniformities. Peirce calls this odd view of his "objective idealism" since it takes feelings and ideas to be the ultimate elements of the objective world, "ultimate" in the sense that they are not reducible to or explainable by mechanical laws.

The history of philosophic systems contains only one-sided and inadequate appreciations of the three categories of Felt Quality, External Reaction, and Habitual Law, more abstractly designated by Peirce as Firstness, Secondness, Thirdness. We see here that by 1890, when Peirce was past fifty, he was no longer content to deal with specific problems of logic or method, but ventured into a bold philosophic synthesis of the sciences. Despite the lacunae in this highly speculative synthesis, there are many valuable suggestions to future cosmological world-builders in this essay.]

Of the fifty or hundred systems of philosophy that have been advanced at different times of the world's history, perhaps the larger number have been, not so much results of historical evolution, as happy thoughts which have accidently occurred to their authors. An idea which has been found interesting and fruitful has been adopted, developed, and forced to yield explanations of all sorts of phenomena. The English have been particularly given to this way of philosophizing; witness, Hobbes, Hartley, Berkeley, James Mill. Nor has it been by any means useless labor; it shows us what the true nature and value of the ideas developed are, and in that way affords serviceable materials for philosophy. Just as if a man, being seized with the conviction that paper was a good material to make things of, were to go to work to build a papier-mâché house, with roof of roofing-paper, foundations of pasteboard, windows of paraffined paper, chimneys, bath tubs, locks, etc., all of different forms of paper, his experiment would probably afford valuable lessons to builders, while it would certainly make a detestable house, so those one-idea'd philosophies are exceedingly interesting and instructive, and yet are quite unsound.

The remaining systems of philosophy have been of the nature of reforms, sometimes amounting to radical revolutions, suggested by certain difficulties which have been found to beset systems previously in vogue; and such ought certainly to be in large part the motive of any new theory. This is like partially rebuilding a house. The faults that have been committed are, first, that the repairs of the dilapidations have generally not been sufficiently thorough-going, and second, that not sufficient pains had been taken to bring the additions into deep harmony with the really sound parts of the old structure.

When a man is about to build a house, what a power of thinking he has to do, before he can safely break ground! With what pains he has to excogitate the precise wants that are to be supplied! What a study to ascertain the most available and suitable materials, to determine the mode of construction to which those materials are best adapted, and to answer a hundred such questions! Now without riding the metaphor too far, I think we may safely say that the studies preliminary to the construction of a great theory should be at least as deliberate and thorough as those that are preliminary to the building of a dwelling-house.

That systems ought to be constructed architectonically has been preached since Kant, but I do not think the full import of the maxim has by any means been apprehended. What I would recommend is that every person who wishes to form an opinion concerning fundamental problems should first of all make a complete survey of human knowledge, should take note of all the valuable ideas in each branch of science, should observe in just what respect each has been successful and where it has failed, in order that in the light of the thorough acquaintance so attained of the available materials for a philosophical theory and of the nature and strength of each, he may proceed to the study of what the problem of philosophy consists in, and of the proper way of solving it. I must not be understood as endeavoring to state fully all that these preparatory studies should embrace; on the contrary, I purposely slur over many points, in order to give emphasis to one special recommendation, namely, to make a systematic study of the conceptions out of which a philosophical theory may be built, in order to ascertain what place each conception may fitly occupy in such a theory, and to what uses it is adapted.

The adequate treatment of this single point would fill a volume, but I shall endeavor to illustrate my meaning by glancing at several sciences and indicating conceptions in them serviceable for philosophy. As to the results to which long studies thus commenced have led me, I shall just give a hint at their nature.

We may begin with dynamics—field in our day of perhaps the grandest conquest human science has ever made—I mean the law of the conservation of energy. But let us revert to the first step taken by modern scientific thought—and a great stride it was—the inauguration of dynamics by Galileo. A modern physicist on examining Galileo's works is surprised to find how little experiment had to do with the establishment of the foundations of mechanics. His principal appeal is to common sense and *il lume naturale*.[2] He always assumes that the true theory will be found to be

[2] *The natural light* of reason was the classical phrase expressing the mind's power of illuminating and reflecting such general truths as reveal the structure of space, time, causality, moral, religious, and esthetic principles.—Editor's note.

a simple and natural one. And we can see why it should indeed be so in dynamics. For instance, a body left to its own inertia moves in a straight line, and a straight line appears to us the simplest of curves. In *itself*, no curve is simpler than another. A system of straight lines has intersections precisely corresponding to those of a system of like parabolas similarly placed, or to those of any one of an infinity of systems of curves. But the straight line appears to us simple, because, as Euclid says, it lies evenly between its extremities; that is, because viewed endwise it appears as a point. That is, again, because light moves in straight lines. Now, light moves in straight lines because of the part which the straight line plays in the laws of dynamics. Thus it is that our minds having been formed under the influence of phenomena governed by the laws of mechanics, certain conceptions entering into those laws become implanted in our minds, so that we readily guess at what the laws are. Without such a natural prompting, having to search blindfold for a law which would suit the phenomena, our chance of finding it would be as one to infinity. The further physical studies depart from phenomena which have directly influenced the growth of the mind, the less we can expect to find the laws which govern them "simple," that is, composed of a few conceptions natural to our minds.

The researches of Galileo, followed up by Huygens and others, led to those modern conceptions of *Force* and *Law*, which have revolutionized the intellectual world. The great attention given to mechanics in the seventeenth century soon so emphasized these conceptions as to give rise to the Mechanical Philosophy, or doctrine that all the phenomena of the physical universe are to be explained upon mechanical principles. Newton's great discovery imparted a new impetus to this tendency. The old notion that heat consists in an agitation of corpuscles was now applied to the explanation of the chief properties of gases. The first suggestion in this direction was that the pressure of gases is explained by the battering of the particles against the walls of the containing vessel, which explained Boyle's law of the compressibility of air.[3] Later, the expansion of gases, Avogadro's chemical law, the diffusion and viscosity of gases, and the action of Crookes's radiometer were shown to be consequences of the same kinetical theory; but other phenomena, such as the ratio of the specific heat at constant volume to that at constant pressure, require additional hypotheses, which we have little reason to suppose are simple, so that we find ourselves quite afloat. In like manner with regard to light. That it consists of vibrations was almost proved by the phenomena of diffraction, while those of polarization showed the excursions of the particles to be perpendicular to the line of propagation; but the phenomena of dispersion, etc., require additional hypotheses which may be very complicated. Thus, the further progress of molecular speculation appears quite uncertain. If hypotheses are to be tried haphazard, or simply because they will suit certain phenomena, it will occupy the mathematical physicists of the world, say, half a century on the average to bring each theory to the test, and since the number of possible theories may go up into the trillions, only one of which can be true, we have little prospect of making further solid additions to the subject in our time.

When we come to atoms, the presumption in favor of a simple law seems very slender. There is room for serious doubt whether the fundamental laws of mechanics hold good for single atoms,[4] and it seems quite likely that they are capable of motion in more than three dimensions.

To find out much more about molecules and atoms, we must search out a natural history of laws of nature, which may fulfill that function which the presumption in favor of simple laws fulfilled in the early days of dynamics, by showing us what kind of laws we have to expect and by answering such questions as this: Can we with reasonable prospect of not wasting time, try the supposition that atoms

[3] Volume varies inversely with the pressure of a confined gas kept at a constant temperature. Boyle's law holds only within certain limits or boundary conditions.—Editor's note.

[4] A remarkable anticipation of quantum-mechanical type of statistical laws, as in Heisenberg's principle of indeterminacy. —Editor's note.

attract one another inversely as the seventh power of their distances, or can we not? To suppose universal laws of nature capable of being apprehended by the mind and yet having no reason for their special forms, but standing inexplicable and irrational, is hardly a justifiable position. Uniformities are precisely the sort of facts that need to be accounted for. That a pitched coin should sometimes turn up heads and sometimes tails calls for no particular explanation; but if it shows heads every time, we wish to know how this result has been brought about. Law is *par excellence* the thing that wants a reason.

Now the only possible way of accounting for the laws of nature and for uniformity in general is to suppose them results of evolution. This supposes them not to be absolute, not to be obeyed precisely. It makes an element of indeterminacy, spontaneity, or absolute chance in nature. Just as, when we attempt to verify any physical law, we find our observations cannot be precisely satisfied by it, and rightly attribute the discrepancy to errors of observation, so we must suppose far more minute discrepancies to exist owing to the imperfect cogency of the law itself, to a certain swerving of the facts from any definite formula.

Mr. Herbert Spencer wishes to explain evolution upon mechanical principles. This is illogical, for four reasons. First, because the principle of evolution requires no extraneous cause; since the tendency to growth can be supposed itself to have grown from an infinitesimal germ accidentally started. Second, because law ought more than anything else to be supposed a result of evolution. Third, because exact law obviously never can produce heterogeneity out of homogeneity; and arbitrary heterogeneity is the feature of the universe the most manifest and characteristic. Fourth, because the law of the conservation of energy is equivalent to the proposition that all operations governed by mechanical laws are reversible; so that an immediate corollary from it is that growth is not explicable by those laws, even if they be not violated in the process of growth. In short, Spencer is not a philosophical evolutionist, but only a half-evolutionist—or, if you will, only a semi-Spencerian. Now philosophy requires thoroughgoing evolutionism or none.

The theory of Darwin was that evolution had been brought about by the action of two factors: first, heredity, as a principle making offspring nearly resemble their parents, while yet giving room for "sporting," or accidental variations—for very slight variations often, for wider ones rarely; and, second, the destruction of breeds or races that are unable to keep the birth rate up to the death rate. This Darwinian principle is plainly capable of great generalization. Wherever there are large numbers of objects, having a tendency to retain certain characters unaltered, this tendency, however, not being absolute but giving room for chance variations, then, if the amount of variation is absolutely limited in certain directions by the destruction of everything which reaches those limits, there will be a gradual tendency to change in directions of departure from them. Thus, if a million players sit down to bet at an even game, since one after another will get ruined, the average wealth of those who remain will perpetually increase. Here is indubitably a genuine formula of possible evolution, whether its operation accounts for much or little in the development of animal and vegetable species.

The Lamarckian theory also supposes that the development of species has taken place by a long series of insensible changes, but it supposes that those changes have taken place during the lives of the individuals, in consequence of effort and exercise, and that reproduction plays no part in the process except in preserving these modifications. Thus, the Lamarckian theory only explains the development of characters for which individuals strive, while the Darwinian theory only explains the production of characters really beneficial to the race, though these may be fatal to individuals.[5] But more broadly and philosophically conceived, Darwinian evolution is evolution by the operation of chance, and the destruction of bad results, while Lamarckian evolution is evolution by the effect of habit and effort.

A third theory of evolution is that of Mr. Clarence King. The testimony of monuments and of rocks is that species

[5] The neo-Darwinian, Weismann, has shown that mortality would almost necessarily result from the action of the Darwinian principle.

are unmodified, or scarcely modified, under ordinary circumstances, but are rapidly altered after cataclysms or rapid geological changes. Under novel circumstances, we often see animals and plants sporting excessively in reproduction, and sometimes even undergoing transformations during individual life, phenomena no doubt due partly to the enfeeblement of vitality from the breaking up of habitual modes of life, partly to changed food, partly to direct specific influence of the element in which the organism is immersed. If evolution has been brought about in this way, not only have its single steps not been insensible, as both Darwinians and Lamarckians suppose, but they are furthermore neither haphazard on the one hand, nor yet determined by an inward striving on the other, but on the contrary are effects of the changed environment, and have a positive general tendency to adapt the organism to that environment, since variation will particularly affect organs at once enfeebled and stimulated. This mode of evolution, by external forces and the breaking up of habits, seems to be called for by some of the broadest and most important facts of biology and paleontology; while it certainly has been the chief factor in the historical evolution of institutions as in that of ideas; and cannot possibly be refused a very prominent place in the process of evolution of the universe in general.

Passing to psychology, we find [that] the elementary phenomena of mind fall into three categories.[6] First, we have Feelings, comprising all that is immediately present, such as pain, blue, cheerfulness, the feeling that arises when we contemplate a consistent theory, etc. A feeling is a state of mind having its own living quality, independent of any other state of mind. Or, a feeling is an element of consciousness which might conceivably override every other state until it monopolized the mind, although such a rudimentary state cannot actually be realized, and would not properly be consciousness. Still, it is conceivable, or supposable, that

[6] The next three paragraphs illustrate Peirce's broadest principles of philosophical explanation: Firstness, Secondness, Thirdness. He applied these not only to psychology but to logic, biology, and cosmology.—Editor's note.

the quality of blue should usurp the whole mind, to the exclusion of the ideas of shape, extension, contrast, commencement and cessation, and all other ideas, whatsoever. A feeling is necessarily perfectly simple, *in itself*, for if it had parts these would also be in the mind, whenever the whole was present, and thus the whole could not monopolize the mind.[7]

Besides Feelings, we have Sensations of reaction; as when a person blindfold suddenly runs against a post, when we make a muscular effort, or when any feeling gives way to a new feeling. Suppose I had nothing in my mind but a feeling of blue, which were suddenly to give place to a feeling of red; then, at the instant of transition there would be a shock, a sense of reaction, my blue life being transmuted into red life. If I were further endowed with a memory, that sense would continue for some time, and there would also be a peculiar feeling or sentiment connected with it. This last feeling might endure (conceivably I mean) after the memory of the occurrence and the feelings of blue and red had passed away. But the *sensation* of reaction cannot exist except in the actual presence of the two feelings blue and red to which it relates. Wherever we have two feelings and pay attention to a relation between them of whatever kind, there is the sensation of which I am speaking. But the sense of action and reaction has two types: it may either be a perception of relation between two ideas, or it may be a sense of action and reaction between feeling and something out of feeling. And this sense of external reaction again has two forms; for it is either a sense of something happening to us, by no act of ours, we being passive in the matter, or it is a sense of resistance, that is, of our expending feeling upon something without. The sense of reaction is thus a sense of connection or comparison between feelings, either, A, between one feeling and another, or B, between feeling and its absence or lower degree; and under B we have, First, the sense of the access of feeling, and Second, the sense of remission of feeling.

Very different both from feelings and from reaction-

---

[7] A feeling may certainly be compound, but only in virtue of a perception which is not that feeling nor any feeling at all.

sensations or disturbances of feeling are general conceptions. When we think, we are conscious that a connection between feelings is determined by a general rule, we are aware of being governed by a habit. Intellectual power is nothing but facility in taking habits and in following them in cases essentially analogous to, but in non-essentials widely remote from, the normal cases of connections of feelings under which those habits were formed.

The one primary and fundamental law of mental action consists in a tendency to generalization. Feeling tends to spread; connections between feelings awaken feelings; neighboring feelings become assimilated; ideas are apt to reproduce themselves. These are so many formulations of the one law of the growth of mind. When a disturbance of feeling takes place, we have a consciousness of gain, the gain of experience; and a new disturbance will be apt to assimilate itself to the one that preceded it. Feelings, by being excited, become more easily excited, especially in the ways in which they have previously been excited. The consciousness of such a habit constitutes a general conception.

The cloudiness of psychological notions may be corrected by connecting them with physiological conceptions. Feeling may be supposed to exist, wherever a nerve-cell is in an excited condition. The disturbance of feeling, or sense of reaction, accompanies the transmission of disturbance between nerve-cells or from a nerve-cell to a muscle-cell or the external stimulation of a nerve-cell. General conceptions arise upon the formation of habits in the nerve-matter, which are molecular changes consequent upon its activity and probably connected with its nutrition.

The law of habit exhibits a striking contrast to all physical laws in the character of its commands. A physical law is absolute. What it requires is an exact relation. Thus, a physical force introduces into a motion a component motion to be combined with the rest by the parallelogram of forces; but the component motion must actually take place exactly as required by the law of force. On the other hand, no exact conformity is required by the mental law. Nay, exact conformity would be in downright conflict with the law; since it would instantly crystallize thought and prevent all further formation of habit. The law of mind only makes a given feeling *more likely* to arise. It thus resembles the "non-conservative" forces of physics, such as viscosity and the like, which are due to statistical uniformities in the chance encounters of trillions of molecules.

The old dualistic notion of mind and matter, so prominent in Cartesianism, as two radically different kinds of substance, will hardly find defenders today. Rejecting this, we are driven to some form of hylopathy, otherwise called monism. Then the question arises whether physical laws on the one hand, and the psychical law on the other are to be taken—

(A) as independent, a doctrine often called *monism*, but which I would name *neutralism;* or,

(B) the psychical law as derived and special, the physical law alone as primordial, which is *materialism;* or,

(C) the physical law as derived and special, the psychical law alone as primordial, which is *idealism.*

The materialistic doctrine seems to me quite as repugnant to scientific logic as to common sense; since it requires us to suppose that a certain kind of mechanism will feel, which would be a hypothesis absolutely irreducible to reason—an ultimate, inexplicable regularity; while the only possible justification of any theory is that it should make things clear and reasonable.

Neutralism is sufficiently condemned by the logical maxim known as Ockham's razor, i.e., that not more independent elements are to be supposed than necessary. By placing the inward and outward aspects of substance on a par, it seems to render both primordial.

The one intelligible theory of the universe is that of objective idealism, that matter is effete mind, inveterate habits becoming physical laws. But before this can be accepted it must show itself capable of explaining the tridimensionality of space, the laws of motion, and the general characteristics of the universe, with mathematical clearness and precision; for no less should be demanded of every philosophy.

Modern mathematics is replete with ideas which may be applied to philosophy. I can only notice one or two. The manner in which mathematicians generalize is very instructive. Thus, painters are accustomed to think of a picture as consisting geometrically of the intersections of its plane by rays of light from the natural objects to the eye. But geometers use a generalized perspective. For instance, in the figure let O be the eye, let $A\ B\ C\ D\ E$ be the edge-

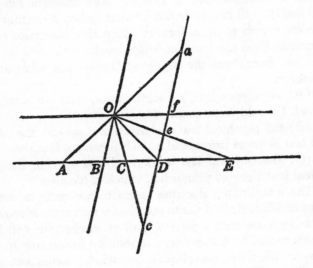

wise view of any plane, and let $a\ f\ e\ D\ c$ be the edgewise view of another plane. The geometers draw rays through O cutting both these planes, and treat the points of intersection of each ray with one plane as representing the point of intersection of the same ray with the other plane. Thus, e represents E, in the painter's way. D represents itself. C is represented by c, which is further from the eye; and A is represented by a which is on the other side of the eye. Such generalization is not bound down to sensuous images. Further, according to this mode of representation every point on one plane represents a point on the other, and every point on the latter is represented by a point on the former. But how about the point f which is in a direction from O parallel to the represented plane, and how about the point B which is in a direction parallel to the representing plane? Some will say that these are exceptions; but modern mathematics does not allow exceptions which can be annulled by generalization. As a point moves from C to D and thence to E and off toward infinity, the corresponding point on the other plane moves from c to D and thence to e and toward f. But this second point can pass through f to a; and when it is there the first point has arrived at A. We therefore say that the first point has passed *through infinity*, and that every line joins in to itself somewhat like an oval. Geometers talk of the parts of lines at an infinite distance as points. This is a kind of generalization very efficient in mathematics.

Modern views of measurement have a philosophical aspect. There is an indefinite number of systems of measuring along a line; thus, a perspective representation of a scale on one line may be taken to measure another, although of course such measurements will not agree with what we call the distances of points on the latter line. To establish a system of measurement on a line we must assign a distinct number to each point of it, and for this purpose we shall plainly have to suppose the numbers carried out into an infinite number of places of decimals. These numbers must be ranged along the line in unbroken sequence. Further, in order that such a scale of numbers should be of any use, it must be capable of being shifted into new positions, each number continuing to be attached to a single distinct point. Now it is found that if this is true for "imaginary" as well as for real points (an expression which I cannot stop to elucidate), any such shifting will necessarily leave two numbers attached to the same points as before. So that when the scale is moved over the line by any continuous series of shiftings of one kind, there are two points which no numbers on the scale can ever reach, except the numbers fixed there. This pair of points, thus unattainable in measurement, is called the Absolute. These two points may be distinct and real, or they may coincide, or they may be both imaginary. As an example of a linear quantity with a double absolute we may take probability, which ranges from an unattainable absolute certainty *against* a proposition to an equally unattainable absolute certainty *for* it. A line, according to ordinary notions, we have seen is a linear quantity where the two points at in-

finity coincide. A velocity is another example. A train going
with infinite velocity from Chicago to New York would be
at all the points on the line at the very same instant, and if
the time of transit were reduced to less than nothing it
would be moving in the other direction. An angle is a familiar example of a mode of magnitude with no real immeasurable values. One of the questions philosophy has to
consider is whether the development of the universe is like
the increase of an angle, so that it proceeds forever without
tending toward anything unattained, which I take to be the
Epicurean view, or whether the universe sprang from a
chaos in the infinitely distant past to tend toward something different in the infinitely distant future, or whether
the universe sprang from nothing in the past to go on indefinitely toward a point in the infinitely distant future,
which, were it attained, would be the mere nothing from
which it set out.

The doctrine of the absolute applied to space comes to
this, that either—

First, space is, as Euclid teaches, both *unlimited* and
immeasurable, so that the infinitely distant parts of any
plane seen in perspective appear as a straight line, in which
case the sum of the three angles of a triangle amounts to
180 degrees; or,

Second, space is *immeasurable* but *limited,* so that the
infinitely distant parts of any plane seen in perspective
appear as a circle, beyond which all is blackness, and in
this case the sum of the three angles of a triangle is less
than 180 degrees by an amount proportional to the area of
the triangle; or,

Third, space is *unlimited* but *finite* (like the surface of
a sphere), so that it has no infinitely distant parts; but a
finite journey along any straight line would bring one back
to his original position, and looking off with an unobstructed
view one would see the back of his own head enormously
magnified, in which case the sum of the three angles of a
triangle exceeds 180 degrees by an amount proportional to
the area.

Which of these three hypotheses is true we know not.
The largest triangles we can measure are such as have the

earth's orbit for base, and the distance of a fixed star for altitude. The angular magnitude resulting from subtracting the sum of the two angles at the base of such a triangle from 180 degrees is called the star's *parallax*. . . .[8] I think we may feel confident that the parallax of the furthest star lies somewhere between −0.″05 and +0.″15, and within another century our grandchildren will surely know whether the three angles of a triangle are greater or less than 180 degrees—that they are *exactly* that amount is what nobody ever can be justified in concluding. It is true that according to the axioms of geometry the sum of the three sides of a triangle are precisely 180 degrees; but these axioms are now exploded, and geometers confess that they, as geometers, know not the slightest reason for supposing them to be precisely true. They are expressions of our inborn conception of space, and as such are entitled to credit, so far as their truth could have influenced the formation of the mind. But that affords not the slightest reason for supposing them exact.

Now, metaphysics has always been the ape of mathematics. Geometry suggested the idea of a demonstrative system of absolutely certain philosophical principles; and the ideas of the metaphysicians have at all times been in large part drawn from mathematics. The metaphysical axioms are imitations of the geometrical axioms; and now that the latter have been thrown overboard, without doubt the former will be sent after them. It is evident, for instance, that we can have no reason to think that every phenomenon in all its minutest details is precisely determined by law. That there is an arbitrary element in the universe we see—namely, its variety. This variety must be attributed to spontaneity in some form.

Had I more space, I now ought to show how important for philosophy is the mathematical conception of continuity. Most of what is true in Hegel is a darkling glimmer of a conception which the mathematicians had long before made pretty clear, and which recent researches have still further illustrated.

[8] Peirce's examples of negative parallax known in 1891 are omitted.—Editor's note.

Among the many principles of Logic which find their application in Philosophy, I can here only mention one. Three conceptions are perpetually turning up at every point in every theory of logic, and in the most rounded systems they occur in connection with one another. They are conceptions so very broad and consequently indefinite that they are hard to seize and may be easily overlooked. I call them the conceptions of First, Second, Third. First is the conception of being or existing independent of anything else. Second is the conception of being relative to, the conception of reaction with, something else. Third is the conception of mediation, whereby a first and second are brought into relation. To illustrate these ideas, I will show how they enter into those we have been considering. The origin of things, considered not as leading to anything, but in itself, contains the idea of First, the end of things that of Second, the process mediating between them that of Third. A philosophy which emphasizes the idea of the One is generally a dualistic philosophy in which the conception of Second receives exaggerated attention; for this One (though of course involving the idea of First) is always the other of a manifold which is not one. The idea of the Many, because variety is arbitrariness and arbitrariness is repudiation of any Secondness, has for its principal component the conception of First. In psychology Feeling is First, Sense of reaction Second, General conception Third, or mediation. In biology, the idea of arbitrary sporting is First, heredity is Second, the process whereby the accidental characters become fixed is Third. Chance is First, Law is Second, the tendency to take habits is Third. Mind is First, Matter is Second, Evolution is Third.

Such are the materials out of which chiefly a philosophical theory ought to be built, in order to represent the state of knowledge to which the nineteenth century has brought us. Without going into other important questions of philosophical architectonic, we can readily foresee what sort of a metaphysics would appropriately be constructed from those conceptions. Like some of the most ancient and some of the most recent speculations it would be a Cosmogonic Philosophy. It would suppose that in the beginning

—infinitely remote—there was a chaos of unpersonalized feeling, which being without connection or regularity would properly be without existence. This feeling, sporting here and there in pure arbitrariness, would have started the germ of a generalizing tendency. Its other sportings would be evanescent, but this would have a growing virtue. Thus, the tendency to habit would be started; and from this with the other principles of evolution all the regularities of the universe would be evolved. At any time, however, an element of pure chance survives and will remain until the world becomes an absolutely perfect, rational, and symmetrical system, in which mind is at last crystallized in the infinitely distant future.

That idea has been worked out by me with elaboration. It accounts for the main features of the universe as we know it—the characters of time, space, matter, force, gravitation, electricity, etc. It predicts many more things which new observations can alone bring to the test. May some future student go over this ground again, and have the leisure to give his results to the world.

9. The Doctrine of Necessity[1]

[Among the three main features of the universe outlined by Peirce in the preceding essay ("The Architecture of Theories"), Chance and Law have been and are still usually regarded as diametrically opposed to each other. Historically, the belief in the universal reign of absolute law (from the Stoics to Laplace) relegated chance to a mere illusion because of our ignorance of the inevitable necessity compelling everything to conform strictly to precise laws. Peirce here boldly challenges the doctrine holding sway in the mechanical philosophy of nature, in the logic of induction (where generalizations from enough particular observations were supposed to attain certainty), and in the human sciences.

The mechanical philosophy of nature was most clearly expressed by the great mathematical scientist of the French Revolution, Laplace, who applied Newton's universal laws of motion and gravitation to the evolution of the solar system from a gaseous nebula. He claimed that the whole past, present, and future are absolutely determined by Newton's laws, given the initial positions and velocities of the components of the material world. Any act of free will was as

1 *The Monist* (April 1892), pp. 321–337. This is the second of the series of five articles in *The Monist*: III. "The Law of Mind" (July 1892), pp. 533–559; IV. "Man's Glassy Essence" (Jan. 1893), pp. 1–22; V. "Evolutionary Love" (April 1893), pp. 176–200. They are a mature formulation of his philosophy of the sciences and of history.—Editor's note.

absolutely determined as the next lover's sigh. This supreme confidence in the predictive power of mathematical equations of motion dominated the Age of Reason and persisted through most of the nineteenth century. It culminated in Herbert Spencer's attempt to deduce the evolution of life, mind, and society from purely mechanical laws.

Peirce argues against mechanical necessity in physics by pointing to the phenomena of heat transfer which are *irreversible:* bodies giving up heat energy cannot generally regain it from colder bodies; but according to the classical laws of mechanics, all changes of state are reversible. In biology also we have the irreversible phenomena of growth which cannot be explained by mechanical laws alone. In psychology the association theory of ideas had reduced mental life to the mechanical combination of sensations, images, and feelings, or in the later form of behaviorism to the mechanics of conditioned reflexes. Since the mind, for Peirce, has its irreducible qualities of chance feelings and spontaneous growth of habits in the process of development, the doctrine of mechanical necessity again fails. The common-sense belief in moral choice and responsibility is regarded by Peirce as incompatible with and preferable to the doctrine of the "necessitarians."

It is clear that Peirce does not wish us to regard the world as a pure chaos simply because it contains chance as one of its pervasive features, as everybody assumes in noticing that luck favors some people at one time or another or that time must be seized by the forelock. The logic of induction (rules for valid generalizations from experience) is based on random sampling and arrives at laws having a certain probability rather than absolute necessity. Scientific laws are inductive generalizations from phenomena showing recurrent properties arising from what Peirce calls "habits of nature" but also revealing in the motions of their minute parts slight departures from absolute conformity to precise law or fixed regularity; else we overlook or omit the ever-present variety and novelty of emergent properties of nature. As a physicist and astronomer, Peirce was competent to note that the most precise instruments of measurement cannot establish absolute confirmation of mathematically exact laws, for there are always small fluctuations or unpredictable perturbations in physical phenomena. These are subsumed under "probable errors" but the limits of exact laws are not due to merely personal errors, according to Peirce, but to objective chance. Even if all individual phenomena are determined by laws, the totality of the laws holding for the actual universe in our epoch would be contingent, and thus incompatible with the doctrine of necessity.]

In *The Monist* for January 1891, I endeavored to show what elementary ideas ought to enter into our view of the universe. I may mention that on those considerations I had already grounded a cosmical theory, and from it had deduced a considerable number of consequences capable of being compared with experience. This comparison is now in progress, but under existing circumstances must occupy many years.

I propose here to examine the common belief that every single fact in the universe is precisely determined by law. It must not be supposed that this is a doctrine accepted everywhere and at all times by all rational men. Its first advocate appears to have been Democritus, the atomist, who was led to it, as we are informed, by reflecting upon the "impenetrability, translation, and impact of matter (*antitypia kai phora kai plege tes hyles*)." That is to say, having restricted his attention to a field where no influence other than mechanical constraint could possibly come before his notice, he straightway jumped to the conclusion that throughout the universe that was the sole principle of action—a style of reasoning so usual in our day with men not unreflecting as to be more than excusable in the infancy of thought. But Epicurus, in revising the atomic doctrine and repairing its defenses, found himself obliged to suppose that atoms swerve from their courses by spontaneous chance; and thereby he conferred upon the theory life and entelechy. For we now see clearly that the peculiar function of the molecular hypothesis in physics is to open an entry for the calculus of probabilities. Already, the prince of philosophers [Aristotle] had repeatedly and emphatically condemned the dictum of Democritus (especially in the *Physics*, Book II, Chapters iv, v, vi), holding that events come to pass in three ways, namely (1) by external compulsion, or the action of efficient causes, (2) by virtue of an inward nature, or the influence of final causes, and (3) irregularly without definite cause, but just by absolute chance; and this doctrine is of the inmost essence of Aristotelianism. It affords, at any rate, a valuable enumeration of the possible ways in which anything can be supposed to have come about. The freedom of the will, too, was admitted both by Aristotle and by Epicurus. But the Stoa [Stoicism], which in every department seized upon the most tangible, hard, and lifeless element, and blindly denied the existence of every other, which, for example, impugned the validity of the inductive method and wished to fill its place with the *reductio ad absurdum*, very naturally became the one school of ancient philosophy to stand by a strict necessitarianism, thus returning to a single principle of Democritus that Epicurus had been unable to swallow. Necessitarianism and materialism with the Stoics went hand in hand, as by affinity they should. At the revival of learning, Stoicism met with considerable favor, partly because it departed just enough from Aristotle to give it the spice of novelty, and partly because its superficialities well adapted it for acceptance by students of literature and art who wanted their philosophy drawn mild. Afterwards, the great discoveries in mechanics inspired the hope that mechanical principles might suffice to explain the universe; and though without logical justification, this hope has since been continually stimulated by subsequent advances in physics. Nevertheless, the doctrine was in too evident conflict with the freedom of the will and with miracles to be generally acceptable, at first. But meantime there arose that most widely spread of philosophical blunders, the notion that associationalism belongs intrinsically to the materialistic family of doctrines; and thus was evolved the theory of motives; and libertarianism became weakened. At present, historical criticism has almost exploded the miracles, great and small; so that the doctrine of necessity has never been in so great vogue as now.

The proposition in question is that the state of things

existing at any time, together with certain immutable laws, completely determine the state of things at every other time (for a limitation to *future* time is indefensible). Thus, given the state of the universe in the original nebula, and given the laws of mechanics, a sufficiently powerful mind could deduce from these data the precise form of every curlicue of every letter I am now writing.

Whoever holds that every act of the will as well as every idea of the mind is under the rigid governance of a necessity co-ordinated with that of the physical world, will logically be carried to the proposition that minds are part of the physical world in such a sense that the laws of mechanics determine everything that happens according to immutable attractions and repulsions. In that case, that instantaneous state of things from which every other state of things is calculable consists in the positions and velocities of all the particles at any instant. This, the usual and most logical form of necessitarianism, is called the mechanical philosophy.

When I have asked thinking men what reason they had to believe that every fact in the universe is precisely determined by law, the first answer has usually been that the proposition is a "presupposition" or postulate of scientific reasoning. Well, if that is the best that can be said for it, the belief is doomed. Suppose it be "postulated": that does not make it true, nor so much as afford the slightest rational motive for yielding it any credence. It is as if a man should come to borrow money, and when asked for his security, should reply he "postulated" the loan. To "postulate" a proposition is no more than to hope it is true. There are, indeed, practical emergencies in which we act upon assumptions of certain propositions as true, because if they are not so, it can make no difference how we act. But all such propositions I take to be hypotheses of individual facts. For it is manifest that no universal principle can in its universality be comprised in a special case or can be requisite for the validity of any ordinary inference. To say, for instance, that the demonstration by Archimedes of the property of the lever would fall to the ground if men were endowed with free-will, is extravagant;

yet this is implied by those who make a proposition in-compatible with the freedom of the will the postulate of all inference. Considering, too, that the conclusions of science make no pretense to being more than probable, and con-sidering that a probable inference can at most only suppose something to be most frequently, or otherwise approxi-mately, true, but never that anything is precisely true with-out exception throughout the universe, we see how far this proposition in truth is from being so postulated.

But the whole notion of a postulate being involved in reasoning appertains to a by-gone and false conception of logic. Non-deductive, or ampliative inference, is of three kinds: induction, hypothesis, and analogy. If there be any other modes, they must be extremely unusual and highly complicated, and may be assumed with little doubt to be of the same nature as those enumerated. For induc-tion, hypothesis, and analogy, as far as their ampliative character goes, that is, so far as they conclude something not implied in the premises, depend upon one principle and involve the same procedure. All are essentially inferences from sampling. Suppose a ship arrives at Liverpool laden with wheat in bulk. Suppose that by some machinery the whole cargo be stirred up with great thoroughness. Sup-pose that twenty-seven thimblefuls be taken equally from the forward, midships, and aft parts, from the starboard, center, and larboard parts, and from the top, half depth, and lower parts of her hold, and that these being mixed and the grains counted, four-fifths of the latter are found to be of quality A. Then we infer, experientially and pro-visionally, that approximately four-fifths of all the grain in the cargo is of the same quality. I say we infer this *ex-perientially* and *provisionally*. By saying that we infer it *experientially*, I mean that our conclusion makes no pre-tension to knowledge of wheat-in-itself, our *alétheia*, as the derivation of that word implies, has nothing to do with *latent* wheat. We are dealing only with the matter of pos-sible experience—experience in the full acceptation of the term as something not merely affecting the senses but also as the subject of thought. If there be any wheat hidden on the ship, so that it can neither turn up in the sample nor be heard of subsequently from purchasers—or if it be half-hidden, so that it may, indeed, turn up, but is less likely to do so than the rest—or if it can affect our senses and our pockets, but from some strange cause or causelessness cannot be reasoned about—all such wheat is to be excluded (or have only its proportional weight) in calculating that true proportion of quality *A*, to which our inference seeks to approximate. By saying that we draw the inference *provisionally*, I mean that we do not hold that we have reached any assigned degree of approximation as yet, but only hold that if our experience be indefinitely extended, and if every fact of whatever nature, as fast as it presents itself, be duly applied, according to the inductive method, in correcting the inferred ratio, then our approximation will become indefinitely close in the long run; that is to say, close to the experience *to come* (not merely close by the exhaustion of a finite collection) so that if experience in general is to fluctuate irregularly to and fro, in a manner to deprive the ratio sought of all definite value, we shall be able to find out approximately within what limits it fluctuates, and if, after having one definite value, it changes and assumes another, we shall be able to find that out, and in short, whatever may be the variations of this ratio in experience, experience indefinitely extended will enable us to detect them, so as to predict rightly, at last, what its ultimate value may be, if it have any ultimate value, or what the ultimate law of succession of values may be, if there be any such ultimate law, or that it ultimately fluctuates irregularly within certain limits, if it do so ultimately fluctuate. Now our inference, claiming to be no more than thus experiential and provisional, manifestly involves no postulate whatever.

For what is a postulate? It is the formulation of a material fact which we are not entitled to assume as a premise, but the truth of which is requisite to the validity of an inference. Any fact, then, which might be supposed postulated, must either be such that it would ultimately present itself in experience, or not. If it will present itself, we need not postulate it now in our provisional inference, since we shall ultimately be entitled to use it as a premise. But if it never would present itself in experience, our conclusion is valid but for the possibility of this fact being otherwise than assumed, that is, it is valid as far as possible experience goes, and that is all that we claim. Thus, every postulate is cut off, either by the provisionality or by the experientiality of our inference. For instance, it has been said that induction postulates that if an indefinite succession of samples be drawn, examined, and thrown back each before the next is drawn, then in the long run every grain will be drawn as often as any other, that is to say, postulates that the ratio of the numbers of times in which any two are drawn will indefinitely approximate to unity. But no such postulate is made; for if, on the one hand, we are to have no other experience of the wheat than from such drawings, it is the ratio that presents itself in those drawings and not the ratio which belongs to the wheat in its latent existence that we are endeavoring to determine; while if, on the other hand, there is some other mode by which the wheat is to come under our knowledge, equivalent to another kind of sampling, so that after all our care in stirring up the wheat, some experiential grains will present themselves in the first sampling operation more often than others in the long run, this very singular fact will be sure to get discovered by the inductive method, which must avail itself of every sort of experience; and our inference, which was only provisional, corrects itself at last. Again, it has been said, that induction postulates that under like circumstances like events will happen, and that this postulate is at bottom the same as the principle of universal causation. But this is a blunder, or *bévue*, due to thinking exclusively of inductions where the concluded ratio is either 1 or 0. If any such proposition were postulated, it would be that under like circumstances (the circumstances of drawing the different samples) different events occur in the same proportions in all the different sets—a proposition which is false and even absurd. But in truth no such thing is postulated, the experiential character of the inference reducing the condition of validity to this, that if a certain result does not occur, the opposite result will be manifested, a condition assured by the provisionality of the inference. But it may be asked whether it is not conceivable that every instance of a certain class destined to be ever employed as a datum of induction should have one character, while every instance destined not to be so employed should have the opposite character. The answer is that in that case, the instances excluded from being subjects of reasoning would not be experienced in the full sense of the word, but would be among these *latent* individuals of which our conclusion does not pretend to speak.

To this account of the rationale of induction I know of but one objection worth mention: it is that I thus fail to deduce the full degree of force which this mode of inference in fact possesses; that according to my view, no matter how thorough and elaborate the stirring and mixing process had been, the examination of a single handful of grain would not give me any assurance, sufficient to risk money upon, that the next handful would not greatly modify the concluded value of the ratio under inquiry, while, in fact, the assurance would be very high that this ratio was not greatly in error. If the true ratio of grains of quality A were 0.80 and the handful contained a thousand grains, nine such handfuls out of every ten would contain from 780 to 820 grains of quality A. The answer to this is that the calculation given is correct when we know that the units of this handful and the quality inquired into have the normal independence of one another, if for instance the stirring has been complete and the character sampled for has been settled upon in advance of the examination of the sample. But in so far as these conditions are not known to be complied with, the above figures cease to be applicable. Random sampling and predesignation of the character sampled for should always be striven after in inductive reasoning, but when they cannot be attained, so long as it is conducted honestly, the inference retains some value. When we cannot ascertain how the sampling has been done or the sample-character selected, induction still has the essential validity which my present account of it shows it to have.

I do not think a man who combines a willingness to be convinced with a power of appreciating an argument upon a difficult subject can resist the reasons which have been given to show that the principle of universal necessity cannot be defended as being a postulate of reasoning. But then the question immediately arises whether it is not proved to be true, or at least rendered highly probable, by observation of nature.

Still, this question ought not long to arrest a person accustomed to reflect upon the force of scientific reasoning. For the essence of the necessitarian position is that certain continuous quantities have certain exact values. Now, how can observation determine the value of such a quantity with a probable error absolutely *nil*? To one who is behind the scenes, and knows that the most refined comparisons of masses, lengths, and angles, far surpassing in precision all other measurements, yet fall behind the accuracy of bank accounts, and that the ordinary determinations of physical constants, such as appear from month to month in the journals, are about on a par with an upholsterer's measurements of carpets and curtains, the idea of mathematical exactitude being demonstrated in the laboratory will appear simply ridiculous. There is a recognized method of estimating the probable magnitudes of errors in physics—the method of least squares. It is universally admitted that this method makes the errors smaller than they really are; yet even according to that theory an error indefinitely small is indefinitely improbable; so that any statement to the effect that a certain continuous quantity has a certain exact value, if well-founded at all, must be founded on something other than observation.

Still, I am obliged to admit that this rule is subject to a certain qualification. Namely, it only applies to continuous[2] quantity. Now, certain kinds of continuous quantity are discontinuous at one or at two limits, and for such limits the rule must be modified. Thus, the length of a line cannot be less than zero. Suppose, then, the question arises how long a line a certain person had drawn from a marked point on a piece of paper. If no line at all can be seen, the observed length is zero; and the only conclusion this observation warrants is that the length of the line is less than the smallest length visible with the optical power employed. But indirect observations—for example, that the person sup-

---

[2] *Continuous* is not exactly the right word, but I let it go to avoid a long and irrelevant discussion.

posed to have drawn the line was never within fifty feet of the paper—may make it probable that no line at all was made, so that the concluded length will be strictly zero. In like manner, experience no doubt would warrant the conclusion that there is absolutely *no* indigo in a given ear of wheat, and absolutely *no* attar in a given lichen. But such inferences can only be rendered valid by positive experiential evidence, direct or remote, and cannot rest upon a mere inability to detect the quantity in question. We have reason to think there is no indigo in the wheat, because we have remarked that wherever indigo is produced it is produced in considerable quantities, to mention only one argument. We have reason to think there is no attar in the lichen, because essential oils seem to be in general peculiar to single species. If the question had been whether there was iron in the wheat or the lichen, though chemical analysis should fail to detect its presence, we should think some of it probably was there, since iron is almost everywhere. Without any such information, one way or the other, we could only abstain from any opinion as to the presence of the substance in question. It cannot, I conceive, be maintained that we are in any *better* position than this in regard to the presence of the element of chance or spontaneous departures from law in nature.

Those observations which are generally adduced in favor of mechanical causation simply prove that there is an element of regularity in nature, and have no bearing whatever upon the question of whether such regularity is exact and universal, or not. Nay, in regard to this *exactitude*, all observation is directly *opposed* to it; and the most that can be said is that a good deal of this observation can be explained away. Try to verify any law of nature, and you will find that the more precise your observations, the more certain they will be to show irregular departures from the law. We are accustomed to ascribe these, and I do not say wrongly, to errors of observation; yet we cannot usually account for such errors in any antecedently probable way. Trace their causes back far enough, and you will be forced to admit they are always due to arbitrary determination, or chance.

But it may be asked whether if there were an element of real chance in the universe it must not occasionally be productive of signal effects such as could not pass unobserved. In answer to this question, without stopping to point out that there is an abundance of great events which one might be tempted to suppose were of that nature, it will be simplest to remark that physicists hold that the particles of gases are moving about irregularly, substantially as if by real chance, and that by the principles of probabilities there must occasionally happen to be concentrations of heat in the gases contrary to the second law of thermodynamics, and these concentrations, occurring in explosive mixtures, must sometimes have tremendous effects. Here, then, is in substance the very situation supposed; yet no phenomena ever have resulted which we are forced to attribute to such chance concentration of heat, or which anybody, wise or foolish, has ever dreamed of accounting for in that manner.

In view of all these considerations, I do not believe that anybody, not in a state of case-hardened ignorance respecting the logic of science, can maintain that the precise and universal conformity of facts to law is clearly proved, or even rendered particularly probable, by any observations hitherto made. In this way, the determined advocate of exact regularity will soon find himself driven to *a priori* reasons to support his thesis. These received such a socdolager from Stuart Mill in his Examination of Hamilton, that holding to them now seems to me to denote a high degree of imperviousness to reason; so that I shall pass them by with little notice.

To say that we cannot help believing a given proposition is no argument, but it is a conclusive fact if it be true; and with the substitution of "I" for "we," it is true in the mouths of several classes of minds, the blindly passionate, the unreflecting and ignorant, and the person who has overwhelming evidence before his eyes. But that which has been inconceivable today has often turned out indisputable on the morrow. Inability to conceive is only a stage through which every man must pass in regard to a number of beliefs—unless endowed with extraordinary obstinacy and obtuseness.

His understanding is enslaved to some blind compulsion which a vigorous mind is pretty sure soon to cast off.

Some seek to back up the *a priori* position with empirical arguments. They say that the exact regularity of the world is a natural belief, and that natural beliefs have generally been confirmed by experience. There is some reason in this. Natural beliefs, however, if they generally have a foundation of truth, also require correction and purification from natural illusions. The principles of mechanics are undoubtedly natural beliefs; but, for all that, the early formulations of them were exceedingly erroneous. The general approximation to truth in natural beliefs is, in fact, a case of the general adaptation of genetic products to recognizable utilities or ends. Now, the adaptations of nature, beautiful and often marvelous as they verily are, are never found to be quite perfect; so that the argument is quite *against* the absolute exactitude of any natural belief, including that of the principle of causation.

Another argument, or convenient commonplace, is that absolute chance is *inconceivable*. (This word has eight current significations. The *Century Dictionary*[3] enumerates six.) Those who talk like this will hardly be persuaded to say in what sense they mean that chance is inconceivable. Should they do so, it would easily be shown either that they have no sufficient reason for the statement or that the inconceivability is of a kind which does not prove that chance is non-existent.

Another *a priori* argument is that chance is unintelligible; that is to say, while it may perhaps be conceivable, it does not disclose to the eye of reason the how or why of things; and since a hypothesis can only be justified so far as it renders some phenomenon intelligible, we never can have any right to suppose absolute chance to enter into the production of anything in nature. This argument may be considered in connection with two others. Namely, instead of going so far as to say that the supposition of chance can *never* properly be used to explain any observed fact, it may

[3] Peirce was one of the editors, and his interleaved copy with his critical notes may be profitably studied at the Houghton Library.—Editor's note.

THE DOCTRINE OF NECESSITY

be alleged merely that no facts are known which such a supposition could in any way help in explaining. Or again, the allegation being still further weakened, it may be said that since departures from law are not unmistakably observed, chance is not a *vera causa,* and ought not unnecessarily to be introduced into a hypothesis.

These are no mean arguments, and require us to examine the matter a little more closely. Come, my superior opponent, let me learn from your wisdom. It seems to me that every throw of sixes with a pair of dice is a manifest instance of chance.

"While you would hold a throw of deuce-ace to be brought about by necessity?" (The opponent's supposed remarks are placed in quotation marks.)

Clearly one throw is as much chance as another.

"Do you think throws of dice are of a different nature from other events?"

I see that I must say that *all* the diversity and specificalness of events is attributable to chance.

"Would you, then, deny that there is any regularity in the world?"

That is clearly undeniable. I must acknowledge there is an approximate regularity, and that every event is influenced by it. But the diversification, specificalness, and irregularity of things I suppose is chance. A throw of sixes appears to me a case in which this element is particularly obtrusive.

"If you reflect more deeply, you will come to see that *chance* is only a name for a cause that is unknown to us."

Do you mean that we have no idea whatever what kind of causes could bring about a throw of sixes?

"On the contrary, each die moves under the influence of precise mechanical laws."

But it appears to me that it is not these *laws* which made the die turn up sixes; for these laws act just the same when other throws come up. The chance lies in the diversity of throws; and this diversity cannot be due to laws which are immutable.

"The diversity is due to the diverse circumstances under which the laws act. The dice lie differently in the box, and the motion given to the box is different. These are the un-known causes which produce the throws, and to which we give the name of chance; not the mechanical law which regulates the operation of these causes. You see you are already beginning to think more clearly about this subject."

Does the operation of mechanical law not increase the diversity?

"Properly not. You must know that the instantaneous state of a system of particles is defined by six times as many numbers as there are particles, three for the co-ordinates of each particle's position, and three more for the com-ponents of its velocity. This number of numbers, which ex-presses the amount of diversity in the system, remains the same at all times. There may be, to be sure, some kind of relation between the co-ordinates and component velocities of the different particles, by means of which the state of the system might be expressed by a smaller number of numbers. But, if this is the case, a precisely corresponding relationship must exist between the co-ordinates and com-ponent velocities at any other time, though it may doubt-less be a relation less obvious to us. Thus, the intrinsic com-plexity of the system is the same at all times."

Very well, my obliging opponent, we have now reached an issue. You think all the arbitrary specifications of the universe were introduced in one dose, in the beginning, if there was a beginning, and that the variety and complica-tion of nature has always been just as much as it is now. But I, for my part, think that the diversification, the speci-fication, has been continually taking place. Should you con-descend to ask me why I so think, I should give my reasons as follows:

(1) Question any science which deals with the course of time. Consider the life of an individual animal or plant, or of a mind. Glance at the history of states, of institutions, of language, of ideas. Examine the successions of forms shown by paleontology, the history of the globe as set forth in geology, of what the astronomer is able to make out con-cerning the changes of stellar systems. Everywhere the main fact is growth and increasing complexity. Death and corruption are mere accidents or secondary phenomena.

Among some of the lower organisms, it is a moot point with biologists whether there be anything which ought to be called death. Races, at any rate, do not die out except under unfavorable circumstances. From these broad and ubiquitous facts we may fairly infer, by the most unexceptionable logic, that there is probably in nature some agency by which the complexity and diversity of things can be increased; and that consequently the rule of mechanical necessity meets in some way with interference.

(2) By thus admitting pure spontaneity or life as a character of the universe, acting always and everywhere though restrained within narrow bounds by law, producing infinitesimal departures from law continually, and great ones with infinite infrequency, I account for all the variety and diversity of the universe, in the only sense in which the really *sui generis* and new can be said to be accounted for. The ordinary view has to admit the inexhaustible multitudinous variety of the world, has to admit that its mechanical law cannot account for this in the least, that variety can spring only from spontaneity, and yet denies without any evidence or reason the existence of this spontaneity, or else shoves it back to the beginning of time and supposes it dead ever since. The superior logic of my view appears to me not easily controverted.

(3) When I ask the necessitarian how he would explain the diversity and irregularity of the universe, he replies to me out of the treasury of his wisdom that irregularity is something which from the nature of things we must not seek to explain. Abashed at this, I seek to cover my confusion by asking how he would explain the uniformity and regularity of the universe, whereupon he tells me that the laws of nature are immutable and ultimate facts, and no account is to be given of them. But my hypothesis of spontaneity does explain irregularity, in a certain sense; that is, it explains the general fact of irregularity, though not, of course, what each lawless event is to be. At the same time, by thus loosening the bond of necessity, it gives room for the influence of another kind of causation, such as seems to be operative in the mind in the formation of associations, and enables us to understand how the uniformity of nature

could have been brought about. That single events should be hard and unintelligible, logic will permit without difficulty: we do not expect to make the shock of a personally experienced earthquake appear natural and reasonable by any amount of cogitation. But logic does expect things *general* to be understandable. To say that there is a universal law, and that it is a hard, ultimate, unintelligible fact, the why and wherefore of which can never be inquired into, at this a sound logic will revolt; and will pass over at once to a method of philosophizing which does not thus barricade the road of discovery.

(4) Necessitarianism cannot logically stop short of making the whole action of the mind a part of the physical universe. Our notion that we decide what we are going to do, if as the necessitarian says, it has been calculable since the earliest times, is reduced to illusion. Indeed, consciousness in general thus becomes a mere illusory aspect of a material system. What we call red, green, and violet are in reality only different rates of vibration. The sole reality is the distribution of qualities of matter in space and time. Brain-matter is protoplasm in a certain degree and kind of complication—a certain arrangement of mechanical particles. Its feeling is but an inward aspect, a phantom. For, from the positions and velocities of the particles at any one instant, and the knowledge of the immutable forces, the positions at all other times are calculable; so that the universe of space, time, and matter is a rounded system uninterfered with from elsewhere. But from the state of feeling at any instant, there is no reason to suppose the states of feeling at all other instants are thus exactly calculable; so that feeling is, as I said, a mere fragmentary and illusive aspect of the universe. This is the way, then, that necessitarianism has to make up its accounts. It enters consciousness under the head of sundries, as a forgotten trifle; its scheme of the universe would be more satisfactory if this little fact could be dropped out of sight. On the other hand, by supposing the rigid exactitude of causation to yield, I care not how little—be it but by a strictly infinitesimal amount—we gain room to insert mind into our scheme, and to put it into the place where it is needed, into the position which, as the

sole self-intelligible thing, it is entitled to occupy, that of the fountain of existence; and in so doing we resolve the problem of the connection of soul and body.

(5) But I must leave undeveloped the chief of my reasons, and can only adumbrate it. The hypothesis of chance-spontaneity is one whose inevitable consequences are capable of being traced out with mathematical precision into considerable detail. Much of this I have done and find the consequences to agree with observed facts to an extent which seems to me remarkable. But the matter and methods of reasoning are novel, and I have no right to promise that other mathematicians shall find my deductions as satisfactory as I myself do, so that the strongest reason for my belief must for the present remain a private reason of my own, and cannot influence others. I mention it to explain my own position; and partly to indicate to future mathematical speculators a veritable gold mine, should time and circumstances and the abridger of all joys prevent my opening it to the world.

If now I, in my turn, inquire of the necessitarian why he prefers to suppose that all specification goes back to the beginning of things, he will answer me with one of those last three arguments which I left unanswered.

First, he may say that chance is a thing absolutely unintelligible, and, therefore, that we never can be entitled to make such a supposition. But does not this objection smack of naïve impudence? It is not mine, it is his own conception of the universe which leads abruptly up to hard, ultimate, inexplicable, immutable law, on the one hand, and to inexplicable specification and diversification of circumstances on the other. My view, on the contrary, hypothetizes nothing at all, unless it be hypothesis to say that all specification came about in some sense, and is not to be accepted as unaccountable. To undertake to account for anything by saying boldly that it is due to chance would, indeed, be futile. But this I do not do. I make use of chance chiefly to make room for a principle of generalization, or tendency to form habits, which I hold has produced all regularities. The mechanical philosopher leaves the whole specification of the world utterly unaccounted for, which is pretty nearly as bad as to boldly attribute it to chance. I attribute it altogether to chance, it is true, but to chance in the form of a spontaneity which is to some degree regular. It seems to me clear at any rate that one of these two positions must be taken, or else specification must be supposed due to a spontaneity which develops itself in a certain and not in a chance way, by an objective logic like that of Hegel. This last way I leave as an open possibility, for the present; for it is as much opposed to the necessitarian scheme of existence as my own theory is.

Secondly, the necessitarian may say there are, at any rate, no observed phenomena which the hypothesis of chance could aid in explaining. In reply, I point first to the phenomenon of growth and developing complexity, which appears to be universal, and which though it may possibly be an affair of mechanism perhaps, certainly presents all the appearance of increasing diversification. Then, there is variety itself, beyond comparison the most obtrusive character of the universe: no mechanism can account for this. Then, there is the very fact the necessitarian most insists upon, the regularity of the universe which for him serves only to block the road of inquiry. Then, there are the regular relationships between the laws of nature—similarities and comparative characters, which appeal to our intelligence as its cousins, and call upon us for a reason. Finally, there is consciousness, feeling, a patent fact enough, but a very inconvenient one to the mechanical philosopher.

Thirdly, the necessitarian may say that chance is not a *vera causa*, that we cannot know positively there is any such element in the universe. But the doctrine of the *vera causa* has nothing to do with elementary conceptions. Pushed to that extreme, it at once cuts off belief in the existence of a material universe; and without that necessitarianism could hardly maintain its ground. Besides, variety is a fact which must be admitted; and the theory of chance merely consists in supposing this diversification does not antedate all time. Moreover, the avoidance of hypotheses involving causes nowhere positively known to act—is only a recommendation of logic, not a positive command. It cannot be formulated in any precise terms without at once betraying its untenable character—I mean as rigid rule, for as a recommendation it is wholesome enough.

I believe I have thus subjected to fair examination all the important reasons for adhering to the theory of universal necessity, and have shown their nullity. I earnestly beg that whoever may detect any flaw in my reasoning will point it out to me, either privately or publicly; for if I am wrong, it much concerns me to be set right speedily. If my argument remains unrefuted, it will be time, I think, to doubt the absolute truth of the principle of universal law; and when once such a doubt has obtained a living root in any man's mind, my cause with him, I am persuaded, is gained.

10.   What Pragmatism Is[1]

[In his poverty and isolation at the turn of the century Peirce was encouraged by James's publicly crediting him with having first formulated pragmatism during the lively philosophical conversations of their informal club at Harvard in the early 1870s. At the age of sixty-four he was partly relieved of the hack work he had been doing in the form of reviews and articles for the Smithsonian Institution, Baldwin's *Dictionary of Philosophy and Psychology,* and semipopular periodicals, by being invited to give a series of lectures on Pragmatism at Harvard University and at the Lowell Institute (1903). The flood of polemical articles on pragmatism that appeared in the next two decades was started not by Peirce's lectures or published articles but by William James and John Dewey, who were both deeply influenced by Peirce. Most of the critics of American pragmatism assailed James's vivid but vulnerable rhetoric: "Truth is what works," "The true is the expedient," "The cash-value of true theories," "Faith in a fact helps create the fact." In order to avoid such literary, metaphorical language, Peirce defended pragmatism by attaching his own version of it to the logical habits of the typical experimenter or laboratory mind. In the same essay he explains the need for philosophers to adopt the same scrupulous regard for precise and universally acceptable definitions of new terms and doctrines as scientists require in

[1] *The Monist,* Vol. 15 (April 1905), pp. 161–181.

their technical terminology. His excursus on the "ethics of terminology" explains why Peirce labels his own doctrine "pragmaticism."

The chief difference between Peirce's pragmaticism and James's pragmatism arises from the fact that Peirce's point of view is logical, while James's is psychological. Whereas Peirce sought the meaning of a proposition in its logical and experimentally testable consequences, James looked for more immediately felt sensations or personal reactions. There is a vast difference between the effects of radiation fall-out as conceived and analyzed by the medical chemist and the effects of one's belief that such radiation is poisonous; the latter belief may be based on fear alone, which cannot influence the experimenter's conception of the measurable effects of the objects exposed to radiation. However, in situations where we are concerned entirely with psychological effects, say, in judging the meaning of self-reproach by its consequential improvement of the habit of self-control, there is no difference between Peirce and James.

In a series of footnotes to his famous pragmatic essay on "How to Make Our Ideas Clear," Peirce explained more fully what ethical considerations guided his principle of pragmaticism: "Consider what effects, that might conceivably have practical bearings, we conceive the object of our conception to have. Then, our conception of these effects is the whole of our conception of the object."

"Before we undertake to apply this rule," Peirce added in 1893, "let us reflect a little upon what it implies. It has been said to be a skeptical and materialistic principle. But it is only an application of the sole principle of logic recommended by Jesus: 'Ye may know them by their fruits,' and it is very intimately related with the ideas of the Gospel. We must certainly guard ourselves against understanding this rule in too individualistic a sense." This was James's error according to Peirce.]

The writer of this article has been led by much experience to believe that every physicist, and every chemist, and, in short, every master in any department of experimental science, has had his mind molded by his life in the laboratory to a degree that is little suspected. The experimentalist himself can hardly be fully aware of it, for the reason that the men whose intellects he really knows about are much like himself in this respect. With intellects of widely different training from his own, whose education has largely been a thing learned out of books, he will never become inwardly intimate, be he on ever so familiar terms with them; for he and they are as oil and water, and though they be shaken up together, it is remarkable how quickly they will go their several mental ways, without having gained more than a faint flavor from the association. Were those other men only to take skillful soundings of the experimentalist's mind—which is just what they are unqualified to do, for the most part—they would soon discover that, excepting perhaps upon topics where his mind is trammeled by personal feeling or by his bringing up, his disposition is to think of everything just as everything is thought of in the laboratory, that is, as a question of experimentation. Of course, no living man possesses in their fullness all the attributes characteristic of his type: it is not the typical doctor whom you will see every day driven in buggy or coupé, nor is it the typical pedagogue that will be met with in the first schoolroom you enter. But when you have found, or ideally constructed upon a basis of observation, the typical experimentalist, you will find that whatever assertion you may make to him, he will either understand as meaning that if a given prescription for an experiment ever can be and ever is carried out in act, an experience of a given description will result, or else he will see no sense at all in what you say. If you talk to him as Mr. Balfour talked not long ago to the British Association[2] saying that "the physicist . . . seeks for something deeper than the laws connecting possible objects of experience," that "his object is physical reality" unrevealed in experiments, and that the existence of such non-experiential reality "is the unalterable faith of science," to all such ontological meaning, you will find the experimentalist mind to be color-blind. What adds to that

[2] *Reflections Suggested by the New Theory of Matter;* Presidential Address, British Association for the Advancement of Science, August 17, 1904.

confidence in this, which the writer owes to his conversations with experimentalists, is that he himself may almost be said to have inhabited a laboratory from the age of six until long past maturity; and having all his life associated mostly with experimentalists, it has always been with a confident sense of understanding them and of being understood by them.

That laboratory life did not prevent the writer (who here and in what follows simply exemplifies the experimentalist type) from becoming interested in methods of thinking; and when he came to read metaphysics, although much of it seemed to him loosely reasoned and determined by accidental prepossessions, yet in the writings of some philosophers, especially Kant, Berkeley, and Spinoza, he sometimes came upon strains of thought that recalled the ways of thinking of the laboratory, so that he felt he might trust to them; all of which has been true of other laboratory-men.

Endeavoring, as a man of that type naturally would, to formulate what he so approved, he framed the theory that a *conception*, that is, the rational purport of a word or other expression, lies exclusively in its conceivable bearing upon the conduct of life; so that, since obviously nothing that might not result from experiment can have any direct bearing upon conduct, if one can define accurately all the conceivable experimental phenomena which the affirmation or denial of a concept could imply, one will have therein a complete definition of the concept, and *there is absolutely nothing more in it.* For this doctrine he invented the name *pragmatism.* Some of his friends wished him to call it *practicism* or *practicalism* (perhaps on the ground that *praktikós* is better Greek than *pragmatikós*). But for one who had learned philosophy out of Kant, as the writer, along with nineteen out of every twenty experimentalists who have turned to philosophy, had done, and who still thought in Kantian terms most readily, *praktisch* and *pragmatisch* were as far apart as the two poles, the former belonging in a region of thought where no mind of the experimentalist type can ever make sure of solid ground under his feet, the latter expressing relation to some definite human purpose. Now quite the most striking feature of the new theory was its recognition of an inseparable connection between rational cognition and rational purpose; and that consideration it was which determined the preference for the name *pragmatism*.

Concerning the matter of philosophical nomenclature, there are a few plain considerations which the writer has for many years longed to submit to the deliberate judgment of those few fellow-students of philosophy who deplore the present state of that study, and who are intent upon rescuing it therefrom and bringing it to a condition like that of the natural sciences, where investigators, instead of condemning each the work of most of the others as misdirected from beginning to end, co-operate, stand upon one another's shoulders, and multiply incontestable results; where every observation is repeated, and isolated observations go for little; where every hypothesis that merits attention is subjected to severe but fair examination, and only after the predictions to which it leads have been remarkably borne out by experience is trusted at all, and even then only provisionally; where a radically false step is rarely taken, even the most faulty of those theories which gain wide credence being true in their main experiential predictions. To those students, it is submitted that no study can become scientific in the sense described until it provides itself with a suitable technical nomenclature, whose every term has a single definite meaning universally accepted among students of the subject, and whose vocables have no such sweetness or charms as might tempt loose writers to abuse them—which is a virtue of scientific nomenclature too little appreciated. It is submitted that the experience of those sciences which have conquered the greatest difficulties of terminology, which are unquestionably the taxonomic sciences, chemistry, mineralogy, botany, zoology, has conclusively shown that the one only way in which the requisite unanimity and requisite ruptures with individual habits and preferences can be brought about is so to shape the canons of terminology that they shall gain the support of *moral principle* and of every man's sense of decency; and that, in particular (under defined restrictions), the general feeling shall be

that he who introduces a new conception into philosophy
is under an obligation to invent acceptable terms to express
it, and that when he has done so, the duty of his fellow-
students is to accept those terms, and to resent any wresting
of them from their original meanings, as not only a gross
discourtesy to him to whom philosophy was indebted for
each conception, but also as an injury to philosophy itself;
and furthermore, that once a conception has been supplied
with suitable and sufficient words for its expression, no
other *technical* terms denoting the same things, considered
in the same relations, should be countenanced. Should this
suggestion find favor, it might be deemed needful that the
philosophians in congress assembled should adopt, after
due deliberation, convenient canons to limit the application
of the principle. Thus, just as is done in chemistry, it might
be wise to assign fixed meanings to certain prefixes and
suffixes. For example, it might be agreed, perhaps, that the
prefix *prope-* should mark a broad and rather indefinite extension of the meaning of the term to which it was prefixed;
the name of a doctrine would naturally end in *-ism,* while
-icism might mark a more strictly defined acception of that
doctrine, etc. Then again, just as in biology no account is
taken of terms antedating Linnæus, so in philosophy it
might be found best not to go back of the scholastic terminology. To illustrate another sort of limitation, it has
probably never happened that any philosopher has attempted to give a general name to his own doctrine without that name's soon acquiring in common philosophical
usage a signification much broader than was originally intended. Thus, special systems go by the names Kantianism,
Benthamism, Comteanism, Spencerianism, etc., while tran-
scendentalism, utilitarianism, positivism, evolutionism, synthetic philosophy, etc., have irrevocably and very conveniently been elevated to broader governments.

After awaiting in vain, for a good many years, some
particularly opportune conjuncture of circumstances that
might serve to recommend his notions of the ethics of terminology, the writer has now, at last, dragged them in over
head and shoulders, on an occasion when he has no specific

proposal to offer nor any feeling but satisfaction at the
course usage has run without any canons or resolutions of
a congress. His word "pragmatism" has gained general recognition in a generalized sense that seems to argue power
of growth and vitality. The famed psychologist, James, first
took it up,[3] seeing that his "radical empiricism" substantially answered to the writer's definition of pragmatism, albeit with a certain difference in the point of view. Next, the
admirably clear and brilliant thinker, Mr. Ferdinand C. S.
Schiller, casting about for a more attractive name for the
"anthropomorphism" of his *Riddle of the Sphinx,* lit, in that
most remarkable paper of his on "Axioms as Postulates,"[4]
upon the same designation "pragmatism," which in its
original sense was in generic agreement with his own doctrine, for which he has since found the more appropriate
specification "humanism," while he still retains "pragmatism" in a somewhat wider sense. So far all went happily.
But at present, the word begins to be met with occasionally
in the literary journals, where it gets abused in the merciless
way that words have to expect when they fall into literary
clutches. Sometimes the manners of the British have ef-
floresced in scolding at the word as ill-chosen—ill-chosen,
that is, to express some meaning that it was rather designed
to exclude. So then, the writer, finding his bantling "pragmatism" so promoted, feels that it is time to kiss his child
good-by and relinquish it to its higher destiny; while to
serve the precise purpose of expressing the original definition, he begs to announce the birth of the word "pragmaticism," which is ugly enough to be safe from kidnappers.[5]

Much as the writer has gained from the perusal of what
other pragmatists have written, he still thinks there is a de-

[3] See his *Pragmatism,* p. 47.

[4] In *Personal Idealism,* ed. by H. Sturt (1902), p. 63.

[5] To show how recent the general use of the word "pragmatism" is, the writer may mention that, to the best of his belief,
he never used it in copy for the press before today, except by
particular request, in *Baldwin's Dictionary.* Toward the end of
1890, when this part of the *Century Dictionary* appeared, he
did not deem that the word had sufficient status to appear in
that work. But he has used it continually in philosophical
conversation since, perhaps, the mid-seventies.

cisive advantage in his original conception of the doctrine. From this original form every truth that follows from any of the other forms can be deduced, while some errors can be avoided into which other pragmatists have fallen. The original view appears, too, to be a more compact and unitary conception than the others. But its capital merit, in the writer's eyes, is that it more readily connects itself with a critical proof of its truth. Quite in accord with the logical order of investigation, it usually happens that one first forms an hypothesis that seems more and more reasonable the further one examines into it, but that only a good deal later gets crowned with an adequate proof. The present writer, having had the pragmatist theory under consideration for many years longer than most of its adherents, would naturally have given more attention to the proof of it. At any rate, in endeavoring to explain pragmatism, he may be excused for confining himself to that form of it that he knows best. In the present article there will be space only to explain just what this doctrine (which, in such hands as it has now fallen into, may probably play a pretty prominent part in the philosophical discussions of the next coming years) really consists in. Should the exposition be found to interest readers of *The Monist,* they would certainly be much more interested in a second article which would give some samples of the manifold applications of pragmaticism (assuming it to be true) to the solution of problems of different kinds. After that, readers might be prepared to take an interest in a proof that the doctrine is true—a proof which seems to the writer to leave no reasonable doubt on the subject, and to be the one contribution of value that he has to make to philosophy. For it would essentially involve the establishment of the truth of synechism.[6]

The bare definition of pragmaticism could convey no satisfactory comprehension of it to the most apprehensive of minds, but requires the commentary to be given below. Moreover, this definition takes no notice of one or two other

[6] Synechism is the principle that continuity prevails in all thought, in the evolution of life and of human societies and institutions as well as in the logic of science.—Editor's note.

doctrines without the previous acceptance (or virtual acceptance) of which pragmaticism itself would be a nullity. They are included as a part of the pragmatism of Schiller, but the present writer prefers not to mingle different propositions. The preliminary propositions had better be stated forthwith.

The difficulty in doing this is that no formal list of them has ever been made. They might all be included under the vague maxim, "Dismiss make-believes." Philosophers of very diverse stripes propose that philosophy shall take its start from one or another state of mind in which no man, least of all a beginner in philosophy, actually is. One proposes that you shall begin by doubting everything, and says that there is only one thing that you cannot doubt, as if doubting were "as easy as lying." Another proposes that we should begin by observing "the first impressions of sense," forgetting that our very percepts are the results of cognitive elaboration. But in truth, there is but one state of mind from which you can "set out," namely, the very state of mind in which you actually find yourself at the time you do "set out"—a state in which you are laden with an immense mass of cognition already formed, of which you cannot divest yourself if you would; and who knows whether, if you could, you would not have made all knowledge impossible to yourself? Do you call it *doubting* to write down on a piece of paper that you doubt? If so, doubt has nothing to do with any serious business. But do not make believe; if pedantry has not eaten all the reality out of you, recognize, as you must, that there is much that you do not doubt, in the least. Now that which you do not at all doubt, you must and do regard as infallible, absolute truth. Here breaks in Mr. Make Believe: "What! Do you mean to say that one is to believe what is not true, or that what a man does not doubt is *ipso facto* true?" No, but unless he can make a thing white and black at once, *he* has to regard what he does not doubt as absolutely true. Now you, *per hypothesiu,* are that man. "But you tell me there are scores of things I do not doubt. I really cannot persuade myself that there is not some one of them about which I am mistaken." You are adducing one of your make-believe facts, which, even if it were established, would only go to show that doubt has a *limen*, that is, is only called into being by a certain finite stimulus. You only puzzle yourself by talking of this metaphysical "truth" and metaphysical "falsity," that you know nothing about. All you have any dealings with are your doubts and beliefs,[7] with the course of life that forces new beliefs upon you and gives you power to doubt old beliefs. If your terms "truth" and "falsity" are taken in such senses as to be definable in terms of doubt and belief and the course of experience (as for example they would be if you were to define the "truth" as that to a belief in which belief would tend if it were to tend indefinitely toward absolute fixity), well and good: in that case, you are only talking about doubt and belief. But if by truth and falsity you mean something not definable in terms of doubt and belief in any way, then you are talking of entities of whose existence you can know nothing, and which Ockham's razor would clean shave off. Your problems would be greatly simplified if, instead of saying that you want to know the "Truth," you were simply to say that you want to attain a state of belief unassailable by doubt.

Belief is not a momentary mode of consciousness; it is a habit of mind essentially enduring for some time, and mostly (at least) unconscious; and like other habits, it is (until it meets with some surprise that begins its dissolution) perfectly self-satisfied. Doubt is of an altogether contrary genus. It is not a habit, but the privation of a habit. Now a privation of a habit, in order to be anything at all, must be a condition of erratic activity that in some way must get superseded by a habit.

Among the things which the reader, as a rational person, does not doubt is that he not merely has habits, but also can exert a measure of self-control over his future actions; which means, however, *not* that he can impart to them any arbitrarily assignable character, but, on the contrary, that a process of self-preparation will tend to impart to action

[7] It is necessary to say that "belief" is throughout used merely as the name of the contrary to doubt, without regard to grades of certainty or to the nature of the proposition held for true, i.e., "believed."

(when the occasion for it shall arise) one fixed character, which is indicated and perhaps roughly measured by the absence (or slightness) of the feeling of self-reproach, which subsequent reflection will induce. Now, this subsequent reflection is part of the self-preparation for action on the next occasion. Consequently, there is a tendency, as action is repeated again and again, for the action to approximate indefinitely toward the perfection of that fixed character, which would be marked by entire absence of self-reproach. The more closely this is approached, the less room for self-control there will be; and where no self-control is possible there will be no self-reproach.

These phenomena seem to be the fundamental characteristics which distinguish a rational being. Blame, in every case, appears to be a modification, often accomplished by a transference, or "projection," of the primary feeling of self-reproach. Accordingly, we never blame anybody for what had been beyond his power of previous self-control. Now, thinking is a species of conduct which is largely subject to self-control. In all their features (which there is no room to describe here), logical self-control is a perfect mirror of ethical self-control—unless it be rather a species under that genus. In accordance with this, what you cannot in the least help believing is not, justly speaking, wrong belief. In other words, for you it is the absolute truth. True, it is conceivable that what you cannot help believing today, you might find you thoroughly disbelieve tomorrow. But then there is a certain distinction between things you "cannot" do, merely in the sense that nothing stimulates you to the great effort and endeavors that would be required, and things you cannot do because in their own nature they are insusceptible of being put into practice. In every stage of your excogitations, there is something of which you can only say, "I cannot think otherwise," and your experientially based hypothesis is that the impossibility is of the second kind.

There is no reason why "thought," in what has just been said, should be taken in that narrow sense in which silence and darkness are favorable to thought. It should rather be understood as covering all rational life, so that an experi-

ment shall be an operation of thought. Of course, that ultimate state of habit to which the action of self-control
ultimately tends, where no room is left for further self-control, is, in the case of thought, the state of fixed belief, or
perfect knowledge.

Two things here are all-important to assure oneself of
and to remember. The first is that a person is not absolutely
an individual. His thoughts are what he is "saying to himself," that is, is saying to that other self that is just coming
into life in the flow of time. When one reasons, it is that
critical self that one is trying to persuade; and all thought
whatsoever is a sign, and is mostly of the nature of language. The second thing to remember is that the man's
circle of society (however widely or narrowly this phrase
may be understood) is a sort of loosely compacted person,
in some respects of higher rank than the person of an individual organism. It is these two things alone that render
it possible for you—but only in the abstract, and in a Pick-
wickian sense—to distinguish between absolute truth and
what you do not doubt.

Let us now hasten to the exposition of pragmaticism itself. Here it will be convenient to imagine that somebody to
whom the doctrine is new, but of rather preternatural per-
spicacity, asks questions of a pragmaticist. Everything that
might give a dramatic illusion must be stripped off, so that
the result will be a sort of cross between a dialogue and a
catechism, but a good deal more like the latter—something
rather painfully reminiscent of Mangnall's *Historical Questions*.

Questioner: I am astounded at your definition of your
pragmatism, because only last year I was assured by a person above all suspicion of warping the truth—himself a
pragmatist—that your doctrine precisely was "that a conception is to be tested by its practical effects." You must
surely, then, have entirely changed your definition very
recently.

Pragmatist: If you will turn to Volumes VI and VII
of the *Revue Philosophique*, or to the *Popular Science
Monthly* for November 1877 and January 1878, you will
be able to judge for yourself whether the interpretation you

mention was not then clearly excluded. The exact wording of the English enunciation (changing only the first person into the second) was: "Consider what effects that might conceivably have practical bearing you conceive the object of your conception to have. Then your conception of those effects is the WHOLE of your conception of the object."

Questioner: Well, what reason have you for asserting that this is so?

Pragmatist: That is what I specially desire to tell you. But the question had better be postponed until you clearly understand what those reasons profess to prove.

Questioner: What, then, is the *raison d'être* of the doctrine? What advantage is expected from it?

Pragmatist: It will serve to show that almost every proposition of ontological metaphysics is either meaningless gibberish—one word being defined by other words, and they by still others, without any real conception ever being reached—or else is downright absurd; so that all such rubbish being swept away, what will remain of philosophy will be a series of problems capable of investigation by the observational methods of the true sciences—the truth about which can be reached without those interminable misunderstandings and disputes which have made the highest of the positive sciences a mere amusement for idle intellects, a sort of chess—idle pleasure its purpose, and reading out of a book its method. In this regard, pragmaticism is a species of prope-positivism. But what distinguishes it from other species is, first, its retention of a purified philosophy; secondly, its full acceptance of the main body of our instinctive beliefs; and thirdly, its strenuous insistence upon the truth of scholastic realism (or a close approximation to that, well stated by the late Dr. Francis Ellingwood Abbot in the Introduction to his *Scientific Theism*). So, instead of merely jeering at metaphysics, like other prope-positivists, whether by long-drawn-out parodies or otherwise, the pragmaticist extracts from it a precious essence, which will serve to give life and light to cosmology and physics. At the same time, the moral applications of the doctrine are positive and potent; and there are many other uses of it not easily classed.

On another occasion, instances may be given to show that it really has these effects.

Questioner: I hardly need to be convinced that your doctrine would wipe out metaphysics. Is it not as obvious that it must wipe out every proposition of science and everything that bears on the conduct of life? For you say that the only meaning that, for you, any assertion bears is that a certain experiment has resulted in a certain way: nothing else but an experiment enters into the meaning. Tell me, then, how can an experiment, in itself, reveal anything more than that something once happened to an individual object and that subsequently some other individual event occurred?

Pragmatist: That question is, indeed, to the purpose—the purpose being to correct any misapprehensions of pragmaticism. You speak of an experiment in itself, emphasizing *in itself*. You evidently think of each experiment as isolated from every other. It has not, for example, occurred to you, one might venture to surmise, that every connected series of experiments constitutes a single collective experiment. What are the essential ingredients of an experiment? First, of course, an experimenter of flesh and blood. Secondly, a verifiable hypothesis. This is a proposition[8] relating to the universe environing the experimenter, or to some well-known part of it and affirming or denying of this only some experimental possibility or impossibility. The third indispensable ingredient is a sincere doubt in the experimenter's mind as to the truth of that hypothesis.

Passing over several ingredients on which we need not dwell, the purpose, the plan, and the resolve, we come to the act of choice by which the experimenter singles out certain identifiable objects to be operated upon. The next is

---

[8] The writer, like most English logicians, invariably uses the word *proposition* not as the Germans define their equivalent, *Satz,* as the language-expression of a judgment (*Urtheil*), but as that which is related to any assertion, whether mental and self-addressed or outwardly expressed, just as any possibility is related to its actualization. The difficulty of the, at best, difficult problem of the essential nature of a Proposition has been increased, for the Germans, by their *Urtheil,* confounding, under one designation, the mental *assertion* with the *assertable.*

the external (or quasi-external) ACT by which he modifies those objects. Next, comes the subsequent *reaction* of the world upon the experimenter in a perception; and finally, his recognition of the teaching of the experiment. While the two chief parts of the event itself are the action and the reaction, yet the unity of essence of the experiment lies in its purpose and plan, the ingredients passed over in the enumeration.

Another thing: in representing the pragmaticist as making rational meaning to consist in an experiment (which you speak of as an event in the past), you strikingly fail to catch his attitude of mind. Indeed, it is not in an experiment, but in *experimental phenomena,* that rational meaning is said to consist. When an experimentalist speaks of a *phenomenon,* such as "Hall's phenomenon," "Zeemann's phenomenon" and its modification, "Michelson's phenomenon," or "the chessboard phenomenon," he does not mean any particular event that did happen to somebody in the dead past, but what *surely will* happen to everybody in the living future who shall fulfill certain conditions. The phenomenon consists in the fact that when an experimentalist shall come to *act* according to a certain scheme that he has in mind, then will something else happen, and shatter the doubts of skeptics, like the celestial fire upon the altar of Elijah.

And do not overlook the fact that the pragmaticist maxim says nothing of single experiments or of single experimental phenomena (for what is conditionally true *in futuro* can hardly be singular), but only speaks of *general kinds* of experimental phenomena. Its adherent does not shrink from speaking of general objects as real, since whatever is true represents a real. Now the laws of nature are true.

The rational meaning of every proposition lies in the future. How so? The meaning of a proposition is itself a proposition. Indeed, it is no other than the very proposition of which it is the meaning: it is a translation of it. But of the myriads of forms into which a proposition may be translated, what is that one which is to be called its very meaning? It is, according to the pragmaticist, that form in which the proposition becomes applicable to human conduct, not

in these or those special circumstances, nor when one en-
tertains this or that special design, but that form which is
most directly applicable to self-control under every situation, and to every purpose. This is why he locates the meaning in future time; for future conduct is the only conduct
that is subject to self-control. But in order that that form
of the proposition which is to be taken as its meaning should
be applicable to every situation and to every purpose upon
which the proposition has any bearing, it must be simply
the general description of all the experimental phenomena which the assertion of the proposition virtually predicts. For an experimental phenomenon is the fact asserted
by the proposition that action of a certain description will
have a certain kind of experimental result; and experimental results are the only results that can affect human
conduct. No doubt, some unchanging idea may come to
influence a man more than it had done; but only because
some experience equivalent to an experiment has brought
its truth home to him more intimately than before. Whenever a man acts purposively, he acts under a belief in some
experimental phenomenon. Consequently, the sum of the
experimental phenomena that a proposition implies makes
up its entire bearing upon human conduct. Your question,
then, of how a pragmaticist can attribute any meaning to
any assertion other than that of a single occurrence is substantially answered.

Questioner: I see that pragmaticism is a thoroughgoing
phenomenalism. Only why should you limit yourself to the
phenomena of experimental science rather than embrace all
observational science? Experiment, after all, is an uncom-
municative informant. It never expiates: it only answers
"yes" or "no"; or rather it usually snaps out "No!" or, at
best, only utters an inarticulate grunt for the negation of
its "no." The typical experimentalist is not much of an observer. It is the student of natural history to whom nature
opens the treasury of her confidence, while she treats the
cross-examining experimentalist with the reserve he merits.
Why should your phenomenalism sound the meagre jew's-
harp of experiment rather than the glorious organ of observation?

Pragmaticist: Because pragmaticism is not definable as "thoroughgoing phenomenalism," although the latter doctrine may be a kind of pragmatism. The *richness* of phenomena lies in their sensuous quality. Pragmaticism does not intend to define the phenomenal equivalents of words and general ideas, but, on the contrary, eliminates their sential element, and endeavors to define the rational purport, and this it finds in the purposive bearing of the word or proposition in question.

Questioner: Well, if you choose so to make Doing the Be-all and the End-all of human life, why do you not make meaning to consist simply in doing? Doing has to be done at a certain time upon a certain object. Individual objects and single events cover all reality, as everybody knows, and as a practicalist ought to be the first to insist. Yet, your meaning, as you have described it, is *general*. Thus, it is of the nature of a mere word and not a reality. You say yourself that your meaning of a proposition is only the same proposition in another dress. But a practical man's meaning is the very thing he means. What do you make to be the meaning of "George Washington"?

Pragmaticist: Forcibly put! A good half dozen of your points must certainly be admitted. It must be admitted, in the first place, that if pragmaticism really made Doing to be the Be-all and the End-all of life, that would be its death. For to say that we live for the mere sake of action, as action, regardless of the thought it carries out, would be to say that there is no such thing as rational purport. Secondly, it must be admitted that every proposition professes to be true of a certain real, individual object, often the environing universe. Thirdly, it must be admitted that pragmaticism fails to furnish any translation or meaning of a proper name, or other designation of an individual object. Fourthly, the pragmaticistic meaning is undoubtedly general; and it is equally indisputable that the general is of the nature of a word or sign. Fifthly, it must be admitted that individuals alone exist; and sixthly, it may be admitted that the very meaning of a word or significant object ought to be the very essence of reality of what it signifies. But when those admissions have been unreservedly made, if you find the pragmaticist still constrained most earnestly to deny the force of your objection, you ought to infer that there is some consideration that has escaped you. Putting the admissions together, you will perceive that the pragmaticist grants that a proper name (although it is not customary to say that it has a *meaning*) has a certain denotative function peculiar, in each case, to that name and its equivalents; and that he grants that every assertion contains such a denotative or pointing-out function. In its peculiar individuality, the pragmaticist excludes this from the rational purport of the assertion, although *the like* of it, being common to all assertions, and so, being general and not individual, may enter into the pragmaticistic purport. Whatever exists, *ex-sists*, that is, really acts upon other existents, so obtains a self-identity, and is definitely individual. As to the general, it will be a help to thought to notice that there are two ways of being general. A statue of a soldier on some village monument, in his overcoat and with his musket, is for each of a hundred families the image of its uncle, its sacrifice to the Union. That statue, then, though it is itself single, represents any one man of whom a certain predicate may be true. It is *objectively* general. The word "soldier," whether spoken or written, is general in the same way; while the name "George Washington" is not so. But each of these two terms remains one and the same noun, whether it be spoken or written, and whenever and wherever it be spoken or written. This noun is not an existent thing: it is a *type*, or *form*, to which objects, both those that are externally existent and those which are imagined, may *conform*, but which none of them can exactly be. This is subjective generality. The pragmaticistic purport is general in both ways.

As to reality, one finds it defined in various ways; but if that principle of terminological ethics that was proposed be accepted, the equivocal language will soon disappear. For *realis* and *realitas* are not ancient words. They were invented to be terms of philosophy in the thirteenth century,[9] and the meaning they were intended to express is

---

[9] See Prantl, *Geschichte der Logik*, III, 91, Anm. 362.

perfectly clear. That is *real* which has such and such characters, whether anybody thinks it to have those characters or not. At any rate, that is the sense in which the pragmaticist uses the word. Now, just as conduct controlled by ethical reason tends toward fixing certain habits of conduct, the nature of which (as, to illustrate the meaning, peaceable habits and not quarrelsome habits) does not depend upon any accidental circumstances, and *in that sense* may be said to be *destined;* so, thought, controlled by a rational experimental logic, tends to the fixation of certain opinions, equally destined, the nature of which will be the same in the end, however the perversity of thought of whole generations may cause the postponement of the ultimate fixation. If this be so, as every man of us virtually assumes that it is, in regard to each matter the truth of which he seriously discusses, then, according to the adopted definition of "real," the state of things which will be believed in that ultimate opinion is real. But, for the most part, such opinions will be general. Consequently, *some* general objects are real. (Of course, nobody ever thought that *all* generals were real; but the scholastics used to assume that generals were real when they had hardly any, or quite no, experiential evidence to support their assumption; and their fault lay just there, and not in holding that generals could be real.) One is struck with the inexactitude of thought even of analysts of power, when they touch upon modes of being. One will meet, for example, the virtual assumption that what is relative to thought cannot be real. But why not, exactly? *Red* is relative to sight, but the fact that this or that is in that relation to vision that we call being red is not *itself* relative to sight; it is a real fact.

Not only may generals be real, but they may also be *physically efficient,* not in every metaphysical sense, but in the common-sense acception in which human purposes are physically efficient. Aside from metaphysical nonsense, no sane man doubts that if I feel the air in my study to be stuffy, that thought may cause the window to be opened. My thought, be it granted, was an individual event. But what determined it to take the particular determination it did, was in part the general fact that stuffy air is unwholesome, and in part other *Forms,* concerning which Dr. Carus[10] has caused so many men to reflect to advantage— or rather, *by* which, and the general truth concerning which Dr. Carus's mind was determined to the forcible enunciation of so much truth. For truths, on the average, have a greater tendency to get believed than falsities have. Were it otherwise, considering that there are myriads of false hypotheses to account for any given phenomenon, against one sole true one (or if you will have it so, against every true one), the first step toward genuine knowledge must have been next door to a miracle. So, then, when my window was opened, because of the truth that stuffy air is *malsain,* a physical effort was brought into existence by the efficiency of a general and non-existent truth. This has a droll sound because it is unfamiliar; but exact analysis is with it and not against it; and it has besides, the immense advantage of not blinding us to great facts—such as that the ideas "justice" and "truth" are, notwithstanding the iniquity of the world, the mightiest of the forces that move it. Generality is, indeed, an indispensable ingredient of reality; for mere individual existence or actuality without any regularity whatever is a nullity. Chaos is pure nothing.

That which any true proposition asserts is *real,* in the sense of being as it is regardless of what you or I may think about it. Let this proposition be a general conditional proposition as to the future, and it is a real general such as is calculated really to influence human conduct; and such the pragmaticist holds to be the rational purport of every concept.

Accordingly, the pragmaticist does not make the *summum bonum* to consist in action, but makes it to consist in that process of evolution whereby the existent comes more and more to embody those generals which were just now said to be *destined,* which is what we strive to express in calling them *reasonable.* In its higher stages, evolution takes place more and more largely through self-control, and this gives the pragmaticist a sort of justification for making the rational purport to be general.

[10] "The Foundations of Geometry," by Paul Carus, *The Monist,* XIII, p. 370.

There is much more in elucidation of pragmaticism that might be said to advantage were it not for the dread of fatiguing the reader. It might, for example, have been well to show clearly that the pragmaticist does not attribute any different essential mode of being to an event in the future from that which he would attribute to a similar event in the past, but only that the practical attitude of the thinker toward the two is different. It would also have been well to show that the pragmaticist does not make Forms to be the *only* realities in the world, any more than he makes the reasonable purport of a word to be the only kind of meaning there is. These things are, however, implicitly involved in what has been said. There is only one remark concerning the pragmaticist's conception of the relation of his formula to the first principles of logic which need detain the reader.

Aristotle's definition of universal predication,[11] which is usually designated (like a papal bull or writ of court, from its opening words), as the *Dictum de omni,* may be translated as follows: "We call a predication (be it affirmative or negative), *universal,* when, and only when, there is nothing among the existent individuals to which the subject affirmatively belongs, but to which the predicate will not likewise be referred (affirmatively or negatively, according as the universal predication is affirmative or negative)." . . .[12] The important words "existent individuals" have been introduced into the translation (which English idiom would not here permit to be literal); but it is plain that "existent individuals" were what Aristotle meant. The other departures from literalness only serve to give modern English forms of expression. Now, it is well known that propositions in formal logic go in pairs, the two of one pair being convertible into another by the interchange of the ideas of antecedent and consequent, subject and predicate, etc. The parallelism extends so far that it is often assumed to be perfect; but it is not quite so. The proper mate of this sort to the *Dictum de omni* is the following definition of affirmative

---

[11] *Prior Analytics,* 24b, 28–30.
[12] The Greek text of Aristotle, given by Peirce, is omitted here.—Editor's note.

predication: We call a predication *affirmative* (be it universal or particular) when, and only when, there is nothing among the sensational effects that belong universally to the predicate which will not be (universally or particularly, according as the affirmative predication is universal or particular) said to belong to the subject. Now, this is substantially the essential proposition of pragmaticism. Of course, its parallelism to the *Dictum de omni* will only be admitted by a person who admits the truth of pragmaticism.

Suffer me to add one word more on this point. For if one cares at all to know what the pragmaticist theory consists in, one must understand that there is no other part of it to which the pragmaticist attaches quite as much importance as he does to the recognition in his doctrine of the utter inadequacy of action or volition or even of resolve or actual purpose, as materials out of which to construct a conditional purpose or the concept of conditional purpose. Had a purposed article concerning the principle of continuity and synthetizing the ideas of the other articles of a series in the early volumes of *The Monist* ever been written, it would have appeared how, with thorough consistency, that theory involved the recognition that continuity is an indispensable element of reality, and that continuity is simply what generality becomes in the logic of relatives, and thus, like generality, and more than generality, is an affair of thought, and is the essence of thought. Yet even in its truncated condition, an extra-intelligent reader might discern that the theory of those cosmological articles made reality to consist in something more than feeling and action could supply, inasmuch as the primeval chaos, where those two elements were present, was explicitly shown to be pure nothing. Now, the motive for alluding to that theory just here is that in this way one can put in a strong light a position which the pragmaticist holds and must hold, whether that cosmological theory be ultimately sustained or exploded, namely, that the third category—the category of thought, representation, triadic relation, mediation, genuine thirdness, thirdness as such—is an essential ingredient of reality, yet does not by itself constitute reality, since this category (which in that cosmology appears as the element of habit) can have no concrete being without action, as a separate object on which to work its government, just as action cannot exist without the immediate being of feeling on which to act. The truth is that pragmaticism is closely allied to the Hegelian absolute idealism, from which, however, it is sundered by its vigorous denial that the third category (which Hegel degrades to a mere stage of thinking) suffices to make the world, or is even so much as self-sufficient. Had Hegel, instead of regarding the first two stages with his smile of contempt, held on to them as independent or distinct elements of the triune Reality, pragmaticists might have looked up to him as the great vindicator of their truth. (Of course, the external trappings of his doctrine are only here and there of much significance.) For pragmaticism belongs essentially to the triadic class of philosophical doctrines, and is much more essentially so than Hegelianism is. (Indeed, in one passage, at least, Hegel alludes to the triadic form of his exposition as to a mere fashion of dress.)

Milford, Pa.,
September, 1904

POSTSCRIPT. During the last five months, I have met with references to several objections to the above opinions, but not having been able to obtain the text of these objections, I do not think I ought to attempt to answer them. If gentlemen who attack either pragmatism in general or the variety of it which I entertain would only send me copies of what they write, more important readers they could easily find, but they could find none who would examine their arguments with a more grateful avidity for truth not yet apprehended, nor any who would be more sensible of their courtesy.

February 9, 1905

11. Issues of Pragmaticism[1]

[The ensuing essay aims at making clear the main tenets
of Peirce's pragmaticism: (1) following his 1868 article in
the *Journal of Speculative Philosophy* (Selection 2, above),
Peirce again regards all thought as a sign whose meaning
is expressible and elucidated by other signs which show
the practical bearings or effects of the objects represented
by the sign; (2) statements about "being" (ontological
metaphysics) are meaningless insofar as they have no conceivable effects, so that what philosophy should investigate
is general problems capable of being studied by scientific
methods; (3) the sum of the experimental phenomena that
a proposition implies will make up its entire bearing on
human conduct and thus its whole meaning; (4) the truth
is that opinion which is ultimately agreed upon by those
who continually subject their opinions to experimental investigation, and the real is the object of such inquiry; (5)
while not all general ideas represent the real (e.g., fictions
like mermaids that have no physical effects), some general
ideas do, e.g., laws of nature which determine the regular
motions of bodies, and justice which affects the moral conduct of persons; (6) the highest aim or good of thought
does not consist in action but in the process of evolution
when men exercise habits of self-control guided by general
or socially reasonable purposes.]

[1] *The Monist*, Vol. 15 (Oct. 1905), pp. 481–499.

Pragmaticism was originally enounced[2] in the form of a maxim, as follows: Consider what effects that might *conceivably* have practical bearings you *conceive* the objects of your *conception* to have. Then, your *conception* of those effects is the whole of your *conception* of the object.

I will restate this in other words, since ofttimes one can thus eliminate some unsuspected source of perplexity to the reader. This time it shall be in the indicative mood, as follows: The entire intellectual purport of any symbol consists in the total of all general modes of rational conduct which, conditionally upon all the possible different circumstances and desires, would ensue upon the acceptance of the symbol.

Two doctrines that were defended by the writer about nine years before the formulation of pragmaticism may be treated as consequences of the latter belief. One of these may be called Critical Common-sensism. It is a variety of the Philosophy of Common Sense, but is marked by six distinctive characters, which had better be enumerated at once.

Character I. Critical Common-sensism admits that there not only are indubitable propositions but also that there are indubitable inferences. In one sense, anything evident is indubitable; but the propositions and inferences which Critical Common-sensism holds to be original, in the sense one cannot "go behind" them (as the lawyers say), are indubitable in the sense of being acritical. The term "reasoning" ought to be confined to such fixation of one belief by another as is reasonable, deliberate, self-controlled. A reasoning must be conscious; and this consciousness is not mere "immediate consciousness," which (as I argued in 1868)[3] is simple Feeling viewed from another side, but is in its ultimate nature (meaning in that characteristic element of it that is not reducible to anything simpler) a

[2] *Popular Science Monthly,* Vol. 12 (Jan. 1878), p. 293. An introductory article opens the volume, in the number for November 1877. Peirce's references here are to his "How to Make Our Ideas Clear" and to "The Fixation of Belief," respectively, reprinted above, Selections 6 and 5.—Editor's note.

[3] See above, Selection 2, "Questions Concerning Certain Faculties Claimed for Man."

sense of taking a habit, or disposition to respond to a given kind of stimulus in a given kind of way. As to the nature of that, some *éclaircissements* will appear below and again in my third paper, on the Basis of Pragmaticism.[4] But the secret of rational consciousness is not so much to be sought in the study of this one peculiar nucleolus, as in the review of the process of self-control in its entirety. The machinery of logical self-control works on the same plan as does moral self-control, in multiform detail. The greatest difference, perhaps, is that the latter serves to inhibit mad puttings forth of energy, while the former most characteristically insures us against the quandary of Buridan's ass. The formation of habits under imaginary action (see the paper ["How to Make Our Ideas Clear"] of January, 1878) is one of the most essential ingredients of both; but in the logical process the imagination takes far wider flights, proportioned to the generality of the field of inquiry, being bounded in pure mathematics solely by the limits of its own powers, while in the moral process we consider only situations that may be apprehended or anticipated. For in moral life we are chiefly solicitous about our conduct and its inner springs, and the approval of conscience, while in intellectual life there 'is a tendency to value existence as the vehicle of forms. Certain obvious features of the phenomena of self-control (and especially of habit) can be expressed compactly and without any hypothetical addition, except what we distinctly rate as imagery, by saying that we have an occult nature of which and of its contents we can only judge by the conduct that it determines, and by phenomena of that conduct. All will assent to that (or all but the extreme nominalist), but anti-synechistic thinkers wind themselves up in a factitious snarl by falsifying the phenomena in representing consciousness to be, as it were, a skin, a separate tissue, overlying an unconscious region of the occult nature, mind, soul, or physiological basis. It appears to me that in the present state of our knowledge a sound methodeutic prescribes that, in adhesion to the appearances, the difference is only relative and the demarcation not precise.

[4] "Prolegomena to an Apology for Pragmaticism," *The Monist* Vol. 16 (Oct. 1906), pp. 492–546.

According to the maxim of Pragmaticism, to say that determination affects our occult nature is to say that it is capable of affecting deliberate conduct; and since we are conscious of what we do deliberately, we are conscious *habitualiter* of whatever hides in the depths of our nature; and it is presumable (and *only* presumable,[5] although curious instances are on record) that a sufficiently energetic effort of attention would bring it out. Consequently, to say that an operation of the mind is controlled is to say that it is, in a special sense, a conscious operation; and this no doubt is the consciousness of reasoning. For this theory requires that in reasoning we should be conscious, not only of the conclusion, and of our deliberate approval of it, but also of its being the result of the premiss from which it does result, and furthermore that the inference is one of a possible class of inferences which conform to one guiding principle. Now in fact we find a well-marked class of mental operations, clearly of a different nature from any others which do possess just these properties. They alone deserve to be called *reasonings;* and if the reasoner is conscious, even vaguely, of what his guiding principle is, his reasoning should be called a *logical argumentation.* There are, however, cases in which we are conscious that a belief has been determined by another given belief, but are not conscious that it proceeds on any general principle. Such is St. Augustine's *"cogito, ergo sum."* Such a process should be called, not a reasoning, but an *acritical inference.* Again, there are cases in which one belief is determined by another, without our being at all aware of it. These should be called *associational suggestions of belief.*

Now the theory of Pragmaticism was originally based, as anybody will see who examines the papers of November 1877 and January 1878, upon a study of that experience of the phenomena of self-control which is common to all grown men and women; and it seems evident that to some extent, at least, it must always be so based. For it is to conceptions of deliberate conduct that Pragmaticism would

[5] But see the experiments of J. Jastrow and me "On Slight Differences of Sensation" in the *Memoirs of the National Academy of Sciences*, Vol. III (1884), pp. 1–11.

trace the intellectual purport of symbols; and deliberate conduct is self-controlled conduct. Now control may itself be controlled, criticism itself subjected to criticism; and ideally there is no obvious definite limit to the sequence. But if one seriously inquires whether it is possible that a completed series of actual efforts should have been endless or beginningless (I will spare the reader the discussion), I think he can only conclude that (with some vagueness as to what constitutes an effort) this must be regarded as impossible. It will be found to follow that there are, besides perceptual judgments, original (i.e., indubitable because uncriticized) beliefs of a general and recurrent kind, as well as indubitable acritical inferences.

It is important for the reader to satisfy himself that genuine doubt always has an external origin, usually from surprise; and that it is as impossible for a man to create in himself a genuine doubt by such an act of the will as would suffice to imagine the condition of a mathematical theorem, as it would be for him to give himself a genuine surprise by a simple act of the will.

I beg my reader also to believe that it would be impossible for me to put into these articles over two per cent of the pertinent thought which would be necessary in order to present the subject as I have worked it out. I can only make a small selection of what it seems most desirable to submit to his judgment. Not only must all steps be omitted which he can be expected to supply for himself, but unfortunately much more that may cause him difficulty.

Character II. I do not remember that any of the old Scotch philosophers ever undertook to draw up a complete list of the original beliefs, but they certainly thought it a feasible thing, and that the list would hold good for the minds of all men from Adam down. For in those days Adam was an undoubted historical personage. Before any waft of the air of evolution had reached those coasts how could they think otherwise? When I first wrote, we were hardly orientated in the new ideas, and my impression was that the indubitable propositions changed with a thinking man from year to year. I made some studies preparatory to an investigation of the rapidity of these changes, but the matter was neglected, and it has been only during the last two years [1903–1905] that I have completed a provisional inquiry which shows me that the changes are so slight from generation to generation, though not imperceptible even in that short period, that I thought to own my adhesion, under inevitable modification, to the opinion of that subtle but well-balanced intellect, Thomas Reid, in the matter of Common Sense (as well as in regard to immediate perception, along with Kant).[6]

Character III. The Scotch philosophers recognized that the original beliefs, and the same thing is at least equally true of the acritical inferences, were of the general nature of instincts. But little as we know about instincts, even now, we are much better acquainted with them than were the men of the eighteenth century. We know, for example, that they can be somewhat modified in a very short time. The great facts have always been known; such as that instinct seldom errs, while reason goes wrong nearly half the time, if not more frequently. But one thing the Scotch failed to recognize is that the original beliefs only remain indubitable in their application to affairs that resemble those of a primitive mode of life. It is, for example, quite open to reasonable doubt whether the motions of electrons are confined to three dimensions, although it is good methodeutic to presume that they are until some evidence to the contrary is forthcoming. On the other hand, as soon as we find that a belief shows symptoms of being instinctive, although it may seem to be dubitable, we must suspect that experiment would show that it is not really so; for in our artificial life, especially in that of a student, no mistake is more likely than that of taking a paper-doubt for the genuine metal. Take, for example, the belief in the criminality of incest. Biology will doubtless testify that the practice is inadvisable; but surely nothing that it has to say could warrant the

----

[6] I wish I might hope, after finishing some more difficult work, to be able to resume this study and to go to the bottom of the subject, which needs the qualities of age and does not call upon the powers of youth. A great range of reading is necessary; for it is the belief men *betray* and not that which they *parade* which has to be studied.

intensity of our sentiment about it. When, however, we consider the thrill of horror which the idea excites in us, we find reason in that to consider it to be an instinct; and from that we may infer that if some rationalistic brother and sister were to marry, they would find that the conviction of horrible guilt could not be shaken off.

In contrast to this may be placed the belief that suicide is to be classed as murder. There are two pretty sure signs that this is not an instinctive belief. One is that it is substantially confined to the Christian world. The other is that when it comes to the point of actual self-debate, this belief seems to be completely expunged and ex-sponged from the mind. In reply to these powerful arguments, the main points urged are the authority of the fathers of the church and the undoubtedly intense instinctive clinging to life. The latter phenomenon is, however, entirely irrelevant. For though it is a wrench to part with life, which has its charms at the very worst, just as it is to part with a tooth, yet there is no *moral* element in it whatever. As to the Christian tradition, it may be explained by the circumstances of the early Church. For Christianity, the most terribly earnest and most intolerant of religions (see *The Book of Revelations of St. John the Divine*)—and it remained so until diluted with civilization—recognized no morality as worthy of an instant's consideration except Christian morality. Now the early Church had need of martyrs, i.e., witnesses, and if any man had done with life, it was abominable infidelity to leave it otherwise than as a witness to its power. This belief, then, should be set down as dubitable; and it will no sooner have been pronounced dubitable, than Reason will stamp it as false.

The Scotch School appears to have no such distinction concerning the limitations of indubitability and the consequent limitations of the jurisdiction of original belief.

Character IV. By all odds, the most distinctive character of the Critical Common-sensist, in contrast to the old Scotch philosopher, lies in his insistence that the acritically indubitable is invariably vague.

Logicians have been at fault in giving Vagueness the go-by, so far as not even to analyze it. The present writer has done his best to work out the Stechiology (or Stoicheiology), Critic, and Methodeutic of the subject, but can here only give a definition or two with some proposals respecting terminology.

Accurate writers have apparently made a distinction between the *definite* and the *determinate*. A subject is *determinate* in respect to any character which inheres in it or is (universally and affirmatively) predicated of it, as well as in respect to the negative of such character, these being the very same respect. In all other respects it is *indeterminate*. The *definite* shall be defined presently. A sign (under which designation I place every kind of thought, and not alone external signs) that is in any respect objectively indeterminate (i.e., whose object is undetermined by the sign itself) is objectively *general* in so far as it extends to the interpreter the privilege of carrying its determination further.[7] *Example:* "Man is mortal." To the question, What man? the reply is that the proposition explicitly leaves it to you to apply its assertion to what man or men you will. A sign that is objectively indeterminate in any respect is objectively *vague* in so far as it reserves further determination to be made in some other conceivable sign, or at least does not appoint the interpreter as its deputy in this office. *Example:* "A man whom I could mention seems to be a little conceited." The *suggestion* here is that the man in view is the person addressed; but the utterer does not authorize such an interpretation or *any* other application of what she says. She can still say, if she likes, that

[7] Hamilton and a few other logicians understood the subject of a universal proposition in the collective sense; but every person who is well-read in logic is familiar with many passages in which the leading logicians explain with an iteration that would be superfluous if all readers were intelligent, that such a subject is distributively, not collectively, general. A term denoting a collection is singular, and such a term is an "abstraction" or product of the operation of hypostatic abstraction as truly as is the name of the essence. "Mankind" is quite as much an abstraction and *ens rationis* as is "humanity." Indeed, every object of a conception is either a signate individual or some kind of indeterminate individual. Nouns in the plural are usually distributive and general; common nouns in the singular are usually indefinite.

she does *not* mean the person addressed. Every utterance naturally leaves the right of further exposition in the utterer; and therefore, in so far as a sign is indeterminate, it is vague, unless it is expressly or by a well-understood convention rendered general. Usually an affirmative predication covers *generally* every essential character of the predicate, while a negative predication *vaguely* denies some essential character. In another sense, honest people, when not joking, intend to make the meaning of their words determinate, so that there shall be no latitude of interpretation at all. That is to say, the character of their meaning consists in the implications and non-implications of their words; and they intend to fix what is implied and what is not implied. They believe that they succeed in doing so, and if their chat is about the theory of numbers, perhaps they may. But the further their topics are from such presciss, or "abstract," subjects, the less possibility is there of such precision of speech. In so far as the implication is not determinate, it is usually left vague; but there are cases where an unwillingness to dwell on disagreeable subjects causes the utterer to leave the determination of the implication to the interpreter; as if one says, "That creature is filthy, in every sense of the term."

Perhaps a more scientific pair of definitions would be that anything is *general* in so far as the principle of excluded middle does not apply to it and is *vague* in so far as the principle of contradiction does not apply to it. Thus, although it is true that "Any proposition you please, *once you have determined its identity*, is either true or false"; yet *so long as it remains indeterminate and so without identity*, it need neither be true that any proposition you please is true, nor that any proposition you please is false. So likewise, while it is false that "A proposition *whose identity I have determined* is both true and false," yet until it is determinate, it may be true that a proposition is true and that a proposition is false.

In those respects in which a sign is not vague, it is said to be *definite*, and also with a slightly different mode of application, to be *precise*, a meaning probably due to *præcisus* having been applied to curt denials and refusals.

It has been the well-established, ordinary sense of *precise* since the Plantagenets; and it were much to be desired that this word, with its derivatives *precision*, *precisive*, etc., should, in the dialect of philosophy, be restricted to this sense. To express the act of *rendering precise* (though usually only in reference to numbers, dates, and the like), the French have the verb *préciser*, which, after the analogy of *décider*, should have been *précider*. Would it not be a useful addition to our English terminology of logic to adopt the verb *to precide*, to express the general sense, to render precise? Our older logicians with salutary boldness seem to have created for their service the verb *to prescind*, the corresponding Latin word meaning only to "cut off at the end," while the English word means to suppose without supposing some more or less determinately indicated accompaniment. In geometry, for example, we "prescind" shape from color, which is precisely the same thing as to "abstract" color from shape, although very many writers employ the verb "to abstract" so as to make it the equivalent of "prescind." But whether it was the invention or the courage of our philosophical ancestors which exhausted itself in the manufacture of the verb "prescind," the curious fact is that instead of forming from it the noun *prescission*, they took pattern from the French logicians in putting the word *precision* to this second use. About the same time[8] (see Watts, *Logick*, 1725, I, vi, 9 *ad fin.*) the adjective *precisive* was introduced to signify what *prescissive* would have more unmistakably conveyed. If we desire to rescue the good ship Philosophy for the service of Science from the hands of lawless rovers of the sea of literature, we shall do well to keep prescind, presciss, prescission, and prescissive on the one hand, to refer to dissection in hypothesis, while precide, precise, precision, and precisive are used so as to refer exclusively to an expression of determination which is made either full or free for the interpreter. We shall thus do much to relieve the stem "abstract" from stag-

---

[8] But unfortunately it has not been in the writer's power to consult the *Oxford Dictionary* concerning these words; so that probably some of the statements in the text might be corrected with the aid of that work.

gering under the double burden of conveying the idea of prescission as well as the unrelated and very important idea of the creation of *ens rationis* out of an *épos pteróen* [winged discourse]—to filch the phrase to furnish a name for an expression of non-substantive thought—an operation that has been treated as a subject of ridicule—this hypostatic abstraction—but which gives mathematics half its power.

The purely formal conception that the three affections of terms, *determination, generality,* and *vagueness,* form a group dividing a category of what Kant calls "functions of judgment" will be passed by as unimportant by those who have yet to learn how important a part purely formal conceptions may play in philosophy. Without stopping to discuss this, it may be pointed out that the "quantity" of propositions in logic, that is, the distribution of the *first* subject,[9] is either *singular* (that is, determinate, which renders it substantially negligible in formal logic), or *universal* (that is, general), or *particular* (as the mediæval logicians say, that is, vague or *indefinite*). It is a curious fact that in the logic of relations it is the first and last quantifiers of a proposition that are of chief importance. To affirm of anything that it is a horse is to yield to it *every* essential character of a horse; to deny of anything that it is a horse is vaguely to refuse to it *some* one or more of those essential characters of the horse. There are, however, predicates that are unanalyzable in a given state of intelligence and experience. These are, therefore, determinately affirmed or denied. Thus, this same group of concepts reappears. Affirmation and denial are in themselves unaffected by these concepts, but it is to be remarked that there are cases in which we can have an apparently definite idea of a border line between affirmation and negation. Thus, a point of a

[9] Thus returning to the writer's original nomenclature, in despite of *The Monist* VII, where an obviously defective argument was regarded as sufficient to determine a mere matter of terminology. But the Quality of propositions is there regarded from a point of view which seems extrinsic. I have not had time, however, to re-explore all the ramifications of this difficult question by the aid of existential graphs, and the statement in the text about the last quantifier may need modification.

surface may be in a region of that surface, or out of it, or on its boundary. This gives us an indirect and vague conception of an intermediary between affirmation and denial in general, and consequently of an intermediate, or nascent state, between determination and indetermination. There must be a similar intermediacy between generality and vagueness. Indeed, in an article in the seventh volume of *The Monist*[10] there lies just beneath the surface of what is explicitly said, the idea of an endless series of such *intermediacies*. We shall find below some application for these reflections.

Character V. The Critical Common-sensist will be further distinguished from the old Scotch philosopher by the great value he attaches to doubt, provided only that it be the weighty and noble metal itself, and no counterfeit nor paper substitute. He is not content to ask himself whether he does doubt, but he invents a plan for attaining to doubt, elaborates it in detail, and then puts it into practice, although this may involve a solid month of hard work; and it is only after having gone through such an examination that he will pronounce a belief to be indubitable. Moreover, he fully acknowledges that even then it may be that some of his indubitable beliefs may be proved false.

The Critical Common-sensist holds that there is less danger to heuretic science in believing too little than in believing too much. Yet for all that, the consequences to heuretics of believing too little may be no less than disaster.

Character VI. Critical Common-sensism may fairly lay claim to this title for two sorts of reasons; namely, that on the one hand it subjects four opinions to rigid criticism: its own; that of the Scotch School; that of those who would base logic or metaphysics on psychology or any other special science, the least tenable of all the philosophical opinions that have any vogue; and that of Kant; while on the other hand it has besides some claim to be called Critical

[10] C. S. Peirce, "The Logic of Relatives," *The Monist*, Vol. 7 (1897), pp. 161–217. This is a critical review of E. Schröder's *Algebra und Logik der Relative*, in which Peirce shows his own method of drawing graphs in the logic of relations.—Editor's note.

from the fact that it is but a modification of Kantism. The present writer was a pure Kantist until he was forced by successive steps into Pragmaticism. The Kantist has only to abjure from the bottom of his heart the proposition that a thing-in-itself can, however indirectly, be conceived; and then correct the details of Kant's doctrine accordingly, and he will find himself to have become a Critical Commonsensist.

Another doctrine which is involved in Pragmaticism as an essential consequence of it, but which the writer defended (*North American Review,* Vol. CXIII, pp. 449–472, 1871) before he had formulated, even in his own mind, the principle of pragmaticism, is the scholastic doctrine of realism. This is usually defined as the opinion that there are real objects that are general, among the number being the modes of determination of existent singulars, if, indeed, these be not the only such objects. But the belief in this can hardly escape being accompanied by the acknowledgment that there are, besides, real *vagues,* and especially real possibilities. For possibility being the denial of a necessity, which is a kind of generality, is vague like any other contradiction of a general. Indeed, it is the reality of some possibilities that pragmaticism is most concerned to insist upon. The article of January 1878[11] endeavored to gloze over this point as unsuited to the exoteric public addressed; or perhaps the writer wavered in his own mind. He said that if a diamond were to be formed in a bed of cotton-wool, and were to be consumed there without ever having been pressed upon by any hard edge or point, it would be merely a question of nomenclature whether that diamond should be said to have been hard or not. No doubt this is true, except for the abominable falsehood in the word "merely," implying that symbols are unreal. Nomenclature involves classification; and classification is true or false, and the generals to which it refers are either reals in the one case, or figments in the other. For if the reader will turn to the original maxim of pragmaticism at the be-

[11] See "How to Make Our Ideas Clear," Selection 6, p. 113, above. For the 1871 article see Selection 4.

ginning of this article, he will see that the question is, not what *did* happen, but whether it would have been well to engage in any line of conduct whose successful issue depended upon whether that diamond *would* resist an attempt to scratch it, or whether all other logical means of determining how it ought to be classed *would* lead to the conclusion which, to quote the very words of that article, would be "the belief which alone could be the result of investigation carried *sufficiently far*." Pragmaticism makes the ultimate intellectual purport of what you please to consist in conceived conditional resolutions, or their substance; and therefore, the conditional propositions, with their hypothetical antecedents, in which such resolutions consist, being of the ultimate nature of meaning, must be capable of being true, that is, of expressing whatever there be which is such as the proposition expresses, independently of being thought to be so in any judgment, or being represented to be so in any other symbol of any man or men. But that amounts to saying that possibility is sometimes of a real kind.

Fully to understand this, it will be needful to analyze modality, and ascertain in what it consists. In the simplest case, the most subjective meaning, if a person does not know that a proposition is false, he calls it *possible*. If, however, he knows that it is *true*, it is much more than possible. Restricting the word to its characteristic applicability, a state of things has the Modality of the possible— that is, of the merely possible—only in case the contradictory state of things is likewise possible, which proves possibility to be the vague modality. One who knows that Harvard University has an office in State Street, Boston, and has impression that it is at No. 30, but yet suspects that 50 is the number, would say, "I think it is at No. 30, but it *may be* at No. 50," or "it *is possibly* at No. 50." Thereupon, another, who does not doubt his recollection, might chime in, "It *actually is* at No. 50," or simply "it *is* at No. 50," or "it *is* at No. 50, *de inesse*." Thereupon, the person who had first asked what the number was might say, "Since you are so positive, it *must be* at No. 50," for "I know the first figure is 5. So, since you are both certain the second is a 0, why 50 it *necessarily is*." That is to say, in this most subjective kind of Modality, that which is known by direct recollection is in the Mode of *Actuality,* the determinate mode. But when knowledge is indeterminate among alternatives, either there is one state of things which alone accords with them all, when this is in the Mode of *Necessity,* or there is more than one state of things that no knowledge excludes, when each of these is in the Mode of *Possibility.*

Other kinds of subjective Modality refer to a Sign or Representamen which is assumed to be true, but which does not include the Utterer's (i.e., the speaker's, writer's, thinker's, or other symbolizer's) total knowledge, the different Modes being distinguished very much as above. There are other cases, however, in which, justifiably or not, we certainly think of Modality as objective. A man says, "I *can* go to the seashore if I like." Here is implied, to be sure, his ignorance of how he will decide to act. But this is not the point of the assertion. It is that the complete determination of conduct in the *act* not yet having taken place, the further determination of it belongs to the subject of the action regardless of external circumstances. If he had said, "I *must* go where my employers may send me," it would imply that the function of such further determination lay elsewhere. In "You *may* do so and so," and "You *must* do so," the "may" has the same force as "can," except that in the one case freedom from particular circumstances is in question, and in the other freedom from a law or edict. Hence the phrase, "You *may* if you *can.*" I must say that it is difficult for me to preserve my respect for the competence of a philosopher whose dull logic, not penetrating beneath the surface, leaves him to regard such phrases as misrepresentations of the truth. So an act of hypostatic abstraction which in itself is no violation of logic, however it may lend itself to a dress of superstition, may regard the collective tendencies to variableness in the world, under the name of Chance, as at one time having their way, and at another time overcome by the element of order; so that, for example, a superstitious cashier, impressed by a bad dream, may say to himself of a Monday morning, "*May be,* the

bank has been robbed." No doubt, he recognizes his total
ignorance in the matter. But besides that, he has in mind
the absence of any particular cause which should protect
his bank more than others that are robbed from time to
time. He thinks of the variety in the universe as vaguely
analogous to the indecision of a person, and borrows from
that analogy the garb of his thought. At the other extreme
stand those who declare as inspired (for they have no
rational proof of what they allege) that an actuary's advice
to an insurance company is based on nothing at all but
ignorance.

There is another example of objective possibility: "A pair
of intersecting rays, i.e., unlimited straight lines conceived
as movable objects, *can* (or *may*) move, without ceasing
to intersect, so that one and the same hyperboloid shall be
completely covered by the track of each of them." How
shall we interpret this, remembering that the object spoken
of, the pair of rays, is a pure creation of the Utterer's imagination, although it is required (and, indeed, forced) to
conform to the laws of space? Some minds will be better
satisfied with a more subjective, or nominalistic, others with
a more objective, realistic interpretation. But it must be
confessed on all hands that whatever degree or kind of
reality belongs to pure space belongs to the substance
of that proposition, which merely expresses a property of
space.

Let us now take up the case of that diamond which,
having been crystallized upon a cushion of jeweler's cotton,
was accidentally consumed by fire before the crystal of corundum that had been sent for had had time to arrive, and
indeed without being subjected to any other pressure than
that of the atmosphere and its own weight. The question
is, was that diamond *really* hard? It is certain that no dis-
cernible *actual* fact determined it to be so. But is its hardness not, nevertheless, a *real* fact? To say, as the article of
January 1878 seems to intend, that it is just as an arbitrary
"usage of speech" chooses to arrange its thoughts, is as
much as to decide against the reality of the property, since
the real is that which is such as it is regardless of how it is,
at any time, thought to be. Remember that this diamond's

condition is not an isolated fact. There is no such thing; and an isolated fact could hardly be real. It is an unsevered, though presciss part of the unitary fact of nature. Being a diamond, it was a mass of pure carbon, in the form of a more or less transparent crystal (brittle, and of facile octahedral cleavage, unless it was of an unheard-of variety), which, if not trimmed after one of the fashions in which diamonds may be trimmed, took the shape of an octahedron, apparently regular (I need not go into minutiæ), with grooved edges, and probably with some curved faces. Without being subjected to any considerable pressure, it could be found to be insoluble, very highly refractive, showing under radium rays (and perhaps under "dark light" and X-rays) a peculiar bluish phosphorescence, having as high a specific gravity as realgar or orpiment, and giving off during its combustion less heat than any other form of carbon would have done. From some of these properties hardness is believed to be inseparable. For like it they bespeak the high polemerization of the molecule. But however this may be, how can the hardness of all other diamonds fail to bespeak *some* real relation among the diamonds without which a piece of carbon would not be a diamond? Is it not a monstrous perversion of the word and concept *real* to say that the accident of the non-arrival of the corundum prevented the hardness of the diamond from having the *reality* which it otherwise, with little doubt, would have had?

At the same time, we must dismiss the idea that the occult state of things (be it a relation among atoms or something else), which constitutes the reality of a diamond's hardness, can possibly consist in anything but in the truth of a general conditional proposition. For to what else does the entire teaching of chemistry relate except to the "behavior" of different possible kinds of material substance? And in what does that behavior consist except that if a substance of a certain kind should be exposed to an agency of a certain kind, a certain kind of sensible result *would* ensue, according to our experiences hitherto. As for the pragmaticist, it is precisely his position that nothing else than this can be so much as *meant* by saying that an object possesses a character. He is therefore obliged to subscribe to the doctrine of a real Modality, including real Necessity and real Possibility.

A good question, for the purpose of illustrating the nature of Pragmaticism, is, What is Time? It is not proposed to attack those most difficult problems connected with the psychology, the epistemology, or the metaphysics of Time, although it will be taken for granted, as it must be according to what has been said, that Time is real. The reader is only invited to the humbler question of what we mean by Time, and not of every kind of meaning attached to Past, Present, and Future either. Certain peculiar feelings are associated with the three general determinations of Time; but those are to be sedulously put out of view. That the reference of events to Time is irresistible will be recognized; but as to how it may differ from other kinds of irresistibility is a question not here to be considered. The question to be considered is simply, What is the intellectual purport of the Past, Present, and Future? It can only be treated with the utmost brevity.

That Time is a particular variety of objective Modality is too obvious for argumentation. The Past consists of the sum of *faits accomplis*, and this Accomplishment is the Existential Mode of Time. For the Past really acts upon us, and *that* it does, not at all in the way in which a Law or Principle influences us, but precisely as an Existent object acts. For instance, when a *Nova Stella* bursts out in the heavens, it acts upon one's eyes just as a light struck in the dark by one's own hands would; and yet it is an event which happened before the Pyramids were built. A neophyte may remark that its reaching the eyes, which is all we know, happens but a fraction of a second before we know it. But a moment's consideration will show him that he is losing sight of the question, which is not whether the distant Past can act upon us *immediately*, but whether it acts upon us just as any Existent does. The instance adduced (certainly a commonplace enough fact) proves conclusively that the mode of the Past is that of Actuality. Nothing of the sort is true of the Future, to compass the understanding of which it is indispensable that the reader should divest himself of his Necessitarianism—at best, but a scientific theory—and return to the Common-sense State of Nature. Do you never say to yourself, "I *can* do this or that as well tomorrow as today"? Your Necessitarianism is a theoretical pseudo-belief—a make-believe belief—that such a sentence does not express the real truth. That is only to stick to proclaiming the unreality of that Time, of which you are invited, be it reality or figment, to consider the meaning. You need not fear to compromise your darling theory by looking out at its windows. Be it true in theory or not, the unsophisticated conception is that everything in the Future is either *destined*, i.e., necessitated already, or is *undecided*, the contingent future of Aristotle. In other words, it is not Actual, since it does not act except through the idea of it, that is, as a law acts; but is either Necessary or Possible, which are of the same mode since (as remarked above) Negation being outside the category of modality cannot produce a variation in Modality. As for the Present instant, it is so inscrutable that I wonder whether no skeptic has ever attacked its reality. I can fancy one of them dipping his pen in his blackest ink to commence the assault, and then suddenly reflecting that his entire life is in the Present—the "living present," as we say, this instant when all hopes and fears concerning it come to their end, this Living Death in which we are born anew. It is plainly that Nascent State between the Determinate and the Indeterminate that was noticed above.

Pragmaticism consists in holding that the purport of any concept is its conceived bearing upon our conduct. How, then, does the Past bear upon conduct? The answer is self-evident: whenever we set out to do anything, we "go upon," we base our conduct on facts already known, and for these we can only draw upon our memory. It is true that we may institute a new investigation for the purpose; but its discoveries will only become applicable to conduct after they have been made and reduced to a memorial maxim. In short, the Past is the storehouse of all our knowledge.

When we say that we know that some state of things exists, we mean that it used to exist, whether just long enough for the news to reach the brain and be retransmitted to tongue or pen, or longer ago. Thus, from whatever point of view we contemplate the Past, it appears as the Existential Mode of Time.

How does the Future bear upon conduct? The answer is that future facts are the only facts that we can, in a measure, control; and whatever there may be in the Future that is not amenable to control are the things that we *shall* be able to infer, or *should* be able to infer, under favorable circumstances. There may be questions concerning which the pendulum of opinion never would cease to oscillate, however favorable circumstances may be. But if so, those questions are *ipso facto* not *real* questions, that is to say, are questions to which there is no true answer to be given. It is natural to use the future tense (and the conditional mood is but a mollified future) in drawing a conclusion or in stating a consequence. "If two unlimited straight lines in one plane and crossed by a third making the sum . . . then these straight lines *will* meet on the side, etc." It cannot be denied that acritical inferences may refer to the Past in its capacity as past; but according to Pragmaticism, the conclusion of a Reasoning power must refer to the Future. For its meaning refers to conduct, and since it is a reasoned conclusion, must refer to deliberate conduct, which is controllable conduct. But the only controllable conduct is Future conduct. As for that part of the Past that lies beyond memory, the Pragmaticist doctrine is that the meaning of its being believed to be in connection with the Past consists in the acceptance as truth of the conception that we ought to conduct ourselves according to it (like the meaning of any other belief). Thus, a belief that Christopher Columbus discovered America really refers to the future.[12] It is more difficult, it must be confessed, to account for beliefs that rest upon the double evidence of feeble but direct memory and upon rational

[12] In order to *verify* this belief, one will consult documents, etc. Such future acts of *verification,* the critics of Peirce can say, do not obviate the reference to the past in the *meaning* of the proposition "Columbus discovered America."—Editor's note.

inference. The difficulty does not seem insuperable; but it must be passed by.

What is the bearing of the Present instant upon conduct?

Introspection is wholly a matter of inference.[13] One is immediately conscious of his Feelings, no doubt; but not that they are feelings of an *ego*. The *self* is only inferred. There is no time in the Present for any inference at all, least of all for inference concerning that very instant. Consequently, the present object must be an external object, if there be any objective reference in it. The attitude of the Present is either conative or perceptive. Supposing it to be perceptive, the perception must be immediately known as external—not indeed in the sense in which a hallucination is *not* external, but in the sense of being present regardless of the perceiver's will or wish. Now this kind of externality is conative externality. Consequently, the attitude of the present instant (according to the testimony of Common Sense, which is plainly adopted throughout) can only be a Conative attitude. The consciousness of the present is then that of a struggle over what shall be; and thus we emerge from the study with a confirmed belief that it is the Nascent State of the Actual.

But how is Temporal Modality distinguished from other Objective Modality? Not by any general character since Time is unique and *sui generis.* In other words, there is only one Time. Sufficient attention has hardly been called to the surpassing truth of this for Time as compared with its truth for Space. Time, therefore, can only be identified by brute compulsion. But we must not go further.

[13] See above, "Questions Concerning Certain Faculties Claimed for Man," Selection 2, Question 4, pp. 32–33.

Lessons from
the History of
Scientific Thought

12. Lessons of the History of Science[1]

[That the life of science is essentially a mode of inquiry is affirmed in the very first page of Peirce's unpublished *History of Science;* the Introduction starts with a bow to Francis Bacon's distinction between science as a body of *results* and science as a *method* of discovery:

Lord Bacon remarks that "the sciences, as we now have them, are nothing but certain orderly arrangements of things previously discovered; not methods of discovery, or schemes for obtaining new results" (*Novum Organum,* lib.1, aph.8). This is a first anticipation of the contrast between the way in which an active science appears to any devotee of it and to one who has a general reader's and a news-devourer's interest in the more striking of the discoveries that are from time to time announced. The latter person, if he happens to be a lexicographer, will insist upon defining science as an "organized body of knowledge"; while for the former, science is a mode of life, like the profession of priest, or practicing physician, or active politician; and that which distinguishes the life of science, in the eyes of the scientific man, is not the *attainment* of knowledge, but a single-minded absorption in the *search* for it for its own

[1] Selections 12 to 16 inclusive are from the Widener Library Archives, Peirce MSS, by permission of the Philosophy Department of Harvard University. Copyright by the President and Fellows of Harvard College.

sake—a single-mindedness that forgets every theory the moment the facts of observation appear against it. It is in this sense of the *search after knowledge for its own sake* that this book endeavors to sketch the history of science. No study is excluded, no matter how unsuccessful, provided it was animated by the love of truth for truth's sake. This history is not confined, therefore, to the sciences of external nature. Psychology, archeology, linguistics, history are to be included. So also are pure mathematics, logic, and metaphysics. Our boundary line is run between the pursuit of knowledge for the sake of knowledge alone and the pursuit of knowledge for some ulterior motive, material utility, the support of religion and morality, or the attainment of any other end whatever. For that which the author had at heart throughout his studies of the history of science was to gain an understanding of the whole logic of every pathway to the truth. . . .

Another set of notes (in the Widener archives at Harvard), lying next to the manuscript of the incomplete two volumes sketched by Peirce for his *History of Science,* is an outline of no less than twenty-nine "Lessons of the History of Science." Again, Peirce here rejects the common notion that science is simply "systematic knowledge" as the etymologist would maintain. "In seeking definitions no guide is more treacherous than etymology," he tells us in a communication to the editor of *Science* on "How Did Science Originate?" Science has changed places historically with philosophy, which in ancient times was the love and quest for truth; but "it is science today that is incessantly engaged in struggles to learn the truth, leaving treatises with rounded systematization to the philosophers."

The very first lesson to be learned from the history of science is that the ultimate aim of science "to educe the truth by close observation" is motivated by a sense of wonder or intellectual curiosity. The Egyptians practiced geometry only to aid their tax collectors to measure lands inundated by the overflowing Nile. They knew that a 3, 4, 5 triangle has a right angle, but they never asked the general question raised and answered by the Pythagoreans in the Greek colonies: What is the relationship among the three sides of *any* right triangle? The reader may properly ask what geometry or pure mathematics in general has to do with "close observation," which Peirce made essential to the definition of science. His answer is that "Observation is here used in the broad sense of attention to that which forces itself upon consciousness; and thus this definition of science (the business whose ultimate aim is to educe the truth by close observation) covers mathematics. For mathematics consists in constructing diagrams (continuous in geometry, arrays of signs in algebra) according to general precepts and then observing in the parts of these diagrams relations not explicitly required in the precepts. All necessary reasoning depends upon such observations, a fact which could easily escape attention as long as logicians studied only syllogistic reasoning, where there is but one conclusion from given premises, which may be produced from them by a machine, but which becomes very obvious in the logic of relatives, where any premise whatever will yield an endless series of conclusions, and attention has to be directed to the particular conclusion desired." Now whether Peirce is or is not stretching the use of "observation" too far is a semantic question for philosophers of mathematics and empirical science, but it is clear that Peirce is claiming that, as a matter of historical fact, disinterested observation and curiosity widen the domain of things and relations to be "observed."

His second lesson states that the imagination of the ancient Babylonians was a help rather than a hindrance to their surpassing the Egyptians and even the early Greeks in discovering general truths in geometry, algebra, and astronomy, "the queen of the sciences." Recent research, especially by Otto Neugebauer, has shown to what a remarkable extent the Babylonian cuneiform tablets reveal general solutions to geometrical problems, to quadratic equations, and to astronomical theories. There is much astrological myth-making accompanying their close observations and records of celestial phenomena (e.g., Ishtar, the Goddess of Love, governs the motions of Venus, as other deities govern the other planets and stars), but Peirce points up the historical lesson that any people devoid of poetic imagination and free play of ideas are also lacking in the power to make scientific advances, for such advances require hypotheses or novel ways of seeing relations.

Peirce, above all other logicians in his time, emphasized the role of hypothesis in scientific method, calling the construction of such possible explanations of puzzling phenomena by the name Abduction, which he added to the conventional forms of reasoning known as Deduction and Induction, thus giving us three types of inference. His six essays in the *Popular Science Monthly* of 1876–1878, "Illustrations of the Logic of Science," show how he expounded the logical form and function of Deduction, Induction, and Abduction (sometimes called by Peirce Retroduction), and their interplay in actual problem-solving. It is significant that Peirce regarded the first two of these essays on "The Fixation of Belief" and "How to Make Our Ideas Clear" as the first enunciation of his pragmatism, which he later called "pragmaticism" in order to emphasize his aim to base philosophy on logical rather than on psychological analyses, such as we find in James, F. S. C. Schiller, Bergson, Dewey, and others known as pragmatists.

The selection from Peirce's unpublished Lowell Lectures on the History of Science, entitled "Kepler," illustrates the eleventh Lesson of "Kepler's Logic" in which astrology gave way to what Peirce regarded as the most ingenious use of abductive and inductive reasoning in the history of science, leading to the famous three laws of planetary motion, the first being that the ellipse was the best hypothesis (after Kepler had imaginatively tried nineteen other mathematical possibilities) with which to describe the paths of the planets, with the sun at one of the foci of the ellipse. Kepler's Second Law—that the planets sweep over equal areas in equal times, so that they are accelerated as they swing around the sun—made it possible for Newton to introduce a gravitational force between the sun and the planets, a force whose mathematical formula (Newton's inverse square law) generalizes Kepler's Third Law (the constant ratio between the square of the time of revolution and the cube of the distance of a planet from the sun).

Newton's universal law exemplifies the cumulative continuity of scientific advance. It brought together the Galilean laws of terrestrial motion of falling bodies and the Keplerian laws of planetary motion, and thus removed the formidable block to a unified view of nature rent asunder by the Aristotelian and Scholastic principle of "violent" (sublunar) *versus* "natural" (eternal superlunar) motions. "Do not block the road to inquiry" is the ninth Lesson of the History of Science, and the slogan of all experimental and theoretical inquiry.

Peirce gives only the titles of some of the other Lessons which he listed in his unfinished work and unrealized "Plan for a History of Science." Most of these Lessons were developed in articles and notes for his compendious *Grand Logic* and *Principles of Philosophy*.

Lesson 14 was to show the success of modern mathematics as due to Generalization and Abstraction, with illustrations from the history of Projective Geometry, Theory of Functions, Non-Euclidean Geometry, Galois' Theory of Groups, and Sadi Carnot's Thermodynamics.

Lesson 15 states the Rule of Predesignation for the logic of inductive probability, theory of errors, etc.

Lesson 16 is headed "Prominence of Nominalism (Ockham's razor)" and was to be illustrated by the history of historical criticism, Egyptology, Dr. Thomas Young's linguistic and optical theories; the next Lesson was the neglect by "critics" to observe appropriate probabilities of generalizations like the corpuscular and wave theories of light.

Lesson 19 is on Residual Phenomena and the history of the steam engine, and Lesson 20 asserts that "means of observation create science": history of telegraph and medicine (dispute about the priority of the discovery of ether as an anesthetic), the history of mathematics (1848–1898), e.g., Topology, Transcendental Geometry, Modern Algebra, Logic of Relatives, Groups, etc.

Lesson 21 was to show that the history of metaphysics (1848–1898) aped mathematics insofar as metaphysicians assumed that "existence does not embrace all reality."

Lesson 22 points to the "Evolutionary view of the history of science," to be illustrated by the history of psychology, inductive philology, anthropology, and archeology, the history of physics (the Mechanical Theory of Heat, Law of the Conservation of Energy, Mendeleef's Law of the Periodic Order of the Chemical Elements), and the history of machinery and social combination.

Lesson 23: "Do not trifle with facts": Telepathy and Spiritualism.

Lesson 24: "Advantage of extending the methods of one science to another."

Lesson 25: "The Littleness of Science."

Lesson 27: "Economics of Research."[2]

Lesson 29: "Prospect of the Decadence of Intellect."

These Lessons of the History of Science must not be interpreted as implying that Peirce thought them the sole basis of the logic and philosophy of science. Although he shared with many nineteenth-century thinkers an historical and evolutionary approach to all natural and social phenomena, he was also aware of the "genetic fallacy" of confusing origins with validity. One could not make clear the foundations of exact thought by invoking the less clear and much more questionable ideas of psychology, social ideology, or "dialectical laws" of historical necessity. Convinced that even in physical sciences the reign of mechanical necessity was over, Peirce could hardly accept historical necessity. He always offers historical statements as examples of the use of hypotheses in abductive or retroductive reasoning, never yielding more than a weak probability as compared to scientific induction.]

[2] Peirce had written a "Note on the Theory of the Economy of Research" for the U. S. Coast Survey (Report of 1879, pp. 197–201), and claimed priority for the idea over Mach.

13. Lowell Lectures on the History
of Science (1892)

Ancient Science

What is the oldest scientific book in the world? I should be perplexed to answer. The Babylonian theory of creation, which is embodied in the earlier chapters of the book of Genesis, must, no doubt, be very old. And though it is sheer guesswork, [it] should I think be considered as a scientific production. Tennyson says

> maybe wildest dreams
> Are but the needful preludes of the truth.

But I would doubt the *maybe*. Wildest dreams *are* the necessary first steps toward scientific investigation. Perhaps, then, the cosmogony-book which was translated by George Smith from the Babylonian bricks is the earliest of scientific works. For I should not call the works of magic scientific. There is no conscious prying into things, no research, there. And as for early medicine it is but part and parcel of magic. But if by the oldest scientific book be meant the oldest book which conveys *truths*, the product of a real scientific research, I think we must name the *Arithmetic* of Aahmes. This is an Egyptian papyrus. The very copy we have was made under the Shepherd King, Apophis, no less than seventeen hundred years before Christ. That is, it was more years older than the Ptolemaic system of astronomy as this system is old today. A third such period of time would carry us back to the Great Pyramid.

This book of Aahmes professes to be based upon an older work of the date of the Pyramid. But such statements are attached to almost all Egyptian books, for the Egyptians were convinced that their early ancestors had knowledge far superior to their own. Since they thought so, I think we must allow it probably so, for they were in a better position to judge of this matter than we are. Besides, I know of no people who have entertained such an idea wrongly. I think if mind has an upward movement, it must feel it. Still, I grant that they might be deceived by the superior workmanship and the gigantic scale of the Pyramid, which when still unscathed, as it remained down to a few centuries ago, must have had an air of awful superiority.

But though we have no reason to suppose the book of Aahmes was really based on another as old as the Pyramid, there can be no reasonable doubt that it was based on others which doubtless formed a series going back five hundred or more [years]. This *Arithmetic* therefore represents a state of science nearly as old as our Constellations.

This book is not very methodical. Of course, methodical exposition always comes late. In fact, it marks a decadent period of thought. That is the reason why the great system-makers cannot write their books until age has diminished the fecundity of their thought. The theory that a successful teacher ought to be within the age of military service is as completely refuted by history as random assertion ever was. We do not expect then to find the *Arithmetic* of Aahmes a systematic treatise. It is little more than a book of examples with some approach to orderly arrangement. There is hardly a general rule contained in it; though the procedure is fairly regular.

It begins with a table for converting fractions having 2 for their numerators into the sums of two or more fractions of unlike denominators. Thus $2/5 = 1/3 + 1/15$. What is the object of this truth? you will ask. It is that the Egyptians were accustomed to speak of $1/3$ and $1/15$ instead of $2/5$, of $1/2$ and $1/10$ instead of $3/5$, and so forth. Two-thirds was the only fraction in common use except those with numerator 1. This was so in all ages of Egyptian history. It seems to have been a necessity of their language. Thus, the eminent mathematician Ptolemy, in the second century of our era, always in place of 5/6 speaks of 1/2 [and] 1/3. Of course, they must have been able to conceive of two equal fractions being added together, or else they would not have known addition of fractions at all, or else not how to count, for wanting the addition of equal things. Still, it no doubt appeared abstruse to their minds strongly habituated to another way of thinking. And if language gave their minds this curious kink, that language was after all the product of the national mind. Somehow then it did not come natural to them to think of the aggregation of things without thinking of the differences of the things aggregated. We meet now with minds so feeble in that direction as to say, and even print, that nothing can be in relation to itself. If we speak of adding say the Egyptians, the things added must differ.

It is difficult to imagine a more striking mark of an imagination not pliant to the requirements of mathematics. In fact, it is very remarkable that the Egyptians, though they were such splendid engineers, did nothing for the science of mechanics, but used and have used from the beginnings of history till now the rudest contrivances only; and though they were, perforce, owing to the annual inundations of the

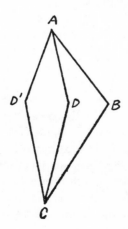

land, the first surveyors, yet their mensuration was most crude. When Aahmes wants to find the area of a field, his invariable proceeding is to multiply the mean of the two opposite sides by the mean of the other two opposite sides. This involves the absurdity that four sticks hinged together to make a plane quadrilateral make a quadrilateral of constant area no matter how much they may turn on their hinges, A B C D being made equal to A B C D'.

We also find that Aahmes calculates as if the ratio of the circumference to the diameter were 3 13/81. History hardly affords us a worse determination of that quantity. The only one much worse is that which comes to us under the sanction of Holy Writ. For we are told that Solomon's brazen sea was 10 cubits in diameter and 30 cubits in circumference. That is the measure of the wisdom of Solomon. If he [Aahmes] had known that the circumference was nearly 3 1/7 diameters, or 3 11/81, he surely would not have reckoned it as 3 13/81 or about 3 8/49. Therefore, he did not know it, and no Egyptian knew it or ever had known it. In fact, no man had ever known it. Some minds will deem that I here go too far. They will say, this thing may very well have been known to the Pyramid builders without being known to Aahmes who lived some two thousand years later, after many and many revolutions, and toward the close of Egypt's Dark Ages. Well! perhaps so. But I do not think if this easily stated and important seeming fact, the circumference is 3 1/7 diameters nearly, had ever been known, it would have failed to spread among all civilized peoples and to have been handed down to the end of time. . . .

That the Babylonians were an infinitely more scientific people than the Egyptians there can be no manner of dispute. In fact, they had much more of the spirit of research than the Greeks. Their natural disposition to make systematic inquiries is seen by their many centuries of observations they must have made before they could have observed an eclipse on every day of the year and noted the effect upon the life of the monarch. Now we have a record showing that they did do this. . . .

In regard to Babylonian astronomy we are now in possession of considerable information from the labors of a learned Jesuit, Epping, who has read and made out the meaning of a good many observations recorded upon bricks found near the Euphrates.

We know that they made observations of quite surprising accuracy by the simple device of stretching a string so that it should bisect two fixed stars at once, and then noting the time at which a given planet crossed the string. In this way, the places were observed with a high degree of accuracy; and considerable progress was made in predictions.

What they did shows the scientific tendency and vast industry of the Babylonians. What they did not do shows how little a scientific spirit and unwearied industry amounts to without the spark of genius.

I now pass to the Greeks. The earliest scientific man of Greece was Thales the Wise. He was born in Miletus, 640 B.C. and died 548 B.C., age about ninety-two years. He is said to have been of Phoenician descent, a merchant and to have conversed with Egyptian priests. In his day Egypt was a place of resort for Greek merchants.

The most remarkable thing told of him is that he foretold an eclipse of the sun, 585 B.C., and that it would be total in a certain place. If he did, he must have learned the fact from Babylonians. It is pretty certain that the eclipse was not total in Miletus where Thales is said to have predicted it. To my mind, it is doubtful whether he did predict it. He, no doubt, first explained to his fellow citizens that solar eclipses are due to the intervention of the moon between earth and sun. And if he said no more, an eclipse happening shortly after and being nearly total would cause people to say, "Why this is just what Thales said." If he did predict the eclipse, which is quite possible, I do not see how he could have known it was going to be total. That requires a very exact knowledge of many different things.

I need hardly say that Thales wrote no book. Consequently, the Greeks themselves did not know precisely what he had accomplished. They knew he was a student of geometry, and being the earliest geometer, any proposition that was very simple they assumed must have been invented by him, without reflecting that he might have learned it from the Egyptians. Thus, Proclus, from whose commentary on Euclid we derive most of our knowledge of early geometry, and who borrowed most of his statements from Geminus, an author of the first century before Christ, tells us that Thales discovered that a circle is bisected by its diameter, a proposition which even Euclid does nothing with proving, for he tacks it on to a definition as a remark, and also that two straight lines that cross each other make the vertical angles equal. But it was the ancient Babylonians who divided the circle into 360 degrees and by the time of Thales that was a perfectly familiar division in Egypt. Now could anybody to whom that division was familiar fail to see that a line which cuts such a circle at points differing by 180 degrees is a diameter? In fact, no point on the circle is distant from another by more than 180 degrees. So the Babylonians and Egyptians must have been perfectly familiar with the fact that a circle is bisected by its diameter. But when that is seen, it must be evident that the vertical angles made by two intersecting lines are equal. For this is seen at once, when a circle is described about the point of crossing as a centre.

I am not by any means a skeptical reader of history. I am disposed to do as the courts of law do, and when the evidence is in, decide according to the testimony. But I really cannot decide that black is white, no matter how concordant the testimony to that effect. Some modern writers have inferred from the statements of Proclus, as well as from other indications, that Thales first made formal demonstrations of propositions, after the fashion of the Greeks.

[Some question] whether he began this wholesome practice [of formal proof], which, however, was carried too far, without entirely effecting its purpose, that of including doubtful propositions. If Thales began this method, for which the Greeks had such a passion, we should, of course, look for his demonstrations among the most awkward. We find it stated, for instance, that the angles at the base of an isosceles triangle are equal was first "set forth and said by" Thales. This is evidently a quotation from a poet and is supposed by Proclus to give the very words of

Thales. Now, everybody sees immediately from the symmetry of the thing (see fig.) that the angles are equal. It is
a triangle with the vertex at the center of a circle, and the
other two on the circumference. It is evident the angles are
equal. But, nevertheless, the Greeks had to *demonstrate* it,
and this Euclid does by means of the singularly awkward
proof, the celebrated *Pons asinorum* [Bridge of asses]

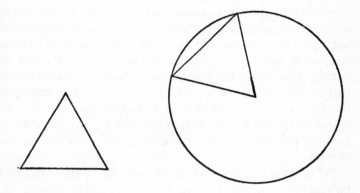

which has made so many boys conclude they have no capacity for Geometry because this proof, the first one of any
difficulty in Euclid, leaves the proposition to their minds
less evident than they found it. It is, perhaps, the most
awkward and ineffective demonstration, not downright fallacious, that ever was given of anything. That is the reason
John Stuart Mill found it especially adapted to illustrate
his theory of reasoning. Now since it is absurd to suppose
that Thales discovered the two angles to be equal, we may
surmise that so much is true, that he gave this demonstration of it. . . .

We now come to one of the greatest names in the history
of science, that of Pythagoras. His life is a touchstone for
methods of historical criticism, for the evidence is manifold,
very contradictory, and decidedly untrustworthy.

Zeller, the well-known historian of philosophy, adopts
rules of evidence, which seem to me very illogical, excludes
all testimony which does not conform to certain artificial
conditions, the result of which is chiefly to cause him to
omit facts of history, which a more intelligent investigation

would regard as sufficiently probable to be admitted into the narrative. What Zeller admits will generally be incontestable. Now what Zeller tells us of Pythagoras is this:

His father's name was Mnesarchus. He was "doubtless" born in the island of Samos. At any rate, that was his home. I will say, however, that Zeller violates his own canons when he says there is *no doubt* he was born there. But an examination of the cases in which Zeller uses the word "doubtless," *zweifellos,* shows that he applies it, not where no doubt is *possible,* but where he accepts a proposition without any evidence, or what *he* considers such. Please remember this. In regard to Pythagoras being born in Samos, if we reject the testimony of those late writers, who had no way that Zeller is certainly aware of, of ascertaining the fact with certainty, whose testimony he calls no evidence at all, then there is no evidence he was born there. But on the other hand, there is some evidence to the contrary.

Zeller goes on. He was "doubtless" born, that is, Zeller indefensibly guesses he was born, say within five or ten years of 582 B.C. And he "doubtless" died within five or ten years of 502 B.C. He *probably* had Pherecydes for a teacher. This Pherecydes lived in Syros, an island well known today to all voyagers in the Aegean. He was a contemporary of Anaximander, who was born 611 B.C. He wrote a book of mythological cosmogony, in which he said that the Creator (identified with the highest heaven), the lower sky, and the earth are the only three eternal things. The Creator to form the universe had first to transform himself into *Eros,* the love-god, etc. This is all that Zeller will admit we know of Pherecydes. Returning to Pythagoras we meet again this gem of criticism: "We cannot pronounce it *impossible* that Pythagoras should have gone to Egypt or Phoenicia or even to Babylon, *but it is on that account all the more undemonstrable.*" Is not this emphatic? "It is more undemonstrable, than if it were impossible." And why? Why, *on that very account;* namely, because it is possible. We have heard of *Credo quia impossible*—"I believe because the thing is impossible"; that is matched by this *Non credo quia possible*—"I reject it because it is too plausible."

Zeller admits that Pythagoras left Samos and went to live in South Italy. This "doubtless" happened within ten or fifteen years of 540 B.C. It seems he has at this time already a high reputation for wisdom. So says Zeller, but I say the reasoning by which he tries to make this out is utterly ridiculous. Zeller's secret reasons for admitting this unfounded idea so readily is that it makes a difficulty in trying to reach any consistent theory of the life of Pythagoras, and thus he hopes to save his canons which will yield no such theory from disgrace.

Zeller further admits that Pythagoras established a school at Crotona, a great commercial city at the southernmost point of the Gulf of Tarentum. (A great commercial city, *let me say*, for that time, but in the conditions of acquaintanceship, more like an isolated little country town of this time.) Pythagoras "doubtless" intended his school should teach piety, temperance, valor, and obedience. Religion seems to have been at the bottom of it. And Pythagoras was a prophet. It is undeniable that the Pythagorean Society had also a political character. It was allied with Dorian aristocracy. It also cultivated science. It went in for music and gymnastics. The teachings had a mathematical character. Still, the only doctrine of Pythagoras which we know as such is that of the transmigration of souls. *Probably* the scholars ate together, at least occasionally. They had a few insignificant peculiarities of dress and food. They certainly had *no* community to speak of whatever. I will just say that I consider this last the most monstrous perversion of history. It is very improbable that any doctrines, except possibly religious ones, were kept secret.

A democratic revolution broke up the meeting houses, probably after the death of Pythagoras. But it is possible he moved from Crotona to Metapontum, if he did do so, in consequence of some political opposition.

Only after this breaking up of the school did the Pythagorean philosophy become known in Greece; or was widely heard of, although Pythagorean mysteries were celebrated there by a few persons. . . .

Aristoxenus, a direct disciple of Aristotle, cites the authority of the Pythagoreans to uphold him in the idea that a certain reticence is to be used. (Diag. Laer. VIII. xv.) He, also, mentions the cryptic modes of expression of the Pythagoreans.

Timaeus of Taormina, who was about one generation later than Aristotle, says that Empedocles and Plato were both refused admission into the Pythagorean School because they were given to blabbing.

Moreover, although Aristotle does not [inform us] in the works which have come down to us, yet in the fragments of his treatise on the Pythagoreans which Rose has collected, there are at least two which do relate to their secrets. There is one where he speaks of something as one of the doctrines which the Pythagoreans kept secret (No. 187). There is another passage reported both by Porphyry and Aelian where Aristotle explains sundry secret modes of expression of the Pythagoreans.

That there are not more citations to this effect from Aristotle is easily accounted for. It was not necessary to quote an authority for what was perfectly notorious.

As for Plato, I do not think that in those writings which are generally considered genuine there are more than two passages alluding to the Pythagoreans. One of these speaks of their following a peculiar mode of life, but does not say what it is. But the *Epinomis*, which is generally believed to be written by an immediate disciple of Plato, refers to the fidelity of the Pythagoreans in keeping secrets.

In view of all this mass of testimony, it seems to me few things so distant in time are better established than that the Pythagoreans had secrets.

There is one objection, however, which I am bound to mention. It is that Neanthes of Cyzicum, an esteemed historian of about the middle of the third century before Christ, says that he understands that the early Pythagoreans did *not* keep their doctrines secret. This is admitting they did so in his day. Now it is not possible to publish a thing first and afterwards keep it secret. Besides, he only says this in order to find an excuse for the conduct of two Pythagoreans who wrote books. But because they wrote books, it does not follow they gave away any important secret.

When we have once convinced ourselves that the Pythagoreans formed a secret society, it is plain that this fact must be taken account of in estimating the value of evidence respecting them. For instance, we at once see that the sudden appearance of additional information in the second century after Christ does not necessarily imply that this information is false. It may be simply that for some reason a good many secrets got told about that time.

Let us ask, how long did ancient secret societies generally contrive to keep their secrets? Of course, a secret is liable to be betrayed at any time, just as a man may die at any time. But there are two reasons why a secret of a given description should have a more constant duration than a man's life. One is that infants and the young are tender and particularly apt to die of certain diseases; and this tends to spread out the period of deaths; while a secret is more apt to be revealed the older it is, and this tends to bring it to a speedy end when the danger point is once reached. In the next place, men die of a thousand causes, and die but once; but secrets are betrayed for very few reasons, and even if betrayed may still be hushed up, till the time comes when they are frequently betrayed.

Let us consider, then, some of these great secret societies. In the first place, there were the religious mysteries of the ancients. The chief of these were derived from the Pelasgians in prehistoric times. Admission to them was quite easy; but the secret was kept substantially, that is, we do not read it until the third century after Christ. Other mysteries came in later, but were not published; then, there are mysteries, or were until very modern times, in all the trades; there are some professions which are altogether mysteries, as that of the Indian jugglers. Yet we do not learn that the secrets are ever divulged.

Now the question arises, what was the character of the Pythagorean secrets? One of Zeller's arguments is that if we admit Pythagoreans had secrets, other than religious mysteries, then we shall be forced by this evidence to conclude that what they most particularly desired to keep secret were propositions of mathematics. Now this he says is improbable.

But I am far from thinking that this is improbable. On the contrary, I think it is most likely the Pythagoreans depended upon their superior skill in mathematics to earn their livelihood. Philosophers must live like ordinary mortals, and when they belong to secret societies, they naturally seek to live by the application of those secrets. Now in surveying, mensuration, bookkeeping, etc., there was use enough for mathematics; and a most powerful motive for keeping the knowledge secret. I will add that there are some facts to support this conjecture. Thus, when what we call the Arabic numbers were first mentioned, namely by Boethius about A.D. 500, he says they were used by the Pythagoreans, that is, the innermost circle of the Pythagoreans.

Besides, as soon as we admit the secret society, the Oath of the Pythagoreans becomes of not impossible genuineness; and this makes much of the secret of the tetractys, that is of *ten,* which is called the "support of life." So it was, if by the practice of arithmetic they gained their living. This becomes still more probable if the Pythagoreans had to some extent their goods in common. Observe that all communities do this more or less, and none do it completely. But Epicurus, a man of great research and lofty intelligence, declared the Pythagoreans had their goods in common, and so did Timaeus of Taormina, another early and excellent authority. This need not be understood to mean that they carried their principle to its furthest extent, but they carried it so far as to constitute a peculiar mode of life. "A peculiar mode of life" are the words in which Plato describes it. It seems to me stubborn in Zeller to say that all this evidence is fabulous, when he has absolutely no testimony to the contrary.

In this point of view, other secrets would be trivial compared with those of mathematics.

All this goes to show that in regard to a school like this, late testimony is not to be rejected, as it properly would be in other cases, because it may rest on secret evidence.

According to Zeller's theory, this remarkable development of thought, Pythagoreanism, one of the most singular in the whole history of thought, and very powerful, sprang out from the island of Samos, without any historical development to speak of, although it is most unlike anything else the Hellenic mind produced. It is true that he says the doctrine of metempsychosis was familiar in Greece; but what did the Greeks who first heard of Pythagoreanism say to it? The philosopher Xenophanes finds the transmigration of souls a comical idea, and writes humorous verses about it. Now that which so moves the risible must be novel. We do not go into convulsions of laughter over very familiar ideas, however absurd they may seem. But Heraclitus, another great philosopher, says that Pythagoreanism is an aggregate of many unrelated doctrines borrowed from various sources. That is a good criticism, and well describes Pythagoreanism as we know it. It is very wanting in that *unity* which the Greeks always required. But from whom were those doctrines borrowed? I do not see what Zeller can answer to that.

Another thing, although Zeller apparently does not believe it, yet we have the testimony of Aristotle, which is the highest possible, is that Pythagoras professed to be a superhuman being, and was considered by his followers as such; so that they spoke of gods, men, and beings like Pythagoras. This being so, we hardly require the testimony which we have in abundance, that strict conformity to his teachings was expected, and all doubt silenced by *autos epha*—"himself has said it." That would tend to fix the doctrine, and prevent rapid accretions to it. Therefore, all this *mélange* of doctrine, or the bulk of it, must have come from Pythagoras himself.

But I remark that this autocracy in philosophy was perfectly foreign to the Greek mind. Nothing could have been more so.

The idea of metempsychosis, or the transmigration of souls, although so novel to Xenophanes, was familiar enough to non-Greek peoples.

This brings us to the question, what stock did Pythagoras and his followers mostly spring from? And what intercourse did he have with non-Greeks?

Now considering how the Pythagoreans regarded their master, I ask whether it is conceivable that they should not have preserved an approximately correct tradition of his biography?

At first, everything about him was so sacred that they did not even name him unnecessarily. The idea of keeping silent about sacred things was a familiar one to Greeks and Pelasgians. But after a while, it seems to have been thought best to give some information to the outside world, for Apollonius of Tyana, a Pythagorean born a few years before the Christian era, wrote a life of him, from which the biographies in our possession are probably chiefly drawn.

But Zeller says that Apollonius had no private information about Pythagoras, because the Pythagorean School had "disappeared" more than three centuries before.

A secret society might "disappear" in Athens where the witness of its disappearance lived without becoming extinct. The later Pythagoreans aver that they possessed a continuous tradition. That seems to me the most probable, especially if they had secret knowledge of mathematics, of the nature of a trade secret, helping them to earn their living.

Pythagoreanism was something like Christianity. That is, it had the most earnest and practical moral basis, and profound belief in the superhuman character of their master. And the lofty morals of the Pythagoreans were praised by all witnesses from Plato down.

Now lofty morals made a deep impression on the Greeks at all times. The Socratic schools, Stoicism, Christianity, are examples of it.

But in one point Pythagoreanism differed from Christianity. Instead of being the belief of the ignorant and the weak-minded, it was the belief of the intellectual *élite* of Magna Grecia.

Further Lectures on the History of Science

Lecture I

The subject of this course of lectures is the History of Science from Copernicus to Newton. This period of a century and a half, from 1543 to 1686, is deeply interesting from many points of view. The elementary phenomena in most of the branches of physics were then discovered. The science of dynamics which is the foundation of all exact science was substantially settled, and from the physical point of view, completed. But that which especially interests me in this era is that it was then that was developed the modern idea of the absolute regularity of causation, according to which if the laws of nature were fully known, and the state of things at any instant, it would be possible, for a mind sufficiently gigantic, to embrace such complication to calculate the precise state of everything at every other instant of time, past and future. This, I say, is the general belief today. It is firmly established that when religion or any other belief whatever conflicts with it, this other belief is weakened and substantially destroyed even in the minds of those who cling to it the most strongly.

In order to demonstrate the extraordinary hold which this belief in universal mechanical necessity has upon all the world, let me recall to your memory what happened a few years ago about Tyndall's proposed prayer-test. . . .

. . . If it [prayer] has any objective efficacy at all, it must have some slight effect which the delicate apparatus of modern meteorology would be able to detect. For my part, I do not hesitate to say that if the clergy had accepted the challenge, there would have been found among the body of the faithful that fraction of a grain of mustard seed that was requisite to produce such an effect. But the miserable dastards had not even the courage to try the experiment. They made the usual excuses of cowards and evaded the trial. Why? Because they believed so strongly in mechanical necessity that they thought it wiser to let religion go discredited than to set it up to fight the laws of nature.

I have had particular occasion myself to experience how strong this belief is, because I have been making what my opponents call an onslaught upon the doctrine of necessity; that is, I hold that while there is a certain force of necessity in the universe, there is a certain power of spontaneity too. I have presented my reasons, and it is generally acknowledged, I believe, that they are pretty strong. But the number of persons whose belief in absolute necessity has been shaken by them is very few.

Now it was in the interval between Copernicus and Newton, and in the time that immediately followed, that the wonderful faith in necessity grew up; and it came from the study of nature. Hence, I for one have been deeply interested in reading the history of natural science during that age, and in tracing the growth of the idea which has so dominated the whole world ever since.

Though my chief interest is with this particular doctrine, yet if we had nothing else in view than the understanding of its development, I should not wish to confine myself too narrowly to this subject. To really comprehend this special question, it is necessary to consider it in its relations to intellectual development as a whole. It is as with the ordinary use of the eyes. When I open my eyes and look at something, there is but a very small area indeed where things are seen sharply in focus; all the rest of the field of vision is ill-defined, but it is very necessary to enable me to see how the little thing that is in focus is situated with reference to other things. So we must not altogether neglect any part of the scientific history of the period in question. We must even go outside that period; we must sketch vaguely the whole history of science before that period and its whole history since.

Where and when did science begin? Of course, the beginnings of knowledge antedate the human race itself. All animals, even the lowest, have some rudimentary ideas of force; and the higher animals have a concrete idea of space, which is a greater discovery than any that deliberate science has ever made. Among the remains of the Stone Age we find implements fashioned into shapes upon which a modern engineer could not easily improve. But all that was knowledge gained by instinctive processes and not deliberately or with a full consciousness of making an investigation, and cannot, therefore, be classed as scientific.

The stars were grouped into constellations in Babylon about twenty-two hundred years before Christ, so that Babylonian astronomy must have already begun. If we cast our mental eye back for eight hundred years, say, to the Norman Conquest, we find a state of ideas on all subjects so very remote from our own that it is with great difficulty that

arduous and long-continued studies will enable us to put
ourselves in any degree into the attitudes of mind of that
time. Go back eight hundred years more, and again you
are in the days of Constantine, an epoch so utterly different
intellectually from that of the Dark Ages as can be imagined. Go back another eight hundred years, and you have
reached the early dawn of Greek philosophy, with the alphabet hardly in use in making books. Another backward
leap of eight hundred years, and Troy had not yet been
built perhaps. The Pharaohs were flourishing. Eight hundred years before that time, the same constellations that we
know were in use by the Babylonians.

Eight hundred years before the beginnings of Babylonian
astronomy, the Great Pyramid was standing as a monument
of the forgotten skill of those who built it. . . . More
learned foolishness has been written of late years about the
Great Pyramid than upon all other subjects. . . .

It is wonderful how many people are to be met with who
know nothing about reasoning. The popular opinion seems
to be that if you find any similar relationship between
things, and then find a supposed condition from which
this relationship would certainly result, you have there
some evidence that that condition really exists. A certain
curious numerical relationship is found to exist between two
dimensions of a building. Such a relation would exist if it
had been intended. Therefore, it was intended. Some of you
will laugh and say, "Of course, this is not good reasoning
because it violates the rules of syllogism"; but you will permit me, as an old student of reasoning, to put it this way:
"It is not good reasoning, *although* it violates the rules of
syllogism." Reasoning which does not violate these rules is
pretty sure to be bad. It is bad reasoning to conclude that
because a curious approximate relation exists between magnitudes, therefore it must have been intended, because there
are a million curious approximate relations between any
two magnitudes. . . . I shall say no more about the Pyramid, although it presents some problems in engineering of
some interest. . . .

14. Kepler

Johann Kepler[1] it was who discovered the form of the planets' paths in coursing round the sun and the law of their varying speeds. This achievement, by. far the most triumphant unravelment of facts ever performed—cunninger than any deciphering of hieroglyphics or of cuneiform inscriptions—occupied its author's whole time from October 1600 to October 1604, and the greater part of four years more. That fairylike town Prague was the scene of these studies and there in April 1609 was published the immortal *Commentaries on the Motions of the Star (Planet) Mars.* To gain any idea of a scientific research, one must look with one's own eyes and brain at the things with which it deals. Now the [present] year 1892 happens to be a good one for watching Mars, and if one will, from his own naked-eye observations, set down upon a star-map (say upon the figures in the *Century Dictionary*) the course of the planet from the third week in March to the end of the year, as it traverses the constellations Sagittarius, Capricornus, and Aquarius, the true greatness of Kepler will begin to dawn upon him. For the telescope was only invented in the year in which Kepler's book was published; so that he had before him only naked-eye observations, and saw only what anybody may see.

During the year 1892 [the year of this Lowell Lecture] Mars will describe a loop among the stars, moving first eastward, then gradually bending to the south, then to the west,

1 Peirce used the spelling "Keppler" throughout this manuscript.—Editor's note.

then to the north, and last to the east again, so that on October 6 he will cross his previous path at the point where he was on June 10. This motion in a loop is characteristic of all the planets; and to account for it, the ancients very naturally supposed each to move round in a circle itself carried round another circle, within which, though not at the centre, the earth was immovably fixed. They could not make the centre of the first circle move at a uniform rate round the circumference of the second, but took within the latter, at the same distance from its centre that the earth was, but on the opposite side, another fixed point, round which the centre of the first circle described equal angles in equal times. They found themselves further obliged to suppose that the first circle had a perpetual tilting, or reciprocating, motion, around an axis tangent to the second. Copernicus, however, had shown that it was better to suppose earth and planets to move round a common centre very near the sun, while still continuing to make them move on circles that were carried round on other circles and balanced back and forth.

Kepler was the scientific executor of the astronomer Tycho Brahe, who had measured as well as he could with the rude instruments of those days the celestial latitude and longitude of Mars in ten alternate years. From the study of these observations, together with a few of his own of inferior value (for he was both nearsighted and awkward) and three by the ancient observer Ptolemy, Kepler found out and proved conclusively that there are no such tiltings, or librations, as had been supposed but that all the motions of Mars take place in a plane having an excessively slow motion if any, and furthermore, what Copernicus had failed to discover, that the sun lies in this plane, and also that Mars does not move in one circle carried by another, but simply in an ellipse having the sun at one of its foci,[2] and also that this ellipse itself turned round at a very slow rate, and also that the line from the Sun to Mars describes

---

[2] The foci of an ellipse are two points within it such that if from them lines be drawn to any point on the ellipse, these lines are equally inclined to the curve at that point and their sum is equal to the greatest diameter of the ellipse.

in its motion equal elliptical sections in equal times. Was it not wonderful to make out all this, and with perfect certainty too, from mere naked-eye observations which anybody could nowadays improve upon with the commonest instruments?

The Kepler family had once been noble; but Johann's new ancestors were artisans of Nuremberg, coarse people, hard and shrewd, but not long-lived. His grandfather, a bookbinder, had removed to Weil der Stadt near Stuttgart, where, owing to his reputation for sagacity, he had risen to be burgomaster, and where Johann was born. His father was a soldier and inn-keeper; his mother, a yellow blonde, little and spare, with a terrible tongue that was a curse to herself and to all that were near her, in later life narrowly escaped being burnt as a witch. Her husband abandoned her when Johann was eighteen and his only brother fourteen years old. Johann, who had been born prematurely, was physically puny and ailing all his life; yet was rather pleasing in appearance, and vivacious in his movements. Though not a precocious child, he was a clever lad, especially at mathematics, eager to learn, curious about all the ways of nature, and, in short, manifesting that gigantic power of right reasoning that distinguished him from other men. It was this reasoning, no doubt, that stimulated him even as a boy to the indomitable industry for which he is celebrated and which was all the more extraordinary that, not to speak of his delicate health, his was a nature to which all drudgery was uncommonly irksome. His success in his studies, together with his weak body, naturally pointed to his becoming a Lutheran minister, and to that end he was sent to the University of Tübingen as a stipendiary scholar. But when later astronomy seemed to offer a better opening, he turned from theology and devoted himself to the study of the stars under Professor Maestlin. In this he was governed, as in all the affairs of life, by careful calculation, for he assures us that predilection for astronomy he had not.

In those days, by a "mathematicus," or *Sternseher*, was understood a man that earned his living by making astrological predictions. Into this study Kepler threw himself with energy, and was more or less addicted to it all his life. He soon came to rate it as nonsense and trickery, and therefore disliked to practice it. Yet, said he, astrology has been the nurse of astronomy. He meant that astronomy could only be advanced by students wholly given up to it, and that the world could hardly be persuaded to give people a livelihood for doing only that. For astronomy seemed to be of no practical use, and was in fact of none except to posterity; though by calling modern mathematics and physics into being it has indirectly been the source of all the conveniencies and inventions of our time.

At twenty-two, Kepler was appointed professor of mathematics at Gratz in Styria, a hundred miles south of Vienna. At twenty-five, he succeeded in marrying a wealthy young grass widow. Meantime, his position in Gratz was becoming untenable on account of his Protestantism; for though so far from a bigot that he was called half-Catholic and was finally read out of the Lutheran Church for his too easy opinion, yet he would not join the Catholic Church. He used so much policy that the Jesuits took his part, and remained after the other Protestant professors and most of the other scholars had gone. But, at last, he was glad at twenty-eight to accept the great Tycho Brahe's invitation to become, under him, assistant astronomer to the Emperor Rudolph II. On Tycho's death in the following year, Kepler was made chief "mathematicus," with an additional allowance for preparing planetary tables from Tycho's observations. A strange appointment this, wherein power missed a rare opportunity of doing a stupid thing; but the explanation of it is that Kepler was designated by the dying Brahe for the task. Besides, Rudolph really had some knowledge of astronomy. These tables were computed in twenty-six years, and were published under the title of the *Rudolphine Tables*. During their preparation, Kepler had many a tussle with the representatives of the noble house of Brahe, who, as long as Tycho lived, had frowned upon one who would demean himself with stargazing, but who now insisted that his theories should govern the new tables; for what nature's truth might be, if they ever so much as reflected that there was such a thing, they neither knew nor cared. The last breath of the dying Tycho himself had been expended in imploring Kepler to follow his system; but then, that was before Kepler's great discoveries. At thirty-seven, he published his great work on the motions of Mars. About that time discord arose between Emperor Rudolph and his brother. Prague in 1611 found itself the focus of the theatre of war. That year all of Kepler's family were very ill. His favorite son died, and his wife followed. She left no will, so that the property was divided among her children to the exclusion of the father. Meantime, Rudolph was forced to surrender Bohemia to his brother Matthew; and Kepler moved to Linz in Austria proper. After Rudolph's death Matthew, succeeding to the Imperial throne, continued his brother's bounty to Kepler. In 1613, Kepler, being forty-two years old, married after the maturest deliberation a poor girl eighteen years younger than himself. At forty-six, he discovered the "third law," that the squares of the periodic times are proportional to the cubes of the mean distances, not a discovery involving any difficult reasoning, yet leading at once, had he only been able to see it, to the corollary that the planets are attracted to the sun inversely with the square of the distance.

The same year began the Thirty Years' War. Then Emperor Matthew died and was succeeded by the bigoted Ferdinand II. Kepler's books were prohibited in some places for teaching that the sun does not move round the earth. There was little hope of further salary, even if he should not be proceeded against; and he received private intimations from the emperor that it would be well for him to renounce astronomy. Then came the invention of logarithms, requiring the planetary tables, now nearly ready, to be entirely reconstructed. In 1620, in the midst of his greatest difficulties, the learned James I warmly invited Kepler to go to England; but he would not accept the succor, lest the tale should be told to the disgrace of his country; and at last by prudent conduct he overcame his chief difficulties. In 1630, at the age of fifty-nine, while on a journey he died rather suddenly at Ratisbon of an infectious fever. He had had in all twelve children.

All the endowments of Kepler's intellect and heart seem

to have been concentrated upon one function, that of reasoning. In his great work on Mars, he has laid bare to us all the operations of his mind during the whole research; and what better sign of the perfection of his ratiocination could there be than that no better pathway could be found by which to lead another thought to the same conclusion than that his own had broken in the first instance. His admirable method of thinking consisted in forming in his mind a diagrammatic or outline representation of the entangled state of things before him, omitting all that was accidental, observing suggestive relations between the parts of his diagram, performing divers experiments upon it, or upon the natural objects, and noting the results.

The first quality required for this process, the first elements of high reasoning power, is evidently imagination; and Kepler's fecund imagination strikes every reader. But "imagination" is an ocean-broad term, almost meaningless, so many and so diverse are its species. What kind of an imagination is required to form a mental diagram of a complicated state of facts? Not that poet-imagination that "bodies forth the forms of things unknowne," but a devil's imagination, quick to take Dame Nature's hints. The poet-imagination riots in ornaments and accessories; a Kepler's makes the clothing and the flesh drop off, and the apparition of the naked skeleton of truth to stand revealed before him. Accordingly, we are not surprised to find that Kepler looked upon life with an eye of sadness, without tears, yet without illusion.

No man was ever more coolly sensible of his own faults and weaknesses, as well as of his own superior powers. In coming to an understanding with Brahe, he recommends himself as follows: "in observing I am under the disadvantage of nearsightedness, and am awkward in handling instruments; while in transacting business, my own or others, I betray an impertinent and choleric nature; nor can I bear to sit long at work, without getting up and moving about, nor to pass my regular hours for meals, even when I am not downright ill." There is no looking at himself through soft violet glass here.

He never was able to put aside a puzzle until he had

completely resolved it. Early in his studies of Mars he obtained a theory which so accurately represented its heliocentric longitudes, that he ever after called it his "vicarious theory," inasmuch as it obviated the necessity of reverting to the observations. He saved the appearances as far as heliocentric longitudes went; and that would have satisfied many an astronomer. But Kepler could not be satisfied, since the theory did not agree with the latitudes or geocentric longitudes; and by far the greater part of his labor came after he had obtained this *vicarious hypothesis*.

Kepler was forever trying experiments with his figures. No bad luck, not dozens of negative results, which other men reckon failures, could discourage him from trying again. Yet it would be a great mistake to suppose that he was addicted to wasting time on wild-cat theories, or what Darwin used to call "nonsense-experiments." Each step was made deliberately, and for sound reasons; and few of Kepler's "failures" failed to throw some light on the problems he had in hand.

When the slightest clue presented itself, Kepler's promptitude to seize upon it was amazing. The last and most essential step of his great discovery was made, according to his own account, by accident. Namely, it was due to his remarking that two numbers which seemed to have no connection with one another were nearly equal, one 429, the other 432. Kepler does not remark that an ordinary man's attention would not have been struck by this near equality, or if it had, would never have divined its significance.

There is one moral quality without which a reasoner cannot escape fallacies, and that is a sturdy honesty of purpose. For the lack of that, we every day see creatures in the guise of men losing fortune, health, and happiness too, deluded by their own sophisms. But Kepler, while not altogether devoid of astuteness and diplomacy, could hardly bring himself to aid his fellowmen to dupe themselves with astrological predictions; and this certainly was the nearest approach to duplicity that he ever made. It had its effect, no doubt, in blinding him to the fanciful character of some of his speculations—another instance of the inevitable intellectual retribution which follows upon guile.

15. Conclusion of the History of Science Lectures

I have now expounded to you as much of the history of science as I found myself able to do in twelve hours. Of course, a great deal remains to be considered; but even the few facts we have collected will do something to answer the questions with which I set out.

We have found as I suggested at the outset that there are three ways by which human thought grows, by the formation of habits, by the violent breaking up of habits, and by the action of innumerable fortuitous variations of ideas combined with differences in the fecundity of different variations.

As for the last mode of development which I have called Darwinism, however important it may be in reference to some of the growths of mind—and I will say that in my opinion we should find it a considerable factor in individual thinking—yet in the history of science it has made as far as we have been able to see, no figure at all, except in retrograde movements. In all these cases it betrays itself infallibly by its two symptoms of proceeding by insensible steps and of proceeding in a direction different from that of any strivings. Whether or not it may not be more or less influential in other cases, in which its action is masked, the means of investigation which I have so far been able to bring to bear fail to disclose.

The manner in which the great and startling advances

in scientific thought have been made appears very clearly. It is by the violent breaking up of certain habits, combined with the action of other habits not broken up. Thus, the highest level of Egyptian thought seems to have been reached at a very early age. So it appears to us, and so it always appeared to the Egyptians, for they always reverence the ideas of antiquity, as superior to those of their own time. Now the great factor in the development of the Egyptian mind was undoubtedly the physical geography of the country which probably produced its effects in a reasonably small number of generations after it was first felt. So with the Greeks. Their thought remained in its primeval condition until the extension of commerce brought them within the sphere of influence of other peoples, the Phoenicians, the Egyptians, and the Babylonians, and then within a few generations they made great strides in thought, to be succeeded by a slower movement of another kind. At first, we have a rather servile copying of the ideas of those countries, a syncretism such as we see in Pythagoras. But soon the foreign ideas begin to react with the ideas and faculties peculiar to the Greeks, and a great original life commences. So it was again, when in the thirteenth century the ideas of the Dark Ages were rudely shaken up by contact with the more civilized Saracens; although as far as science was concerned that movement was quickly stifled by the rapid development of theological ideas.

The Renaissance in Italy was of slower growth, because foreign ideas had been slowly filtering in since the thirteenth century uninterrupted. However, after the fall of Constantinople in 1454, there was a much more rapid movement. That movement was first strongest in the direction of art, which I take to be a mark of rapidly growing minds, of minds receiving nutrition too rapidly to be packed down into the forms of science. But the scientific development came later. Galileo was born the very day of Michelangelo's death.

In this early development of science there were two great factors. In the first place, the direct strivings of the astronomers, the European successors of the Arabians, who brought to astronomy more masculine intellects than the

Arabians had, had brought out at length a world-shaking idea, the Copernican conception. In the existing state of the church, this was more easily accomplished in Northern Europe, and there it was brought to its perfection by Kepler, and I have traced out the birth of this conception with some minuteness because it is remarkable as being a birth from within, not an influence from without. Although the authors of this, Copernicus, Tycho, and Kepler, were all Teutons, the value of their work was better understood and more accurately appreciated in Italy than north of the Alps.

The other great factor, which chiefly influenced the development of dynamics, was the study of the works of Archimedes; and a strongly Hellenic color is apparent everywhere in that branch of science down to the time of Newton. It is shown in the great fondness for demonstrations from axioms, in the desire to put all special experimentation out of sight, and to rely on the Light of Nature. It is also shown in the geometrical methods which are preferentially employed.

As to the third [Lamarckian] mode of intellectual development, we should see more of it if we were to trace out the history of science into its later era. Though it is not so startlingly manifest, it is certainly the method of the ordinary successful prosecution of scientific inquiring.

We see its action clearly in the history of astronomy at all periods, and especially in Kepler's gigantic work. It is growth by exercise, or by direct efforts in the direction of the growth. If we have seen little of it, it is because I felt it necessary to the understanding of the subject to begin at the beginning, and I would not in twelve hours carry you on to the point in which science, except in astronomy and to some extent in the last developments of dynamics, was really settled down to its work. I will mention, however, that in the January number of *The Monist*,[1] I have endeavored to give an analysis of this kind of evolution, and especially have connected it with the Christian theory of the way in which the world is to be made better and wiser.

[1] "Evolutionary Love," *The Monist*, Vol. 3 (Jan. 1893), pp. 176–200. Here Peirce attempted a cyclical theory of cultural history based on periods of roughly 500 years.—Editor's note.

I have to thank the company very gratefully for the patience and kind indulgence with which my lectures have been listened to. I have done what lay in my power to present as much of the history of science as I have been able to treat in a lucid manner, and to show that it is governed by law like other departments of nature. But these laws are not of the nature of mechanical forces, such that the individual and the spirit of man is swallowed up in cosmical movements, but on the contrary it is a law by virtue of which lofty results require for their attainment lofty thinkers of original power and individual value. You cannot silence or stifle or starve a single one of them without a loss to civilization from which it never can wholly recover. It is not more certain that the inches of a man's stature will be affected all his life by an attack of fever as a baby, than that we are now less happy because of the many great geniuses whom untoward circumstances have put down. The country that can first find the means, not to provide the million with miscellaneous reading matter, and elementary education, but to utilize its superior intellects for the general good, will expend a wonderful acceleration of civilization from which the benefit of the million, in much more valuable ways, will come about of itself.

16. The Nineteenth Century: Notes[1]

[The two chief ideas of the nineteenth century were for Peirce the idea of continuity and the idea of evolutionary progress. He tried in his philosophy to combine the two ideas by means of his logic of relations and probability, his notion of thought as "the melody that runs through our sensations," and the evolution of laws in a universe striving for reasonableness.]

Two Chief Ideas

If we survey the work of the nineteenth century, it is surprising to find to what an extent its successes have been due to the recognition of the idea of Continuity, and its failures to the want of such recognition. The work of Mr. Peirce consists in carrying the idea of Continuity into all parts of philosophy. First, it is necessary to define Continuity with accuracy; and it is necessary to show why it should have so mighty a function in the world of ideas. To do this is impossible without a full development of the Logic of Relations and of "Objective" Logic. This last phrase is used in a peculiar sense, and refers to the manner in which one idea, as a pure idea, suggests another, and to the law of the evolution of ideas.

[1] From Widener Library Archives, Peirce MSS. By permission of the Philosophy Department of Harvard University. Unpublished miscellaneous Notes, Copyright by the President and Fellows of Harvard College.

The nineteenth century has been a century of Progress, and this naturally inclines us to favor Evolution. But we must not *assume* evolution; we must find out whether or not there is direct evidence, first, that things in general do not drift from a state of evolution to a state of regression—so that we are only in an accidentally progressive situation. Second, even if there be a general march of events and ideas, the pessimists have heaped up solid arguments going to show that march ultimately brings up the nothingness from which it set out.

The Reigning Philosophy: Büchnerism

The Büchnerites [who define thought as a secretion of the brain] undertake to make use of the truths of physics to answer questions [the nature of life, the relation of mind to body] which are the furthest removed from physics that any question can possibly be. . . .

The Leading Ideas of the Nineteenth Century [Listed]

Continuity—Historical Idea; Napoleonic Idea; Centennials; Scientific Associations; Labor Unions; Socialism; Galvanism; Emigration; Modern Idealism; Chemistry; Neptune; Sewing Machine; Anaesthetics; English Poetry; French Novels; Modern Music; Utilitarianism; Theory of Gases; Theory of Heat; Conservation of Energy; Darwinism; Spectrum Analysis; Theory of Functions; Modern Mathematics; Imaginaries; Boolian Logic; Objective Logic; Statistics and Probabilities.

Chance and Great Men

The native capacity of the lesser great men, like that of the merely eminent men, is due to the accidental co-operation of a thousand minute independent causes such as operate one way or another upon all of us, while the greater ones do somewhat partake of the nature of monstrous births in that their exceptional natures are largely due to causes that very rarely operate at all.

Nineteenth-Century Philosophy

The schools of Hegel, Comte, J. S. Mill, Schopenhauer, and Herbert Spencer are coteries of philodoxers, almost, if not quite, as narrow-minded as Italian monks, Thomists, or Rosminians. The only upheaval of the century that stands amid the tempest of philosophical opinion unshaken and citadel-crowned is the exact logic of Boole and De Morgan; and this was the product of pure scientific study. Its authors could never have foreseen that it would leave no practical maxim of reasoning unaffected, but would extend some, curtail others. It is needless to remark that those teachers of logic who have not yet waked up to the doctrine of probability, which for more than a century has been the logic of the exact sciences, will pass into another stage of fossilization without knowing what modern scientific logic is.

. . . The hypothesis of Natural Selection is another idea that occurred simultaneously to two different men, one of them a sort of paradoxer [Hegel?], while the other [Darwin] has stirred science and philosophy as no man since Newton had done.

Nineteenth-Century Music

Nineteenth-century music has the same tendency as nineteenth-century mathematics, for both seek to satisfy a purely inward ideal, in contradistinction to the ideals formed upon outward experience which the imitative arts, poetry, and even architecture pursue.

Just as nineteenth-century mathematics has disdained utility, so our music has disdained the office of merely diverting and amusing people, and expects to be listened to for the sake of the pure beauty it embodies. The point is that both adore an eternal inward voice. And just as we have seen that this passion of the nineteenth-century mathematician is quite at one with the spirit of ardor, energy, and severe earnestness with which throughout the same era, distinctively objective fact has been sought in every special science, psychical and physical, both tendencies being but outcomes of a thorough spiritual awakening to the pettiness of self, of our traditional ideas, even of man at large, so we can perceive that the obsequience to nature and objective truth that has put its plain stamp on the other nineteenth-century arts has sprung from the very same source as the Platonism of our music; for objectivity in art is nothing but universal validity, and our striving for it has consisted simply in aiming at that which any observer could see whose attention was sufficiently trained and who could lay aside the limitations of fashion, of convention, or, in one word, of self. Thus the science and the art of the century, as I seem to myself to see them, have undergone one common regeneration. . . .

It may be said that the romanticism of our literature is a contrary tendency to replace the universal and abstract by the personal and idiosyncratic. But such an objection is based on a comparison that was cleared up in the early years of the century by Hegel, and which exact logic has rendered still more patent. Namely, the universal is not necessarily the abstracted. The abstractly universal is only the lower kind of universal. Whatever is true is universal in a better sense, and the personality of romantic literature is, in that sense, more truly universal than the labels of classicism.

17. The Century's Great Men in Science[1]

[Peirce's Lowell Lectures of 1892–93 on the History of Science from the ancients to Newton did not terminate his interest in or writing on the history of thought. He outlined a cosmic philosophy of intellectual history in his essay on "Evolutionary Love" for *The Monist* in 1893, planned a twelve-volume work on *The Principles of Philosophy,* whose first volume was written under the title: *A Review of the Leading Ideas of the Nineteenth Century.* He wrote a "Note on the Age of Basil Valentine" for *Science* (August 12, 1898), thus continuing his earlier researches in medieval science (e.g., in 1884 he started to edit and translate Petrus Peregrinus' "Letter on the Magnet," a fourteenth-century MS. on magnetism); but always the continuity of the thought of his own century with that of the past was foremost in his mind. As a physicist he appreciated the tremendous advances made by giants like Faraday, Maxwell, and Helmholtz; as a chemist, the unifying periodic table of Mendeleef; and as a religious philosopher, the impact of Darwin's theory on the human sciences. It is on a religious note that Peirce ends his essay on the century's great men of science: "To an earlier age knowledge was power . . . ; to us it is life and the *summum bonum.*"]

[1] From *Annual Report of the Smithsonian Institution for year ending June 30, 1900* (Washington, D.C., 1901), pp. 693–699. Reprinted from *New York Evening Post* (Jan. 12, 1901), "Review of the Nineteenth Century."

How shall we determine that men are great? Who, for instance, shall we say are the great men of science? The men who have made the great and fruitful discoveries? Such discoveries in the nineteenth century have mostly been made independently by two or more persons. Darwin and Wallace simultaneously put forth the hypothesis of natural selection. Clausius, Rankine, and Sadi Carnot, perhaps Kelvin, worked out the mechanical theory of heat. Krönig, Clausius, Joule, Herapath, Waterston, and Daniel Bernouilli independently suggested the kinetical theory of gases. I do not know how many minds besides Robert Mayer, Colding, Joule, and Helmholtz hit upon the doctrine of the conservation of energy. Faraday and Joseph Henry brought magneto-electricity to light. The pack of writers who were on the warm scent of the periodic law of the chemical elements approached two hundred when the discovery itself, a most difficult inference, was partly achieved by Lothar Meyer, wholly by Mendeleef. When great discoveries were thus in the air, shall that brain necessarily be deemed great upon which they happened earliest to condense, or the man supereminent who, by the unmeaning rule of priority of publication, gets the credit in brief statements? No, this method of estimation, natural as it is to make success the standard of measure, will not do.

Shall we, then, by a logical analysis, draw up an abstract definition of greatness and call those men great who conform to it? If there were no dispute about the nature of greatness, this might probably prove the most convenient plan. It would be like a rule of grammar adduced to decide whether a phrase is good English or not. Nor would the circumstance that the definition could not be as explicit and determinate as a rule of grammar constitute a serious difficulty. Unfortunately, however, among the few writers who have seriously studied the question, the most extreme differences prevail as to the nature of great men. Some hold that they are fashioned of the most ordinary clay, and that only their rearing and environment, conjoined with fortunate opportunities, make them what they are. The heaviest weight, intellectually, among these writers maintains,[2] on the other hand, that circumstances are as powerless to suppress the great man as they would be to subject a human being to a nation of dogs. But it was only the blundering Malvolio who got the notion that some are born great. The sentence of the astute Maria was: "Some are become great: some atcheeves greatnesse, and some have greatnesse thrust uppon em."[3] Amid this difference of opinion any definition of greatness would be like a disputed rule of grammar. Just as a rule of grammar does not render an expression bad English, but only generalizes the fact that good writers do not use it, so, in order to establish a definition of greatness, it would be necessary to begin by ascertaining what men were and what men were not great, and that having been done the rule might as well be dispensed with. My opinion will, I fear, be set down by some intellectual men as foolishness, though it has not been lightly formed nor without long years of experimentation—that the way to judge of whether a man was great or not is to put aside all analysis, to contemplate attentively his life and works, and then to look into one's heart and estimate the impression one finds to have been made. This is the way in which one would decide whether a mountain were sublime or not. The great man is the impressive personality, and the question whether he is great is a question of impression.

The glory of the nineteenth century has been its science, and its scientific great men are those whom I mean here to consider. Their distinctive characteristic throughout the century, and more and more so in each succeeding generation, has been devotion to the pursuit of truth for truth's sake. In this century we have not heard a Franklin asking, "What signifies a philosophy which does not apply itself to some use?"—a remark that could be paralleled by utterances of Laplace, of Rumford, of Buffon, and of many another well-qualified spokesman of eighteenth-century science. It was in the early dawn of the nineteenth that Gauss (or was it Dirichlet?) gave as the reason of his passion for the

[2] Cf. William James, "Great Men, Great Thoughts, and the Environment," *Atlantic Monthly* (October 1880).—Editor's note.
[3] *Twelfth Night*, Act II, Scene 5.—Editor's note.

Theory of Numbers that "it is a pure virgin that never has been and never can be prostituted to any practical application whatsoever."

It was my inestimable privilege to have felt as a boy the warmth of the steadily burning enthusiasm of the scientific generation of Darwin, most of the leaders of which at home I knew intimately and some very well in almost every country of Europe. I particularize that generation without having any reason to suspect that that flame has since burned dimmer or less purely, but simply because if a word belonged to one's mother tongue, one may be supposed to know unerringly the meaning the teachers of one's boyhood attached to it.

The word "science" was one often in those men's mouths, and I am quite sure they did not mean by it "systematized knowledge," as former ages had defined it, nor anything set down in a book; but, on the contrary, a mode of life; not knowledge, but the devoted, well-considered life pursuit of knowledge; devotion to truth—not "devotion to truth as one sees it," for that is no devotion to truth at all, but only to party—no, far from that, devotion to the truth that the man is not yet able to see but is striving to obtain. The word was thus, from the etymological point of view, already a misnomer. And so it remains with the scientists of today. What they meant and still mean by "science" ought, etymologically, to be called philosophy. But during the nineteenth century it was only a metaphysical professor of a now obsolescent type, as I hope, who could sit in his academic chair, puffed up with his "systematized knowledge" —no true philosopher, but a mere philodoxer. For a snapshot at the nineteenth-century man of science one may take Sir Humphrey Davy, willing, as early as 1818, seriously to investigate the liquefaction of the blood of St. Januarius; or John Tyndall, with scientific ingenuousness proposing that prayer test to which no clerical Elijah has yet been found with the faith and good faith to respond; or William Crookes, devoting years of his magnificent powers to examining the supposed evidences of the direct action of mind upon matter in the face of the world's scorn. Contrast these instances with the refusal of Laplace and Biot in the closing years of the previous century to accept the evidence that stones fall from heaven (evidence proving that they do so daily), simply because their prepossessions were the other way. One of the geologist brothers De Luc declared that he would not believe such a thing though he saw it with his own eyes; and a scientifically given English ecclesiastic who happened to be sojourning in Siena when a shower of aerolites were dashed in broad daylight into an open square of that town, wrote home that having seen the stones he had found the testimony of eyewitnesses so unimpeachable and so trustworthy—that he accepted the fact, you will say? by no means—that he knew not what to think! Such was the *bon sens* that guided the eighteenth century—a pretty phrase for ineradicable prejudice.

To this self-effacement before the grandeur of reason and truth is traceable the greatness of nineteenth-century science, most obviously in mathematics. In the minds of eighteenth-century mathematicians their science existed for the sake of its applications. Forgetfulness of this was in their eyes reprehensible, immoral. The question was, what would a given piece of mathematics do? They liked smooth-running and elegant machinery—there was economy in that; but they were not sedulous that it should have symmetry; idle admiration of its beauty they hardly approved. If it was excessively complicated and intricate, that was regarded rather as a feature to be proud of than as a blemish. Were the complete revolution that the nineteenth century wrought upon the ideal of mathematics not notorious, one could soon convince himself of it by looking over almost any modern treatise—say, Salmon on Higher Plane Curves. That volume, for example, would be found replete with theorems hardly any of which hold good for any curves that could really exist. Realizable curves have hardly been studied at all, for the reason that they do not yield a beautiful theory, such as is now exacted. Modern mathematics is highly artistic. A simple theme is chosen, some conception pretty and charming in itself. Then it is shown that by simply holding this idea up to one's eye and looking through it a whole forest that before seemed a thick and tangled jungle of brushes and briers is seen to be in reality an orderly garden. The word "generalization" really cannot be fully understood without studying modern mathematics; nor can the beauty of generalization be in any other way so well appreciated. There is here no need of throwing out "extreme cases." Far from that, it is precisely in the extreme cases that the power and beauty of the magic eyeglass is most apparent and most marvellous. Let me take back the word "magic," though, for the reasonableness of it is just its crowning charm. I must not be led away from my point, to expatiate upon the reposefulness of the new mathematics, upon how it relieves us of that tiresome imp, man, and from the most importunate and unsatisfactory of the race, one's self. Suffice it to say that it is so reasonable, so simple, so easy to read, when the right view has once been attained, that the student may easily forget what arduous labors were expended in constructing the first convenient pathway to that lofty summit, that mastery over intricacies, far beyond that of the eighteenth-century master. "It must not be supposed," said C. G. J. Jacobi, one of the simplifying pioneers, "that it is to a gift of nature that I owe such mathematical power as I possess. No; it has come by hard work, hard work. Not mere industry, but brain-splitting thinking—hard work; hard work that has often endangered my health." Such reflections enable us to perceive that if modern mathematics is great, so also were the men who made it great.

The science next in abstractness after mathematics is logic. The contributions of the eighteenth century to this subject were enormous. In pure logic the doctrine of chances, which has been the logical guide of the exact sciences and is now illuminating the pathway of the theory of evolution, and is destined to still higher uses, received at the hands of Jacob Bernouilli and of Laplace developments of the first importance. In the theory of cognition Berkeley and Kant laid solid foundations; their personal greatness is incontestable. This is hardly true of Hume. In the nineteenth century Boole created a method of miraculous fruitfulness, which aided in the development of the logic of relatives, and threw great light on the doctrine of probability, and thereby upon the theory and rules of inductive reasoning.

De Morgan added an entirely new kind of syllogism, and brought the logic of relatives into existence, which revolutionizes general conceptions of reasoning. The works of Comte, Whewell, J. S. Mill, Jevons, and others upon the philosophy of inductive science were less successful or fruitful. In the more metaphysical part of logic the philosophy of Hegel, though it cannot be accepted on the whole, was the work of a great man. In metaphysics and general cosmology the attitude of the century has been expectant. Herbert Spencer has been proclaimed as a sort of scientific Messiah by a group of followers more ardent than philosophic, which does not seem to be gathering strength.

At the head of the physical sciences stands nomological physics. Dr. Thomas Young was here the earliest great man of the century, whose intellect illuminated every corner to which it was directed, taking the first difficult steps in the decipherment of the hieroglyphics, originating the doctrine of color-mixtures, propounding the correct theory of light, and illuminative everywhere. It gives a realizing sense of the century's progress that this great man in its early years should have opined that experimentation in general had then been pushed about far enough. On that occasion it was not his usual logic, but the eighteenth-century watchword *le bon sens,* that was his guide, with the sort of result it is continually turning out when used beyond its proper sphere of every-day practical affairs. The advance of years, with their experience, has led physicists to expend more and vastly more effort upon extreme precision, against every protest of good sense. What has come of it? Marconi's wireless telegraphy, for one thing. For it was the precision with which the velocity of light on the one hand and the ratio of statical and dynamical constants of electricity on the other had been determined that proved to Maxwell that the vibrating medium of light was the substance of electricity, a theory that his great follower, Hertz, applied to making giant light waves less affected by obstructions than even those of sound. I dare say, sapient "good sense" pooh-poohs those wonderful new substances, helium and the rest, that seem the connecting link between ordinary matter and the ether. So it would be useless to point out that their discovery was entirely due to Lord Rayleigh's fastidiousness in the determination of the density of nitrogen. But it has to be noted as a characteristic of the great physicists of the nineteenth century that their reverence for every feature of the phenomenon, however minute, has been in thorough disaccord with the older "good sense." The greatest advances in physics during the century were made by several men at once. Certain ideas would come somehow to be in the air; and by the time they had crystallized for a student here and there, he would hesitate to announce as original conceptions what he had reason to suppose many men shared, while he knew that the larger body would not be yet ready to accept them. Under those circumstances priority of publication can signify nothing except haste.

Of all men of the century Faraday had the greatest power of drawing ideas straight out of his experiments and making his physical apparatus do his thinking, so that experimentation and inference were not two proceedings, but one. To understand what this means, read his *Researches on Electricity*. His genius was thus higher than that of Helmholtz, who fitted a phenomenon with an appropriate conception out of his store, as one might fit a bottle with a stopper. The most wonderful capacity for "catching on" to the ideas of nature when these were of a complicated kind was shown by Mendeleef in making out the periodic law of the chemical elements, as one might make out the meaning of a pantomime, from data so fragmentary, and in some cases erroneous, that the interpretation involved the correction of sundry facts, corrections since confirmed, as well as the prediction of the very peculiar properties of the unknown gallium, scandium, and germanium, which were soon afterwards actually met with. Minute examination of all his utterances convinces one that Mendeleef's mental processes in this unparalleled induction were largely subconscious and, as such, indicate an absorption of the man's whole being in his devotion to the reason in facts.

A great naturalist, as well as I can make out, is a man whose capacious skull allows of his being on the alert to a hundred different things at once, this same alertness being connected with a power of seeing the relations between different complicated sets of phenomena when they are presented in their entirety. The eighteenth century had its Linnæus, whose greatness even I can detect as I turn over his pages; its Huber, discovering through others' eyes what others could not discern with their own; its Goethe, its Haller, its Hunter, and mixed with practical greatness, its Pinel and its Jenner. Then, there was Lavater, who showed how pure æsthetic estimation might be turned to the discovery of truth—a man depreciated because logicians and philodoxers can so much more easily detect his weakness than discern his strength. The nineteenth century, with its great thinker, Darwin; its Pasteur (great in chemistry as well as in biology, a man who impressed me personally, and impresses me in his works, as much as any but two or three of the century); its Lamaroll, Weissmann, Cuvier, Agassiz, von Baer, Bichat, Johannes Müller, Robert Brown, and I know not whom besides, has certainly garnered a magnificent harvest of great men from this field.

Those sciences which study individual objects and seek to explain them upon physical principles—astronomy, geology, etc., corresponding to history and biography on the psychical side—demand the greatest assemblage of different powers. Those who pursue them have first to be mathematicians, physicists, chemists, naturalists, all at once, and, after that, astronomers or geologists in addition. It is almost beyond human power. In the eighteenth century A. G. Werner broke ground in geology, William Herschel, Kant, and Laplace did great things in astronomy. In the nineteenth century geology was first really made a science, and among its great men one recalls at once Lyell, Agassiz, Kelvin. This country has become its home. In astronomy, too, this country has been eminent, especially in the new astronomy which has afforded the needed scope for greatness, instead of the narrow rut that Bessel and Argelander had left behind them. Thus it happens that we have a magnificent group of great astronomers living among us today. We stand too close to them to take in their true proportions. But it is certain that the names of Chandler, Langley, Newcomb, Pickering, and several others are indelibly inscribed upon the heavens. In England it is only this year that Sir Norman Lockyer has brought the extraordinary research to which his life has been devoted to completion, so far as such work can be said to be capable of completion. It is an attribute of its greatness that it is endless.

When we compare all the men I have glanced at, with a view to eliciting a common trait somewhat distinctive of the nineteenth century, we cannot but see that science has been animated by a new spirit, till the very word has become a misnomer. It is the man of science, eager to have his every opinion regenerated, his every idea rationalized, by drinking at the fountain of fact, and devoting all the energies of his life to the cult of truth, not as he understands it, but as he does not yet understand it, that ought properly to be called a philosopher. To an earlier age knowledge was power, merely that and nothing more; to us it is life and the *summum bonum*. Emancipation from the bonds of self, of one's own prepossessions, importunately sought at the hands of that rational power before which all must ultimately bow—this is the characteristic that distinguishes all the great figures of the nineteenth-century science from those of former periods.

18. Letters to Samuel P. Langley, and "Hume on Miracles and Laws of Nature"*

[By 1901 Peirce's lack of a steady position and income left him poverty-stricken and dependent on reviewing and hack work like translating scientific papers for the Smithsonian Institution, whose Secretary, then Samuel P. Langley, took a generous interest in helping to support Peirce. The first letter (April 1, 1901) of the correspondence printed below between Peirce and Langley contains a plea by Peirce to use the Appendices of the Annual Report of the Secretary as a medium for the publication of his lifelong and original researches in logic and the nature of reasoning. Peirce refers to a paper by Poincaré (which he had translated for Langley) on the use of hypotheses in science, and condemned Poincaré's conventionalism as an example of a dangerous advocacy of "loose and desultory thought" in line with the equally bad nominalism of Karl Pearson's *Grammar of Science*. Peirce had just reviewed this book severely for Cattell[1] who had written him that it "was so much used by students that something ought to be done to counteract some of its tendencies." Peirce enclosed a copy of his review, along with a newspaper article on "The Cen-

* Reprinted from my article in *Proc. Amer. Philos. Soc.*, Vol. 91, 1947, pp. 201–228, with the kind permission of the American Philosophical Society and the Smithsonian Institution. —Editor's note.

[1] *Popular Science Monthly*, Jan. 1901. See Selection 7, above.

tury's Great Men in Science"[2] and a review in the *Nation* (Vol. 72, No. 1865) of Rev. John M. Bacon's *By Land and Sea*, consisting of scientific observations made from a balloon. In the latter Peirce indicates the "natural way in which science advances. . . . A man first acquires some peculiar facilities for making a certain class of observations, and then he applies these facilities as best he can." In "The Century's Great Men in Science" Peirce elaborated his favorite theme of the historical continuity and objective reality of general ideas, namely, that great scientific discoveries have mostly been made independently by two or more persons. This is illustrated by the leading scientific discoveries of the nineteenth century: "Darwin and Wallace simultaneously put forth the hypothesis of natural selection. Clausius, Rankine, and Sadi-Carnot, perhaps, Kelvin . . . the mechanical theory of heat. Krönig, Clausius, Joule, Herapath, Waterston, and Daniel Bernouilli . . . the kinetic theory of gases, etc." Ironically enough, Langley and the Wright brothers were soon to illustrate Peirce's point by engaging in the controversy over the priority of inventing the airplane.

In Secretary Langley's reply (April 3, 1901), we note that he recalls "with pleasure" his reading "The Fixation of Belief" (1877), the first of Peirce's six papers ("Illustrations of the Logic of Science").[3] Langley, in the postscript to this letter, invited Peirce to write on the change in the idea of "laws of nature" since Hume's time. Langley thought that Hume's skepticism about reason in religion, as expressed in his essay on Miracles, had been the beginning of the break with the eighteenth-century rationalistic and deistic belief in the certainty of the laws of nature. But, as the correspondence and manuscripts submitted by Peirce

---

[2] *New York Evening Post*, Jan. 12, 1901, Sec. IV, "Review of the Nineteenth Century." See Selection 17, above. In this section, alongside of Peirce's article, there are articles of considerable interest to historians of nineteenth-century scientific thought, by Leslie Stephen on science and religion, by Simon Newcomb on astronomy, and by Oliver Lodge on physics.

[3] *Popular Science Monthly* 12: 1–15, Nov. 1877, contains this first paper, which together with the second, "How To Make Our Ideas Clear" in the same volume (12: 286–302, Jan. 1898), constituted Peirce's "Plea for Pragmatism [1903]."

emphatically indicate, Peirce was adamant in his belief that Hume's psychological nominalism was inadequate to support the modern notion of scientific laws as probabilities. It is doubtful whether the good Secretary, who was an eminent physicist and not a historian or metaphysician, understood the subtleties of Peirce's scholastic and tychistic realism. Lester F. Ward, who was asked by Langley for an opinion of Peirce's manuscript, replied (April 17, 1901) that he was puzzled by Peirce's statement, based on his tychistic evolutionism, that scientific ideas are becoming "more theological" because "there is less confidence than formerly that laws of nature are unchangeable."

It took Peirce less than a week (April 3–9) to write his first manuscript on "Hume and the Laws of Nature."[4] Langley was not too satisfied and asked in his letter of April 19 that Peirce add "a few words . . . concerning the change of the common view about the meaning of the laws of Nature between Hume's time and our own," to which Peirce immediately replied (April 20) that he would have to write a new article going into the history of the phrase "laws of nature" and into the logic of Hume's argument based on the "balancing of probabilities." This would include a statement of Peirce's own "pragmatical" logic of hypotheses, which he "had been in possession of for five or six years"; perhaps, Peirce is referring to his "Grand Logic" of 1893 in which Abduction, Deduction, and Induction were worked out as the principal types of scientific inference. In any case Peirce's second manuscript entitled "The Proper Treatment of Hypotheses" was received at the Smithsonian Institution on May 13 and returned on May 18 as "too hard reading."[5]

[4] Cf. *Collected Papers of Charles Sanders Peirce*, ed. C. Hartshorne and P. Weiss, I: 54–56, Harvard Univ. Press, 1931, with the date guessed by the editors as "c. 1894" and with no reference to Secretary Langley. Hume is criticized by Peirce's reference to mathematics as "a large part of philosophy" and to "simple" observations as not easy because they are permeated with uncriticized opinions.

[5] *Ibid.*, VI: 356–369, 1935. Here the editors guessed the date correctly "c. 1901" but were still unaware of the Peirce-Langley correspondence and the Peirce manuscripts of June 1, 1901, and September 5, 1901, reproduced below.

Peirce then began to insist in stronger language that Langley was mistaken in thinking there was any logical connection between Hume's argument against miracles and the older metaphysical notion of the laws of nature, and sent on June 1, 1901, a third manuscript, "Hume on Miracles and Laws of Nature." I have incorporated this autoscript in the "final draft" printed below which includes Peirce's final changes on the draft of Langley's edited version. The excisions and revisions of Peirce's autoscript were proposed by Langley in order to get *The Century Review* to pay $100 for the article, and thus help Peirce financially. But Peirce refused to accept all the changes (for the reasons given in his letter of Sept. 5, 1901), and added further historical and logical comments on Hume's theory of induction and probability that are inserted in the text below with footnotes to indicate where his original autoscript draft differs from this final version.

When the Smithsonian Report for 1901 finally appeared, there was a paper on "The Laws of Nature" but it was not by C. S. Peirce. It was by S. P. Langley who still maintained, despite all of Peirce's arguments to the contrary, that the laws of nature are "laws of our own minds—and a simple product of our human nature"; the good Secretary in offering to help Peirce was apparently unable philosophically to be helped by the metaphysical realism of Peirce.

These documents, then, not only throw additional light on Peirce's personal and intellectual biography, but also on the history and philosophy of science at the opening of the twentieth century when scientists were wondering how aeronautics, x-rays, radioactivity, De Vries' biological mutations,[6] and new developments in mathematics and the logic of probability, were going to change our conception of "laws of nature." In fact, Ludwig Boltzmann, at the International Congress of scientists and scholars in 1904 (St. Louis Expo-

---

[6] I owe to my friend, Mr. Jerome Rosenthal, the suggestion that Peirce and James were impressed by the Curies' discovery of radioactivity (1895) and De Vries' *Die Mutations Theorie* (1901) as evidences of internal energy that seemed to be independent of the environment, and hence evidence of internal relations that transcend external "mechanical" forces.

sition), sketched the new statistical conception of laws of nature as superseding Maxwell's preference for the "dynamic" type of causal explanation in classical mechanics. Peirce's premonition of this statistical idea of laws of nature was obscured by his metaphysical attempts to link the new idea with older, scholastic ideas of the teleological order of nature.]

The Peirce-Langley Correspondence

Milford, Pa.   1901, April 1

My dear Professor Langley:

I have been studying your Reports, and I think I understand just what you want the Appendices to be. I write now to persuade you to employ me to write, say, 12,000 words for your next report upon a subject on which I have much to say which would really be useful to a great many people; and it would be a pity if, after the many years of hard thinking that I have devoted to making the matter clear to my own mind, the results which could be put into a very forcible and clear statement, amounting to proof, should die with me, or go unexpressed until my powers decay. What I mean is the nature of scientific reasoning. It is singular that men who are very exact in their conceptions upon other subjects, such as Poincaré—I don't mention logicians who are only superficially exact in any of their thinking—should not only deem loose and desultory thought about the relations of theories to facts and like subjects to be permissible, but even have a notion that thinking of that sort on those subjects is particularly commendable. I should undertake to convince thinking men that that whole method—as well as other methods that are in vogue, the psychological, the grammatical—are wrong. That it is necessary to begin by ascertaining upon what principles the doctrine of legitimate inference should rest, and to adhere to them. Then I should go on to show what it must rest upon, namely, upon experience; but no desultory experience but experience of certain kinds and treated in a certain way. Then I would show that this method leads to definite practical and useful maxims. . . .

[—C. S. Peirce]

Milford, Penn.   1901, Apr. (10)

My dear Professor Langley:

I have done the best I could with the subject you set for me, and enclose the result. It belongs, however, to an entirely different class of topics from those which I profess to be able to bring within the comprehension of the common farmer. Having lived among farmers for a great many years, and having carefully studied their ways of thinking, I know how to talk to them about anything within their comprehension. Logical subjects, if taken up in their proper order, are quite within their comprehension, because every step can be illustrated by a reasoning sufficiently like those upon which they have to think hard and anxiously every year. I know better than to insult them by drawing my examples as if they were able to think of nothing but farming; but I make my illustrations precisely analogous to reasonings of their own. I have very often written for them in the journals they read to their high satisfaction.

As to treating logical topics in newspaper articles, of course that is precisely what I am constantly doing; but the city daily paper addresses a totally different kind of intelligence from the country weekly.

As for boys of fourteen, they are incomparably below the farmer in logical intelligence, because they never have done any very serious and strenuous thinking. On other subjects I have had much success in writing to them.

Readers of Smithsonian Reports form a class rather different from farmers, and in some respects more intelligent. Still I do not think it would be possible to discuss before them to any advantage a question of metaphysics, such as is that which you assign to me to write about. Probably you regarded it as a scientific question. To my mind, it is quite clear that it is a question upon which no special science can throw any particular light, although the scientist has to make some sort of assumption about it.

I have just multiplied the space you gave me by two, so as to bring the task a little nearer to the region of possibility; and in that space, I have treated the subject as nearly as possible so as to be of benefit to your readers. Probably it might do *some* of them good to read what I have written.

I am glad you find my Pop. Sci. Monthly article so totally unsuitable for your readers. It was written for a totally different class, which I carefully defined in my letter to you, and had it been the least suitable to your readers, it must have been utterly unsuitable to those for whom it was intended. I exhibited a boat of my making as evidence of my handiness with tools, and your comment upon it was that it would not do for a rattrap at all. I should hope not!

Although I forward what I have written, I do not think it very suitable for your readers. The subject set me was too impossible. So you need feel under no obligation to keep it.

If you do not like the idea of my writing for your readers about logic, about which I have much to say which they would understand, is there not a "first-intentional" subject upon which you would accept an article from me? Suppose, for example, I were to describe my method of studying great men, which is elaborate and interesting?

Although, as you can see, I am far from charmed with the subject you assigned to me, and not altogether reconciled to your rejection of the subject I would have liked to write about, yet I beg you, my dear Prof. Langley, to understand that I fully appreciate the great kindness and friendliness with which you treat me, and that I am deeply grateful for the material succor which it brings and of which I am very much in need, indeed. My wife whom I sent to N. Y. to see the doctors, came back with their verdict that a second great operation has to be performed just as quick as she can be brought up into condition to undergo it.

Yours very faithfully,

C. S. Peirce

Milford, Pa.   1901, Apr. 20

My dear Professor Langley:

I have just received yours of 19th with my screed, and regret that I should have misunderstood your desires, which you now make plain to me. I shall have to write quite a new article, which will not prevent your taking the one I have already written, if you like; but as I said before, there is no obligation. I must re-read several things before writing, and I have no books here, not even a Hume. I shall have to go to New York.

Meantime, I can say that there is no great significance in the occurrence of the word *law* in Hume's definition of a miracle. His definition was drawn directly or indirectly from Aquinas, who says, *Miraculum propriae dicitur, cum aliquid fit praeter ordinem naturae.*[7] Of course, "law of nature" meant something entirely different for Aquinas. In fact, it was so, even in Hume's time, out of England, as one can see from Baumeister (1738) who says, *Miraculum est, cujus ratio sufficiens in essentia et natura entis non continetur,*[8] and who goes on, in this connection to define *ordo naturae,* and *cursus naturae,* but not at all *lex naturae,* about which he only talks in connection with ethics. However, it was different in England and in a measure in France. The expression "law of nature" is as old as Pindar in Greek, as Lucretius in Latin. But until modern times, it was used, as "law" ought to be, of something that *can* be broken but *ought* not to be. On the other hand, our *idea* of a law of nature was not foreign to the Greek mind. Only, the difficulty was that everybody then thought about Physics what today everybody but me and a select few think about Logic, namely, that minute and exact studies were out of place, and that broad and rough sketches were wanted. Thus Cicero, *De Natura Deorum,* says: *Alii naturam censent esse vim quondam sine ratione, cientem motus in corporibus necessarios: alii autem,* vim participem *rationis,* atque ordinis; *tanquam via progredientem, declarantemque, quid cujusque rei causa efficiat, quid sequatur, cujus sollertium nulla ars, nulla manus, nemo opifex consequi possit imitando.*[9] I believe that the modern application of

[7] "Miracle in the strict sense is used when something takes place outside the order of nature."

[8] "Miracle is that whose adequate cause (sufficient reason) is not contained in the essence and nature of the thing."

[9] "Some consider nature at certain times an irrational force exciting necessary motions in bodies; others again, as a force

the word "law" to something that cannot be broken, took its rise from Descartes, with his undeveloped occasionalism. He said the three angles of a triangle were equal to two right angles, because God chose to have them so; while he held at the same time, that all the purposes of God, without exception, are alike inscrutable. In Boyle, we see this very idea leading, as it naturally would, to the phrase *law of nature*, in the modern sense. See his Free Inquiry into the received Notion of Nature. Section vii. "Nature is not to be looked on as a distinct or separate agent, but as a rule, or rather a system of rules, according to which those agents, and the bodies they work on, are, by the great Author of things, determined to act and suffer. . . . We may usefully distinguish between the *laws of nature*, more properly so called, and the custom of nature, or, if you please, between the fundamental and general constitutions among bodily things," etc.

Returning to miracles, Bishop Butler, in his Analogy, 1736, holds it to be presumable that miracles follow certain higher laws.

The fathers of the church use no metaphysics in defining miracles. Thus, St. Augustine says, *Miraculum voco, quicquid arduum aut insolitum supra spem et facultatem mirantis apparet.*[10]

Hume's argument does not turn upon any metaphysical definition, any more than that of Woolston did. There is some force in the argument. But he makes the balancing of probabilities the sole consideration in judgment concerning testimony. From the pragmatical principle, which I still regard as highly useful, although not as the ultimate principle, a different conception of the function of hypothesis and of the logic of hypothesis necessarily results. As I have been in possession of this doctrine of the logic of hypothesis for five or six years, carefully considering and criticizing it, and am now quite ready to publish my con-

---

endowed with reason and order, declaring she acts according to a plan which is the cause of the thing, and whose skill no art, no hand, no artisan can accomplish by imitating."

[10] "Miracle, I call, what seems to one difficult or unusual, surpassing his ability and expectation."

clusions, I shall be very glad to have an opportunity to do so. I make the question of probability a secondary factor.

As to the state of the public mind at the time of Hume, as compared with that of today, I cannot speak with so much confidence. Nevertheless, I think the emptiness of the churches shows that miracles are less believed now. At the same time, my own impression, for which I can give some reasons, is, that the pendulum is now swinging the other way.

To say what is the cause of such phenomena is far more difficult, if not quite idle, at present. But I certainly do not think it comes from any deep thought or from any cause for which a rational thinker need entertain any respect. It is easy enough to suggest possible explanations in plenty.

Holding, as I do, that there is no intimate connection between the conception of the Laws of Nature and Hume's argument against miracles, I think you can understand how when you asked me to treat of "the Laws of Nature as understood by Hume's contemporaries and by our own, with special reference to his argument on miracles," I quite failed to see that it was a *logical* question about Hume's argument against miracles and not the *metaphysical* question of *law* which you wanted me to make my principal subject. I much prefer to do so.

Yours very truly,

C. S. Peirce

If your Disbursing Agent would send that $4. it would pay my fare to N. Y. and return. I have had to pay off more than half my mortgage this spring amounting to $1,700 and had to dump every cent I got from you into that. Then I had a suit which I felt confident would bring me $800. Unfortunately one of our "Lay Judges" had a suit against the same party, and thought if I got all that, there would not be enough left for him, and he managed iniquitously so that I only get $200, not enough to pay expenses hardly. I can appeal; but meantime, I am just as hard up as can be, with Mrs. Peirce's operation coming shortly.

[Undated]   Received May 13, 1901

My dear Professor Langley:

On careful consideration of the matter, I have decided that the only possible way of discussing the question you propose in your Appendices, is to separate it into at least three chapters and even then those chapters must be quite long. They may be made so far independent that they can be published in different years.

I now send you one, the first one. It would be much clearer if it were half as long again—because the sequence of thought could be better enforced upon the reader unaccustomed to consecutive thought. It would be still better for all classes of readers if another considerable addition were made to it in order to give historical illustrations. In fact several of these I actually wrote, but cut them out to save space.

Let me say again that you are not obliged to take the thing. As it is, it is no doubt hard reading. Yet there [are] bits of it that may please the readers who really don't understand it.

My plan would be to add another on the Rationale of Historic Criticism and finally wind up with the one sent back to me which I retain in order to improve it.

I was in New York eleven days hoping to earn a sum much needed. Unfortunately the gentleman for whom I worked very hard and increased greatly the value of his extraordinary library by my discoveries (as he fully acknowledged) took the view that as I was a personal friend and under obligations to him it wasn't necessary for him to pay *more* than my expenses, if quite that. He said he thought he had paid half my expenses. In fact, it was rather more than the total, but not so much as I could have earned in, say, driving a team. However, I must not permit myself to blame my friend. I mention it merely to show that if so be as any further money could be sent, I should be relieved. I fear I did not write and thank you for your splendid response to my previous appeal. If I did not, it was because I went off in a great hurry and was working day and night all the time I was gone.

I found a magnificent passage from St. Augustine about miracles, saying substantially what Bishop Butler said, but saying in Augustine's grand style that we cannot really know what is or is not in true accord with the course of nature.

I met in New York an old friend of mine, a Frenchman, who told me how he had known very well the elder Alexandre Dumas, who used to come to his country place. I remarked that Dumas must have been a splendid shot. On the contrary, said he, he was a remarkably bad shot. A new proof of the brilliancy of his imagination.

Very truly and with particular gratitude for your prompt response,

C. S. Peirce

Milford, Pa.   1901, June 1

My dear Professor Langley:

Your returning me a copy of your former letter leads me to believe that you supposed I had not read it attentively.

That was not it. Certainly nothing can be farther from my desire than to quarrel with any task you may set me, but the difficulty of bringing subjects so remote from one another, and so complex, as Hume's argument and the Laws of Nature into one piece was extreme. *Hume's argument has nothing to do with the Laws of Nature.* That is the difficulty.

I now send you another attempt. I have made pencil marks of different colors along the margin against different classes of parts which could be omitted. Omitting all these parts, it contains on a rough estimate 3,200 words. I think you may be yourself interested in reading the whole of the marked parts, and may very likely wish to include some of them. I therefore give my estimate of the number of words contained in each: Marked in yellow 1,800 words. . . .

I have withheld some notes containing chiefly quotations. If you want to see them, I will send them.

It is pleasing to see a man with Jannsen's spirit. Thanks for your communication to the C. R.   [*Century Review*]

Very respectfully, C. S. Peirce

[The next letter was written after the entire affair of Peirce's differences with Langley on the subject of Hume and the laws of nature had been consigned to the files of the Smithsonian Institution. Langley in his reply which terminates the correspondence regretted that he had no authority over the trustees of the Carnegie Institution, and could not help Peirce. Peirce never received a Carnegie grant.]

Milford, Pa.   1902, May 6

My dear Langley:

I wish you could give me some employment for a few months. I have lately written a section of my big book on logic, this section dealing with the Classification of the Sciences. How much thought and labor has gone into it, you will understand when I tell you that the MS. is 50,000 words long, and that in preparing it I consulted very close to a hundred different schemes that had been proposed. I am not entirely satisfied with what I have done and am now at work examining how scientific men in different branches felt themselves affiliated. This may lead to my making some changes.

I don't undertake to classify all possible sciences, but to produce a *natural* classification of the sciences as they now exist.

I think if I were to revise the work and bring it down to about 25,000 words, there are various classes of men, librarians, arrangers of sections of scientific societies, and scientific men of all kinds, who would be thankful to have it.

It is confined to the theoretical sciences, and does not include technology. To classify that would be a tremendous task. I have done a good deal of work on it. But my classification includes not only the psychical sciences, ethnology, linguistics, history, etc., but also the philosophical sciences and mathematics. It is carried out quite minutely.

Another subject on which I could give you an essay would

be the different theories now held concerning the connection between soul and body, and the nature of the soul, glancing at unconscious mind. I have a new theory of the relation between body and soul which I have not yet published or said anything about. Whether it is correct or not is a question which elaborate researches would be necessary in order to ascertain; but the mere possibility of the thing at once knocks the bottom out of the principal argument for "psycho-physical parallelism," which is the theory most widely entertained at present.

I have been working on this big book pretty steadily since last summer, and have a large mass done; but it is but a small fraction of the whole. Some friends have been buying the copyrights of the separate parts in order to enable me to go on. But their money has given out. Since it will represent about forty years of industry, I am strongly in hopes the Carnegie Institution will do something for me in the autumn. Under clauses 1, 2, and 6 of Carnegie's statement of the purposes of that institution, it seems to me their plain duty to enable me to get this work done. But some of the trustees are determined to put me down.

I hate to break off this work. There will be waste in doing so. If I could get something to write for you which would tide me over, writing on some subject allied to those of my book, it would be a great thing for me.

(People often write to me to ask me to write about the new doctrines of multitude, number, continuity, geometry, on which I have much to say, but I cannot say it because all my time has to go to bread and butter.)

Mrs. Peirce is in an extremely critical state of health, in which it is most necessary she should have the luxuries that her physician prescribes; and that is an additional reason why I should think only of work that brings in something. There is a lot of work people want me to do, which is right in my line, but they are unable to keep me alive while I do it.

Yours faithfully, C. S. Peirce

The Laws of Nature and Hume's Argument Against Miracles[11]

BY C. S. PEIRCE

I. What is a Law of Nature?

Having consented to write upon the subject or two subjects of this paper, I begin by remarking that[12] this phrase "Law of Nature" is used by physicists pretty vaguely and capriciously, in several respects. It is felt to be particularly appropriate as the designation of a physical truth of a widely general kind, exact in its definition, and found to be true without exception, to a high degree of precision. Yet there are truths of this description to which the title is refused; while others, special, rough in their statement, merely approximate in their truth, even subject to out-and-out exceptions, are, nevertheless, so called.

But there are two common characters of all the truths called laws of nature. The first of these characters is that every such law is a generalization from a[13] collection of results of observations, *gathered* upon the principle that the observing was done so well to conform to outward conditions; but not *selected* with any regard to what the results

[11] Peirce's holograph, 55 autoscript half-pages (hereafter designated as AS), sent with his letter of June 1, 1901, was entitled "Hume on Miracles and Laws of Nature." It was changed by Peirce to the one printed in the text above after he crossed out Langley's suggested title: "On the Meaning of the Words 'Laws of Nature' in Modern Scientific Thought." The editor's notes indicate how Peirce's autoscript of June 1, 1901, differs from his final draft of Sept. 5, 1901, in the combined version printed here.—Editor's note.

[12] Peirce's AS begins here: "This phrase is used by physicists . . . ," which Peirce changed in the final draft to the opening clauses printed above.—Editor's note.

[13] From here to the end of the paragraph, Peirce's AS reads: ". . . selection of observations; the principle of the selection having reference to the outward conditions under which the observations were made, and not to those results of them which are taken as the subject of generalization. That is to say, we do not cull those observations which show any peculiarity, and then call it a 'law of nature' that they show the very peculiarity which they were selected for showing."—Editor's note.

themselves were found to be—a harvest or a gleaning of the fruit of known seed, not culled or select, but fairly representative.

The second character is that a law of nature is neither a mere chance coincidence among the observations on which it has been based, nor is it a subjective generalization, but is of such a nature that from it can be drawn an endless series of prophecies, or predictions, respecting other observations not among those on which the law was based; and experiment shall verify these prophecies, though perhaps not absolutely (which would be the ideal of a law of nature), yet in the main. Nor is a proposition termed a "law of nature" until its predictive power has been tried and proved so thoroughly that no real doubt of it remains.[14] But the[15] expression "subjective generalization" calls for explanation. Augustus De Morgan very simply demonstrated[16] that, taking any selection of observations whatever, propositions without number can always be found which shall be strictly true of all those observations (and it may be added that they may be propositions not going beyond the matter of the observations), and yet no one of them likely to be true of any other observations which the same principle of selection might add to the collection. Such a generalization, a mere fabrication of ingenuity, which I term a subjective generalization, is often proposed by an amateur in science as an induction. "Bode's law"[17] was a subjective generali-

[14] This sentence beginning with "Nor" is not in AS; it was added by Pierce in final draft.—Editor's note.

[15] AS: "my" instead of "the."—Editor's note.

[16] A. De Morgan (1806–1871). Cf. article "Logic" in the *English Cyclopedia* (1860), *Essay on Probabilities* (1838), *Formal Logic, or the Calculus of Inference, Necessary and Probable* (1847).—Editor's note.

[17] J. Jeans, *The Universe Around Us*, pp. 237–238: N. Y., Macmillan, 4th ed., 1944, "Modern science is no longer concerned to look for numerical order in the distances between the planets, but is very much concerned to see whether the various observed regularities can be explained on evolutionary lines as the result of the operation of natural forces." Bode's Law (1772) has the form $d = 4 + 3.2^n$ where d is the distance of a planet from the sun, taking the earth's distance as 10, and n is the order of the planets. The "law" fails badly for Neptune and Pluto.—Editor's note.

zation. Let the artificers of such false inductions dare to set up predictions upon them, and the first blast of nature's verity will bring them down, houses of cards that they are.

So, then, I do not think a better definition of a *law of nature* can be given than this: it is a foreknowing[18] generalization of observations.

This said, the question is instantly started, How can the reason of a man attain such foreknowledge?[19]

How shall we answer? Must we not say that the fact that he can so attain proves that there is an energizing reasonableness that shapes phenomena in some sense, and that this same working reasonableness has molded the reason of man into something like its own image? These questions must remain for the reader to decide to his own satisfaction.

II.[20] *What conception of a Law of Nature was entertained in England in Hume's day, not by those who wrote upon the subject, but by the silent mass of educated men?*

In Hume's day, more than at other times, the great mass of educated Englishmen were grossly "practical." They did not waste thought upon anything not pretty directly concerning their own comfort, security, or amusement. They went to church, because doing so set a good example to the people, and so tended to maintain the supremacy of the upper classes. That was commonly regarded among university graduates as the chief function of the church; and consequently, anything that tended to weaken the church awoke in such men horror and dread.[21]

---

[18] AS: "prognostic." Langley changed this to "forecasting" which Peirce finally changed to "foreknowing," and in some passages (*infra*) to "predictive" and "forecastive."—Editor's note.

[19] AS: "to prognosis" instead of "such foreknowledge." Langley had "such forecasting."—Editor's note.

[20] Langley deleted some of the paragraphs in Part II of Peirce's AS and revised others. Peirce accepted with changes certain portions of Langley's version, after writing in the margin: "The simplest way is for me to adopt the paragraphs of Prof. Langley and make such modifications as seem to me called for." I refer to these changes by Peirce of Langley's version as "the final draft."—Editor's note.

[21] For a picture of Oxford in 1721, see Amhurst's "Terrae Filius."

The small remainder who really had any philosophical opinions, and yet did not write, were divided among three different ways of thinking. The Scotistic opinion, which had ruled the universities before the Reformation, had, in Hume's day, quite disappeared. That opinion, it is necessary to remember, had been that, in addition to Actual Existence, there are various modes of Imperfect Being, all of them varieties of Being *in futuro*—which we talk of when we say that "Christmas *really is coming*"—and in one of those modes of being, it was held that there really was something, which we of today should call a "law of nature," but which in the Latin language is simply a "nature"; and the Being *in future* of this law of nature was held to *consist in* this, that future events would conform to it. The theoretical element in that opinion lay precisely in the supposition that that which the ordinary course of things is bound (if not hindered) to bring about, already has a Germinal Being. That was no scholastic invention: it was the very heart of Aristotle's philosophy. But in Hume's day, nobody any longer believed in any such thing as that.[22]

In the last century an argument against miracles by David Hume attained celebrity and was generally regarded by the common of educated men as conclusive.[23] The great variety of attempts to answer it and their unsuccess[24] are the best evidence of the importance which attached to it in the century following its promulgation.

Briefly Hume accepts the definition of[25] a miracle which had become common in England in his day,[26] as a "violation of the laws of nature." It might be added that the

[22] The next four paragraphs were added by Langley to AS, and then modified by Peirce.—Editor's note.

[23] Peirce deleted from the rest of this sentence of Langley's version: "at least as against the Christian miracles," and wrote in the margin: "This is not my writing; but the men referred to were fully so much convinced of the absurdity of non-christian as of christian miracles."—Editor's note.

[24] Langley had "uniform failure" which Peirce changed to "unsuccess."—Editor's note.

[25] Langley had "defines" which Peirce changed to "accepts the definition of."—Editor's note.

[26] Peirce inserted after "miracle": "which . . . day."—Editor's note.

whole of modern "higher criticism" of ancient history in general, and of biblical history in particular is based upon the same logic that is used by Hume.[27] He says there must[28] "be an uniform experience against every miraculous event, otherwise the event would not merit that appellation, and as an uniform experience amounts to a proof, there is here a direct and full proof from the nature of the fact against the existence of any miracle." This does not exhibit the line of argument[29] which appeared so convincing to the century that followed Hume; but it is a curtailed statement given by Hume, no doubt for the benefit of those to whom the full argument seemed too abstruse.[30] Within the past generation, especially[31] within the past decade,[32] there have been symptoms that this true argument, and not merely this abridgment of it, is beginning to satisfy minds less completely than it used to do and that without having been refuted by any formal argument but partly because in some influential branches of science, it is out of harmony

[27] Peirce inserted the foregoing sentence into Langley's version.—Editor's note.

[28] Peirce inserted "there must," a typist's omission.—Editor's note.

[29] Langley's version: "This in briefest terms was the argument."—Editor's note.

[30] The clause "but . . . abstruse" was inserted by Pierce.—Editor's note.

[31] Langley's version "perhaps" instead of "especially."—Editor's note.

[32] After "decade," Langley's version: "it seems to have lost its force in the eyes of scientific men and is losing it in that of the laity and without having been refuted by any formal argument but by the mere change of attitude of educated thought toward its underlying assumption. For now, if not entirely without weight it has at any rate ceased to influence men's opinions. What the laws of nature mean in our contemporary thought we can very well assist ourselves by considering the change of our attitude to this argument. Now, what conception of the law of nature was entertained in England in Hume's day by the mass of educated men? To sum up, as has been said by another, the definition of a miracle as a supposition or a contravention of the order of nature is self-contradictory, because all we know of the order of nature is derived from our observation of the course of events of which the so-called 'miracle' is a part."

with modern ways of reasoning, and partly, no doubt, because archaeological research has refuted so many conclusions to which the same method of reasoning had brought the critics of history. At any rate, whatever the cause may be, the argument is certainly falling from its high renown. Professor Langley is of opinion that what "Laws of Nature" are coming to mean to our contemporary thought we can assist ourselves to understand by considering the change of our attitude toward this argument.

Now, what conception of a "Law of Nature" was entertained in England in Hume's day by the mass of educated men?

It has often been remarked that the definition of a miracle as a contravention of the order of nature is self-contradictory, because all we know of the order of nature is derived from our observation of the course of events of which the so-called "miracle" is a part.[33] St. Augustine, for example, in his glowing language, the Latin of the Vulgate, points out that it is only the order of nature so far as we can penetrate it that can be violated by a miracle; for the true order of nature is the ordinance of God; and the usual definition of a miracle among the fathers of the church is a performance which seems clearly to be beyond the power of man without divine assistance. In fact, the argument of Hume in no way turns upon any metaphysical definition of a miracle. Had it done so, it would have been refuted easily enough. It is, indeed, not properly an argument against miracles, in general, but only against *historical* miracles; and Hume does not lay himself open to so puerile an objection as that "all we know of the order of nature is derived from our observation of the course of events of which the so-called miracle is a part"; for nobody was more alive to that than he. It was against those miracles which did *not* form a part of our perceptual data, but were only hypotheses to account for the testimony of documents, that his argumentation was directed. Precisely, the same line of reasoning can be, and frequently is, applied to extraordinary events that are not miraculous. The reaction of thought

[33] The rest of this paragraph was inserted by Peirce and is not in AS.—Editor's note.

which now prevails consists in a suspiciousness concerning all reasoning of this description. The suspicion is thoroughly justified. The reasoning which Hume defends as highly scientific and as based upon mathematical principles, is shown by modern exact logic to amount to nothing but a peculiarly unfounded sort of presumption, only permissible in the extremest cases; and its pomp of mathematics is but a lion's skin disguising an obstinacy of adherence to preconceived opinions. But although it would thus appear that no two topics could be less germane, the one to the other, than Hume's argument and the conception of a law of nature, there is, nevertheless, a certain connection between them. Let us begin by examining the state of ideas in England in Hume's day.

The oldest opinion rife at that time was that of the Ockhamists, which was developed in the first half of the fourteenth century, and has had a very strong following in England from that day even to our own, without yet betraying any great signs of enfeeblement. This opinion is that there is but one mode of Being, that of individual objects or facts; and that this is sufficient to explain everything, provided it be borne in mind that among such objects are included *signs,* that among signs there are *general* signs, i.e., signs applicable each to more than a single object, and that among such general signs are included the different individual *conceptions* of the mind. This theory opens a labyrinthine controversy, full of pitfalls, which ninety-nine readers out of every hundred lack the patience to thread to the last; so that they finally leap the hedge and decide the question according to their personal predilections. I will simply aver, from having analyzed the whole argument, that the Ockhamists are forced to say of a law of nature that it is a similarity between phenomena, which similarity consists in the fact that somebody *thinks* the phenomena similar. But when they are asked why *future* phenomena conform to the law, they are apt to evade the question as long as they can. Held[34] to it, they have their choice between three replies.

[34] From "Held" to "a quite common answer" (three paragraphs below) was deleted by Langley from AS.—Editor's note.

The reply which the stricter Ockhamists usually give is that the conformity of future observations to inductive predictions is an "ultimate fact." They mostly endeavor to generalize this reply, so that, as they phrase it, it is the "uniformity of nature," or something of the sort, that is the ultimate fact. Such a generalization is inherently vague; and besides, a general fact has, for them, no being at all except as somebody's thought about its particulars; so that there seems to be no inaccuracy in saying that they make each fulfillment of a prognostication an "ultimate," that is to say, an utterly inexplicable, fact. But they cannot, and do not, maintain that the fulfillment of the prophecy is *self-evidently* an ultimate fact. Indeed, the Ockhamists are justly very chary of admitting "self-evidence." No, they admit that the "ultimacy" of the prognostication is their *theory* of it. But at this point, Logic puts in a demurrer. For the only possible logical justification that a theory can have, must be that it furnishes a rational explanation of the relation between the observed facts; while to say that a relation between observations is an "ultimate fact," is nothing more than another way of saying that it is *not susceptible* of rational explanation. That, one would think, ought to put this first answer out of court, at once.

There remain two other possible answers, though neither is much in the Ockhamistic taste. To the question how true prognostication was possible, an answer sometimes given in Hume's time was that it was rendered so "by the courteous revelations of spirits." If these were finite spirits, as some of the Cambridge men thought, one does not see how they could prognosticate better than their superior, redeemed man.

Finally, a quite common answer was that predictions[35] come true because God chooses so to govern the universe that they may come true. I term this style of explanation, that things happen as they do because God chooses that they shall so happen, "explanation *à la turque*."[36] It is a right handy contrivance for explaining all past, present, and

[35] AS: "prognostications"; Langley's version: "forecastings." —Editor's note.
[36] Langley deleted "explanation *à la turque*."—Editor's note.

future phenomena, without stirring from one's sofa, in one brief sentence which no monotheist can deny. Some may think it a disadvantage in this theory that it refuses to lend itself to any definite prediction, for all its making prediction such a simple matter. But then, it so escapes all danger of refutation. Ockhamists do not commonly attach much importance to prediction anyway, and often seem to hate to hear it talked about.

Under the head of Ockhamists I mean to include, first, Hobbes, more extreme than Ockham himself; then Berkeley, Hume, the Mills, etc.;[37] then Locke, and many others less decidedly of this turn of thought.[38] But the truth is that all modern philosophy is more or less tainted with this malady.

Another[39] philosophy which had some currency in England in Hume's time was the theory of a "plastic nature," that is to say, a slightly intelligent agent, intermediate between the Creator and the universe, God's factotum, which attended to the ordinary routine of administration of the universe. This theory was so much out of date that I should not have mentioned it were it not that I suspect it aided considerably in bringing into vogue the phrase "law of nature" in England, an expression which the sectaries of the plastic nature might very naturally, and in fact early did, employ. One of them, for example, Lord Brooke, in a work published in 1633, but "written in his Youth and familiar Exercise with Sir Philip Sidney," has the following:

> "And where the progresse was to finde the cause
> First by effects out, now her regresse should
> Forme Art directly under *Natures Lawes,*
> And all effects so in their causes mould
> As fraile Man lively, without School of smart,
> Might see Successes comming in an Art."

Here, "Nature's Laws" are nothing but prognostic generali-

---

[37] AS added: "typical Ockhamists, all."—Editor's note.
[38] AS: "who are less decidedly Ockhamistic."—Editor's note.
[39] This paragraph in Peirce's AS was deleted in Langley's version.—Editor's note.

zations of observations. However, a stray poetical example does not argue much.

Another philosophy, famous even in England, was that of Descartes, who made all connections between events to be due solely to the direct intervention of the Deity. In short, he held the explanation *à la turque* to be the only true one.[40] It followed that if we can attain any foreknowledge,[41] this is because the Deity has chosen somehow to make the order of events in some measure comprehensible to us. But the conclusion which Descartes *held* to be deducible, for he it was who set that fashion of loose reasoning to which all subsequent metaphysicians have so religiously conformed, went a good deal further; for from the bare thought "I think, and so I exist," he professed to demonstrate that whatever appears to us clear and distinct must be true—another of those modern conveniences by which Descartes rendered philosophizing so reposeful! Meantime, one might expect that Descartes' opinion would lead to his calling predictive generalizations of observations by the name of "laws of nature"; and so, accordingly we read, in his *Principia Philosophiæ*, published in 1644: "Moreover, from this same immutability of God, certain rules, or laws of nature, can be known, which are secondary and particular causes of the different movements which we observe in bodies."[42] It will be observed that Descartes does not acknowledge that his laws of nature are generalizations from experience, although they are prognostic. He was as extreme in attributing almost the whole achievement of science to the light of reason as the Ockhamists are in altogether denying it any part in that achievement.

The branch of philosophy in which the Britain of Hume's time really takes a distinguished place was ethics. The great light at the time Hume's argument was published was

[40] This sentence from Peirce's AS was deleted by Langley.—Editor's note.

[41] AS: "make any prognoses" instead of "attain any foreknowledge."—Editor's note.

[42] Atque ex eadem immutabilitate Dei, regulae quaedam, sive leges naturae cognosci possunt, quae sunt causae secundariae et particulares diversorum motuum, quos in singulis corporibus advertimus. Pars II, xxxvii.

Hutcheson. Hume considered his own greatest work to be his *Principles of Morals* (1751), which merely modified Hutcheson's doctrine. The book which reading Englishmen were talking most about when Hume's argument appeared was Wollaston's *Religion of Nature*. It had gone, I believe, through seven editions. Its main doctrine was that all vice is, at bottom, lying; and the one virtue, truthfulness. But as far as I am aware, there is little in all that literature to illuminate the problem we have before us.

In asking what speculations were passing in the minds of men who lived near two centuries ago, and never set pen to paper, I found myself before a pretty enigma. Still, having made my little research (all too hasty, I confess) I ought, at least, to know more about the matter than the average man. Now, however, I have to take up a question where I can only rely on personal observation within an area of acquaintance very likely no wider than my reader's —perhaps less so. The question lies across my path, however, not to be avoided. I must briefly consider it.[43]

III. *What conception of laws of nature is entertained to-day by the generality of educated men?*

I should say, most commonly, the same Ockhamistic conception which was commonest in Hume's time; for most men whom I meet, when they refer to such matters, talk the language of Mill's *Logic*. In particular, the explanation of foreknowledge[44] most common is that it is rendered possible by the uniformity of nature, which is an "ultimate fact." This adapts itself well to the atheistic opinion which has always been common among Ockhamists—more so, perhaps, about 1870 than at any other time.

Today, the idea uppermost in most minds is Evolution. In their genuine nature, no two things could be more hostile than the idea of evolution and that individualism upon which Ockham erected his philosophy. But this hostility has not yet made itself obvious; so that the lion cub and the lamb still lie down together in one mind, until a certain one of them shall have become more mature. Whatever in the

[43] This last AS paragraph was deleted in Langley's version.— Editor's note.
[44] AS: "prognosis."—Editor's note.

philosophies of our day (as far as we need consider them) is not Ockhamism is evolutionism of one kind or another; and every evolutionism must in its evolution eventually restore that rejected idea of law as a reasonableness energizing in the world (no matter through what mechanism of natural selection or otherwise) which belonged to the essentially evolutionary metaphysics of Aristotle, as well as to the scholastic modifications of it by Aquinas and Scotus.[45] To this wing of philosophy belongs, too, that theory of Gassendi which the present writer endeavored, a few years ago, to reawaken (in a perfected form), and of which, for the sake of the evolutionary conception of law which it illustrates, may here be inserted a description by an opponent of it, which was published in 1678:

"But because men may yet be puzzled with the universality and constancy of this regularity, and its long continuance through so many ages that there are no records to the contrary anywhere to be found, the atomic atheist further adds, that the senseless atoms, playing and toying up and down, without any care or thought, and from eternity

[45] [Footnote added by Peirce to take the place of the rest of part III of AS, deleted by Langley.] The acute reader (and it has become known to me that the Smithsonian Reports number among their readers men who, though they be children in scientific methods, yet surpass the average of the great scientists in the precision and vigor of their thought) will ask what I mean by a "reasonableness energizing in the world." I do not *define* the reasonable as that which accords with men's natural ways of thinking, when corrected by careful consideration; although it is a *fact* that men's natural ways of thinking are more or less reasonable. I had best explain myself by degrees. By reasonableness, I mean, in the first place, such unity as reason apprehends—say, generality. "Humph! By generality I suppose you mean that different events resemble one another." Not quite: let me distinguish. The green shade over my lamp, the foliage I see through the window, the emerald on my companion's finger, have a resemblance. It consists in an impression I get on comparing those and other things, and exists by virtue of their being as they are. But if a man's whole life is animated by a desire to become rich, there is a general character in all his actions, which is not caused by, but is formative of his behavior. "Do you mean then that it is a purpose in nature?" I am not insisting that it is a purpose; but it is the law that shapes the event, not a chance resemblance between the events that

trying all manner of tricks and conclusions and experiments, were at length (they know not how) taught, and by the necessity of things themselves, as it were, driven, to a certain kind of trade of artificialness and methodicalness; so that, though their motions were at first all casual and fortuitous, yet in length of time they became orderly and artificial, and governed by a certain *law,* they contracting as it were upon themselves, by long practice and experience, a kind of habit of moving regularly." Cudworth's *True Intellectual System of the Universe.*

IV. *What is the conception of law entertained today by typical scientific men?*

It does not belong to the function of a scientific man to ascertain the metaphysical essence of laws of nature. On the contrary, that task calls for talents widely different from those which he requires. Still, the metaphysician's account of law ought to be in harmony with the practice of the scientific man in discovering the laws; and in the mind of the typical scientific man, untroubled by dabbling with

---

constitute the law. "But are you so ignorant as not to know that generality only belongs to the figments of the mind?" That would seem to be my condition. If you will have it that generality takes its origin in mind alone, that is beside the question. But if things can only be *understood* as generalized, generalized they really and truly *are;* for no idea can be attached to a reality essentially incognizable. However, Generality, as commonly understood, is not the whole of my "reasonableness." It includes *Continuity,* of which, indeed, Generality is but a cruder form. Nor is this all. We refuse to call a design reasonable unless it be feasible. There are certain ideas which have a character which our reason can in some measure appreciate but which it by no means creates, which character insures their sooner or later getting realized. What machinery may be requisite for this I do not ask. But the laws of nature have, I suppose, been brought about in some way; and if so, it would seem that they were of such a nature as inevitably to realize themselves. These, then, are the naked abstract characters that must be recognized in the "reasonableness" of a law of nature. Whether or no it be a legitimate presumption from those characters that nature has an intelligent author, I certainly do not see how the abstractions could, better than in that statement, be clothed in the concrete forms which many minds require, or how they could better be connected with appropriate sentiments.

metaphysical theories, there will grow up a notion of law rooted in his own practice.

The scientific man finds himself confronted by phenomena which he seeks to generalize or to explain. His first attempts to do this, though they will be suggested by the phenomena, can yet, after all, be reckoned but mere conjectures; albeit, unless there be something like inspiration in them, he never could make a successful step. Of those conjectures—to make a long matter short—he selects one to be tested. In this choice, he ought to be governed solely by considerations of economy. If, for example, the prospect is that a good many hypotheses to account for any one set of facts, will probably have to be taken up and rejected, and if it so happens that, among these hypotheses, one that is unlikely to be true can probably be disposed of by a single easy experiment, it may be excellent economy to begin by taking up that. In this part of his work, the scientist can learn something from the business man's wisdom. At last, however, a hypothesis will have been provisionally adopted, on probation; and now, the effort ought to be to search out the most unlikely necessary consequence of it that can be thought of, and that is among those that are readily capable of being brought to test of experiment. The experiment is made. If the prediction from the hypothesis fails, its failure may be so utter[46] as to be conclusive; or, maybe, nothing more than an alteration of the defective theory need be undertaken. If, notwithstanding its unlikelihood, the prediction be verified, and if the same thing happen again and again, although each time the most unlikely of the (convenient) predictions has been tried, one begins to doff one's cap to the rising star that nature herself seems to favor.

The scientific man certainly looks upon a law, if it really *be* a law, as a matter of fact as objective as fact can be. The only way in which, to the scientist's apprehension, a newly recognized law differs from a fact directly observed is, that he is, perhaps, not quite sure that it *is* a law. Ultimately, the law becomes for him much *more* reliable than

[46] AS: "it may fail so utterly" instead of "its failure may be so utter" which Peirce inserted in final draft.—Editor's note.

any single observation. It now begins to stand before the scientific man, the hardest of hard facts, by no means a fabrication of his; his exhumation rather, almost to be called a thing of power; although, even now, it might conceivably be brought to naught by a sufficient array of new observations; and, indeed, the presumption is that the time will come when it will have to be reformed, or perhaps even superseded.

V. *What was Hume's argument against miracles?*

[The argument consists of two parts. In the following analysis of it, I number the paragraphs of the first part which contains the gist of the whole. My comments are inclosed in square brackets, and each paragraph containing a condensation of one or more of Hume's is preceded by his name.] (Brackets in text to p. 315 below are Peirce's. —Ed.)

HUME: An argument of Archbishop Tillotson against the real presence is of a very broad nature, showing decisively that no testimony whatever can prove propositions of a certain kind.   ¶1.

HUME: Announces that he has discovered a similar general and decisive argument against all miracles, than which nothing could be more convenient.   ¶2. [The allusion here, well understood by every contemporary reader, was to the fact that all through Hume's boyhood (he was born 1711) and down to within four years of his present publication, the island of Great Britain had rung with the vigorous attacks of a very pious Christian, Rev. Thomas Woolston, and of his successor Peter Annet, upon the literal truth of the gospel miracles. Woolston's first publication in this line was in 1705; and from 1720 to 1728 his publications were almost incessant. He was then imprisoned,[47] and died in prison in 1733. But the same cudgels were taken up by Annet, another clergyman, who took pains to make himself intelligible to the common people. His attack on the resurrection reached its third edition in 1744. Hume's

---

[47] He was not incarcerated, but was fined, and put in the debtor's prison for not paying the fine. He "purchased the liberties," and was thus allowed to enter certain streets. [This footnote was inserted by Peirce in final draft.]

argument appeared in 1748. The sale of Woolston's books had been absolutely unprecedented; and they provoked no less than sixty published replies. There can, therefore, be no doubt that a very large part of Christian England was already thoroughly persuaded of the incredibility of the gospel miracles at the time Hume's argument appeared. But former methods of attack upon them had involved a minute analysis of each story. To illustrate this, I will summarize Woolston's treatment of the casting of the devils into the herd of swine. He begins by ridiculing the statement that a man with an unclean spirit was permitted to remain in a public place "night and day crying out," as well as the assertion that "no man could any more bind him, no, not with a chain; because he had been often bound with fetters and chains, and the chains had been rent asunder by him, and the fetters broken in pieces: and no man had strength to tame him." In the next place there could not have been "a great herd of swine feeding" in that public place, because for centuries the keeping of swine in any part of Palestine had been forbidden by law under severe penalties. Finally, far from proving the divine nature of Jesus, such a performance would simply have evinced a shocking disregard for the rights of property; and any jury in England would have brought in a verdict of heavy damages against him. In this fashion, it had been necessary minutely to examine every one of the gospel narratives of miracles. No reader could carry such a voluminous argument in his mind; so that all must have appreciated Hume's remark that it would be found a great convenience to be furnished with one decisive argument, not only against all gospel miracles, but against all the "prodigies to be found *in history*, sacred and profane," where he doubtless had in mind prophecies, traditions of stones having fallen out of the heavens, ghost-stories, tales of cures wrought by psychical agency and the like. But it will be noted that he expressly limits the argument to history. What ought to be said to a directly experienced miracle is a question which he does incidentally touch upon; but it is aside from his main argument.]

HUME: Like events do not, indeed in every case, uniformly happen under like circumstances; yet experience will commonly show how often an occurrence of one kind is usually accompanied by an occurrence of another kind. ¶3. A wise man proportions his belief to the excess of cases in experience in which facts resembling a fact in question have been found true over the cases in which such facts have been found false. In all cases we must balance the opposite experiments. ¶4. [The remarks that "a wise man proportions his belief to the evidence," ¶4, and that he "weighs opposite experiments" or "balances opposite circumstances," ¶6, merit careful scrutiny. If belief is what a man goes upon, the first statement suggests that, if the evidence is imperfect, the wise man in question will act a little on one theory and a little on the opposite theory, which is commonly called sitting on two stools. It may, however, mean that the man reckons on being disappointed once in so many times. If that be the meaning, the expression of "weighing opposite experiments" is correct enough, but the subsequent and principal application of this, that of balancing the improbability of a witness giving false testimony against the improbability of the occurrences to which he testifies, is not only inaccurate but irremediably and radically wrong.[48] It is to be noted that Hume was not the first to apply the doctrine of chances to testimony; for that had been done by Nicolas Bernouilli, the first of that name, two years before Hume (1711–1776) was born; and general attention had been called to the matter four years before Hume's *Essay* (1748) appeared by the circumstance that a lawsuit had then been decided against Nicolas Bernouilli upon the strength of the very rule which he himself had laid down. Without speaking of the great posthumous work of Jakob Bernouilli, which gave shape to the mathematical doctrine of probabilities in 1713, which Hume probably never looked into, two important works had appeared into one or another of which Hume must have looked, but without thoroughly understanding it. These were Dean Rémond de Montfort's *Essai d'Analyse sur les Jeux de Hazard* (1708; second much improved edition, 1713) and De Moivre's

[48] The next six sentences on the history of probability were inserted by Peirce in final draft.—Editor's note.

Doctrine of Chances (1716; second altered and enlarged edition, 1738). This branch of science was just coming to maturity; and the early writers are excusable for supposing, as Laplace and Poisson did later, that it was applicable to testimony. Although Hume's notions are foggy in the extreme, they are not without value and are decidedly original in part. It is next to impossible clearly to expound ideas which are themselves far from clear.[49] But the fairest rule of exegesis will be to attach such definitions to Hume's vague terms as to bring his final application of them to testimony (to which all that goes before is merely preparatory), as nearly into harmony with the truth as its essential falsity will permit. Guided by this rule of exegesis, I find that, in order to interpret the sentence *"a wise man proportions his belief to the evidence,"* the first necessary step is to define an "evidence," or "item of evidence" in a way which is so complicated, in its abstract statement, that it will be necessary to lead up to it by an example. Suppose, then, that it is known that into an empty urn have been placed a black ball and ten white balls. This knowledge assures us that if the balls are well stirred up and then one be drawn out, looked at, and thrown back, and this be repeated again and again, indefinitely, and if, at regular intervals, as the drawing goes on (as, for example, at the end of every 10th, 20th, 30th, etc., drawing) the ratio of *all* the white drawings to black drawings *from the beginning* be ascertained, then the only value which each ascertained ratio, as compared with the last previously ascertained ratio, will not, on the whole, depart from more often than it will approach, is the value 10:1. We commonly express this briefly by saying that "in the long run" ten white drawings will be made for every one black drawing. Such a known fact (as that ten white balls and one black ball are contained in the urn), which assures us that under circumstances definitely related to that fact (the drawings being made as prescribed), a kind of result (the drawing of a white ball) definitely related to the same fact will occur

---

[49] AS: "It is plainly useless to ask what Hume meant, the fogginess of whose ideas in this place penetrates to the reader's bones."

with a definite frequency in the long run, is to be termed an "evidence," or "item of evidence." It is to be carefully noted that, in all that follows, the word "evidence" is used in this excessively peculiar sense. The next step in the interpretation must be to define in what sense "belief" is to be understood. For that purpose, Hume must be understood to postulate that when a man holds any fact to be an "evidence" in the sense just defined a feeling is excited in his breast *upon the contemplation of any one of those possible future results* to the aggregate of which the "evidence" relates; as, for example, upon wondering whether the fifth drawing will give a white ball. To this feeling, which I might perhaps incline to call an expectation, Hume prefers to attach the name of "belief." It may be "belief" *pro* or "belief" *con*. Finally, we have to ask what sense we are to attach to the wise man's "proportioning" his belief to the evidence. I must here entreat the reader's close attention to one of the niceties of this important theory of probabilities, upon which, in Hume's view and that of the "higher critics," our whole judgment of testimony ought to turn. Nothing can be more important, to every man, than to understand clearly how far they are in the right. I am sure, therefore, that the reader will not object to being called upon for somewhat close thought here. Suppose, then, it were known that the contents of an urn were as follows:

1 black ivory ball,   10 white ivory balls,
3 black wooden balls,   30 white wooden balls.

This knowledge would be an "evidence," in Hume's peculiar sense of the term, that if balls were drawn at random and replaced, in the long run ten white drawings would be made for every black one, and three wooden drawings for every ivory one. Furthermore, these two "evidences" would be *independent*, in the sense in which that term is used in the doctrine of probabilities. That is to say, we should have "evidence," not only that 10 white balls would be drawn to every black one, but that this would equally be true among those which produced ivory balls. We should, likewise, have "evidence" that 3 wooden balls would be drawn to every ivory one, and this, not only among all the drawings, but also among the drawings of white balls and among the drawings of black balls. This is the meaning of the term *independent* as it is used in the doctrine of probabilities. But now, suppose that we were to employ a boy to make the drawings, with instructions to look at each ball after he had drawn it, and if it were either black and wooden or both white and ivory, to show it; but if it were either black and ivory or white and wooden to throw it back into the urn without showing it. According to Hume's view and that of many mathematical writers, under this last supposition the knowledge we have of the contents of the urn, regarded as "evidence" (in the same extraordinary sense) of what the character of any one ball that the boy shows will be, is analogous to our knowledge that a witness tells the truth 3 times for every time he falsifies, but that the like of the story he tells will be false 10 times for every time that it is true, considered as bearing upon the question of whether we shall believe him or not. Three wooden balls will be drawn for every ivory[50] one, just as the witness tells 3 truths against every falsehood. Ten white balls will be drawn against a black one; just as stories like that the witness tells will be ten times false to every time they are true. Under this supposition, the correct rule of probabilities is that the odds, 3/1, that the witness tells the truth, is to be multiplied by the odds, 1/10, that such a story will be true, to get 3/10, which is the odds (or ratio of favorable to unfavorable cases) in favor of such a story told by such a witness. Hume talks of "balancing" as though addition or subtraction were to be used instead of multiplication or division. This may have been a simple blunder on his part; but my rule of exegesis would require me to interpret him as meaning that the intensity of that feeling which he calls "belief" is proportional to the logarithm of the odds which excite it, according to an extension of Fechner's law. Hume was so gifted a psychologist that it is not quite impossible that he may have seen this.

In ¶4, Hume falls into an error which is very characteristic of the kinds of mistake which the Ockhamists fre-

---

[50] The MS. reads "black" instead of "ivory," but this is obviously a slip of Peirce's pen.—Editor's note.

quently commit, and particularly of their conception of laws of nature. Namely, he thinks that when a man is led to expect a certain sort of result in a given case, because it is, on the whole, more comfortable to the analogous instances in his past experience than the opposite result would be, those single experiential instances, or "experiments," as he calls them, can logically be "balanced" against one another, as if they were independent "evidences." But this is not so. The single instances though they may be evidences in the ordinary sense of the word are not "evidences," in the sense his argument requires. If I do not know what balls have been put into an urn, the drawing of a ball and finding it to be blue, affords me no assurance that any definite proportion of future drawings (and no more) will be of blue balls. This blunder has been committed, even by great mathematicians; but nobody but Hume ever fell into the manifest absurdity of holding the single instances to be *independent* "evidences." Were that the case, a man who merely knew of a certain urn of balls that a hundred white drawings had been made from it, would, in the absence of all information in regard to the black drawings, be entitled to a definite intensity of "belief" in regard to the next drawing, and not only so, but the degree of this "belief" would remain quite unaffected by the further information that the number of black drawings that had ever been made from the urn was zero!

It must not be supposed that because a sign that anything is a fact is highly convincing, therefore that sign must be an "evidence," in the sense here required. An "evidence," in what we are bound to take as Hume's meaning, is an argument from which it *necessarily* follows that a given sort of result must happen in the long run just so often, neither more nor less. Past experience is no "evidence" of future experience, because it is quite conceivable that the arrangements of the universe should change. Nor is there any sense in speaking of "evidence" of any single event; for "evidence" only shows how often a certain *kind* of event occurs. In short, "evidence" properly relates only to a purely hypothetical state of things, which quite *other* kinds of reasons may induce us to believe approximately agrees with the real state of things.

It is proper here to explain the analogy between Hume's erroneous assumption that the single instances of an induction are *independent* "evidences," and the opinion he and his followers entertain that when an event occurs in accordance with a law of nature, there is no real "necessity" in it. I do not accuse them of saying that there is no necessity in such an occurrence in *any* sense. On the contrary, they are fond of calling themselves "necessitarians." In the strict scholastic sense, necessity, as all the old logics containing the doctrine of modals explain, is a species of universality. To say that an event is necessary, in the strict sense, means that it not only does happen, but would happen under *all* circumstances. In this sense, the Humists are not peculiar in denying that any experiential knowledge is necessary. Almost all philosophers agree to that. In the usual sense of every-day life, that is necessary which would happen under all circumstances *that would ordinarily be considered.* Thus, we do not say that the alternation of day and night is necessary, because it depends upon the circumstance that the earth continually rotates. But we do say that by virtue of gravity every body near the surface of the earth *must* be continually receiving a component downward acceleration. For that will happen under all circumstances we are likely to take into account. Nor do Hume or his followers dream of denying that. But what they mean when they say there is no "necessity" in gravitation is that every "event" which gravitation formulates is in reality totally *independent* of every other; just as Hume supposes the different instances of induction to be *independent* "evidences." One stone's falling has no real connection with another's fall. The fact that the acceleration, which is what gravitation consists in, is continual, would make it necessary for such theorists to suppose time to be composed of discrete instants; and, of course, the Ockhamist doctrine that nothing really *is* but individual objects is contrary to any true continuity. The objection to Hume's conception of a Law of Nature is that it supposes the universe to be utterly unintelligible, while, in truth, the only warrant for any hypothesis must be that it renders phenomena intelligible. The Humists are very fond of representing their conception of a law of nature as a scientific result; but unfortunately metaphysics has not yet reached the scientific stage, and when it shall at length be so far matured, every indication today is that it will be a metaphysics as far as possible from this fourteenth-century Ockhamism. Anybody who maintains that there is any sense (except the strict scholastic sense) in which it is a result of science that a law of nature is not necessary, may at least be required to explain very distinctly just what that sense is; and to avoid the imputation of insisting upon a truism, he will probably vouchsafe to tell us who are the philosophers of the present day with any following who hold the contrary opinion.

The treatises on probabilities, which are written exclusively in the interest of the mathematical developments, and are weak upon their logical side, treat testimonies as "evidences" to be balanced along with and against one another. That is to say, they think that the character of a witness, etc., will in itself afford an absolute assurance that he will falsify just once in so often, neither more nor less. This seems to me absurd. How often he will answer wrongly depends on how the questions are put. If they are so put as to be answered by "yes" or "no," mere haphazard answers will, *we are told,* be half the time right; but a person who should answer correctly half the questions in such a book as *Mangnall's Historical Questions,* would not have answered at random. If it be said that what is meant is the ordinary course of questions in the long run, I doubt very much whether there is any long run in such a case. This phrase implies a series of ratios converging (though irregularly) toward a definite value. There is no necessity that there should be such a convergence; and if there is not, there is no long run and no such thing as probability in the case.

Without going deeper into the discussion, I will only say that if I am right in contending that there is no such thing as the numerical "veracity" of a witness; that the idea is essentially absurd; then, whether I am right or not in maintaining that a similar remark holds good of the "credibil-

ity" of a narrative, taken in itself, Hume's argument is hopelessly wrong and past all mending. But if I am wrong in
both respects, then with the proper definitions, there can
be no doubt that his method of "balancing evidences" is
profound and excellent, and that his argument does refute
all very extraordinary histories.]

HUME: Belief in testimony is merely a case of judgment
based upon the knowledge that there is a certain degree
of uniformity in certain phenomena (namely, the degree
of uniformity with which testimony of a given character is
true) and, as such, that belief should be governed by the
same principles as other reasoning from the uniformities of
experience. ¶5. Testimony must, therefore, be accepted
or not, according to the balance of likelihoods. ¶6.
(Hume says, "balance of opposite circumstances.") We
have to consider the character and number of witnesses,
etc. ¶7.

HUME: When the fact testified to partakes of the extraordinary and marvellous, or is such as has seldom fallen
under our observation, this should have a weight in the
other scale. ¶8. A corollary supported by a Roman prov-
erb. ¶9. Nor did the Indian think unwisely in refusing
to believe in ice. ¶10. [Here, a note, interesting for its
acute reference to the rule of continuity, has little relevancy to the main argument.] What ought we to conclude
in case the character of the witnesses, to be put into one
scale of our balance, is all that could be desired, while the
extraordinariness of their story, to be put into the other
scale, also reaches its maximum, in being a miracle? ¶11.
A miracle is a violation of X. [A violation of "the laws of
nature," says Hume. But since the problem before us is to
ascertain the precise logical bearing of a particular conception of the laws of nature upon Hume's argument, we must,
according to the rule of logic, substitute for that phrase a
symbol, which shall render it impossible to set forth the
argument without explicitly stating so much of the logical
content of the suppressed phrase as has any real relevancy
to the argument.] But a firm and unalterable experience
has established the truth of X. Therefore, the argument
against the miracle is as cogent as any argument from ex-

perience can be. A miracle is an event against which there is a uniform experience. ¶12. [This is the only definition of a miracle which is pertinent to the argument. As he elsewhere has it, a miracle is that which has not only never been known to happen in any age or country, but which is positively counter to all experience. At this point, Hume inserts a footnote to deal with the trifling objection that in many miracles the effect is not at all unparalleled; as when that effect is that an Ananias in apparent health falls dead, or that a storm immediately abates. The answer is that such circumstances are, in no case, the whole story, all of whose items together make up an unprecedented complex. In the course of this note, Hume gives the scholastic definition of a miracle in its full shape, to which I shall revert below. The whole footnote is mere eddy in the current of the argumentation.]

HUME: It follows that in order to establish a miracle by testimony, it would be requisite to adduce testimony of such a character that its falsehood would constitute a miracle—and a miracle much greater than that to which it should testify. ¶13.

[To refute the widely spread and extremely important error, as I hold it to be, that testimony ought to be treated by the balancing of likelihoods, and to show upon what principles it ought to be treated, with a sufficiency of illustrative examples, would require a separate essay; and its connection with the conception of a law of nature is not very close. I may mention, however, among the objections to that method, that it confounds two totally different things; objective probabilities, which are statistical facts, such as form the basis of the insurance business; and subjective probabilities, or likelihoods, which are nothing more than the expression of our preconceived notions. It was not "likely" that a stone would fall from the sky as long as men had a violent prejudice that it did not. But that is not all. The notion that a man tells a falsehood once in so often, *independently* of what the subject matter is, is a theory too far from the truth to be of the slightest service. Moreover, the practice of German writers on those branches of ancient history with which I am acquainted (which do not include biblical history) of frequently rejecting all the evidence there is, in favor of their notions of what is likely, without attempting to explain just how that testimony came to be what it is, is quite unwarrantable. The true method is in all cases to explain the testimony; and then, to put the explanation to every test possible. But examples would be required to show clearly what I mean.[51]]

HUME begins Part II of his argument [which is unimportant for our purpose] by enunciating the proposition which he is to prove, namely, that no testimony to a miracle ever had the requisite degree of certainty. ¶1. This is, indeed, sufficiently proved by the consideration that, with no human witnesses, could the event of their making up any story by a mixture of error and exaggeration be deemed a miraculous event, or anything approaching to miracle. ¶2.

In addition, people are more likely to tell false stories that are marvelous than false stories that have nothing remarkable about them. ¶¶3–6. Further, we are in possession of special information which increases the improbability of stories of this nature. ¶¶7–10. Further, the miracles of each religion are opposed by the miracles, and other evidences, of all other religions. ¶11. Three well-authenticated uses of miracles are adduced which any ordinary English contemporary of Hume would reject. ¶¶12–14. [They appear weakish under modern light.] Seven arguments follow (¶¶15–21) all of which are special, except the first, which is not developed. In ¶22 the argument is summed up, in full agreement with the above analysis. [The three next paragraphs, ¶¶23–25, appear to involve bad reasoning, since Hume only considers what he should say in certain cases, without showing to what conclusions his principles would lead. At all events, they are merely intended to confirm the principles employed by

[51] This bracketed paragraph was inserted by Peirce in final draft, after Langley had deleted the rest of part V and inserted: "In common if not correct language, a law of nature is a sequence of events where all that we observe is simply that these events do follow each other so far as our observation extends, to which we are in no way whatever entitled to say that there is any *necessity* in their so following."—Editor's note.

showing that they agree with the dicta of good sense.]
Francis Bacon seems to have embraced the same principles of reasoning. ¶26. [The two concluding paragraphs, ¶¶27, 28, merely fling a gratuitous insult to Christians, in order to give *éclat* to the chapter and to provoke angry replies.]

VI. *What is the bearing upon this argument of any particular conception of the laws of nature, or of the metaphysical essence of a miracle?*

The fathers of the church defined a miracle as a performance so far beyond ordinary human powers as to show that the agent must have had extraordinary super-human aid. This definition, which contains nothing about laws of nature or anything else, of a metaphysical character, would have suited Hume's purpose to admiration. He would have said, here we have two alternatives before us; either we have to believe that falsity has in some way crept into the testimony, or we have to believe that a man did something which all experience is against the possibility of his having done. Which is the more likely? Since experience is the only source of knowledge, we ought to accept the former alternative, which is quite conformable to experience, rather than the latter, which is altogether against it. This is Hume's argument, unmodified. It thus appears that that argument does not require any particular view to be taken of the regularities of phenomena or of the nature of a miracle—further than that it is something opposed to all experience.

Hume did not employ the patristic definition, because that definition was no longer usual. He simply adopted the definition of Aquinas, translating *ordo naturae* by the phrase "laws of nature," which had been familiar in England for more than two generations.[52]

---

[52] The earliest instance of its use (in the modern sense) with which I am acquainted occurs in a poem of Fulke Greville, "written in his Youth and familiar Exercise with Sir Philip Sidney" (says the title page) and printed in 1633 . . . [In this footnote, inserted by Peirce in final draft because Langley had deleted the poem with the paragraphs of AS at the end of part II, the first four lines of that poem are quoted by Peirce.]

It, no doubt, seemed to Hume preferable to allow the current definition of a miracle to stand, rather than to perplex the main question by disputing this point. And yet, were that usual definition accepted, either in its original sense or in the sense which the Cartesians and others among Hume's contemporaries would put upon it, it ought logically to preclude the admission of Hume's argument. For it is a vital postulate of that argument that experience is absolutely the sole source of our knowledge; while by the "order of nature" the scholastic realists had understood something like thought, or reasonableness, really active in shaping the phenomena of the cosmos. But to grant that there is such an energizing reasonableness is to give some hope that the inborn light of man's reason may contribute something to knowledge. Now if any place for such hope be allowed, then in cases where experience seems to be wholly in default,[53] as (apart from the gospel narratives) it seems to be wholly in default as to what would happen if the Son of God commanded a man to rise from the dead, then we shall inevitably resort, in such cases, to that inward "light of nature," to the discomfiture of Hume's argument. It thus appears that a strictly Ockhamist conception of the world, and consequently of the laws of nature, is presupposed in Hume's argument.

VII. *What effect did Hume's argument produce upon the minds of those of Hume's contemporaries who did not publish their opinions?*[54]

[53] Langley's version of the remainder of part VI: "then we shall inevitably resort in such cases to that inward 'light of nature,' to the discomfiture of Hume's argument. Everybody must have seen that to regard a regularity in phenomenon as due simply to a special decree of the Almighty, which is [nearly] the implication of the phrase 'law of nature,' was a view eminently favorable to miracles; to such a degree, that it could, and did, lead men to argue that what would [usually] be exceedingly improbable might become highly probable when God wished to reveal himself. Yet no doubt there were swarms of men for whom such reasoning was too abstruse." [Words inserted in brackets were added by Peirce.]—Editor's note.

[54] Langley's version deleted most of parts VII and VIII and incorporated the remainder of these parts in part VI, so that parts IX and X of Peirce's AS became parts VII and VIII of Langley's version.—Editor's note.

The majority of such people are not affected by any reasoning apart from the authority of its author; and Hume's name carried no weight at the date of this publication. Many others would remark that Hume only offered his argument as a brief substitute for other arguments of which they had heard a great deal—arguments which certainly demanded no *more*, perhaps less, to be conceded than Hume's. It could not have had much effect on any of those who had been sufficiently interested in the subject to read Woolston and Annet. It really only appealed to Ockhamists, very few of whom were not already dead-against miracles. As for the majority of educated men, who looked upon the church as a mere adjunct to the state, they could only regard it as a reprehensible performance.

VIII. *What bearing did those persons who did not express their opinions in print conceive that the metaphysical essence of a law of nature had upon Hume's argument?*

Everybody must have seen that to regard a regularity in phenomena as due simply to a special decree of the Almighty, which is the implication of the phrase "law" of nature, was a view eminently favorable to miracles; to such a degree, that it could, and did, lead men to argue that what would be exceedingly improbable under ordinary circumstances, might become highly probable when God wished to reveal himself. Yet no doubt there were swarms of men for whom such reasoning (which from the Ockhamistic standpoint is quite nonsensical) was far too abstruse, and who would simply say, "Although this gentleman shows his disposition to concede everything he possibly can, yet he cannot admit miracles because he is such a wonderful reasoner, whom we cannot follow. So, no doubt, he is right." Others, seeing that "laws of nature" were talked about, and well knowing that no Hobbes or other strict Ockhamist could endure such a phrase, were probably blinded by it to the fact that Hume's argument could have no standing except upon Ockhamistic ground.

IX. *Does Hume's argument affect the educated men of our day differently; and if so, why?*

I have little doubt (for here again I can only state what lies within my own narrow horizon) that the argument has lost a good deal of the *prestige* which it enjoyed at an intermediate period when philosophy was in a confused state and metaphysical questions were not as well understood as they were in Hume's time or as they are now.

Many men are now doubtful whether there is sufficient evidence that there was any one Jesus to whom the Gospels mainly relate; and under those circumstances they can hardly think it worth while to examine Hume's argument. Others opine that, independently of Hume's argument, which may be questionable, miracles performed in the midst of such a mob as would seem to have surrounded Jesus, could not possibly be sufficiently attested. Very few Christians now rest their faith on the gospel miracles. They believe in the religion because of some personal experience of their own; and if they believe in the miracles, in a literal sense, it is because they seem inseparable from the religion. Then again, Hume's main principle, that historic testimony ought to be judged by the balance of probabilities, has now been so exploited by the German critics, and carried so much further than Hume's innocence permitted his doubts to wander, that it has lost all its novelty, and most of its lustre.

In addition to these general causes, two special features of Hume's argument tend now to render it unacceptable to many. The first is his teaching that all human knowledge rests upon a quasi-mechanical examination of statistics, without allowing the smallest part to the natural light of reason, which is counter to the tendencies of thought of our day, when evolution has already caused us to recede somewhat from pure Ockhamism. Another thing is that Hume, after having made all reasoning an application of the calculus of probabilities, promptly displays such ignorance of the calculus himself[55] as to cause those who know something of it to take him to be more superficial than he really was. Anyway, we are now in the mood of dwelling on the superficiality of eighteenth-century skepticism; so that

[55] In final draft, Peirce added: "that very calculus of probabilities from which he makes such a parade of drawing his argument."—Editor's note.

such a symptom inclines us to contempt for Hume, who was really one of the great geniuses in psychology.

X. *Has any change in the usual conception of a law of nature been influential in causing the change of attitude toward Hume's argument?*

The very same conception of a law of nature which was most widely adopted in Hume's day is certainly the one most widely adopted now. The difference is that the progress of scientific applications has now forced everybody to ponder upon the regularity of nature,[56] so that, whereas in Hume's day, as well as we can judge, a good majority of the Protestant clergy not only persuaded themselves that they believed in miracles, but really did so, in our day a man may, during a long season of severe drought, make a point of going to one church after another, on different Sundays, without once hearing a prayer for rain.

I dare say people are now more given to fortune telling, chiromancy, communications from the other world, and other similar means of nervous titillation, which they class with wireless telegraphy, telephony, X-rays, and bicycles, as things incomprehensible, than they were in Hume's day, when good sense was in fashion. But I see no analogy between that state of mind and belief in miracles.

It is true that a section of the scientific world has of late been considerably occupied with the essentially provisional character of scientific theories. There is nothing new about this. St. Augustine, in connection with miracles, remarked that the unregenerate man can know nothing of the real order of nature, and that a miracle is but a violation of the laws of nature *so far as we know them;* and Bishop Butler, in Hume's day, repeated the remark.[57] But to say that the formulas we have found reason to accept as laws of nature are likely, in time, to be superseded, far from being necessarily hostile to Ockhamism, is quite in accord with that philosophy, and has, in our time, been urged chiefly by Ockhamists. Neither is there anything in Ockhamism to make miracles impossible. What *is* illogical, from the Ockhamistic standpoint, is the making of either of those

[56] Langley deleted the rest of this sentence.—Editor's note.
[57] Langley deleted the rest of this paragraph.—Editor's note.

propositions a ground for admitting any particular miracle. For upon Ockhamistic principles, the only logical support for any belief is positive experience, and to argue from what you do *not* know is simple nonsense.

So far as there are, in our times, evolutionary tendencies, which already begin to cause us to regard laws from a different point of view, there is the germ of ideas destined to destroy Ockhamism, and with it the argument of Hume against miracles.

XI. *What are the real merits of Hume's argument?*

It is one of the strongest applications that ever has been made of the general method of judging testimonies by balancing likelihoods.

That method rests on the assumption that experience is the sole source of knowledge, and the inductive process the only way of passing from the known to the unknown.

Not only is our knowledge not exclusively derived from experience, but every item of science came originally from conjecture, which has only been pruned down by experience.

The inductive process is inexplicable upon the assumption that all our knowledge comes from experience alone, and would be impossible if it were the only way of passing from the known to the unknown.

The entire matter of our works of solid science consists of conjectures checked by experience. The entire matter of those works which have been written upon the method of judging of testimony by balancing likelihoods consists of conjecture riding rough-shod over all the pertinent facts.

This method has never been put into practice without yielding fruit either ridiculous or horrible, according as the application was speculative[58] or practical.

It has been applied speculatively by modern German critics of ancient history, with whom it is a constant practice to deny the testimony of all the witnesses and to set down what seems likely in a German university town in the place of history. But wherever those critical denials have been struck by the spade of the archaeological ex-

---

[58] Peirce in final draft changed "speculative" to "purely scientific."—Editor's note.

plorer, the attitude of criticism has made a laughable picture.[59]

The same principle has been practically applied on the continent of Europe to judicial evidence; and if anybody is shocked by the hideous wrongs perpetrated by our own courts and district attorneys' offices, he can find some balm for his wounded Americanism in studying the results of the method in question in continental "justice."

[59] Langley's version ended here, deleting the last paragraph of Peirce's AS, printed above.—Editor's note.

Science
and Education

19. Research and Teaching in Physics[1]

[In this letter of January 13, 1878, Peirce, who was being considered, along with Henry Rowland, by President D. C. Gilman of the new Johns Hopkins University to head the Physics Department, offered his ideas concerning the aims and organization of such a department, the qualifications of its director, and his own interests in the logic of science. Henry Rowland, who perfected the diffraction-grating technique, became the Professor of Physics, and Peirce was invited to lecture on Logic without relinquishing his post at the U. S. Coast and Geodetic Survey in Washington, D.C.]

I venture to think that a frank expression of my ideas with reference to your physical department and other connected topics will not be unwelcome to you.

In the first place, I note the considerable number of rather promising young physicists in the country; and I am inclined to think that American genius has a bent in that direction. If so, it makes the proper organization of this department all the more important. For the head of it three sets of qualities are requisite:

First, those which go to make a talent for physical research,

Second, the mathematical and general ability to lay out

[1] Letter of Peirce to Gilman, among the Gilman letters at the Johns Hopkins University Library, printed with the kind permission of that University.—Editor's note.

large and judicious plans of research which may guide that talent to great results, and

Third, the capacity for organization and administration for making the laboratory and carrying on the work and business of the department.

In regard to Mr. Rowland, it is easy to see his strength in the first respect and his relative weakness in the third; but I cannot in the short time I passed with him make a complete estimate of his powers. Some things, however, I noted with great pleasure. In the first place, his energies were not occupied with improving "lecture experiments." Such matters are not only utterly trivial, but they are also untrue instruction; the professor's object ought to be to let the pupil as much into the interior of the scientific way of thinking as possible, and for that purpose he should make his lecture experiments resemble real ones as much as possible, and he should avoid those exhibitions of natural magic which impress the mind with a totally perverted idea of science. For this reason, I would have a doubt of any man's real capacity for teaching physics as it ought to be taught, who should seem to delight as much in a "lecture experiment" as in one undertaken *bona fide* to find out something. There is as far as I can see nothing of that in Rowland. His apparatus for demonstration is good, sensible, not too elaborate, not mixed with the apparatus for research.

In the next place, the solidity of the questions he is putting to nature pleases me. Physical research is of three kinds: first, the making out of new phenomena; second, the investigation of their laws; and third, the measurement of constants. The order of the importance of the discoveries is

1. Phenomena
2. Laws
3. Constants

The order of technical skill and discipline required is just the reverse. Physicists have a tendency to rate men's talents according to the purely technical standard, but they ought to be rated from a mixture of both considerations. To find a new phenomenon is more or less a matter of chance. But to observe it and to recognize it as new and to take the first steps in analyzing it and determining its frequency of occurrence requires a real genius. Still, the new phenomena which now remain to be discovered are probably only of secondary importance, and moreover the kind of reasoning here brought into action wants the salutary severity of exact science. It is not so good for the pupils. On the other hand, the exact measurement of constants, though I should be the last to disparage it, does not in my opinion call for as high qualities of mind as the investigation of laws. In Mr. Rowland's work so far as I could see everything was designed for the study of constants, but they were all constants of a very fundamental kind. It is work of real solidity and importance, and appears inspired by a sound mathematical conception of the subject. Mr. Rowland's work is ambitious; sometimes too much so. Thus, he talks of making an original subdivision of the metre, one of the most difficult problems of metrology. In my opinion he will not succeed in the manner he proposes to do it. Mr. Hilgard, I think, would be of the same opinion. I also observe that Mr. Rowland is not always acquainted with important researches intimately connected with his own. On the whole, I have conceived a very high opinion of him, without, at the same time, in my present lights placing him upon such a pinnacle at all as Mr. Sylvester seems to do.

It seems to me that, the question of funds apart, the happiest solution of the difficulty would be to have two full professors of physics. The subject admits of division in various ways; for instance, into physics of ponderable bodies and physics of the ether, the latter to include electricity, magnetism, and physical optics, certainly a sufficient field for any man; and the former to embrace heat, gravitation, cohesion, etc. The ponderable professor to be the administrative head of the department, and Mr. Rowland to be free in his own department, under that limitation. One laboratory to be built.

In regard to my own *persönlichen Wenigkeit*, I understand that my father has suggested my name for the place of general professor of physics. But supposing it were determined to call me to the University (a call which would be very agreeable to me), I think it would be more advantageous to make use of me, first, to fill the precise want of the physical department, and second, to utilize my logical studies.

What I would do in the physical department would depend on the amount of funds. A physical laboratory is, however, wanted which should be a solid brick building in which requisite conditions of stability, temperature, electricity, magnetism, and light could be obtained, and in which convenience of arrangement and adaptability to new purposes should be studied. In the next place, a comprehensive plan of physical investigation to cover, say, ten years, should be carefully matured, in order to make the work done by professors and pupils as efficient as possible. A good instrument-making shop with an energetic and capable head should be attached to the department and should be self-supporting, or nearly so, the university paying for its purchases. It would be one of the main duties of the professor to bring the work here done to the highest pitch of perfection.

In regard to the system of instruction, the special pupils would give little trouble. They should be apprentices in establishment, above all. They should be made to feel that they were doing real and important work which was to appear in the digests of science and for the accuracy of which they were responsible. They should be left to work out the mathematics of practical problems in order that their mathematics might not be up in the air; they should also be made to study out new methods and make designs for new instruments, the instructor measuring their strength. Everything so done by them should be subjected in their presence to serious criticism, as a result, without saying whether it was good or bad for them. Deliberations by the professor upon the course he ought to pursue in any research should be as much as possible thrown open to the pupils in order that they might see the whole way of working. Some of the merits of this method are that from the first the pupil feels himself an apprentice—a learned but yet a real worker; he is introduced to a great and important investigation (I would not tell him too much about it at first; I would make him feel that I am going to use him for my purposes and that if he desires to use me for his he must put forth a strong volition to do so) and of this investigation he has a necessary part to do; he is not working for practice merely; his investigation is not burdened with fancying he is doing something serious, nor is he made to consider things serious which are not so. In the next place, he gets clearly in his mind the high place occupied by the organizing element. He sees a great whole of investigation, and he escapes the frequent destiny of clever men who do not know how to lay out their work to advantage. Then, his theoretical knowledge takes from the outset the shape in his mind in which it appears in practice, so that it is entirely clear. Boys destined to be physicists *ought* to enter the laboratory at nine or ten and remain there most of the time for two or three years. They should then return at eighteen or twenty. Of course that would very rarely be done.

The method with general students, in my opinion, is a much more difficult problem than that with special students. For them are lessons. A lesson should be neither a recitation nor a lecture but something like a mixture of the two. The teacher should consider what he expects the pupil to carry into after life of his instruction. He should aim for something attainable in that respect, and strike for that. First, the moral lessons of physics and its logical lessons should be branded on the soul of the scholar. Second, he should get an idea of what a physicist is: his purposes, his ideas, his methods, his life. Third, the main laws of physics should be taught him in a hundred applications. But calculations of vapor densities and all such things, as well as all that is calculated only to produce a confused effect on the memory, should be omitted.

But as for me I am a logician. The data for the generalizations of logic are the special methods of the different sciences. To penetrate these methods the logician has to study various sciences rather profoundly. In that way, I have learned nearly the whole trade of the physicist, though there are a good many instruments relative to electricity particularly with which I am not practically familiar. However, being a delicate manipulator in other branches of physics and in chemistry, I should not fear taking hold of anything, especially as I have seen most of the instruments, the quadrant electrometer, etc., worked and know the points to be attended to. Thus though I am a logician, I consider it necessary to have a laboratory.

In logic, I am the exponent of a particular tendency, that of physical science. I make the pretension to be the most thoroughgoing and fundamental representative of that element who has yet appeared. I believe that my system of logic (which is a philosophical method to which mathematical algebra only affords aid in a particular part of it) must stand, or else the whole spirit of the physical sciences must be revolutionized. If this is to happen, it cannot be brought about in any way so quickly as by the philosophical formularization of it and the carrying of it to its furthest logical consequences. If on the other hand it is to abide, its general statement will be of consequence for mankind. I have measured my powers against those of other men; I know what they are. It is my part to announce with modest confidence what I can do. My system has been sketched out but not so that its bearings can be appreciated. If the world thinks it worth developing, they have only to give me the means of doing it. But if not, I shall follow another path, with perfect contentment.

It would be a great pleasure to me to enter the society of scholars in Baltimore, the idea of which I approve from the bottom of my heart. You are the only real university in America. . . .

20. Definition and Function of a University

[The definition is from the *Century Dictionary* (New York, 1889) of which Peirce was one of the editors. His interleaved copy, in twenty volumes, at the Houghton Library of Harvard University, with his many emendations written on the blank interleaved pages, can still be profitably consulted by the lexicographer. The following excerpts are from Peirce's review of *Clark University, 1889–1899: Decennial Celebration* (Worcester, Mass., 1899) in *Science* (April 20, 1900), pp. 620–622, and from a Fourth of July address in Paris, 1880.]

A University

An association of men for the purpose of study, which confers degrees which are acknowledged as valid throughout Christendom, is endowed, and is privileged by the state in order that the people may receive intellectual guidance, and that the theoretical problems which present themselves in the development of civilization may be resolved.

Of the three verbs to *be*, to *do*, and to *know*, the great majority of young men unhesitatingly regard the second as expressing the ultimate purpose and end of life. This is, as a matter of course, the idea of the practical man, who knows what he wants, and does not desire to want anything else. The average trustee of an American college will think it a commendable thing for a professor to employ all the time he can possibly save in making money; but if he devotes much energy to any purely theoretical research, the trustees will look upon him askance, as a barely respectable squanderer of his opportunities. In England, this notion takes a turn that really makes it a little less gross; yet, being foreign, perhaps we can discern its error more easily than in its more familiar guise. Thus, Dr. Karl Pearson, in the introduction to his *Grammar of Science*,[1] deliberately lays down the principle that no end whatever is to be approved without a reason, except the end of the preservation of society; and applying this rule, declares that the only valid excuse for the encouragement of scientific activity lies in its tending to maintain "the stability of society." This is truly a British phrase, meaning the House of Lords and vested rights and all that. Only recently we have seen an American man of science and of weight discuss the purpose of education, without once alluding to the only motive that animates the genuine scientific investigator. I am not guiltless in this matter myself, for in my youth I wrote some articles to uphold a doctrine I called Pragmatism, namely, that the meaning and essence of every conception lies in the application that is to be made of it. That is all very well, when properly understood. I do not intend to recant it. But the question arises, *what is* the ultimate application; at that time I seem to have been inclined to subordinate the *conception* to the *act,* knowing to doing. Subsequent experience of life has taught me that the only thing that is really desirable without a reason for being so, is to render ideas and things reasonable. One cannot well demand a reason for reasonableness itself. Logical analysis shows that reasonableness consists in association, assimilation, generalization, the bringing of items together into an organic whole—which are so many ways of regarding what is essentially the same thing. In the emotional sphere this tendency towards union appears as Love; so that the Law of Love and the Law of Reason are quite at one.

There was a simple fellow who, in a benighted age and

---

[1] See Peirce's review of Karl Pearson's positivistic *Grammar of Science* (London, 1900) in *Popular Science Monthly* for January 1901, taking the statistician Pearson to task for limiting the value of science to perpetuation of the race, "social stability," and the "happiness of mankind."—Editor's note.

land, wandered about uttering appreciations of the elements of human life which have made an extraordinary impression upon most of us. Of all his sayings there is none whose truth has been brought home to me more strongly by what I have been able to detect in successful men and women than this: Whoever makes his own welfare his object will simply ruin it utterly.

American education, for the most part, is directed to no other object than the welfare of individual scholars; and thereby incites *them* to pursue that object exclusively. A great university bears upon its seal the remark of its founder: "I wish to found an institution where any man can learn anything." It was a noble idea; and it would be mean to pick flaws in it—especially as he did not say what ulterior purpose he might have in view. But the university which parades this casual remark as its motto seems to proclaim to its students that their individual well-being is its only aim. Our scientific schools distribute circulars which dwell chiefly upon the handsome incomes their alumni are making, thereby calling up such images as a handsomely laid table with a pair of Havre de Grace ducks and a bottle of Château Margaux. What comes of such a conception of education and of life, for surely the purpose of education is not different from the purpose of life? The result is that, notwithstanding all the devices and tricks of the American teachers' art, it may be doubted whether any teaching ever anywhere did less to make happy men and women. At any rate, the spiritual meagreness of the typical American school-book is extreme. The great mediæval universities, the modern German universities, the new science colleges of England, which did, and do, great things for their students personally, were never in the least founded for their students' individual advantage, but, on the contrary, because of the expectation that the truths that would be brought to light in such institutions would benefit the state. This end was, and is, so constantly in view that the scholars are led to regard their own lives as having a purpose beyond themselves.

Yet even this is a low view of learning and science. No reader of this Journal [*Science*] is likely to be content

with the statement that the searching out of the ideas that
govern the universe has no other value than that it helps
human animals to swarm and feed. He will rather insist
that the only thing that makes the human race worth perpetuation is that thereby rational ideas may be developed,
and the rationalization of things furthered.

No other occupation of man is so purely and immediately directed to the one end that is alone intrinsically rational as scientific investigation. It so strongly influences
those who pursue it to subordinate all motives of ambition,
fame, greed, self-seeking of every description, that other
people, even those who have relatively high aspirations,
such as theologians and teachers, altogether fail, in many
cases, to divine the scientific man's simple motives. The
Clark University, in recognizing the pursuit of science as
its first object, with teaching—of course, an indispensable
means of securing continuity of work—as only a subordinate, or at most a secondary object, has perhaps the most
elevated ideal of any university in the world; and I believe
it to be so much the better for the individual students. . . .

[The following is an excerpt from Peirce's address of
July 4, 1880.][2]

One university in our country, the Johns Hopkins University at Baltimore, has been carried on upon principles
directly contrary to those which have governed the other
colleges. That is to say, it has here alone been recognized
that the function of a university is the production of knowledge, and that teaching is only a necessary means to that
end. In short, instructors and pupils here compose a company who are all occupied in studying together, some under leading strings and some not. From this small institution with half a dozen professors and a hundred and fifty
students, I am unable to tell you how much valuable work

[2] From an address before a Fourth of July gathering of
Americans in Paris, 1880, as excerpted by Max H. Fisch and
Jackson I. Cope, "Peirce at the Johns Hopkins University," in
Studies in the Philosophy of C. S. Peirce, ed. Philip P. Wiener
and Frederic H. Young (Harvard University Press, 1952), p.
277.—Editor's note.

has emanated in the four years of its existence in philology and biology. A great deal, I am sure. With its work in mathematical and physical science, I am better acquainted, and I am proud to say—because it shows the real capability of America for such work—that in those four short years the members of this little university have published some one hundred original researches, some of them of great value—fairly equal to the sum of what all the other colleges in the land have done (except in astronomy) in the last twenty years.

21. Logic and a Liberal Education[1]

This is the age of Methods; and the university which is to be the exponent of the living condition of the human mind must be the university of methods.

Now I grant you that to say this is the age of the development of new methods of research is so far from saying it is the age of the theory of methods that it is almost to say the reverse. Unfortunately practice generally precedes theory, and it is the usual fate of mankind to get things done in some boggling way first, and find out afterwards how they could have done them much more easily and perfectly. And it must be confessed that we students of modern methods are as yet but a voice crying in the wilderness, and saying prepare ye the way for this lord of the sciences which is to come.

. . . The theory of any act in no wise aids the doing of it, so long as what is to be done is of a narrow description, so that it can be governed by the unconscious part of our organism. . . . But when new paths have to be struck out, a spinal cord is not enough; a brain is needed, and that brain an organ of mind, and that mind perfected by a liberal education. And a liberal education—so far as its relation

[1] From the Johns Hopkins University Circulars (Nov. 1882) as excerpted by Max H. Fisch and Jackson I. Cope, "Peirce at the Johns Hopkins University," in *Studies in the Philosophy of C. S. Peirce,* ed. Philip P. Wiener and Frederic H. Young (Harvard University Press, 1952), pp. 289–90.—Editor's note.

to the understanding goes—means *logic*. That is indispensable to it, and no other one thing is. . . .

The scientific specialists—pendulum swingers and the like—are doing a great and useful work, each one very little, but altogether something vast. But the higher places in science in the coming years are for those who succeed in adapting the methods of one science to the investigation of another. . . .

Now although a man needs not the theory of a method in order to apply it as it has been applied already, yet in order to adapt to his own science the method of another with which he is less familiar, and to properly modify it so as to suit it to its new use, an acquaintance with the principles upon which it depends will be of the greatest benefit. For that sort of work a man needs to be more than a specialist; he needs such a general training of his mind and such knowledge as shall show him how to make his powers most effective in a new direction. That knowledge is logic.

In short, if my view is the true one, a young man wants a physical education and an aesthetic education, an education in the ways of the world and a moral education, and with all these logic has nothing in particular to do; but so far as he wants an intellectual education, it is precisely logic that he wants; and whether it be in one lecture-room or another, his ultimate purpose is to improve his logical power and his knowledge of methods. To this great end a young man's attention ought to be directed when he first comes to the university; he ought to keep it steadily in view during the whole period of his studies; and finally, he will do well to review his whole work in the light which an education in logic throws upon it.

22. Logic of Mathematics in Relation to Education[1]

. . . A simple way of arriving at a true conception of the mathematician's business is to consider what service it is to which he is called in to render in the course of any scientific or other inquiry. Mathematics has always been more or less a trade. An engineer, or a business company (say, an insurance company or a buyer, say, of land), or a physicist, finds it suits his purpose to ascertain what the necessary consequences of possible facts would be; but the facts are so complicated that he cannot deal with them in his usual way. He calls upon a mathematician and states the question. Now the mathematician does not conceive it to be part of his duty to verify the facts stated. He accepts them absolutely without question. He does not in the least care whether they are correct or not. He finds, however, in almost every case that the statement has one inconvenience, and in many cases that it has a second. The first inconvenience is that, though the statement may not at first sound very complicated, yet, when it is accurately analyzed, it is found to imply so intricate a condition of things that it far surpassed the power of the mathematician to say with exactitude what its consequence would be. At the same time, it frequently happens that the facts, as stated, are insufficient to answer the question that is put.

[1] From *Educational Review* (1898), pp. 209–16.

Accordingly, the first business of the mathematician, often a most difficult task, is to frame another, simpler but quite fictitious problem (supplemented, perhaps, by some supposition), which will be within his powers, while at the same time it is sufficiently like the problem set before him to answer, well or ill, as a substitute for it.

This substituted problem differs also from that which was set before the mathematician in another respect; namely, that it is highly abstract. All features that have no bearing upon the relations of the premises to the conclusion are effaced and obliterated. The skeletonization or diagrammatization of the problem serves more purposes than one, but its principal purpose is to strip the significant relations of all disguise. Only one kind of concrete clothing is permitted —namely, such as, whether from habit or from the constitution of the mind, has become so familiar that it decidedly aids in tracing the consequences of the hypothesis. Thus, the mathematician does two very different things: first, he frames a pure hypothesis stripped of all features which do not concern the drawing of consequences from it, and this he does without inquiring whether it agrees with the actual facts or not; and, secondly, he proceeds to draw necessary consequences from that hypothesis.

Kant is entirely right in saying that, in drawing those consequences, the mathematician uses what, in geometry, is called a "construction," or in general a diagram or visual array of characters or lines. Such a construction is formed according to a precept furnished by the hypothesis. Being formed, the construction is submitted to the scrutiny of observation, and new relations are discovered among its parts, not stated in the precept by which it was formed, and are found, by a little mental experimentation, to be such that they will always be present in such a construction. Thus, the necessary reasoning of mathematics is performed by means of observation and experiment, and its necessary character is due simply to the circumstance that the subject of this observation and experiment is a diagram of our own creation, the conditions of whose being we know all about.

But Kant, owing to the slight development which formal

logic had received in his time, and especially owing to his total ignorance of the logic of relatives, which throws a brilliant light upon the whole of logic, fell into error in supposing that mathematical and philosophical necessary reasoning are distinguished by the circumstance that the former uses constructions. This is not true. All necessary reasoning whatsoever proceeds by constructions; and the only difference between mathematical and philosophical necessary deductions is that the latter are so excessively simple that the construction attracts no attention and is overlooked. The construction exists in the simplest syllogism in Barbara.[2] Why do the logicians like to state a syllogism by writing the major premiss on one line and the minor below it, with letters substituted for the subject and predicates? It is merely because the reasoner has to notice that relation between the parts of those premisses which such a diagram brings into prominence. If the reasoner makes use of syllogistic (reasoning) in drawing his conclusion, he has such a diagram or construction in his mind's eye, and observes the result of eliminating the middle term. If, however, he trusts to his unaided reason, he still uses some kind of a diagram which is familiar to him personally.

The true difference between the necessary logic of philosophy and mathematics is merely one of degree. It is

[2] A line of reasoning made up of three universal affirmative statements: All M is P, all S is M; therefore, all S is P (e.g., All men are philosophers and all sailors are men as premisses yield the conclusion that all sailors are philosophers). The major premiss contains the predicate term P of the conclusion, the minor contains the subject S of the conclusion, and both contain the middle term M. Aristotle regarded the syllogism as the most perfect type of demonstration, and Kant thought formal logic was a science in which no further progress could be made since all the valid forms of the syllogism had been completely exhibited. The extension of logic beyond the syllogism was due to mathematical philosophers like Leibniz, inventor of the symbolism of the calculus and of determinants, and the modern systems of Symbolic Logic stem from George Boole, John Venn, Charles S. Peirce, Ernst Schroeder, Peano, and Frege (whose work was not known at all to Peirce, or for that matter to many other logicians who had to await Bertrand Russell's discovery of the importance of Frege's neglected writings).—Editor's note.

that, in mathematics, the reasoning is frightfully intricate, while the elementary conceptions are of the last degree of familiarity; in contrast to philosophy, where the reasonings are as simple as they can be, while the elementary conceptions are abstruse and hard to get clearly apprehended. But there is another much deeper line of demarcation between the two sciences. It is that mathematics studies nothing but hypotheses, and is the only science which never inquires what the actual facts are; while philosophy, although it uses no microscopes or other apparatus of special observation, is really an experimental science which is common to us all; so that its principal reasonings are not mathematically necessary at all, but are only necessary in the sense that all the world knows beyond all doubt those truths of experience upon which philosophy is founded. This is why the mathematician holds the reasoning of the metaphysician in supreme contempt, while he himself, when he ventures into philosophy, is apt to reason fantastically and not solidly, because he does not recognize that he is upon ground where elaborate deduction is of no more avail than it is in chemistry or biology.

Science
and Religion

23. Science and Immortality[1]

[Peirce was critical of both pseudoscientific proofs of immortality and of dogmatic rejections of all religious aspirations. He steered clear of the vague commitments of the romantic Transcendentalists of the Concord School (Emerson, Thoreau, Theodore Parker, and others whose writings have been recently anthologized by Perry Miller: *The Transcendentalists*), although he greatly respected their spiritual revolt against philistinism. He shot holes through the alleged evidence of communication with the dead offered by the Psychical Research Society of which William James was president for many years. However, he had the highest disdain for the positivist followers of Comte and Spencer who tried to replace religious yearning by dubious sociological laws and a mechanical philosophy of evolution, respectively. The main point of Peirce's diatribe with these romantic and positivistic movements of the nineteenth century was to strip them of their claims to infallible certainty, and thus keep open the possibility of discovering a rational reconciliation of science with religious values as expressions of human needs. The following articles range over a period of twenty years during which time Peirce from his retreat at Milford, Pennsylvania, was strenuously developing his

---

[1] First published in a Symposium in the *Christian Register*, Boston, April 7, 1887. Reprinted from *Science and Immortality*, The Christian Register Symposium, Revised and Enlarged, edited by S. J. Barrows; Geo. H. Ellis (Boston, 1887).

thoughts on cosmology, pragmaticism, lessons from the history of science, the ethics of science, and the philosophy of religion. They may be regarded as the more mature development of the ideas touched upon in his youthful oration of 1863, the first of our selections above, on "The Place of Our Age in the History of Civilization."]

What is the bearing of positively ascertained facts upon the doctrine of a future life? By the doctrine of a future life, I understand the proposition that after death we shall retain or recover our individual consciousness, feeling, volition, memory, and, in short (barring an unhappy contingency), all our mental powers unimpaired. The question is, laying aside all higher aspects of this doctrine, its sacredness and sentiment—concerning which a scientific man is not, as such, entitled to an opinion—and judging it in the same cold way in which a proposition in physics would have to be judged, what facts are there leading us to believe or to disbelieve it?

Under the head of direct positive evidence to the affirmative would be placed that of religious miracles, of spiritualistic marvels, and of ghosts, etc. I have little to say to all this. I take the modern Catholic miracles to be the best attested. Three members of the English Psychical Research Society have lately published a vast book of fourteen hundred pages, large octavo, under the title of *Phantasms of the Living*. This work gives some seven hundred cases of apparitions, etc., of a dying person to another person at a distance. The phenomenon of telepathy, or perception under conditions which forbid ordinary perception, though not fully established, is supported by some remarkable observations. But the authors of the book I am speaking of—Messrs. Gurney, Myers, and Podmore—think they have proved a kind of telepathy by which dying persons appear to others at great distances. Their most imposing arguments are based upon the doctrine of probabilities, and these I have examined with care. I am fully satisfied that these arguments are worthless, partly because of the uncertainty and error of the numerical data, and partly because the authors have been astonishingly careless in the admission of cases ruled out by the conditions of the argumentation.

But, granting all the ghost stories that ever were told, and the reality of all spiritual manifestation, what would they prove? These ghosts and spirits exhibit but a remnant of mind. Their stupidity is remarkable. They seem like the lower animals. If I believed in them, I should conclude that, while the soul was not always at once extinguished on the death of the body, yet it was reduced to a pitiable shade, a mere ghost, as we say, of its former self. Then these spirits and apparitions are so painfully solemn. I fancy that, were I suddenly to find myself liberated from all the trials and responsibilities of this life, my probation over, and my destiny put beyond marring or making, I should feel as I do when I find myself on an ocean steamer, and know that for ten days no business can turn up, and nothing can happen. I should regard the situation as a stupendous frolic, should be at the summit of gayety, and should only be too glad to leave the vale of tears behind. Instead of that, these starveling souls come mooning back to their former haunts, to cry over spilled milk.

Under the head of positive evidence apparently unfavorable to the doctrine, we may reckon ordinary observations of the dependence of healthy mind-action upon the state of the body. There are, also, those rare cases of double consciousness where personal identity is utterly destroyed or changed, even in this life. If a man or woman, who is one day one person, another day another, is to live hereafter, pray tell me which of the two persons that inhabit the one body is destined to survive?

There is certainly a large and formidable mass of facts, which, though not bearing directly upon the question of a future life, yet inclines us to a general conception of the universe which does not harmonize with that belief. We judge of the possibility of the unseen by its analogy with the seen. We smile at Aladdin's lamp or the elixir of life, because they are extremely unlike all that has come under our observation. Those of us who have never met with spirits, or any fact at all analogous to immortality among the things that we indubitably know, must be excused if we smile at that doctrine. As far as we see, forms of beauty,

of sentiment, and of intelligence are the most evanescent
of phenomena.

"The flower that once has bloomed forever dies."

Besides, scientific studies have taught us that human testimony, when not hedged about with elaborate checks, is a
weak kind of evidence. In short, the utter unlikeness of an
immortal soul to anything we cannot doubt, and the slightness of all the old arguments of its existence, appear to me
to have tremendous weight.

The Breakdown of the Mechanical Philosophy

On the other hand, the theory of another life is very
likely to be strengthened, along with spiritualistic views
generally, when the palpable falsity of that mechanical philosophy of the universe which dominates the modern world
shall be recognized. It is sufficient to go out into the air
and open one's eyes to see that the world is not governed
altogether by mechanism, as Spencer, in accord with
greater minds, would have us believe. The endless variety
in the world has not been created by law. It is not of the
nature of uniformity to originate variation, nor of law to
beget circumstance. When we gaze upon the multifarious-
ness of nature we are looking straight into the face of a
living spontaneity. A day's ramble in the country ought to
bring that home to us.

Then there is the great fact of growth, of evolution. I
know that Herbert Spencer endeavors to show that evolution is a consequence of the mechanical principle of the conservation of energy. But his chapter[2] on the subject is
mathematically absurd, and convicts him of being a man
who will talk pretentiously of what he knows nothing about.
The principle of the conservation of energy may, as is well
known, be stated in this form: whatever changes can be
brought about by forces can equally happen in the reverse
order (all the movements taking place with the same velocities, but in the reverse directions), under the govern-

[2] *First Principles,* Bk. II, Ch. 18.

ment of the same forces. Now, the essential of growth is that it takes place in one determinate direction, which is *not* reversed. Boys grow into men, but not men into boys. It is thus an immediate corollary from the doctrine of the conservation of energy that growth is not the effect of force alone.

The world, then, is evidently not governed by blind law. Its leading characteristics are absolutely irreconcilable with that view. When scientific men first began to understand dynamics, and had applied it with great success to the explanation of some phenomena, they jumped to the anticipation that the universe could be explained in that way; and thus what was called the Mechanical Philosophy was set up. But a further study of the nature of force has shown that it has this conservative character, which absolutely refutes that mechanical notion of the universe. As well as I can read the signs of the times, the doom of necessitarian metaphysics is sealed. The world has done with it. It must now give place to more spiritualistic views, and it is very natural now to anticipate that a further study of nature may establish the reality of a future life.

For my part, I cannot admit the proposition of Kant—that there are certain impassable bounds to human knowledge; and, even if there are such bounds in regard to the infinite and absolute, the question of a future life, as distinct from the question of immortality, does not transcend them. The history of science affords illustrations enough of the folly of saying that this, that, or the other can never be found out. Auguste Comte said that it was clearly impossible for man ever to learn anything of the chemical constitution of the fixed stars,[3] but before his book had reached its readers the discovery which he announced as impossible had been made. Legendre said of a certain proposition in the theory of numbers that, while it appeared to be true, it was most likely beyond the powers of the human mind to prove it; yet the next writer on the subject gave six independent demonstrations of the theorem. I really cannot see why the dwellers upon earth should not, in some future

[3] *Cours de philosophie positive,* 19ᵉ leçon. Vol. 2, p. 8 (Paris, 1835).

day, find out for certain whether there is a future life or not. But at present I apprehend that there are not facts enough in our possession to warrant our building any practical conclusion upon them. If anyone likes to believe in a future life, either out of affection for the venerable creed of Christendom or for his private consolation, he does well. But I do not think it would be wise to draw from that religious or sentimental proposition any practical deduction whatever —as, for instance, that human happiness and human rights are of little account, that all our thoughts ought to be turned away from the things of this world, etc.—unless such deduction has the independent sanction of good sense.

The Marriage of Religion and Science[4]

What is science? The dictionary will say that it is systematized knowledge. Dictionary definitions, however, are too apt to repose upon derivations; which is as much as to say that they neglect too much the later steps in the evolution of meanings. Mere knowledge, though it be systematized, may be a dead memory; while by science we all habitually mean a living and growing body of truth. We might even say that knowledge is not necessary to science. The astronomical researches of Ptolemy, though they are in great measure false, must be acknowledged by every modern mathematician who reads them to be truly and genuinely scientific. That which constitutes science, then, is not so much correct conclusions, as it is a correct method. But the method of science is itself a scientific result. It did not spring out of the brain of a beginner: it was a historic attainment and a scientific achievement. So that not even this method ought to be regarded as essential to the beginnings of science. That which is essential, however, is the scientific spirit, which is determined not to rest satisfied with existing opinions, but to press on to the real truth of nature. To science once enthroned in this sense, among any people, science in every other sense is heir apparent.

And what is religion? In each individual it is a sort of sentiment, or obscure perception, a deep recognition of a

4 *The Open Court*, Vol. 7 (1893), pp. 3559-60.

something in the circumambient All, which, if he strives to express it, will clothe itself in forms more or less extravagant, more or less accidental, but ever acknowledging the first and last, the A and Ω, as well as a relation to that Absolute of the individual's self, as a relative being. But religion cannot reside in its totality in a single individual. Like every species of reality, it is essentially a social, a public affair. It is the idea of a whole church, welding all its members together in one organic, systemic perception of the Glory of the Highest—an idea having a growth from generation to generation and claiming a supremacy in the determination of all conduct, private and public.

Now, as science grows, it becomes more and more perfect, considered as science; and no religionist can easily so narrow himself as to deny this. But as religion goes through the different stages of its history, it has, I fear we must confess, seldom been seen so vitalized as to become more and more perfect, even as judged from its own standpoint. Like a plucked flower, its destiny is to wilt and fade. The vital sentiment that gave it birth loses gradually its pristine purity and strength, till some new creed treads it down. Thus it happens quite naturally that those who are animated with the spirit of science are for hurrying forward, while those who have the interests of religion at heart are apt to press back.

While this double change has been taking place, religion has found herself compelled to define her position; and, in doing so, has inevitably committed herself to sundry propositions, which, one by one, have been, first questioned, then assailed, and finally overthrown by advancing science. Seeing such a chasm open before her feet, religion has at first violently recoiled, and at last has leapt it; satisfying herself as best she might with an altered creed. In most cases the leap has not seemed to hurt her; yet internal injuries may have been sustained. Who can doubt that the church really did suffer from the discovery of the Copernican system, although infallibility, by a narrow loophole, managed to escape? In this way, science and religion become forced into hostile attitudes. Science, to specialists, may seem to have little or nothing to say that directly con-

cerns religion; but it certainly encourages a philosophy
which, if in no other respect, is at any rate opposed to the
prevalent tendency of religion, in being animated by a progressive spirit. There arises, too, a tendency to pooh-pooh
at things unseen.

It would be ridiculous to ask to whose fault this situation
is chargeable. You cannot lay blame upon elemental forces.
Religion, from the nature of things, refuses to go through
her successive transformations with sufficient celerity to
keep always in accord with the convictions of scientific
philosophy. The day has come, however, when the man
whom religious experience most devoutly moves can recognize the state of the case. While adhering to the essence of
religion, and so far as possible to the church, which is all
but essential, say, penessential, to it, he will cast aside that
religious timidity that is forever prompting the church to
recoil from the paths into which the Governor of history is
leading the minds of men, a cowardice that has stood
through the ages as the landmark and limit of her little
faith, and will gladly go forward, sure that truth is not split
into two warring doctrines, and that any change that
knowledge can work in his faith can only affect its expression, but not the deep mystery expressed.

Such a state of mind may properly be called a religion of
science. Not that it is a religion to which science or the
scientific spirit has itself given birth; for religion, in the
proper sense of the term, can arise from nothing but the
religious sensibility. But it is a religion, so true to itself,
that it becomes animated by the scientific spirit, confident
that all the conquests of science will be triumphs of its own,
and accepting all the results of science, as scientific men
themselves accept them, as steps toward the truth, which
may appear for a time to be in conflict with other truths,
but which in such cases merely await adjustments which
time is sure to effect. This attitude, be it observed, is one
which religion will assume not at the dictate of science,
still less by way of a compromise, but simply and solely out
of a bolder confidence in herself and in her own destiny.

Meantime, science goes unswervingly its own gait. What

is to be its goal is precisely what it must not seek to determine for itself, but let itself be guided by nature's strong hand. Teleological considerations, that is to say ideals, must be left to religion; science can allow itself to be swayed only by efficient causes; and philosophy, in her character of "queen of the sciences," must not care, or must not seem to care, whether her conclusions be wholesome or dangerous.

What Is Christian Faith?[5]

It is easy to chop logic about matters of which you have no experience whatever. Men color-blind have more than once learnedly discussed the laws of color-sensation, and have made interesting deductions from those laws. But when it comes to positive knowledge, such knowledge as a lawyer has of the practice of the courts, that can only rest on long experience, direct or indirect. So, a man may be an accomplished theologian without ever having felt the stirring of the spirit; but he cannot answer the simple question at the head of this article except out of his own religious experience.

There is in the dictionary a word, *solipsism*, meaning the belief that the believer is the only existing person. Were anybody to adopt such a belief, it might be difficult to argue him out of it. But when a person finds himself in the society of others, he is just as sure of their existence as of his own, though he may entertain a metaphysical theory that they are all hypostatically the same *ego*. In like manner, when a man has that experience with which religion sets out, he has as good reason—putting aside metaphysical subtilities—to believe in the living personality of God as he has to believe in his own. Indeed, *belief* is a word inappropriate to such direct perception.

Seldom do we pass a single hour of our waking lives away from the companionship of men (including books); and even the thoughts of that solitary hour are filled with ideas

[5] *The Open Court*, Vol. 7 (1893), pp. 3743-45.

which have grown in society. Prayer, on the other hand, occupies but little of our time; and, of course, if solemnity and ceremony are to be made indispensable to it (though why observe manners toward the Heavenly Father that an earthly father would resent as priggish?), nothing more is practicable. Consequently, religious ideas never come to form the warp and woof of our mental constitution, as do social ideas. They are easily doubted, and are open to various reasons for doubt, which reasons may all be comprehended under one, namely, that the religious phenomenon is sporadic, not incessant.

This causes a degeneration in religion from a perception to a trust, from a trust to a belief, and a belief continually becoming more and more abstract. Then, after a religion has become a public affair, quarrels arise, to settle which watchwords are drawn up. This business gets into the hands of theologians: and the ideas of theologians always appreciably differ from those of the universal church. They swamp religion in fallacious logical disputations. Thus, the natural tendency is to the continual drawing tighter and tighter of the narrowing bounds of doctrine, with less and less attention to the living essence of religion, until, after some *symbolum quodcumque* has declared that the salvation of each individual absolutely and almost exclusively depends upon his entertaining a correct metaphysics of the godhead, the vital spark of inspiration becomes finally quite extinct.

Yet it is absurd to say that religion is a mere belief. You might as well call society a belief, or politics a belief, or civilization a belief. Religion is a life, and can be identified with a belief only provided that belief be a living belief—a thing to be lived rather than said or thought.

The Christian religion, if it has anything distinctive—and must not aspire to be the necessary ultimate outcome of *every* path of religious progress—is distinguished from other religions by its precept about the Way of Life. I appeal to the typical Christian to answer out of the abundance of his spirit, without dictation from priests, whether this be not so. In the recently discovered book, *The Teaching of the Twelve*

Apostles,[6] which dates from about A.D. 100, we see that, long before the Apostles' or any other creed was insisted upon, or at all used, the teaching of the Lord was considered to consist in the doctrine of the Two Ways—the Way of Life and the Way of Death. This it was that at that date was regarded as the saving faith—not a lot of metaphysical propositions. This is what Jesus Christ taught; and to believe in Christ is to believe what he taught.

Now what is this way of life? Again I appeal to the universal Christian conscience to testify that it is simply love. As far as it is contracted to a rule of ethics, it is: Love God, and love your neighbor; "on these two commandments hang all the law and the prophets." It may be regarded in a higher point of view with St. John as the universal evolutionary formula. But in whatever light it be regarded or in whatever direction developed, the belief in the law of love is the Christian faith.

"Oh," but it may be said, "that is not distinctive of Christianity! That very idea was anticipated by the early Egyptians, by the Stoics, by the Buddhists, and by Confucius." So it was; nor can the not insignificant difference between the negative and the positive precept be properly estimated as sufficient for a discrimination between religions. Christians may, indeed, claim that Christianity possesses that earmark of divine truth—namely, that it was anticipated from primitive ages. The higher a religion the more catholic.

Man's highest developments are social; and religion, though it begins in a seminal individual inspiration, only comes to full flower in a great church coextensive with a civilization. This is true of every religion, but supereminently so of the religion of love. Its ideal is that the whole world shall be united in the bond of a common love of God accomplished by each man's loving his neighbor. Without a church, the religion of love can have but a rudimentary existence; and a narrow, little exclusive church is almost worse than none. A great catholic church is wanted.

[6] Edited with translation and notes by Roswell D. Hitchcock and Francis Brown, New York, Scribner's (1884). Also, by Philip Schaff, 3d edition, New York, Funk and Wagnalls (1890).

The invisible church does now embrace all Christendom. Every man who has been brought up in the bosom of Christian civilization does really believe in some form of the principle of love, whether he is aware of doing so or not.

Let us, at any rate, get all the good from the vital element in which we are all at one that it can yield: and the good that it can yield is simply all that is any way possible, and richer than is easily conceivable. Let us endeavor, then, with all our might to draw together the whole body of believers in the law of love into sympathetic unity of consciousness. Discountenance as immoral all movements that exaggerate differences, or that go to make fellowship depend on formulas invented to exclude some Christians from communion with others.

A sapient critic has recently blamed me for defective cocksureness in my metaphysical views. That is no less than an indictment for practicing just as I have always preached. *Absurd* was the epithet ever coming to my tongue for persons very confident in opinions which other minds, as good as they, denied. Can you induce the philosophic world to agree upon any assignable creed, or in condemning any specified item in the current creeds of Christendom? I believe not; though doubtless you can gather a sequacious little flock, quite disposed to follow their bell-bearer into every vagary—if you will be satisfied so. For my part, I should think it more lovely to patch up such peace as might be with the great religious world. This happens to be easy to an individual whose unbiased study of scientific logic has led him to conclusions not discordant with traditional dogmas. Unfortunately, such a case is exceptional; and guilt rests on you who insist on so tautening the lines of churches as to close them against the great body of educated and thinking men, pure and undefiled though the religion of many of them (you are obliged to acknowledge it) be. Surely another generation will witness a sweeping reform in this respect. You will not be permitted to make of those churches a permanent laughing-stock for coming ages. Many things are essential to religion which yet ought not to be insisted on: the law of love is not the rule of angry and bullying insistence. Thus, it seems plain to me, I confess, that miracles are intrinsic elements of a genuine religion. But it is not half so important to emphasize this as it is to draw into our loving communion almost the entire collection of men who unite clear thought with intellectual integrity. And who are you, anyway, who are so zealous to keep the churches small and exclusive? Do you number among your party the great scholars and the great saints? Are you not, on the other hand, egged on by all the notorious humbugs—votaries of Mammon or of Ward McAllister—who deem the attitude of a church-caryatid to be a respectable or a genteel thing? Your voting-power, too, is repleted with many who, as soon as they are a little better informed and educated, will drop away from you; and in these days that education will come speedily.

To those who for the present are excluded from the churches, and who, in the passionate intensity of their religious desire, are talking of setting up a church for the scientifically educated, a man of my stripe must say, Wait, if you can; it will be but a few years longer; but if you cannot wait, why then Godspeed! Only, do not, in your turn, go and draw lines so as to exclude such as believe a little less—or, still worse, to exclude such as believe a little more—than yourselves. Doubtless, a lot of superstition clings to the historical churches; but superstition is the grime upon the venerable pavement of the sacred edifice, and he who would wash that pavement clean should be willing to get down on his knees to his work inside the church.

A religious organization is a somewhat idle affair unless it be sworn in as a regiment of that great army that takes life in hand, with all its delights, in grimmest fight to put down the principle of self-seeking, and to make the principle of love triumphant. It has something more serious to think about than the phraseology of the articles of war. Fall into the ranks then; follow your colonel. Keep your one purpose steadily and alone in view, and you may promise yourself the attainment of your sole desire, which is to hasten the chariot wheels of redeeming love!

A Neglected Argument for the Reality of God[7]

The word "God," so "capitalized" (as we Americans say), is *the* definable proper name, signifying *Ens necessarium;* in my belief Really creator of all three Universes of Experience.

Some words shall herein be capitalized when used, not as vernacular, but as terms defined. Thus an "idea" is the substance of an actual unitary thought or fancy; but "Idea," nearer Plato's idea of *idéa,* denotes anything whose Being consists in its mere capacity for getting fully represented, regardless of any person's faculty or impotence to represent it.

"Real" is a word invented in the thirteenth century to signify having Properties, i.e., characters sufficing to identify their subject, and possessing these whether they be anywise attributed to it by any single man or group of men, or not. Thus, the substance of a dream is not Real, since it was such as it was, merely in that a dreamer so dreamed it; but the fact of the dream is Real, if it was dreamed; since if so, its date, the name of the dreamer, etc., make up a set of circumstances sufficient to distinguish it from all other events; and these belong to it, i.e., would be true if predicated of it, whether *A, B,* or *C* Actually ascertains them or not. The "Actual" is that which is met with in the past, present, or future.

An "Experience" is a brutally produced conscious effect that contributes to a habit, self-controlled, yet so satisfying, on deliberation, as to be destructible by no positive exercise of internal vigor. I use the word "self-controlled" for "controlled by the thinker's self," and not for "uncontrolled" except in its own spontaneous, i.e., automatic, self-development, as Professor J. M. Baldwin[8] uses the word. Take for illustration the sensation undergone by a child that puts its forefinger into a flame with the acquisition of a habit of keeping all its members out of all flames. A compulsion is "Brute," whose immediate efficacy nowise consists in conformity to rule or reason.

[7] *Hibbert Journal,* Vol. 7 (1908), pp. 90–112.
[8] See his *Thought and Things* (London, 1906), p. 261.

Of the three Universes of Experience familiar to us all, the first comprises all mere Ideas, those airy nothings to which the mind of poet, pure mathematician, or another *might* give local habitation and a name within that mind. Their very airy-nothingness, the fact that their Being consists in mere capability of getting thought, not in anybody's Actually thinking them, saves their Reality. The second Universe is that of the Brute Actuality of things and facts. I am confident that their Being consists in reactions against Brute forces, notwithstanding objections redoubtable until they are closely and fairly examined. The third Universe comprises everything whose being consists in active power to establish connections between different objects, especially between objects in different Universes. Such is everything which is essentially a Sign—not the mere body of the Sign, which is not essentially such, but, so to speak, the Sign's Soul, which has its Being in its power of serving as intermediary between its Object and a Mind. Such, too, is a living consciousness, and such the life, the power of growth, of a plant. Such is a living constitution—a daily newspaper, a great fortune, a social "movement."

An "Argument" is any process of thought reasonably tending to produce a definite belief. An "Argumentation" is an Argument proceeding upon definitely formulated premisses.

If God Really be, and be benign, then, in view of the generally conceded truth that religion, were it but proved, would be a good outweighing all others, we should naturally expect that there would be some Argument for His Reality that should be obvious to all minds, high and low alike, that should earnestly strive to find the truth of the matter; and further, that this Argument should present its conclusion, not as a proposition of metaphysical theology, but in a form directly applicable to the conduct of life, and full of nutrition for man's highest growth. What I shall refer to as the N. A.—the Neglected Argument—seems to me best to fulfill this condition, and I should not wonder if the majority of those whose own reflections have harvested belief in God must bless the radiance of the N. A. for that wealth. Its persuasiveness is no less than extraordinary;

while it is not unknown to anybody. Nevertheless, of all those theologians (within my little range of reading) who, with commendable assiduity, scrape together all the sound reasons they can find or concoct to prove the first proposition of theology, few mention this one, and they most briefly. They probably share those current notions of logic which recognize no other Arguments than Argumentations.

There is a certain agreeable occupation of mind which, from its having no distinctive name, I infer is not as commonly practiced as it deserves to be; for indulged in moderately—say through some five to six per cent of one's waking time, perhaps during a stroll—it is refreshing enough more than to repay the expenditure. Because it involves no purpose save that of casting aside all serious purpose, I have sometimes been half-inclined to call it reverie with some qualification; but for a frame of mind so antipodal to vacancy and dreaminess such a designation would be too excruciating a misfit. In fact, it is Pure Play. Now, Play, we all know, is a lively exercise of one's powers. Pure Play has no rules, except this very law of liberty. It bloweth where it listeth. It has no purpose, unless recreation. The particular occupation I mean—a *petite bouchée* with the Universes—may take either the form of æsthetic contemplation, or that of distant castle-building (whether in Spain or within one's own moral training), or that of considering some wonder in one of the Universes, or some connection between two of the three, with speculation concerning its cause. It is this last kind—I will call it "Musement" on the whole—that I particularly recommend, because it will in time flower into the N. A. One who sits down with the purpose of becoming convinced of the truth of religion is plainly not inquiring in scientific singleness of heart, and must always suspect himself of reasoning unfairly. So he can never attain the entirety even of a physicist's belief in electrons, although this is avowedly but provisional. But let religious meditation be allowed to grow up spontaneously out of Pure Play without any breach of continuity, and the Muser will retain the perfect candor proper to Musement.

If one who had determined to make trial of Musement

as a favorite recreation were to ask me for advice, I should reply as follows: The dawn and the gloaming most invite one to Musement; but I have found no watch of the nychthemeron that has not its own advantages for the pursuit. It begins passively enough with drinking in the impression of some nook in one of the three Universes. But impression soon passes into attentive observation, observation into musing, musing into a lively give and take of communion between self and self. If one's observations and reflections are allowed to specialize themselves too much, the Play will be converted into scientific study; and that cannot be pursued in odd half hours.

I should add: Adhere to the one ordinance of Play, the law of liberty. I can testify that the last half century, at least, has never lacked tribes of Sir Oracles, colporting brocards to bar off one or another roadway of inquiry; and a Rabelais would be needed to bring out all the fun that has been packed in their airs of infallibility. Auguste Comte, notwithstanding his having apparently produced some unquestionably genuine thinking, was long the chief of such a band. The vogue of each particular maxim of theirs was necessarily brief. For what distinction can be gained by repeating saws heard from all mouths? No bygone fashion seems more grotesque than a *panache* of obsolete wisdom. I remember the days when a pronouncement all the rage was that no science must borrow the methods of another; the geologist must not use a microscope, nor the astronomer a spectroscope. Optics must not meddle with electricity, nor logic with algebra. But twenty years later, if you aspired to pass for a commanding intellect, you would have to pull a long face and declare that "it is not the business of science to search for origins." This maxim was a masterpiece, since no timid soul, in dread of being thought naïve, would dare inquire what "origins" were, albeit the secret confessor within his breast compelled the awful self-acknowledgment of his having no idea into what else than "origins" of phenomena (in some sense of that indefinite word) man can inquire. That human reason can comprehend some causes is past denial, and once we are forced to recognize a given element in experience, it is reasonable

to await positive evidence before we complicate our acknowledgment with qualifications. Otherwise, why venture
beyond direct observation? Illustrations of this principle
abound in physical science. Since, then, it is certain that
man is able to understand the laws and the causes of some
phenomena, it is reasonable to assume, in regard to any
given problem, that it would get rightly solved by man, if
a sufficiency of time and attention were devoted to it. Moreover, those problems that at first blush appear utterly insoluble receive, in that very circumstance, as Edgar Poe
remarked[9] in his "The Murders in the Rue Morgue," their
smoothly-fitting keys. This particularly adapts them to the
Play of Musement.

Forty or fifty minutes of vigorous and unslackened analytic thought bestowed upon one of them usually suffices
to educe from it all there is to educe, its general solution.
There is no kind of reasoning that I should wish to discourage in Musement; and I should lament to find anybody
confining it to a method of such moderate fertility as logical
analysis. Only, the Player should bear in mind that the
higher weapons in the arsenal of thought are not playthings
but edge-tools. In any mere Play they can be used by way
of exercise alone; while logical analysis can be put to its
full efficiency in Musement. So, continuing the counsels that
had been asked of me, I should say, "Enter your skiff of
Musement, push off into the lake of thought, and leave the
breath of heaven to swell your sail. With your eyes open,
awake to what is about or within you, and open conversation with yourself; for such is all meditation." It is, however, not a conversation in words alone, but is illustrated,
like a lecture, with diagrams and with experiments.

Different people have such wonderfully different ways of
thinking that it would be far beyond my competence to
say what courses Musements might not take; but a brain
endowed with automatic control, as man's indirectly is,
is so naturally and rightly interested in its own faculties
that some psychological and semi-psychological questions

[9] "It appears to me that this mystery is considered insoluble
for the very reason which should cause it to be regarded as
easy of solution. I mean the *outré* character of its features."

would doubtless get touched; such, in the latter class, as this: Darwinians, with truly surprising ingenuity, have concocted, and with still more astonishing confidence have accepted as proved, one explanation for the diverse and delicate beauties of flowers, another for those of butterflies, and so on; but why is all nature—the forms of trees, the compositions of sunsets—suffused with such beauties throughout, and not nature only, but the other two Universes as well? Among more purely psychological questions, the nature of pleasure and pain will be likely to attract attention. Are they mere qualities of feeling, or are they rather motor instincts attracting us to some feelings and repelling others? Have pleasure and pain the same sort of constitution, or are they contrasted in this respect, pleasure arising upon the forming or strengthening of an association by resemblance, and pain upon the weakening or disruption of such a habit or conception?

Psychological speculations will naturally lead on to musings upon metaphysical problems proper, good exercise for a mind with a turn for exact thought. It is here that one finds those questions that at first seem to offer no handle for reason's clutch, but which readily yield to logical analysis. But problems of metaphysics will inevitably present themselves that logical analysis will not suffice to solve. Some of the best will be motived by a desire to comprehend universe-wide aggregates of unformulated but partly experienced phenomena. I would suggest that the Muser be not too impatient to analyze these, lest some significant ingredient be lost in the process; but that he begin by pondering them from every point of view, until he seems to read some truth beneath the phenomena.

At this point a trained mind will demand that an examination be made of the truth of the interpretation; and the first step in such examination must be a logical analysis of the theory. But strict examination would be a task a little too serious for the Musement of hour fractions, and if it is postponed there will be ample remuneration even in the suggestions that there is not time to examine; especially since a few of them will appeal to reason as all but certain.

Let the Muser, for example, after well appreciating, in

its breadth and depth, the unspeakable variety of each Universe, turn to those phenomena that are of the nature of homogeneities of connectedness in each; and what a spectacle will unroll itself! As a mere hint of them I may point out that every small part of space, however remote, is bounded by just such neighboring parts as every other, without a single exception throughout immensity. The matter of Nature is in every star of the same elementary kinds, and (except for variations of circumstance), what is more wonderful still, throughout the whole visible universe, about the same proportions of the different chemical elements prevail. Though the mere catalogue of known carbon-compounds alone would fill an unwieldy volume, and perhaps, if the truth were known, the number of aminoacids alone is greater, yet it is unlikely that there are in all more than about 600 elements, of which 500 dart through space too swiftly to be held down by the earth's gravitation, coronium being the slowest moving of these. This small number bespeaks comparative simplicity of structure. Yet no mathematician but will confess the present hopelessness of attempting to comprehend the constitution of the hydrogen-atom, the simplest of the elements that can be held to earth.

From speculations on the homogeneities of each Universe, the Muser will naturally pass to the consideration of homogeneities and connections between two different Universes, or all three. Especially in them all we find one type of occurrence, that of growth, itself consisting in the homogeneities of small parts. This is evident in the growth of motion into displacement, and the growth of force into motion. In growth, too, we find that the three Universes conspire; and a universal feature of it is provision for later stages in earlier ones. This is a specimen of certain lines of reflection which will inevitably suggest the hypothesis of God's Reality. It is not that such phenomena might not be capable of being accounted for, in one sense, by the action of chance with the smallest conceivable dose of a higher element; for if by God be meant the *Ens necessarium*, that very hypothesis requires that such should be the case. But the point is that that sort of explanation leaves a mental

explanation just as needful as before. Tell me, upon sufficient authority, that all cerebration depends upon movements of neurites that strictly obey certain physical laws,
and that thus all expressions of thought, both external and
internal, receive a physical explanation, and I shall be ready
to believe you. But if you go on to say that this explodes
the theory that my neighbor and myself are governed by
reason, and are thinking beings, I must frankly say that it
will not give me a high opinion of your intelligence. But
however that may be, in the Pure Play of Musement the
idea of God's Reality will be sure sooner or later to be
found an attractive fancy, which the Muser will develop in
various ways. The more he ponders it, the more it will find
response in every part of his mind, for its beauty, for its
supplying an ideal of life, and for its thoroughly satisfactory
explanation of his whole threefold environment.

The hypothesis of God is a peculiar one, in that it supposes an infinitely incomprehensible object, although every
hypothesis, as such, supposes its object to be truly conceived in the hypothesis. This leaves the hypothesis but one
way of understanding itself; namely, as vague yet as true
so far as it is definite, and as continually tending to define
itself more and more, and without limit. The hypothesis,
being thus itself inevitably subject to the law of growth,
appears in its vagueness to represent God as so, albeit this is
directly contradicted in the hypothesis from its very first
phase. But this apparent attribution of growth to God, since
it is ineradicable from the hypothesis, cannot, according to
the hypothesis, be flatly false. Its implications concerning
the Universes will be maintained in the hypothesis, while
its implications concerning God will be partly disavowed,
and yet held to be less false than their denial would be.
Thus the hypothesis will lead to our thinking of features
of each Universe as purposed; and this will stand or fall
with the hypothesis. Yet a purpose essentially involves
growth, and so cannot be attributed to God. Still it will,
according to the hypothesis, be less false to speak so than to
represent God as purposeless.

Assured as I am from my own personal experience that

every man capable of so controlling his attention as to perform a little exact thinking will, if he examines Zeno's argument about Achilles and the tortoise, come to think, as I do,
that it is nothing but a contemptible catch, I do not think
that I either am or ought to be less assured, from what I
know of the effects of Musement on myself and others, that
any normal man who considers the three Universes in the
light of the hypothesis of God's Reality, and pursues that
line of reflection in scientific singleness of heart, will come
to be stirred to the depths of his nature by the beauty of
the idea and by its august practicality, even to the point of
earnestly loving and adoring his strictly hypothetical God,
and to that of desiring above all things to shape the whole
conduct of life and all the springs of action into conformity
with that hypothesis. Now to be deliberately and thoroughly prepared to shape one's conduct into conformity
with a proposition is neither more nor less than the state of
mind called Believing that proposition, however long the
conscious classification of it under that head be postponed.

There is my poor sketch of the Neglected Argument,
greatly cut down to bring it within the limits assigned to
this article. Next should come the discussion of its logicality;
but nothing readable at a sitting could possibly bring home
to readers my full proof of the principal points of such an
examination. I can only hope to make the residue of this
paper a sort of table of contents, from which some may
possibly guess what I have to say; or to lay down a series
of plausible points through which the reader will have to
construct the continuous line of reasoning for himself. In
my own mind the proof is elaborated, and I am exerting my
energies to getting it submitted to public censure. My present abstract will divide itself into three unequal parts. The
first shall give the headings of the different steps of every
well-conducted and complete inquiry, without noticing possible divergencies from the norm. I shall have to mention
some steps which have nothing to do with the Neglected
Argument in order to show that they add no jot nor tittle
to the truth which is invariably brought just as the Neglected
Argument brings it. The second part shall very briefly state,

without argument (for which there is no room), just wherein lies the logical validity of the reasoning character- istic of each of the main stages of inquiry. The third part shall indicate the place of the Neglected Argument in a com- plete inquiry into the Reality of God, and shall show how well it would fill that place, and what its logical value is supposing the inquiry to be limited to this; and I shall add a few words to show how it might be supplemented.

Every inquiry whatsoever takes its rise in the observation, in one or another of the three Universes, of some surprising phenomenon, some experience which either disappoints an expectation, or breaks in upon some habit of expectation of the *inquisiturus;* and each apparent exception to this rule only confirms it. There are obvious distinctions between the objects of surprise in different cases; but throughout this slight sketch of inquiry such details will be unnoticed, es-. pecially since it is upon such that the logic-books descant. The inquiry begins with pondering these phenomena in all their aspects, in the search of some point of view whence the wonder shall be resolved. At length a conjecture arises that furnishes a possible Explanation, by which I mean a syllogism exhibiting the surprising fact as necessarily conse- quent upon the circumstances of its occurrence together with the truth of the credible conjecture, as premisses. On account of this Explanation, the inquirer is led to regard his conjecture, or hypothesis, with favor. As I phrase it, he pro- visionally holds it to be "Plausible"; this acceptance ranges in different cases—and reasonably so—from a mere expres- sion of it in the interrogative mood, as a question meriting attention and reply, up through all appraisals of Plausibility, to uncontrollable inclination to believe. The whole series of mental performances between the notice of the wonderful phenomenon and the acceptance of the hypothesis, during which the usually docile understanding seems to hold the bit between its teeth and to have us at its mercy, the search for pertinent circumstances and the laying hold of them, sometimes without our cognizance, the scrutiny of them, the dark laboring, the bursting out of the startling conjec- ture, the remarking of its smooth fitting to the anomaly, as it is turned back and forth like a key in a lock, and the final estimation of its Plausibility, I reckon as composing the First Stage of Inquiry. Its characteristic formula of reasoning I term Retroduction,[10] i.e., reasoning from consequent to antecedent. In one respect the designation seems inappropriate; for in most instances where conjecture mounts the high peaks of Plausibility—and is *really* most worthy of confidence—the inquirer is unable definitely to formulate just what the explained wonder is; or can only do so in the light of the hypothesis. In short, it is a form of Argument rather than of Argumentation.

Retroduction does not afford security. The hypothesis must be tested.

This testing, to be logically valid, must honestly start, not as Retroduction starts, with scrutiny of the phenomena, but with examination of the hypothesis, and a muster of all sorts of conditional experiential consequences which would follow from its truth. This constitutes the Second Stage of Inquiry. For its characteristic form of reasoning our language has, for two centuries, been happily provided with the name Deduction.

Deduction has two parts. For its first step must be by logical analysis to Explicate the hypothesis, i.e., to render it as perfectly distinct as possible. This process, like Retroduction, is Argument that is not Argumentation. But unlike Retroduction, it cannot go wrong from lack of experience, but so long as it proceeds rightly must reach a true conclusion. Explication is followed by Demonstration, or Deductive Argumentation. Its procedure is best learned from Book I of Euclid's *Elements*, a masterpiece which in real insight is far superior to Aristotle's *Analytics*; and its numerous fallacies render it all the more instructive to a close student. It invariably requires something of the nature of a diagram; that is, an "Icon," or Sign that represents its Object in resembling it. It usually, too, needs "Indices," or Signs that represent their Objects by being actually connected with them. But it is mainly composed of "Symbols," or Signs that represent their Objects essentially because they will be so interpreted. Demonstration should be *Corol-*

[10] Or Abduction. [This is Peirce's contribution to the logic of explanation or method of justifying hypotheses.]

larial when it can. An accurate definition of Corollarial Demonstration would require a long explanation; but it will suffice to say that it limits itself to considerations already introduced or else involved in the Explication of its conclusion; while *Theorematic* Demonstration resorts to a more complicated process of thought.

The purpose of Deduction, that of collecting consequents of the hypothesis, having been sufficiently carried out, the inquiry enters upon its Third Stage, that of ascertaining how far those consequents accord with Experience, and of judging accordingly whether the hypothesis is sensibly correct, or requires some inessential modification, or must be entirely rejected. Its characteristic way of reasoning is Induction. This stage has three parts. For it must begin with Classification, which is an Inductive Non-argumentational kind of Argument, by which general Ideas are attached to objects of Experience; or rather by which the latter are subordinated to the former. Following this will come the testing-argumentations, the Probations; and the whole inquiry will be wound up with the Sentential part of the Third Stage, which, by Inductive reasonings, appraises the different Probations singly, then their combinations, then makes self-appraisal of these very appraisals themselves, and passes final judgment on the whole result.

The Probations, or direct Inductive Argumentations, are of two kinds. The first is that which Bacon ill described as *"inductio illa quæ procedit per enumerationem simplicem"* [that induction which proceeds by simple enumeration.] So at least he has been understood. For an enumeration of instances is not essential to the argument that, for example, there are no such beings as fairies, or no such events as miracles. The point is that there is no well-established instance of such a thing. I call this Crude Induction. It is the only Induction which concludes a logically Universal Proposition. It is the weakest of arguments, being liable to be demolished in a moment, as happened toward the end of the eighteenth century to the opinion of the scientific world that no stones fall from the sky. The other kind is Gradual Induction, which makes a new estimate of the proportion of truth in the hypothesis with every new instance; and given any degree of error there will *sometime* be an estimate (or would be, if the probation were persisted in) which will be absolutely the last to be infected with so much falsity. Gradual Induction is either Qualitative or Quantitative and the latter either depends on measurements, or on statistics, or on countings.

Concerning the question of the nature of the logical validity possessed by Deduction, Induction, and Retroduction, which is still an arena of controversy, I shall confine myself to stating the opinions which I am prepared to defend by positive proofs. The validity of Deduction was correctly, if not very clearly, analyzed by Kant.[11] This kind of reasoning deals exclusively with Pure Ideas attaching primarily to Symbols and derivatively to other Signs of our own creation; and the fact that man has a power of Explicating his own meaning renders Deduction valid. Induction is a kind of reasoning that may lead us into error; but that it follows a method which, sufficiently persisted in, will be Inductively Certain (the sort of certainty we have that a perfect coin, pitched up often enough, will *sometime* turn up heads) to diminish the error below any predesignate degree, is assured by man's power of perceiving Inductive Certainty. In all this I am inviting the reader to peep through the big end of the telescope; there is a wealth of pertinent detail that must here be passed over.

Finally comes the bottom question of logical Critic, What sort of validity can be attributed to the First Stage of inquiry? Observe that neither Deduction nor Induction contributes the smallest positive item to the final conclusion of the inquiry. They render the indefinite definite; Deduction explicates; Induction evaluates: that is all. Over the chasm that yawns between the ultimate goal of science and such ideas of Man's environment as, coming over him during his primeval wanderings in the forest, while yet his very notion of error was of the vaguest, he managed to communicate to some fellow, we are building a cantilever bridge of induction, held together by scientific struts and ties. Yet

11 *Kritik der Reinen Vernunft*, A154–158; B193–197.

every plank of its advance is first laid by Retroduction alone, that is to say, by the spontaneous conjectures of instinctive reason; and neither Deduction nor Induction contributes a single new concept to the structure. Nor is this less true or less important for those inquiries that self-interest prompts.

The first answer we naturally give to this question is that we cannot help accepting the conjecture at such a valuation as that at which we do accept it; whether as a simple interrogation, or as more or less Plausible, or, occasionally, as an irresistible belief. But far from constituting, by itself, a logical justification such as it becomes a rational being to put forth, this pleading, that we *cannot help* yielding to the suggestion, amounts to nothing more than a confession of having failed to train ourselves to control our thoughts. It is more to the purpose, however, to urge that the strength of the impulse is a symptom of its being instinctive. Animals of all races rise far above the general level of their intelligence in those performances that are their proper function, such as flying and nest-building for ordinary birds; and what is man's proper function if it be not to embody general ideas in art-creations, in utilities, and above all in theoretical cognition? To give the lie to his own consciousness of divining the reasons of phenomena would be as silly in a man as it would be in a fledgling bird to refuse to trust to its wings and leave the nest, because the poor little thing had read Babinet,[12] and judged aerostation to be impossible on hydrodynamical grounds. Yes; it must be confessed that *if we knew* that the impulse to prefer one hypothesis to another really were analogous to the instincts of birds and wasps, it would be foolish not to give it play, within the bounds of reason; especially since we must entertain some hypothesis, or else forego all further knowledge than that which we have already gained by that very means. But is it a fact that man possesses this magical faculty? Not, I reply, to the extent of guessing right the first time, nor perhaps the second; but that the well-prepared mind has wonderfully soon guessed each secret of nature is

[12] Jacques Babinet (1794–1872), a popular writer on hydrodynamics and many other scientific subjects.

historical truth. All the theories of science have been so obtained. But may they not have come fortuitously, or by some such modification of chance as the Darwinian supposes? I answer that three or four independent methods of computation show that it would be ridiculous to suppose our science to have so come to pass. Nevertheless, suppose that it can be so "explained," just as that any purposed act of mine is supposed by materialistic necessitarians to have come about. Still, what of it? Does that materialistic explanation, supposing it granted, show that reason has nothing to do with my actions? Even the parallelists will admit that the one explanation leaves the same need of the other that there was before it was given; and this is certainly sound logic. There is a reason, an interpretation, a logic, in the course of scientific advance, and this indisputably proves to him who has perceptions of rational or significant relations, that man's mind must have been attuned to the truth of things in order to discover what he has discovered. It is the very bedrock of logical truth.

Modern science has been builded after the model of Galileo, who founded it, on *il lume naturale*. That truly inspired prophet had said that, of two hypotheses, the *simpler* is to be preferred;[13] but I was formerly one of those who, in our dull self-conceit fancying ourselves more sly than he, twisted the maxim to mean the *logically* simpler, the one that adds the least to what has been observed, in spite of three obvious objections: first, that so there was no support for any hypothesis; secondly, that by the same token we ought to content ourselves with simply formulating the special observations actually made; and thirdly, that every advance of science that further opens the truth to our view discloses a world of unexpected complications. It was not until long experience forced me to realize that subsequent discoveries were every time showing I had been wrong, while those who understood the maxim as Galileo had done, early unlocked the secret, that the scales fell from my eyes and my mind awoke to the broad

13 See "Dialogues Concerning the Two Great Systems of the World," in *Mathematical Collections and Translations* of Thomas Salisbury, Vol. 1, p. 301 (London, 1661).

and flaming daylight that it is the simpler Hypothesis in the sense of the more facile and natural, the one that instinct suggests, that must be preferred; for the reason that, unless man have a natural bent in accordance with nature's, he has no chance of understanding nature at all. Many tests of this principal and positive fact, relating as well to my own studies as to the researches of others, have confirmed me in this opinion; and when I shall come to set them forth in a book, their array will convince everybody. Oh, no! I am forgetting that armor, impenetrable by accurate thought, in which the rank and file of minds are clad! They may, for example, get the notion that my proposition involves a denial of the rigidity of the laws of association: it would be quite on a par with much that is current. I do not mean that logical simplicity is a consideration of no value at all, but only that its value is badly secondary to that of simplicity in the other sense.

If, however, the maxim is correct in Galileo's sense, whence it follows that man has, in some degree, a divinatory power, primary or derived, like that of a wasp or a bird, then instances swarm to show that a certain altogether peculiar confidence in a hypothesis, not to be confounded with rash cocksureness, has a very appreciable value as a sign of the truth of the hypothesis. I regret I cannot give an account of certain interesting and almost convincing cases. The N. A. excites this peculiar confidence in the very highest degree.

We have now to apply these principles to the evaluation of the N. A. Had I space I would put this into the shape of imagining how it is likely to be esteemed by three types of men: the first of small instruction with corresponding natural breadth, intimately acquainted with the N. A., but to whom logic is all Greek; the second, inflated with current notions of logic, but prodigiously informed about the N. A.; the third, a trained man of science who, in the modern spirit, has added to his specialty an exact theoretical and practical study of reasoning and the elements of thought, so that psychologists account him a sort of psychologist, and mathematicians a sort of mathematician.

I should, then, show how the first would have learned that nothing has any kind of value in itself—whether æsthetic, moral, or scientific—but only in its place in the whole production to which it appertains; and that an individual soul with its petty agitations and calamities is a zero except as filling its infinitesimal place, and accepting his little futility as his entire treasure. He will see that though his God would not *really* (in a certain sense) adapt means to ends, it is nevertheless quite true that there are relations among phenomena which finite intelligence must interpret, and truly interpret, as such adaptations; and he will macarize himself for his own bitterest griefs, and bless God for the law of growth with all the fighting it imposes upon him— Evil, i.e., what it is man's duty to fight, being one of the major perfections of the Universe. In that fight he will endeavor to perform just the duty laid upon him and no more. Though his desperate struggles should issue in the horrors of his rout, and he should see the innocents who are dearest to his heart exposed to torments, frenzy, and despair, destined to be smirched with filth, and stunted in their intelligence, still he may hope that it be best *for them*, will tell himself that in any case the secret design of God will be perfected through their agency, and even while still hot from the battle, will submit with adoration to His Holy will. He will not worry because the Universes were not constructed to suit the scheme of some silly scold.

The context of this I must leave the reader to imagine. I will only add that the third man, considering the complex process of self-control, will see that the hypothesis, irresistible though it be to first intention, yet needs Probation; and that though an infinite being is not tied down to any consistency, yet man, like any other animal, is gifted with power of understanding sufficient for the conduct of life. This brings him, for testing the hypothesis, to taking his stand upon Pragmaticism, which implies faith in common sense and in instinct, though only as they issue from the cupel-furnace of measured criticism. In short, he will say that the N. A. is the First Stage of a scientific inquiry, resulting in a hypothesis of the very highest Plausibility, whose ultimate test must lie in its value in the self-controlled growth of man's conduct of life.

Since I have employed the word *Pragmaticism*, and shall have occasion to use it once more, it may perhaps be well to explain it. About forty years ago, my studies of Berkeley, Kant, and others led me, after convincing myself that all thinking is performed in Signs, and that meditation takes the form of a dialogue, so that it is proper to speak of the "meaning" of a concept, to conclude that to acquire full mastery of that meaning it is requisite, in the first place, to learn to recognize the concept under every disguise, through extensive familiarity with instances of it. But this, after all, does not imply any true understanding of it; so that it is further requisite that we should make an abstract logical analysis of it into its ultimate elements, or as complete an analysis as we can compass. But, even so, we may still be without any living comprehension of it; and the only way to complete our knowledge of its nature is to discover and recognize just what general habits of conduct a belief in the truth of the concept (of any conceivable subject, and under any conceivable circumstances) would reasonably develop; that is to say, what habits would ultimately result from a sufficient consideration of such truth. It is necessary to understand the word "conduct," here, in the broadest sense. If, for example, the predication of a given concept were to lead to our admitting that a given form of reasoning concerning the subject of which it was affirmed was valid, when it would not otherwise be valid, the recognition of that effect in our reasoning would decidedly be a habit of conduct.

In 1871, in a Metaphysical Club in Cambridge, Massachusetts, I used to preach this principle as a sort of logical gospel, representing the unformulated method followed by Berkeley, and in conversation about it I called it "Pragmatism." In December [November] 1877 and January 1878 I set forth the doctrine in the *Popular Science Monthly;* and the two parts of my essay were printed in French in the *Revue Philosophique*, Volumes vi and vii. Of course, the doctrine attracted no particular attention, for, as I had remarked in my opening sentence, very few people care for logic. But in 1897 Professor James remodelled the matter, and transmogrified it into a doctrine of philosophy,[14] some parts of which I highly approved, while other and more prominent parts I regarded, and still regard, as opposed to sound logic. About the time Professor Papini[15] discovered, to the delight of the Pragmatist school, that this doctrine was incapable of definition, which would certainly seem to distinguish it from every other doctrine in whatever branch of science, I was coming to the conclusion that my poor little maxim should be called by another name; and accordingly, in April 1905 I renamed it *Pragmaticism*. I had never before dignified it by any name in print, except that, at Professor Baldwin's request, I wrote a definition of it for his *Dictionary of Psychology and Philosophy*. I did not insert the word in the *Century Dictionary*, though I had charge of the philosophical definitions of that work, for I have a perhaps exaggerated dislike of *réclame*.

It is that course of meditation upon the three Universes which gives birth to the hypothesis and ultimately to the belief that they, or at any rate two of the three, have a Creator independent of them, that I have throughout this article called the N. A., because I think the theologians ought to have recognized it as a line of thought reasonably productive of belief. This is the "humble" argument, the innermost of the nest. In the mind of a metaphysician it will have a metaphysical tinge; but that seems to me rather to detract from its force than to add anything to it. It is just as good an argument, if not better, in the form it takes in the mind of the clodhopper.

The theologians could not have *presented* the N. A., because that is a living course of thought of very various forms. But they might and ought to have *described* it, and should have defended it, too, as far as they could, without going into original logical researches, which could not be justly expected of them. They are accustomed to make use

[14] See *The Will to Believe and Other Essays in Popular Philosophy* (1897).

[15] See "What Pragmatism Is Like," *Popular Science Monthly,* Vol. 71 (1907), p. 351.

of the principle that that which convinces a normal man must be presumed to be sound reasoning; and therefore they ought to say whatever can truly be advanced to show that the N. A., if sufficiently developed, will convince any normal man. Unfortunately, it happens that there is very little established fact to show that this is the case. I have not pretended to have any other ground for my belief that it is so than my assumption, which each one of us makes, that my own intellectual disposition is normal. I am forced to confess that no pessimist will agree with me. I do not admit that pessimists are, at the same time, thoroughly sane, and in addition are endowed in normal measure with intellectual vigor; and my reasons for thinking so are two. The first is, that the difference between a pessimistic and an optimistic mind is of such controlling importance in regard to every intellectual function, and especially for the conduct of life, that it is out of the question to admit that both are normal, and the great majority of mankind are naturally optimistic. Now, the majority of every race depart but little from the norm of that race. In order to present my other reason, I am obliged to recognize three types of pessimists. The first type is often found in exquisite and noble natures of great force of original intellect whose own lives are dreadful histories of torment due to some physical malady. Leopardi is a famous example. We cannot but believe, against their earnest protests, that if such men had had ordinary health, life would have worn for them the same color as for the rest of us. Meantime, one meets too few pessimists of this type to affect the present question. The second is the misanthropical type, the type that makes itself heard. It suffices to call to mind the conduct of the famous pessimists of this kind, Diogenes the Cynic, Schopenhauer, Carlyle, and their kin with Shakespeare's Timon of Athens, to recognize them as diseased minds. The third is the philanthropical type, people whose lively sympathies, easily excited, become roused to anger at what they consider the stupid injustices of life. Being easily interested in everything, without being overloaded with exact thought of any kind, they are excellent raw material for *littérateurs*:

witness Voltaire. No individual remotely approaching the calibre of a Leibniz is to be found among them.

The third argument, enclosing and defending the other two, consists in the development of those principles of logic according to which the humble argument is the first stage of a scientific inquiry into the origin of the three Universes, but of an inquiry which produces, not merely scientific belief, which is always provisional, but also a living, practical belief, logically justified in crossing the Rubicon with all the freightage of eternity. The presentation of this argument would require the establishment of several principles of logic that the logicians have hardly dreamed of, and particularly a strict proof of the correctness of the maxim of Pragmaticism. My original essay, having been written for a popular monthly, assumes, for no better reason than that real inquiry cannot begin until a state of real doubt arises and ends as soon as Belief is attained, that "a settlement of Belief," or, in other words, a state of *satisfaction*, is all that Truth, or the aim of inquiry, consists in. The reason I gave for this was so flimsy, while the inference was so nearly the gist of Pragmaticism, that I must confess the argument of that essay might with some justice be said to beg the question. The first part of the essay, however, is occupied with showing that, if Truth consists in satisfaction, it cannot be any *actual* satisfaction, but must be the satisfaction which *would* ultimately be found if the inquiry were pushed to its ultimate and indefeasible issue. This, I beg to point out, is a very different position from that of Mr. Schiller and the pragmatists of today. I trust I shall be believed when I say that it is only a desire to avoid being misunderstood in consequence of my relations with pragmatism, and by no means as arrogating any superior immunity from error which I have too good reason to know that I do not enjoy, that leads me to express my personal sentiments about their tenets. Their avowedly undefinable position, if it be not capable of logical characterization, seems to me to be characterized by an angry hatred of strict logic, and even some disposition to rate any exact thought which interferes with their doctrines as all humbug. At the same time, it seems to me clear that their approximate acceptance of the Prag-

maticist principle, and even that very casting aside of difficult distinctions (although I cannot approve of it), has
helped them to a mightily clear discernment of some fundamental truths that other philosophers have seen but through
a mist, and most of them not at all. Among such truths—all
of them old, of course, yet acknowledged by few—I reckon
their denial of necessitarianism; their rejection of any "consciousness" different from a visceral or other external sensation; their acknowledgment that there are, in a Pragmatis-
tical sense, Real habits (which Really *would* produce
effects, under circumstances that may not happen to get
actualized, and are thus Real generals); and their insistence
upon interpreting all hypostatic abstractions in terms of
what they *would* or *might* (not actually *will*) come to in
the concrete. It seems to me a pity they should allow a
philosophy so instinct with life to become infected with
seeds of death in such notions as that of the unreality of all
ideas of infinity[16] and that of the mutability of truth,[17] and
in such confusions of thought as that of active willing (willing to control thought, to doubt, and to weigh reasons)
with willing not to exert the will (willing to believe).[18]

[16] F. C. S. Schiller, *Humanism* (London, 1903), p. 314, note;
Studies in Humanism (London, 1907), p. 295.

[17] William James, *Pragmatism* (New York, 1908), p. 59ff.

[18] William James, *The Will to Believe* (New York, 1899),
p. 11.

24. Letters to Lady Welby

[Peirce's letters to Lady (Viola) Welby began with his joint review in the *Nation* (October 15, 1903) of her book *What Is Meaning?* and Bertrand Russell's *Principles of Mathematics.* Lady Welby proposed the name "significs" for the study of signs in the development of the mind in general and in the evaluation of the various subjects considered essential to a liberal education. She later wrote the article on "Significs" for the *Encyclopaedia Britannica.* Since Peirce had devoted so many years to the logical theory of signs and the historical evolution of thought, which he had early identified with the use of signs, he was glad to engage in a lengthy correspondence with a cultivated person interested not only in his logical theories of language but also in his philosophical views on ethical and religious questions. Hence, his informal discussions in these letters of his pragmatism, his cosmological categories of Firstness, Secondness, Thirdness, his analyses of different kinds of signs, his view of ethical ideals as symbols, and his account of religious faith not only give us a review of Peirce's philosophy but expositions that are often clearer than his technical articles on these topics. They also throw light on some personal matters touching his solitude and poverty in the last decade of his life. Purely incidental passages in the letters have been omitted.]

Excerpts of Letters to Lady Welby (1903–1911)[1]

[Dec. 1, 1903]

. . . It seems to me that the objections that have been made to my word "pragmatism" are very trifling. It is the doctrine that truth consists in future serviceableness for our ends. "Pragmatism" seems to me to express this. I might have called it "practism," or "practicism" (*praktikós* being rather more classical than *pragmatikós*), but pragmatism is more sonorous.

. . . The greatest analyst of thought that ever lived might spend an indefinite amount of time in endeavoring to express his ideas with perfect accuracy. Expression and thought are one. It would be time and energy spent in making his thoughts themselves perfectly distinct. But he never would perfectly succeed. He would only make his thoughts so involved that they would not be apprehended. I think your extreme insistence on accuracy of metaphor—say about the expression "coining a word"—might well be tempered, without really yielding any point. I fully and heartily agree that the study of what we mean ought to be the—how shall I express it so as not to offend your fastidious requirements?—general purpose of a liberal education, as distinguished from special education—of that education which should be required of everybody with whose society and conversation we are expected to be content. But, then, perfect accuracy of thought is unattainable, *theoretically unattainable*. And undue striving for it is worse than time wasted. It positively renders thought unclear. . . .

P. O. Milford, Pa.
1904, Oct. 12

My dear Lady Welby:

Not a day has passed since I received your last letter that I have not lamented the circumstances that prevented me

[1] Copyright by Whitlock's, Inc., 1953. *Charles S. Peirce's Letters to Lady Welby*, ed. Irwin C. Lieb (Whitlock's, Inc., New Haven, Conn., 1953). Reprinted here with the very kind permission of Dr. Irwin C. Lieb and Mr. Reverdy Whitlock.

from writing that very day the letter that I was intent upon writing to you, without my promising myself that it should soon be done. But living in the country on this side of the Atlantic, unless one is a multimillionaire, is attended with great friction. Though it is done more of late years, it is not yet a usual thing, and in this country one is expected to be just like everybody else. I will venture to say that your imagination could not compass the picture of the sort of domestic servant that an American girl makes. Then too an inconsiderate contract I entered into to get certain definitions for a supplement to the *Century Dictionary* ready by a certain time drives me like the furies. To be sure I might have scribbled a line to explain myself; but I was always telling myself that in a very few days I should get time to write as I desired, until now my idea of what it was I wanted to write is blurred. I hope, however, that you will have had faith to know that only an impossibility could have prevented my writing; for from one who lives in the country one may hope for more of that sort of faith than from a *citadin*.

For one thing, I wanted to express my surprise at finding you rather repelled the designation of a "rationalist," and said that as a woman you were naturally conservative. Of course, the lady of the house is usually the minister of foreign affairs (barring those of money and law) and as an accomplished diplomat, is careful and conservative. But when a woman takes up an idea my experience is that she does so with a singleness of heart that distinguishes her. Some of my very best friends have been very radical women. I do not know that I don't think your recommending a serious consideration of changing the base of numeration is a bit radical.

But I wanted to write to you about signs, which in your opinion and mine, are matters of so much concern. More in mine, I think, than in yours. For in mine, the highest grade of reality is only reached by signs; that is, by such ideas as those of Truth and Right and the rest. It sounds paradoxical; but when I have devolved to you my whole theory of signs, it will seem less so. I think that I will today explain the outlines of my classification of signs.

LETTERS TO LADY WELBY

You know that I particularly approve of inventing new
words for new ideas. I do not know that the study I call
Ideoscopy can be called a new idea, but the word *phenomenology* is used in a different sense. *Ideoscopy* consists in
describing and classifying the ideas that belong to ordinary
experience or that naturally arise in connection with ordinary life, without regard to their being valid or invalid or
to their psychology. In pursuing this study I was long ago
(1867) led, after only three or four years' study, to throw
all ideas into the three classes of Firstness, of Secondness,
and of Thirdness. This sort of notion is as distasteful to me
as to anybody; and for years, I endeavored to pooh-pooh
and refute it; but it long ago conquered me completely.
Disagreeable as it is to attribute such meaning to numbers,
& to a triad above all, it is as true as it is disagreeable.
The ideas of Firstness, Secondness, and Thirdness are simple enough. Giving to being the broadest possible sense, to
include ideas as well as things, and ideas that we fancy
we have just as much as ideas we do have, I should define
Firstness, Secondness, and Thirdness thus:

Firstness is the mode of being of that which is such as it
is, positively and without reference to anything else.

Secondness is the mode of being of that which is such as
it is, with respect to a second but regardless of any third.

Thirdness is the mode of being of that which is such as
it is, in bringing a second and third into relation to each
other.

I call these three ideas the cenopythagorean categories.

The typical ideas of Firstness are qualities of feeling, or
mere appearances. The scarlet of your royal liveries, the
quality itself, independently of its being perceived or remembered, is an example, by which I do not mean that
you are to imagine that you *do not* perceive or remember
it, but that you are to drop out of account that which may
be attached to it in perceiving or in remembering, but
which does not belong to the quality. For example, when
you remember it, your idea is said to be *dim* and when it is
before your eyes, it is *vivid*. But dimness or vividness do not
belong to your idea of the quality. They *might* no doubt,
if considered simply as a feeling; but when you think of

vividness you do not consider it from that point of view. You think of it as a degree of disturbance of your consciousness. The quality of red is not thought of as belonging to you, or as attached to liveries. It is simply a peculiar positive possibility regardless of anything else. If you ask a mineralogist what hardness is, he will say that it is what one predicates of a body that one cannot scratch with a knife. But a simple person will think of hardness as a simple positive possibility the *realization* of which causes a body to be like a flint. That idea of hardness is an idea of Firstness. The unanalyzed total impression made by any manifold not thought of as actual fact, but simply as a quality as simple positive possibility of appearance is an idea of Firstness. Notice the *naïveté* of Firstness. The cenopythagorean categories are doubtless another attempt to characterize what Hegel sought to characterize as his three stages of thought. They also correspond to the three categories of each of the four triads of Kant's table. But the fact that these different attempts were independent of one another (the resemblance of these Categories to Hegel's stages was not remarked for many years after the list had been under study, owing to my antipathy to Hegel) only goes to show that there really are three such elements. The idea of the present instant, which, whether it exists or not, is naturally thought as a point of time in which no thought can take place or any detail be separated, is an idea of Firstness.

The type of an idea of Secondness is the experience of effort, prescinded from the idea of a purpose. It may be said that there is no such experience, that a purpose is always in view as long as the effort is cognized. This may be open to doubt; for in sustained effort we soon let the purpose drop out of view. However, I abstain from psychology which has nothing to do with ideoscopy. The existence of the word *effort* is sufficient proof that people think they have such an idea; and that is enough. The experience of effort cannot exist without the experience of resistance. Effort only is effort by virtue of its being opposed; and no third element enters. Note that I speak of the *experience*, not of the *feeling*, of effort. Imagine yourself to be seated alone at night in the basket of a balloon, far above earth, calmly enjoying the absolute calm and stillness. Suddenly the piercing shriek of a steam-whistle breaks upon you, and continues for a good while. The impression of stillness was an idea of Firstness, a quality of feeling. The piercing whistle does not allow you to think or do anything but suffer. So that too is absolutely simple. Another Firstness. But the breaking of the silence by the noise was an experience. The person in his inertness identifies himself with the precedent state of feeling, and the new feeling which comes in spite of him is the non-ego. He has a two-sided consciousness of an ego and a non-ego. That consciousness of the action of a new feeling in destroying the old feeling is what I call an *experience*. Experience generally is what the course of life has *compelled* me to think. Secondness is either *genuine* or *degenerate*. There are many degrees of genuineness. Generally speaking genuine secondness consists in one thing acting upon another, brute action. I say brute, because so far as the idea of any *law* or *reason* comes in, Thirdness comes in. When a stone falls to the ground, the law of gravitation does not act to make it fall. The law of gravitation is the judge upon the bench who may pronounce the law till doomsday, but unless the strong arm of the law, the brutal sheriff, gives effect to the law, it amounts to nothing. True, the judge can create a sheriff if need be; but he must have one. The stone's actually falling is purely the affair of the stone and the earth at the time. This is a case of *reaction*. So is *existence* which is the mode of being of that which reacts with other things. But there is also action without reaction. *Such is the action of the previous upon the subsequent.* It is a difficult question whether the idea of this one-sided determination is a pure idea of secondness or whether it involves thirdness. At present, the former view seems to me correct. I suppose that when Kant made Time a form of the internal sense alone, he was influenced by some such considerations as the following. The relation between the previous and the subsequent consists in the previous being determinate and fixed for the subsequent, and the subsequent being indeterminate for the previous. But indeterminacy belongs only to ideas; the existent is determinate in every respect; and this is just what the law of causation consists in. Accordingly, the relation of time concerns only ideas. It may also be argued that, according to the law of the conservation of energy, there is nothing in the physical universe corresponding to our idea that the previous determines the subsequent in any way in which the subsequent does not determine the previous. For, according to that law, all that happens in the physical universe consists in the exchange of just so much *vis viva* $\frac{1}{2}$m $(ds/dt)^2$ for so much displacement. Now the square of a negative quantity being positive, it follows that if all the velocities were reversed at any instant, everything would go on just the same, only time going backward as it were. Everything that had happened would happen again in reverse order. These seem to me to be strong arguments to prove that temporal causation (a very different thing from physical dynamic action) is an action upon ideas and not upon existents. But since our idea of the past is precisely the idea of that which is absolutely determinate, fixed, *fait accompli,* and dead, as against the future which is living, plastic, and determinable, it appears to me that the idea of one-sided action, in so far as it concerns the being of the determinate, is a pure idea of Secondness; and I think that great errors of metaphysics are due to looking at the future as something that will have been past. I cannot admit that the idea of the future can be so translated into the Secundal ideas of the past. To say that a given Kind of event never will happen is to deny that there is any date at which its happening will be past; but it is not equivalent to any affirmation about a past relative to any assignable date. When we pass from the idea of an event to saying that it never will happen, or will happen in endless repetition, or introduce in any way the idea of endless repetition, I will say the idea is *mellonized* (*méllon,* about to be, do, or suffer). When I conceive a fact as acting but not capable of being acted upon, I will say that it is *parelélythose* (past) and the mode of being which consists in such action I will call *parelelythosine* (-ine = einai, being). I regard the former as an idea of Thirdness, the latter as an idea of Secondness. I consider the idea of any dyadic relation not involving any third as an idea of Secondness; and I should not call any completely degenerate except the relation of identity. But similarity which is the only possible identity of Firsts is very near to that. Dyadic relations have been classified by me in a great variety of ways; but the most important are first with regard to the nature of the Second in itself and second with regard to the nature of its first. The Second, or *Relate* is, in itself, either a *Referate*, if it is intrinsically a possibility, such as a Quality or it is a *Revelate* if it is of its own nature an Existent. In respect to its first, the Second is divisible either in regard to the dynamic first or to the immediate first. In regard to its dynamic first, a Second is determined either by virtue of its own intrinsic nature, or by virtue of a real relation to that second (an action). Its immediate second is either a Quality or an Existent.

I now come to Thirdness. To me, who have for forty years considered the matter from every point of view that I could discover, the inadequacy of Secondness to cover all that is in our minds is so evident that I scarce know how to begin to persuade any person of it who is not already convinced of it. Yet I see a great many thinkers who are trying to construct a system without putting any thirdness into it. Among them are some of my best friends who acknowledge themselves indebted to me for ideas but have never learned the principal lesson. Very well. It is highly proper that Secondness should be searched to its very bottom. Thus only can the indispensableness and irreducibility of thirdness be made out, although for him who has the mind to grasp it, it is sufficient to say that no branching of a line can result from putting one line on the end of another. My friend Schröder fell in love with my algebra of dyadic relations. The few pages I gave to it in my Note B in the "Studies in Logic by Members of the Johns Hopkins University" were proportionate to its importance.[1] His book is profound,[2]

---

[1] *Studies in Logic by Members of the Johns Hopkins University* was edited by Peirce. It was published by Little, Brown and Company, Boston, in 1883. Peirce's "Note B" is reproduced as Chapter 12 in Volume III of the *Collected Papers.*—Note by Dr. Lieb.

[2] *Vorlesungen über die Algebra der Logik.* B. G. Teubner, Leipzig, 1890–1905.

but its profundity only makes it more clear that Secondness cannot compass Thirdness. (He is careful to avoid ever saying that it can, but he does go so far as to say that Secondness is the more important. So it is, considering that Thirdness cannot be understood without Secondness. But as to its application, it is so inferior to Thirdness as to be in that aspect quite in a different world.) Even in the most degenerate form of Thirdness, and Thirdness has two grades of degeneracy, something may be detected which is not mere secondness. If you take any ordinary triadic relation, you will always find a *mental* element in it. Brute action is secondness, any mentality involves thirdness. Analyze for instance the relation involved in "A gives B to C." Now what is giving? It does not consist A's putting B away from him and C's subsequently taking B up. It is not necessary that any material transfer should take place. It consists in A's making C the possessor according to *Law*. There must be some kind of law before there can be any kind of giving—be it but the law of the strongest. But now suppose that giving *did* consist merely in A's laying down the B which C subsequently picks up. That would be a degenerate form of Thirdness in which the thirdness is externally appended. In A's putting away B, there is no thirdness. In C's taking B, there is no thirdness. But if you say that these two acts constitute a single operation by virtue of the identity of the B, you transcend the mere brute fact, you introduce a mental element. As to my algebra of dyadic relations, Russell in his book which is superficial to nauseating me, has some silly remarks, about my "relative addition" etc., which are mere nonsense.[3] He says, or Whitehead says, that the need for it seldom occurs. The need for it *never* occurs if you bring in the same mode of connection in any other way. It is part of a system which does not bring in that mode of connection in any other way. In that system, it is indispen-

[3] The remarks to which Peirce refers are on page 24 of *The Principles of Mathematics*. Russell there comments that Peirce's methods are so cumbrous as to make useful application of them not feasible, and that the methods very likely involve philosophical errors in interpreting relational propositional forms. According to wide contemporary opinion, Peirce's interpretation of relational propositions is admissible.—Note by Dr. Lieb.

sable. But let us leave Russell and Whitehead to work out their own salvation. The criticism which I make on that algebra of dyadic relations, with which I am by no means in love, though I think it is a pretty thing, is that the very triadic relations which it does not recognize, it does itself employ. For every combination of relatives to make a new relative is a triadic relation irreducible to dyadic relations. Its *inadequacy* is shown in other ways, but in this way it is in a conflict with itself *if it be regarded,* as I never did regard it, *as sufficient for the expression of all relations.* My universal algebra of relations, with the subjacent indices and Σ and Π is susceptible of being enlarged so as to comprise everything and so, still better, though not to ideal perfection, is the system of existential graphs.[4] I have not sufficiently applied myself to the study of the degenerate forms of Thirdness, though I think I see that it has two distinct grades of degeneracy. In its genuine form, Thirdness is the triadic relation existing between a sign, its object, and the interpreting thought, itself a sign, considered as constituting the mode of being of a sign. A sign mediates between the *interpretant* sign and its object. Taking sign in its broadest sense, its interpretant is not necessarily a sign. Any concept is a sign, of course. Ockham, Hobbes, and Leibniz have sufficiently said that. But we may take a sign in so broad a sense that the interpretant of it is not a thought, but an action or experience, or we may even so enlarge the meaning of sign that its interpretant is a mere quality of feeling. A *Third* is something which brings a First into relation to a Second. A sign is a sort of Third. How shall we characterize it? Shall we say that a Sign brings a Second, its Object, into *cognitive* relation to a Third? That a Sign brings a Second into the same relation to a first in which it stands itself to that First? If we insist on *consciousness,* we must say what we mean by consciousness of an object. Shall we say we mean Feeling? Shall we say we mean association, or Habit? These are, on the face of them, psychological distinctions, which I am particular to avoid. What is the essential difference between a sign that is communicated to

[4] See Book II of Volume IV of the *Collected Papers.*—Note by Dr. Lieb.

a mind, and one that is not so communicated? If the question were simply what we *do* mean by a sign, it might soon be resolved. But that is not the point. We are in the situation of a zoologist who wants to know what ought to be the meaning of "fish" in order to make fishes one of the great classes of vertebrates. It appears to me that the essential function of a sign is to render inefficient relations efficient— not to set them into action, but to establish a habit or general rule whereby they will act on occasion. According to the physical doctrine, nothing ever happens but the continued rectilinear velocities with the accelerations that accompany different relative positions of the particles. All other relations, of which we know so many, are inefficient. Knowledge in some way renders them efficient; and a sign is something by knowing which we know something more. With the exception of knowledge, in the present instant, of the contents of consciousness in that instant (the existence of which knowledge is open to doubt) all our thought & knowledge is by signs. A sign therefore is an object which is in relation to its object on the one hand and to an interpretant on the other in such a way as to bring the interpretant into a relation to the object, corresponding to its own relation to the object. I might say "similar to its own," for a correspondence consists in a similarity; but perhaps correspondence is narrower.

I am now prepared to give my division of signs, as soon as I have pointed out that a sign has two objects, its object as it is represented and its object in itself. It has also three interpretants, its interpretant as represented or meant to be understood, its interpretant as it is produced, and its interpretant in itself. Now signs may be divided as to their own material nature, as to their relations to their objects, and as to their relations to their interpretants.[5]

[5] The recognition of two objects and three interpretants enables Peirce to define ten trichotomies and 66 classes of signs. This is a considerable refinement of the doctrine in Book II of Volume II, where Peirce attends mainly to three trichotomies and ten classes of signs. Peirce's letter of December 23, 1908, supplements the account of signs given in this letter. Appendix B contains a catalogue of the ten trichotomies.—Note by Dr. Lieb. Appendix B is in Dr. Lieb's edition.

As it is in itself, a sign is either of the nature of an appearance, when I call it a *qualisign;* or secondly, it is an individual object or event, when I call it a *sinsign* (the syllable *sin* being the first syllable of *sem*el, *sim*ul, *sin*gular, etc.); or thirdly, it is of the nature of a general type, when I call it a *legisign.* As we use the term "word" in most cases, saying that "the" is one "word" and "an" is a second "word," a "word" is a legisign. But when we say of a page in a book, that it has 250 "words" upon it, of which twenty are "the's," the "word" is a sinsign. A sinsign so embodying a legisign, I term a "replica" of the legisign.[6] The difference between a legisign and a qualisign, neither of which is an individual thing, is that a legisign has a definite identity, though usually admitting a great variety of appearances. Thus, &, *and*, and the sound are all one word. The qualisign, on the other hand, has no identity. It is the mere quality of an appearance & is not exactly the same throughout a second. Instead of identity, it has *great similarity,* & cannot differ much without being called quite another qualisign.

In respect to their relations to their dynamic objects, I divide signs into Icons, Indices, and Symbols (a division I gave in 1867). I define an Icon as a sign which is determined by its dynamic object by virtue of its own internal nature. Such is any qualisign, like a vision—or the sentiment excited by a piece of music considered as representing what the composer intended. Such may be a sinsign, like an individual diagram; say, a curve of the distribution of errors. I define an Index as a sign determined by its Dynamic object by virtue of being in a real relation to it. Such is a Proper Name (a legisign); such is the occurrence of a symptom of a disease (the Symptom itself is a legisign, a general type of a definite character. The occurence in a particular case is a sinsign). I define a Symbol as a sign which is determined by its dynamic object only in the sense that it will be so interpreted. It thus depends either upon a convention, a habit, or a natural disposition of its interpretant, or of the field of its interpretant (that of which the interpretant

[6] Peirce's usual term is "sinsign." Instead of "replica" he sometimes uses "token."—Note by Dr. Lieb.

is a determination). Every symbol is necessarily a legisign, for it is inaccurate to call a replica of a legisign a symbol.

In respect to its immediate object a sign may either be a sign of a quality, of an existent, or of a law.

In regard to its relation to its signified interpretant, a sign is either a Rheme, a Dicent, or an Argument. This corresponds to the old triune Term, Proposition, & Argument, modified so as to be applicable to signs generally. A *Term* is simply a class-name or proper-name. I do not regard the common noun as an essentially necessary part of speech. Indeed, it is only fully developed as a separate part of speech in the Aryan languages & the Basque—possibly in some other out-of-the-way tongues. In the Shemitic languages it is generally in form a verbal affair, & usually is so in substance too. As well as I can make out, such it is in most languages. In my universal algebra of logic there is no common noun. A rheme is any sign that is not true nor false, like almost any single word except "yes" and "no," which are almost peculiar to modern languages. A *proposition* as I use that term, is a dicent symbol. A dicent is not an assertion, but is a sign *capable* of being asserted. But an assertion is a dicent. According to my present view (I may see more light in future) the act of assertion is not a pure act of signification. It is an exhibition of the fact that one subjects oneself to the penalties visited on a liar if the proposition asserted is not true. An act of judgment is the self-recognition of a belief; and a belief consists in the acceptance of a proposition as a basis of conduct deliberately. But I think this position is open to doubt. It is simply a question of which view gives the simplest view of the nature of the proposition. Holding, then, that a Dicent does not assert, I naturally hold that an Argument need not actually be submitted or urged. I therefore define an argument as a sign which is represented in its signified interpretant not as a Sign of that interpretant (the conclusion) (for that would be to urge or submit it) but *as if* it were a Sign of the Interpretant or perhaps as if it were a Sign of the state of the universe to which it refers, in which the premisses are taken for granted. I define a dicent as a sign represented in its signified interpretant *as if it were* in a Real

Relation to its Object. (Or as being so, if it is asserted.) A rheme is defined as a sign which is represented in its signi- fied interpretant as *if it were* a character or mark (or as being so).

According to my present view, a sign may appeal to its dynamic interpretant in three ways:

1st,   an argument only may be *submitted* to its interpret- ant, as something the reasonableness of which will be acknowledged.

2nd,   an argument or dicent may be *urged* upon the inter- pretant by an act of insistence.

3rd,   argument or dicent may be and a rheme can only be, presented to the interpretant for *contemplation.*

Finally, in its relation to its immediate interpretant, I would divide signs into three classes as follows:

1st,   those which are interpretable in thoughts or other signs of the same kind in infinite series,

2nd,   those which are interpretable in actual experiences,

3rd,   those which are interpretable in qualities of feelings or appearances.

Now if you think on the whole (as I do) that there is much valuable truth in all this, I should be gratified if you cared to append it to the next edition of your book, after editing it & of course cutting out personalities of a disagree- able kind *especially if accompanied by one or more* (run- ning or other) *close criticisms;* for I haven't a doubt there is more or less error involved. . . .

Dec. 14, 1908

You ask whether, when I speak of religion being "proved" I mean "tested" or "logically proved." I reply that the ques- tion of the truth of religion being a question of what *is* true, and not of what *would be* true under an arbitrary hypothe- sis, such as those of pure mathematics, the only logical proof possible is the testing. If, for example, the question be whether the Koh-inoor diamond if thrown up *in vacuo* will describe a parabola with a vertical axis, it is no proof to say that the Koh-inoor is a body having weight and all bodies having weight so move *in vacuo,* but the whole question is the question of fact whether it has weight or not, that is, the *same* weight at all heights and at all times, and this can only be known by testing; and the sufficient testing is to give a glance at the thing. For it is known already, as a fact, that everything but an optical image or illusion that is visible does have weight. For if, to prove a given experiential proposition, a mixture of testing and mathematical reasoning be required, the latter does not count at all in characterizing the proof, since mathematical reasoning is well understood to be a necessary ingredient of all testing. I object strongly, however, to making mathematical demonstration the sole "logical proof." On the contrary, I maintain that "testing" is the sole logical proof of any question concerning Real objects. Mathematical demonstration only shows that one arbitrary hypothesis involves another; and such reasoning can only concern real matter of fact because, since it appears by testing that an arbitrary hypothesis is approximately fulfilled, we presume that its mathematical consequences will be approximately fulfilled. But this is not proved until it is tested.

You ask me whether, when I said the mind is characterized by its "active power to establish relations between objects," I would extend this to establishing relations between ideas and acts, *also.* In answer, I must explain that, according to my note on the Ethics of Terminology, which I must have sent you, but will now send another copy, I use the term "object" in the sense in which obiectum was first made a substantive early in the thirteenth century; and when I use the word without adding *"of"* what I am speaking of the object, I mean anything that comes before thought or the mind in any usual sense. Stout and Baldwin use the term in the same sense, though not upon the same principle. I will add, while I am about it, that I do not make any contrast between Subject and Object, far less talk about "subjective and objective" in any of the varieties of German senses, which I think have led to a lot of bad philosophy, but I use "subject" as the correlative of "predicate," and speak only of the "subjects" of those signs which have a part which separately indicates what the object of the sign is. A subject of such a sign is that kind of object of the sign which is so separately indicated, or would be if the sign were uttered in more detail. (By "uttered," I mean put forth in speech, on paper, or otherwise.) Of course, your question is already answered, at least, it is so as to ideas; what you mean by establishing relations between *acts,* as distinguished from ideas of acts, is not clear to me. But I will go on to say something more about subjects, since the study of significs must, I should think, involve a good deal of fine logical analysis, i.e., definition. Now what I have to say about subjects is particularly relevant to the doctrine of logical analysis. The subject of a pure symbolic proposition, i.e., one in which no diagram is involved, but only conventional signs, such as words, might be defined as that with which some collateral acquaintance is requisite to the interpretation (the understanding) of the proposition. Thus the statement "Cain killed Abel" cannot be fully understood by a person who has no further acquaintance with Cain and Abel than that which the proposition itself gives. Of course, Abel is as much a subject as Cain. But further, the statement cannot be understood by a person who has no collateral acquaintance with killing. Therefore, Cain, Abel, and the relation of killing are the subjects of this proposition. Of course, an Icon would be necessary to explain what was the relation of Cain to Abel, in so far as this relation was *imaginable* or imageable. To give the necessary acquaintance with any single thing an Index would be required. To convey the idea of causing death in general, according to the operation of a general law, a general sign would be requisite, that is, a *Symbol.* For symbols are founded either upon habits, which are, of course general, or upon conventions or agreements, which are equally general. Here I may remark that *brute* compulsion differs from rational necessitation founded on law, in that one can have an idea of it—a sense of it—in the single case, quite regardless of any law. A law of nature, which I insist, is a reality, and not, as Karl Pearson tries to show, a creature of our minds, an *ens rationis,* I am fond of comparing with a legislative enactment, in that it exercises no compulsion of itself, but only because the people *will* obey it. The judge who passes sentence on a criminal, applies the statutes to an individual case; but his sentence exercises no more force *per se* than the general law. But what the sentence does effect is to bring the execution of it into the field of purpose of the sheriff, whose brute muscles—or those of bailiff or hangman under him, exercise the actual compulsion. Thus the Icon represents the sort of thing that may appear and sometimes does appear; the Index points to the very thing or event that is met with—and I mean by an *Occurrence* such a single thing or state of things; and finally, the Symbol represents that which may be observed under certain general conditions and is essentially general. When we have analyzed a proposition so as to throw into the subject everything that can be removed from the predicate, all that it remains for the predicate to represent is the form of connection between the different subjects as expressed in the propositional *form*. What I mean by "everything that can be removed from the predicate" is best explained by giving an example of something not so removable. But first take something removable. "Cain kills Abel." Here the predicate appears as "—— kills ——." But we can remove killing from the predicate and make the latter "—— stands in the relation —— to ——." Suppose we attempt to remove more from the predicate and put the last into the form "—— exercises the function of relate of the relation —— to ——" and then putting "the function of relate to the relation" into another subject leave as predicate "—— exercises —— in respect to —— to ——." But this "exercises" express "exercises the function." Nay more, it expresses "exercises the function of relate," so that we find that though we may put this into a separate subject, it continues in the predicate just the same. Stating this in another form, to say that "A is in the relation R to B" is to say that A is in a certain relation to R. Let us separate this out thus: "A is in the relation R^1 (where R^1 is the relation of a relate to the relation of which it is the relate,) to R to B." But A is here said to be in a certain relation to the relation R^1. So that we can express the same fact by saying, "A is in the relation R^1 to the relation R^1 to the relation R to B," and so on *ad infinitum*. A predicate which can thus be analyzed into parts all homogeneous with the whole I call a *continuous predicate*. It is very important in logical analysis, because a continuous predicate obviously cannot be a *compound* except of continuous predicates, and thus when we have carried analysis so far as to leave only a continuous predicate, we have carried it to its ultimate elements. I won't lengthen this letter by easily furnished examples of the great utility of this rule. But I proceed to the next point of your letter.

By *belief*, I mean merely holding for true—real, genuine, practical holding for true—whether that which is believed be the atomic theory, or the fact that this is Monday, or the fact that this ink is pretty black, or what you will. You well say that Belief may be mistaken. Yes, the nearest certain of anything is, for example, that this paper is white or whitish—or *appears* so. Yet it is easy to show that this belief may be mistaken. For the judgment can never relate to the appearance at the instant of the judgment, because the subject of any judgment must have been known by *collateral* acquaintance. There can be no judgment of the very judgment itself. The old *Insolubilia*, such as "this proposition is false" are examples of this. If it be false, since this is all that it asserts, it must be true; and if it be true, since it denies this, it must be false. Belief that could not be false would be infallible belief and Infallibility is an Attribute of Godhead. The fruit of the tree of knowledge which Satan told Adam and Eve was to make them equal with God was precisely the doctrine that there is some kind of Infallible belief. This must be so; for after this was rendered still more blasphemous by asserting that the kind of belief that was to be Infallible was belief about God, the most utterly inscrutable of any subject, it became the means of corrupting Christianity until the religion of Love was confounded with the *odium theologicum*.

1908, Dec. 23

Dear Lady Welby, for the past week all my time and all my energy have been taken up with what we Yankees (i.e., the stock of those who came over to Massachusetts before 1645—I forget the exact date,) call "chores." I believe that in standard English the word is lost. It means the menial offices of every day in a household, especially, a primitive household—the hewing of wood and the drawing of water and the like.

I now return to the expression of my abhorrence of the doctrine that any proposition whatever is infallibly true. Unless truth be recognized as *public*—as that of which *any* person would come to be convinced if he carried his inquiry, his sincere search for immovable belief, far enough—then there will be nothing to prevent each one of us from adopting an utterly futile belief of his own which all the rest will disbelieve. Each one will set himself up as a little prophet; that is, a little "crank," a half-witted victim of his own narrowness.

But if Truth be something public, it must mean that to the acceptance of which as a basis of conduct any person you please would ultimately come if he pursued his inquiries far enough—yes, every rational being, however prejudiced he might be at the outset. For Truth has that compulsive nature which Pope well expressed:

The eternal years of God are hers.

But, you will say, I am setting up this very proposition as infallible truth. Not at all; it is a mere definition. I do not say that it is infallibly true that there is any belief to which a person would come if he were to carry his inquiries far enough. I only say that that alone is what I call Truth. I cannot infallibly know that there *is* any Truth.

You say there is a certain "Faith" the object of which is absolutely "certain." Will you have the goodness to tell me what you mean by "certain"? Does it mean anything more than that you personally are obstinately resolved upon sticking to the proposition, *ruat caelum?* It reminds me of an anecdote that was told me in 1859 by a southern darky. 'You know,' says he, 'Massa, that General Washington and General Jackson was great friends, dey was (the fact being that the latter was in irreconcilable opponent of the former, but did not become a figure in national politics until after Washington had retired from public life). Well, one day

Gen'l Washington, he said to Gen'l Jackson, "Gen'l, how tall should you think that horse of mine was?" "I don't know, General," says General Jackson, "how tall is he, General Washington?" "Why," says General Washington, "he is sixteen feet high." "Feet, General Washington," say Gen'ral Jackson, "feet, General Washington? You means *hands*, Gen'ral!" "Did I say *feet*, General Jackson?" said General Washington. "Do you mean to say that I said my horse was sixteen *feet* high?" "You certainly said so, General Washington." "Very well, then, Gen'ral Jackson, if I *said* feet, *if* I said feet, then I sticks to it!" ' Is your "sublime faith" any more "sublime" than that? How?

Now I will tell you the meaning that *I* would, in my turn, attach to the word faith. The New Testament word is *pistis*, which means, in its most proper sense, *trust*; i.e., belief in something *not* as having any knowledge or approach to knowledge about the matter of belief, but "implicit belief," as the Catholics say, i.e., belief in it derived from one's belief that a witness who testifies to it would not so testify if it were not so. Hence, the latest writers of classical Greek, such as Plato and Isocrates, and the earliest writers of common Greek, such as Aristotle, use it for any mediate belief, any belief well founded on another belief. That is, these writers apply *pistis* to an assured belief. They also apply it to an *assurance* of any belief. But the English word "faith" could not be used so without great violence to usage which would be entirely unwarranted by any need. I think that what the word is needed to express, and what it might be restricted to express without too great violence to usage is *that belief which the believer does not himself recognize,* or rather (since that cannot properly be called belief, that which he is prepared to conform his conduct to), without recognizing what it is to which he is conforming his conduct. For example, if I do not know what Liddell & Scott say is the meaning of *pistis* but am convinced that whatever they may say is its meaning really is so, I have a *faith* that it is so. A person who says, "Oh, I could not believe that this life is our only life; for if I did I should be so miserable that I should suicide forthwith," I say he has a *Faith* that things are not intolerably bad for any individual

or at any rate are not so for *him*. Every true man of science,
i.e., every man belonging to a social group all the members
of which sacrifice all the ordinary motives of life to their
desire to make their beliefs concerning one subject conform
to verified judgments of perception together with sound reasoning, and who therefore really believes the universe to
be governed by reason, or in other words by God—but who
does not explicitly recognize that he believes in God—has
Faith in God, according to my use of the term Faith. For
example, I knew a scientific man who devoted his last years
to reading theology in hopes of coming to a belief in God,
but who never could in the least degree come to a consciousness of having the least belief of the sort, yet passionately pursued that very mistaken means of attaining his
heart's supreme desire. He, according to me, was a shining
example of Faith in God. For to believe in reasoning about
phenomena is to believe that they are governed by reason,
that is, by God. That to my mind is a high and wholesome
belief. One is often in a situation in which one is obliged
to assume, i.e., to go upon, a proposition which one ought
to recognize as extremely doubtful. But in order to conduct
oneself with vigorous consistency one must dismiss doubts
on the matter from consideration. There is a vast difference
between that and any holding of the proposition for certain. To hold a proposition to be certain is to puff oneself
up with the vanity of perfect knowledge. It leaves no room
for Faith. It is not absolutely certain that twice two is four.
It is humanly certain that no conception of God can be free
from all error. I once made a careful study of Dr. Schaff's
three solid volumes on *The Creeds of Christendom*. I found
not one that said one word about the principle of love, although that seems to be the leading element of Christian
faith. In order to find out, if I could, the reason for this
passing strange omission, I made a study of the circumstances which determined the formulation of each Symbolum, and ascertained that, with the possible exception of
what we erroneously call "The Apostles' Creed," concerning whose origin we have no definite information, but which
is no exception as regards the information in question, and
certainly does not breathe the spirit of such early docu-

ments as the *Didaché,* every one sprang from the *odium the-ologicum* and the desire to have some certain person excom-municated, with the evident wish that he might be damned. Theology arises from discontent with religious Faith—which implies a lack of such Faith, and with a desire to substitute for that a scientific anatomy and physiology of God, which, rightly considered, is blasphemous and antireligious. It is also in most striking disaccord with the spirit of the son of Mary.

Your pleading that I should not use such a phrase as "attractive fancy" and I suppose you might feel so about the phrase "strictly hypothetical God" seems to show that I quite failed to convey my own sense of the value of the Neglected Argument, in that it does not lead to any the-ology at all, but only to what *I* mean by a purely religious *Faith,* which will have already taken deep root before the subject of it thinks of it at all as a belief. Writing this is like having to explain a joke.

As to the word "play," the first book of philosophy I ever read (except Whately's *Logic,* which I devoured at the age of twelve or thirteen,) was Schiller's *Aesthetische Briefe* where he has so much to say about the Spiel-Trieb; and it made so much impression upon me as to have thoroughly soaked my notion of "play," to this day. . . .

By the way, when I was speaking of creeds, I might have mentioned . . . that I say the creed in church with the rest. By doing so I only signify, as I presume the majority do—& hope they do—my willingness to put aside, most heartily, anything that tends to separate me from my fellow Chris-tians. For the very ground of my criticism of creeds is that every one of them was originally designed to produce such a separation, contrary to the notions of him who said "He that is not against me is for me." By the way, I have been reading, with much study, the book of W. B. Smith entitled *Der vorchristliche Jesus,* which I have little doubt is sound in the main; and I think probably Christianity was a higher development out of Buddhism, modified by Jewish belief in a living god.

Being a convinced Pragmaticist in semeiotic, naturally

and necessarily nothing can appear to me sillier than rationalism; and folly in politics cannot go further than English liberalism. The people ought to be enslaved; only the slaveholders ought to practice the virtues that alone can maintain their rule. England will discover too late that it has sapped the foundations of culture. The most perfect language that ever was spoken was classical Greek; and it is obvious that no people could have spoken it who were not provided with plenty of intelligent slaves. As to us Americans, who had, at first, so much political sense, we always showed a disposition to support such aristocracy as we had; and we have constantly experienced, and felt but too keenly, the ruinous effects of universal suffrage and weakly exercised government. Here are the labor-organizations, into whose hands we are delivering the government, clamoring today for the "right" to persecute and kill people as they please. We are making them a ruling class; and England is going to do the same thing. It will be a healthful revolution; for when the lowest class insists on enslaving the upper class, as they are insisting, and that is just what their intention is, and the upper class is so devoid of manhood as to permit it, clearly that will be a revolution by the grace of God; and I only hope that when they get the power they won't be so weak as to let it slip from their hands. Of course, it will mean going back relatively to the Dark Ages, and working out a new civilization, this time with some hopes that the governing class will use common sense to maintain their rule. The rationalists thought their phrases meant the satisfaction of certain feelings. They were under the hedonist delusion. They will find they spell revolution of the most degrading kind.

The publishers of the *Britannica* have given an earnest of their determination to maintain the eminence of their encyclopaedia in electing editors who would ask you to give a compend of the exact science of "significs."

In a paper of 1867, May 14 (Proc. Am. Acad. Arts & Sci. [Boston] VII, 295), I defined logic as the doctrine of the formal conditions of the truth of symbols; i.e., of the reference of symbols to their objects. Later, when I had recognized that science consists in *inquiry, not* in "doctrine"

(the *history* of words, not their *etymology*, being the key
to their meanings, especially for a word saturated with the
idea of progress as science is), and when I accordingly recognized that, in order that the lines of demarcation between
what we call "sciences" should be real, in view of the rapid
growth of sciences and the impossibility of allowing for future discoveries, those lines of demarcation can only represent the separations between the different groups of men
who devote their lives to the advance of different studies, I
saw that for a long time those who devoted themselves to
discovering the truth about the general reference of symbols to their objects would be obliged to make researches
into the reference to their interpretants, too, as well as into
other characters of symbols, and not *of symbols* alone but
of all sorts of signs. So that, for the present, the man who
makes researches into the reference of symbols to their objects will be forced to make original studies into all branches
of the general theory of signs; and so I should certainly
give the logic-book that I am writing the title "Logic, considered as Semeiotic," if it were not that I foresee that everybody would suppose *that* to be a translation of *Logik,
als Semeiotik dargestellt,* which would not comport with my
disagreement (bordering closely upon contempt) from German logic.

"Significs" would appear, from its name, to be that part
of Semeiotic which inquires into the relation of signs to their
Interpretants (for which, as limited to symbols, I proposed
in 1867 the name Universal Rhetoric), for I am sure you
recognize that no usage of language is better established
among students of semeiotic than that distinction to which
the elegant writer and accurate thinker John of Salisbury
in the twelfth century referred as *"quod fere in omnium ore
celebre est, aliud scilicet esse quod appellatiua significant,
et aliud esse quod nominant. Nominatur singularia, sed uni-
versalia significantur."* (*Metalogicus.* Book II, Chap. xx.
Edition of 1620, p. 111.) But, assuming this to be your
meaning, I should hardly think it possible, in the present
state of the subject, to make much headway in a truly scientific investigation of significs in general without devoting

a very large share of one's work to inquiries into other questions of semeiotic.

It is clearly indispensable to start with an accurate and broad analysis of the nature of a Sign. I define a Sign as anything which is so determined by something else, called its Object, and so determines an effect upon a person, which effect I call its Interpretant, that the latter is thereby mediately determined by the former. My insertion of "upon a person" is a sop to Cerberus, because I despair of making my own broader conception understood. I recognize three Universes, which are distinguished by three Modalities of Being.

One of these Universes embraces whatever has its Being in itself alone, except that whatever is in this Universe must be present to one consciousness, or be capable of being so present in its entire Being. It follows that a member of this universe need not be subject to any law, not even to the principle of contradiction. I denominate the objects of this Universe *Ideas,* or *Possibles,* although the latter designation does not imply capability of actualization. On the contrary, as a general rule, if not a universal one, an Idea is incapable of perfect actualization on account of its essential vagueness if for no other reason. For that which is not subject to the principle of contradiction is essentially vague. For example, geometrical figures belong to this Universe; now since every such figure involves lines which can only be *supposed* to exist as boundaries where three bodies come together, or to be the place common to three bodies, and since the boundary of a solid or liquid is merely the place at which its forces of cohesion are neither very great nor very small, which is essentially vague, it is plain that the idea is essentially vague or indefinite. Moreover, suppose the three bodies that come together at a line are wood, water, and air, then a whole space including this line is at every point either wood, water, or air; and neither wood and water, nor wood and air, nor water and air can together occupy any place. Then plainly the principle of contradiction, were it applicable, would be violated in the idea of a place where wood, water, & air come together. Similar antinomies affect all Ideas. We can only reason about them in respects which the antinomies do not affect, and often by arbitrarily assuming what upon closer examination is found to be absurd. There is this much truth in Hegel's doctrine, although he is frequently in error in applying the principle.

Another Universe is that of, first, Objects whose Being consists in their Brute reactions, and of, second, the Facts (reactions, events, qualities, etc.) concerning those Objects, all of which facts, in the last analysis, consist in their reactions. I call the Objects, Things, or more unambiguously, *Existents,* and the facts about them, I call *Facts.* Every member of this Universe is either a Single Object subject alike to the Principles of Contradiction and to that of Excluded Middle, or it is expressible by a proposition having such a singular subject.

The third Universe consists of the co-being of whatever is in its nature *necessitant,* that is, is a Habit, a law, or something expressible in a universal proposition. Especially, *continua* are of this nature. I call objects of this universe *Necessitants.* It includes whatever we can know by logically valid reasoning. I note that the question you put on the first page of your letter as to whether a certain proposition is "thoroughly tested" and supports the test, or whether it is "logically proved," seems to indicate that you are in some danger of enlisting in that army of "cranks," who insist on calling a kind of reasoning "logical" which leads from true premises to false conclusions, thus putting themselves outside the pale of sanity: people, for example, who maintain that the reasoning of the "Achilles" [and the tortoise] is "logical," though they cannot state it in any sound syllogistic or other form acknowledged by sane reasoners. I knew a gentleman who had mind enough to be a crack chessplayer, but who insisted that it was "logical" to reason

> It either rains or it doesn't rain,
> Now it rains;
> ∴ It doesn't rain.

This is on a perfect level with saying that contemptible Achilles catch is "Logical." The truth is that an inference is "logical," if, and only if, it is governed by a habit that would in the long run lead to the truth. I am confident you will assent to this. Then I trust you do not mean to lend any countenance to notions of logic that conflict with this. It is a part of our duty to frown sternly upon *immoral* principles; and logic is only an application of morality. Is it not?

A Sign may *itself* have a "possible" Mode of Being, e.g., a hexagon inscribed in or circumscribed about a conic. It is a Sign, in that the collinearity of the intersections of opposite sides shows the curve to be a conic, if the hexagon is inscribed; but if it be circumscribed the co-punctuality of its three diameters (joining opposite vertices). Its Mode of Being may be Actuality: as with any barometer. Or Necessitant: as the word "the" or any other in the dictionary. For a "possible" Sign I have no better designation than a *Tone,* though I am considering replacing this by "Mark." Can you suggest a really good name? An Actual sign I call a *Token;* a Necessitant Sign, a *Type.*

It is usual and proper to distinguish two Objects of a Sign, the Mediate without, and the Immediate within the Sign. Its Interpretant is all that the Sign conveys: acquaintance with its Object must be gained by collateral experience. The Mediate Object is the Object outside of the Sign; I call it the *Dynamoid* Object. The Sign must indicate it by a hint; and this hint, or its substance, is the *Immediate* Object. Each of these two Objects may be said to be capable of either of the three Modalities, though in the case of the Immediate Object, this is not quite literally true. Accordingly, the Dynamoid Object may be a Possible; when I term the Sign an *Abstractive;* such as the word Beauty; and it will be none the less an Abstractive if I speak of "the Beautiful," since it is the ultimate reference, and not the grammatical form, that makes the sign an *Abstractive.* When the Dynamoid Object is an Occurrence (Existent thing or Actual fact of past or future), I term the Sign a *Concretive;* any one barometer is an example; and so is a written narrative of any series of events. For a *Sign* whose Dynamoid Object is a Necessitant, I have at present no better designation than a *Collective,* which is not quite so bad a name as it sounds to be until one studies the matter: but for a person, like me, who thinks in quite a different system of symbols to words, it is so awkward and often puzzling to translate one's thought into words! If the Immediate Object is a "Possible," that is, if the Dynamoid Object is indicated (always more or less vaguely) by means of its Qualities, etc., I call the Sign a *Descriptive;* if the Immediate is an Occurrence, I call the Sign a *Designative;* and if the Immediate Object is a Necessitant, I call the Sign a *Copulant;* for in that case the Object has to be so identified by the Interpreter that the Sign may represent a necessitation. My name is certainly a temporary expedient.

It is evident that a possible can determine nothing but a Possible, it is equally so that a Necessitant can be determined by nothing but a Necessitant. Hence it follows from the Definition of a Sign that since the Dynamoid Object determines the Immediate Object,

> Which determines the Sign itself,
> which determines the Destinate Interpretant
> which determines the Effective Interpretant
> which determines the Explicit Interpretant

the six trichotomies, instead of determining 729 classes of signs, as they would if they were independent, only yield 28 classes; and if, as I strongly opine (not to say almost prove), there are four other trichotomies of signs of the same order of importance, instead of making 59,049 classes, these will only come to 66. The additional 4 trichotomies are undoubtedly, first,

Icons (or Simulacra, Aristotle's *homoiómata*),
> caught from Plato, who I guess took it from the Mathematical school of logic, for it earliest appears in the *Phaedrus* which marks the beginning of Plato's being decisively influenced by that school. Lutoslowski is right in saying that the *Phaedrus* is later than the *Republic* but his date 379 B.C. is about eight years too early.

Symbols   Indices

and then 3 referring to the Interpretants. One of these I am pretty confident is into: *Suggestives, Imperatives, Indicatives,* where the Imperatives include the Interrogatives.

Of the other two I *think* that one must be into Signs assuring their Interpretants by

Instinct   Experience   Form

The other I suppose to be what, in my *Monist* exposition of Existential Graphs, I called

Semes   Phemes   Delomes.

You, with your life-long study of "significs" must surely have important teachings about the three Interpretants for me, whose studies have been diluted through the whole subject of semeiotic; and what I have succeeded in assuring myself of in significs has chiefly concerned Critic of Arguments, upon which the question you propound on the first page of your letter makes me think you are not at your best. But I smiled at your speaking of my having been "*kindly* interested" in your work, as if it were a divergence —I should say a *deviation,* from my ordinary line of attention. Know that from the day when at the age of twelve or thirteen I took up, in my elder brother's room a copy of Whately's *Logic,* and asked him what logic was, and getting some simple answer, flung myself on the floor and buried myself in it, it has never been in my power to study anything—mathematics, ethics, metaphysics, gravitation, thermodynamics, optics, chemistry, comparative anatomy, astronomy, psychology, phonetics, economics, the history of science, whist, men and women, wine, metrology—except as a study of semeiotic; and how rarely I have been able to feel a thoroughly sympathetic interest in the studies of other men of science (how far *more* than rarely have met any who [?] understand my own studies), I need not tell you, though fortunately I am a man of an ardently sympathetic nature, I mean fortunately for my scientific development, under chilling circumstances.

I wish you would study my Existential Graphs; for in my opinion it quite wonderfully opens up the true nature and method of logical analysis, that is to say, of definition; though *how* it does so is not easy to make out, until I shall have written my exposition of that art.

I am now working desperately to get written before I

die a book on Logic that shall attract some good minds
through whom I may do some real good, & may after all
hear those wonderful words that will be better by far than
any kind of Heaven I ever heard of. Unless there is going
to be work to do—useful work—I cannot conceive of another
life as very desirable. I wish you with all my heart & soul
a successful year! Don't forget your implied promise about
the proof of the *Britannica* article. My dear wife constantly
though slowly loses ground; & her disposition not to spare
herself is most distressing. Very faithfully,

C. S. Peirce

Milford, Pa.
1909, Jan. 31

My dear Lady Welby:

I yesterday received your beautiful letter of the 21st inst.
which has done me a world of good & which I shall read
again and again. I have not had time to read any of the
enclosures, eager as I am to get at your *Britannica* article;
but I shall do so, I hope, in the course of this week. I must
beg you to let me know if you expect the return of that
MS. or of any of the others.

I will notice at once two odd words I came across last
evening; for if I didn't I should forget all about them, &
they are rather curious. The book in which I found them
was Frank Wigglesworth Clarke's *Data of Geochemistry,*
in which the author spoke of "*salic* rocks and *femic* rocks."
I was completely at a loss to imagine what these words
could mean or whence they were derived; but diligent
search through the volume disclosed the chemist-author's
notion of the way to form words. (Note that I am profes-
sionally a chemist myself, but not enough of a chemist to
fathom the allusions of the two words.) I found out, at
last, that "salic rocks" were rocks predominantly composed
of oxygen, *silicon* (Si) and *aluminum* (Al); so that *si-al*-an
or *si-al*-ian would have been better than "salic"; while
femic rocks were those in which Iron (Fe) and magnesium
(Mg) predominate. If chemists had agreed upon M as the

symbol of *magnesium*, as they would have done but for
the necessity of distinguishing it from *manganese* (originally, the same word), this would have been intelligible,
once one possessed the secret of the general method of formation; but under the circumstances "femgan" seems to me
the proper word. I thought the words were interesting as
specimens of the utterly un-English, and I may say un-
Aryan ways of word-formation that chemists have found so
well adapted to their purposes. Those two words of Frank
Wigglesworth Clarke suddenly bring to my mind something
that I do not believe I have thought of for half a century;
how as a boy I invented a language in which almost every
letter of every word made a definite contribution to its signification. It involved a classification of all possible ideas;
and I need not say that it was never completed. I remember
however a number of features of it. Not only must the ideas
be classified, but abstract and psychical ideas had to be
provided with fixed metaphors; such as *lofty* for pride, ambition, etc. Roget's *Thesaurus* did not exist in those days. I
had no better prompter than Bishop Wilkin's *Real Character*—a book (if you have never seen it) that attempts to
furnish a graphical sign for every idea. The grammar of
my Language was, I need hardly say, modelled in a general way after the Latin Grammar as almost all ideas of
grammar are to this day. It had, in particular, the Latin
parts of speech; and it never dawned upon me that they
could be other than they are in Latin. Since then I have
bought Testaments in such languages as Zulu, Dakota,
Hawaiian, Jagalu, Magyar (Basque I have dipped into
otherwise; and I learned a little Arabic from Edward
Palmer whom I knew in Constantinople & later in Cambridge). These studies have done much to broaden my
ideas of language in general; but they have never made me
a good writer, because my habits of thinking are so different
from those of the generality of people. Besides I am left-
handed (in the literal sense) which implies a cerebral development and connections of parts of the brain so different
from those of right-handed people that the sinister is almost sure to be misunderstood and live a stranger to his
kind, if not a misanthrope. This has, I doubt not, had a

good deal to do with my devotion to the science of logic.
Yet probably my intellectual left-handedness has been serviceable to my studies in that science. It has caused me to
be *thorough* in penetrating the thoughts of my predeces-
sors, not merely their ideas as they understood them, but
the potencies that were in them. I have neglected no school,
nor any logician whose books I could lay hand upon. Thus
I have gained caution in forming my own opinions & still
more in condemning others; and I have produced little, and
that little has been far, far more deeply considered and
debated than anybody dreams of its being. Yet today half
of what I have written seems to me immature and not sufficiently considered.

I place a high valuation upon my Existential Graphs, and
hope you will persevere in the study of the system; and if
you do so, I desire to aid you. . . .

[This letter was started in January, added to in February,
and finished in March, 1909.]

Ash Wednesday
1909, Feb. 24

I think what a lapse of time has intervened in which I
have been working with might & main to get my wife rescued from her failing state of health. We must pull up
stakes & go about to give her *change*. To do that we must
sell this house which is any way too big for her. To accomplish that the outside of it must be made attractive. For
now it looks so forlorn that nobody can be persuaded that
the inside is worth looking at. Besides, its four roofs are all
in need of shingling & a new verandah must replace the
present one. All these things have compelled me to drop
logic for the last days completely. I had intended to make
the last example very elaborate & instructive. But it can
wait, until I ascertain whether or not you are at all interested in my Existential Graphs.

Dear me, I won't deny I am beginning to age; but it
seems to me that it is not nearly so much that it is I that
have grown old as it is that the world in my day has been
settling down to a state of ferocious hum-drumacity—a

positive appetite for the humdrum. I could still enjoy an old-time Roman carnival, or an old-time *bal masque* at the Paris Opera. But how did I celebrate my *mardi gras?* I read all your essay-cules. I had already read your *Britannica* article and had learned something important from it. It is what you are after, what you are well on the *piste* of, in your Sense, Meaning, & Significance.

1909, March 14

Oh, to think that, in the Middle of March, I should not have finished a letter begun in January—a letter to my dear Lady Welby! And, what is much worse still, that I should have let your admirable letter go all this time without one word of response, nor even acknowledgment. It has been because one thing after another has demanded my instant attention, while I was always promising myself that surely in two or three days at the utmost I should get back to this. But what have you been thinking of me? Will you really forgive me? If you knew all that I have been forced to neglect, and how terribly overworked I have been, every night falling asleep while my pen scrawled over the paper, and every morning jumping up at the alarum!

I wrote somewhat further about your *Britannica* article; but as I have, at odd moments, thought considerably of it since my last words, I prefer to begin that subject again. I propose to treat it with the coolest criticism, because it is worth such treatment. I confess I had not realized, before reading it, how fundamental your trichotomy of Sense, Meaning, and Significance really is. It is not to be expected that concepts of such importance should get perfectly defined for a long time.

By the way, I find in my portfolio some part of a letter, if not the whole, dated December 28. I suppose I sent you that. I hope so, because it seems, from the glance I cast upon it, to be concerned with my gropings after *the three kinds of Interpretant.* I now find that my division nearly coincides with yours, as it ought to do exactly, if both are correct. I am not in the least conscious of having been at all influenced by your book in settling my trichotomy, as nearly as it is settled; and I don't believe there was any such influence; though of course there may have been without my being aware of it. In reading your book my mind may quite well have absorbed the ideas without my remembering it; and when I came to search for a division of the Interpretant, those ideas may have seemed to me to have been struck out by processes of thought that I thought then were presenting themselves to me for the first time, when the fact was that they were due to a bent of my thoughts which the perusal of your book had made. However, as I do not believe this did happen, I feel some exultation in finding that my thought and yours nearly agree, for I think it is because we were both trying to get at the truth; and I should not wonder if you have the same feeling. But as far as the public goes, I can only point out the agreement, and confess to having read your book.

Let us see how well we do agree. The greatest discrepancy appears to lie in my Dynamical Interpretant as compared with your "Meaning." If I understand the latter, it consists in the effect upon the mind of the Interpreter that the utterer (whether vocally or by writing) of the sign intends to produce. My Dynamical Interpretant consists in direct effect actually produced by a Sign upon an Interpreter of it. They agree in being effects of the Sign upon an individual mind, I think, or upon a number of actual individual minds by independent action upon each. My Final Interpretant is, I believe, exactly the same as your Significance; namely, the effect the Sign *would* produce upon any mind upon which circumstances should permit it to work out its full effect. My Immediate Interpretant is, I think, very nearly, if not quite, the same as your "Sense"; for I understand the former to be the total unanalyzed effect that the Sign is calculated to produce, or naturally might be expected to produce; and I have been accustomed to identify this with the effect the sign first produces or may produce upon a mind, without any reflection upon it. I am not aware that you have ever attempted to define your term "Sense"; but I gather from reading over what you say that it is the first effect that a sign would have upon a mind well qualified to comprehend it. Since you say it is Sensal and has no Volitional element, I suppose it is of the nature

of an "impression." It is thus, as far as I can see, exactly
my Immediate Interpretant. You have selected words from
vernacular speech to express your varieties, while I have
avoided these and manufactured terms suitable, as I think,
to serve the uses of Science. I might describe my Immediate Interpretation, as so much of the effect of a Sign as
would enable a person to say whether or not the Sign was
applicable to anything concerning which that person had
sufficient acquaintance.

My Interpretant with its three kinds is supposed by me
to be something essentially attaching to anything that acts
as a Sign. Now natural Signs and symptoms have no utterer; and consequently have no Meaning, if Meaning be
defined as the intention of the utterer. I do not allow myself
to speak of the "purposes of the Almighty," since whatever
He might desire is done. Intention seems to me, though I
may be mistaken, an interval of time between the desire
and the laying of the train by which the desire is to be
brought about. But it seems to me that Desire can only
belong to a finite creature.

Your ideas of Sense, Meaning, and Signification seem to
me to have been obtained through a prodigious sensitive-
ness of Perception that I cannot rival, while my three grades
of Interpretant were worked out by reasoning from the definition of a Sign what sort of thing *ought* to be noticeable
and *then* searching for its appearance. My Immediate Interpretant is implied in the fact that each Sign must have
its own peculiar Interpretability before it gets any Interpreter. My Dynamical Interpretant is that which is experienced in each act of Interpretation and is different in each
from that of any other; and the Final Interpretant is the
one Interpretative result to which every Interpreter is destined to come if the Sign is sufficiently considered. The Immediate Interpretant is an abstraction, consisting in a Possibility. The Dynamical Interpretant is a single actual event.
The Final Interpretant is that toward which the actual
tends.

It is now a good while since I read your essay-lets. If I
can recall anything in them, it must have struck me as very
good or else as open to some particular criticism. When you

speak in one of them of Man as *translating* vegetal and Brute strength into intellectual and spiritual vigor, that word *translating* seems to me to contain profound truth wrapped up in it. Then there was one piece dated All-Souls' that I liked in much the same way; that is, as expressing thoughts familiar to me too, but probably not to Tom, Dick, and Harry. I regard Logic as the Ethics of the Intellect—that is, in the sense in which Ethics is the science of the method of bringing Self-Control to bear to gain our Satisfactions. If I had a son, I should instill into him this view of morality, and force him to see that there is but one thing that raises one individual animal above another, Self-Mastery, and should teach him that the Will is Free only in the sense that, by employing the proper appliances, he can make himself behave in the way he really desires to behave. As to what one ought to desire, it is, I should show him, what he will desire if he sufficiently considers it, and that will be to make his life beautiful, admirable. Now the Science of the Admirable is *true* Esthetics. Thus, the Freedom of the Will, such as it is, is a one-sided affair, it is Freedom to become Beautiful, *kalòs k'agathós:* There is no freedom to be or to do anything else. Nor is there any freedom to do right if one has neglected the proper discipline. By these teachings, by showing him that a good dog is more to be respected than an improvident man, who has not prepared himself beforehand to withstand the day of temptation, I should expect to render him eager to submit to a pretty severe discipline.

One remark I approved particularly was that "Language is only the extreme form of expression." Also, "Life, itself, may be considered (I should have said *should be recognized*) as Expression."

But your method of getting at the exact meanings of words is very different from mine. I should be greatly obliged to you if you would give me a statement of what your method is, and of your reasons for adopting it; and if I may petition for still more, I should further like to know, since your *Britannica* article contains much less about the physiology of signs than about efforts that ought to be made for improving our language, what your method is of assur-

ing yourself and others that any given habit of language
ought to be changed, and that a given sort of effort will
pay, that is will cause advantages greater than any other
way of expending the same energy. In this connection, I
will send you, if I can find one, a copy of a study I made
a good many years ago of the *economics of research*.[7]

I ask these things of you because, if you have considered
well your methods—a study which I have just endeavored
to show you is about what Morals amount to—I shall certainly get some good, some practical application to my own
doings from what you tell me, while in any case, it is not
likely to be altogether profitless for you to set down for the
benefit of another what you so often ruminate upon for
yourself; since one generally gains some new *aperçu* in putting one's personal meditations into shape for communication.

Your trichotomy of Sense, Meaning, Signification is a positive earnest of the value of what I ask to myself.

In order at any rate to prove my disposition to recipro-
cate the benefit, I will explain my own methods.

My father was universally acknowledged to be by far the
strongest mathematician in the country, and was a man of
great intellect and weight of character. All the leading men
of science, particularly astronomers and physicists, resorted
to our house; so that I was brought up in an atmosphere
of science. But my father was a broad man and we were
intimate with literary people too. William Story, the sculptor, Longfellow, James Lowell, Charles Norton, Wendell
Holmes, and occasionally Emerson, are among the figures
of my earliest memories. Among them I remember the
Italian Gallenga, who went by the name of Mariotte. The
Quincys we also knew very well, but not the Adamses. My
mother's father had been a Senator in Washington. But his
weak lungs having obliged him to retire, he set up a law
school; and in that way I used to see some of the most
eminent of the political people, such as Webster. Bancroft
had been very intimate with my mother's family, as in his
old age he was a great friend of my wife here. I used occasionally to see him; and Lothrop Motley was one of our

---

[7] [Cf. *U. S. Coast Survey Reports*, 1879, appendix 21.]

friends. My father had strong contempts for certain men whom he considered shams, and among them was Charles Sumner, who was, I must say, one of the absurdest figures of vanity I ever laid eyes on. Among the lawyers I remember Rufus Choate, Judge Story, etc. Another figure of my childhood was Emerson's friend Margaret Fuller (Countess[8] Ossoli). I was brought up with far too loose a rein, except that I was forced to think hard & continuously. My father would sometimes make me sit up all night playing double dummy till sunrise without relaxing my attention.

I was educated as a chemist, and as soon as I had taken my A.B. degree, after a year's work in the Coast Survey, I took first six months under Agassiz in order to learn what I could of his methods, & then went into the laboratory. I had had a laboratory of my own for many years & had every memoir of any consequence as it came out; so that at the end of two or three years, I was the first man in Harvard to take a degree in chemistry *summa cum laude*.

But I had already discovered that my only very unusual gift was for logical analysis. I began with German Philosophy, having read hardly any of the great English school and not very much of such French writers as Maine de Biran, Jouffroy, Cousin, etc. For several years I studied the *Kritik der reinen Vernunft,* and knew it almost word for word, in both editions. Even now, I fancy there are few who know it better. Then I devoted myself for some years chiefly to the scholastics and after that to Locke, Hume, Berkeley, Gay, Hartley, Reid, Hamilton, etc. I had already read the most readable part of Cudworth & all of Hobbes. Gradually, I gained independent views.

By this time the inexactitude of the Germans, and their tottering logic utterly disgusted me. Kant & Leibniz alone seemed to me great. I more and more admired British thought. Its one great and terrible fault, which my severe studies in the schoolmen had rescued me from—or rather, it was because I suspected they were right about this that I took to the study of them & found that they didn't go far enough to satisfy me—was their extreme Nominalism. To be sure *all* modern philosophers were nominalists, even Hegel.

[8] Should be "Marchioness".—Editor's note.

But I was quite convinced they were absolutely wrong. Modern science, especially physics, is and must be, for all the brilliant Lothringian—whose name escapes me—says, essentially on the side of scholastic realism. So is religion; but that cannot be admitted as evidence. I set myself to finding out how it happened that all modern philosophy had put up with that dire nonsense. It did not take very long to solve that problem. It was that all the humanists were no better than *littérateurs,* with the total lack of ratiocinative power which I had seen in the literary men whom I had personally known. Such fools! On the intellectual level of the wine-tasters of Bordeaux. (By the way, I was myself for six months under the tutelage of the *sommelier* of Voisin in Paris before he sold out his great *caves,* to study the red wines of Médoc, and became quite an expert.) Now the Scotists had almost undisputed supremacy in almost all the Universities having gained it by their superiority in Logic. They therefore appeared as the old fogeys whom the Humanists had to fight. The latter called them Dunces after their master Duns Scotus. But for the first generation of the Renaissance a Dunce was far from meaning or suggesting a stupid person. The title rather conveyed the idea of a man so skilled in debate on the wrong side as to be a terror to the pure humanist upon whom he might fall. So since the great adversaries of the Scotists were the Ockhamists, or terminists, who belonged to the class of *nominales,* whom the humanists called nominalists, the humanists allied themselves with the nominalists to cast the Scotists out of the Universities, & not caring a tuppence for the dispute between the two kinds of logicians they conformed to the nominalistic confession in return for the favor of that party; and so, because from that day to this scarcely anybody has examined into the real meaning or merits of the controversy & it was very easy and obvious to say that "Generals are mere words," which moreover is perfectly true in a sense, which was not the point at issue, it follows that everybody has admitted that Nominalism was the correct doctrine, just as everybody in England of any consequence that I saw, in my time, used publicly to assert all the monstrosities of the Athanasian Creed, and just as everybody who

graduated from Oxford for I know not how many centuries
swore to hate and detest one Simon (or I forget the name),
though no English writer whom I ever consulted professed
to know for certain who the Simon he had sworn to devote
himself to putting down was. He was supposed to be somebody who lived under the reign of King John; but nobody
knew what he had ever said or done that was amiss.

It is very easy to prove in two twos that Realism is right
and Nominalism is wrong. The realists are those who declare that *some* generals such as fit each to be predicated
of many subjects are Real. The nominalists said in various
forms that no general was Real. Now the word "real,"—
Latin *realis*—was not an old word. It had been invented
during the controversy to mean that which is not a *figment*,
as of course any word of a particular language is, or, to
express the precise meaning of it in terms intelligible today,
the Real is such that whatever is true of it is not true because some individual person's thought or some individual
group of persons' thought attributes its predicate to its subject, but is true, no matter what any person or group of
persons may think *about* it. Thus a dream, meaning what
is dreamed, is not real because, for example, if it be true
that the dream was about hen's eggs, it is because the action of the dreamer's mind made it to be true. But the *fact*
that a given person did dream of hen's eggs, if it be true *is*
true whether he remembers dreaming it, or thinks he
dreamed it or not. It in truth depends on the action of his
mind, but does *not* depend upon any attribution by his
mind to the *fact* that he dreamed, which is now that whose
reality is in question. All the scholastic philosophy is full of
such subtilties, and it requires *exact thinking*, which few
people except lawyers, mathematicians, etc., are, in our
days trained to, in order to steer one's bark between them
without swamping it. Those humanists broke up the habit
of exact thinking throughout Europe. That of which whatever is true depends for its truth on the action of a mind is
internal or as schoolmen said *objective* (Germans might say
subjective). That of which the truth of whatever is true of
it depends not merely on the action of a person's or a group
of persons' thought but also upon their thought *about* the

substance of the proposition that is true, is unreal. That
which is such that something true about it is either true
independently of the thought of any *definite* mind or minds
or is at least true independently of what any person or any
definite individual group of persons think about that truth,
is real. It was Duns Scotus more than anybody else who
(though he did not first invent the word *real*,) brought it
into use. The word *real* had already been used for *Real
property*. But that had nothing at all to do with the usual
metaphysical sense which attaches to it.

Now that you see what the word *real* means, I ask you,
as to the Law that every body set in motion continues to
move right on at a uniform rate only modified by its coming into the spatial vicinity of some other body that acts
upon it, whether supposing this Law to be true, whether
it be not a *real Law*, Does it depend for its truth upon some
person's *thinking* it to be true? Not so; supposing it to be
true at all. To be sure, you may say, with Kant, that it is
only true of Space which is a form of thought (of course
Kant does not use "thought" in this wide sense; but in English we *do*. Germans often think the English ought to
change their language to conform to German habits, but
this is only an example of the extreme modesty and dif-
fidence of which the Germans are so prodigiously vain.)
But that though it makes the truth of whatever is true of
the law to depend upon *thought* in general, does not make
it depend upon the thought of any particular person or
any particular group of persons. So if you believe that modern science has made any general discovery at all, you believe that general so discovered to be real, and so you *are* a
scholastic realist whether you are aware of it or not. Not
only does all *science* hang upon the decision but so do
Truth and Righteousness! Nominalism and all its ways are
devices of the Devil if devil there be. And in particular it
is the disease which almost drove poor John Mill mad—the
dreary outlook upon a world in which all that can be loved,
or admired, or understood, is figment.

Oh I must skip a great deal; for I can't spend what I
don't own, which is an hour's more time for this letter!

I at first defined logic as the general science of the relation of *symbols* to their *objects*. And I think still that this
defines the Critic of Argument which is the central part of
logic—its heart. But studies of the limits of the sciences in
general convinced me that the Logician ought to broaden
his studies, and take in every *allied* subject that it was no
business of anybody else to study and in short, and above
all, he must *not* confine himself to *symbols* since no reasoning that amounts to much can be conducted with Icons and
Indices. Nor ought he to confine himself to the relations of
signs to their Objects since it had always been considered
the business of the logician and of nobody else to study Definition. Now a definition does not reveal the Object of a
Sign, its Denotation, but only analyzes its Signification, and
that is a question not of the sign's relation to its Object but
of its relation to its Interpretant. My studies must extend
over the whole of general semeiotic. I think, dear Lady
Welby, that perhaps you are in danger of falling into some
error in consequence of limiting your studies so much to
Language and among languages to *one* very peculiar language, as all Aryan Languages are; and within that language so much to *words*.

Now as to English Words, there are only three classes
with which I have any decent acquaintance. The first are
the words of the vernacular of the class of society in which
I am placed—not a very cultivated class of late years but
for a few correspondents. The second are the words of
philosophical and mathematical terminology. The third,
which can hardly be said to be English or any other Aryan
speech, being of a synthetic structure much like those of
the tribes of our brown "red Indians," I mean chemical
words. This third class answer their purpose admirably except for their intolerable length; and they might be enormously cut down & be even more descriptive than they are.
But chemists won't bother to learn a *new* vocabulary. It
wouldn't pay. One route between two places may be far
preferable to another; and yet, when one is more than half-
way over the latter, it won't be worth while to toil back
and take the former.

Well my time is up! I must tell you another time how I discover or try to discover the best use of words.

Very faithfully,

C. S. Peirce

Milford, Pa.
1909, Oct. 11

My dear Lady Welby:

I could not bear to just dot down a line or two upon a post card to you nor to content myself with any hurried note; and in fact I did write you one long letter. But my wife read it and suggested that it might bear an interpretation that had not occurred to me, and so it was not sent. The truth is that there are great obstacles to my writing. In the first place, I am seventy years old and can perceive that my powers of mind are beginning to fail, and I feel that it is my most sacred of all duties to write that book which shall show that many powerful minds have held views apparently the most antipodal upon the subjects of highest concern to all men, merely because they have all alike missed that point of view which would have reconciled them all in one truth, and which will incidentally show any intelligent person how to think in such a way as to reach the truth expeditiously. Since Kant, the majority of logicians nearly sharing his opinion that the principles of reasoning had already been thoroughly investigated—a most superficial and fatal opinion—instead of studying their proper subject have either turned to a barren *Erkenntnisslehre* or to a study of the psychology of thought or to the attempt—like Mill—to found logic on a baseless system of metaphysics, or to the ridiculous trifling of some other of the English logicians; and I feel that I am in possession of truth which must be put into writing before my powers quite fail. This haunts me constantly & I am now, as it were, under orders to give every minute that can be made useful to writing a *preliminary volume* on which I am now engaged which shall give a foretaste of my other & which I hope may in some way enable me to gather together the many books which I have read & whose substance I have in mind, but which of course I cannot discuss on the basis of my unaided memory & so may be enabled to resume the writing of my great book which had to be set aside because I could not refer to the books I had in mind. This preliminary volume I propose to entitle *Essays on Meaning,* where I use Meaning in a general way as it is used by persons who have not thought much about it. If it recalls your "What Is Meaning?" so much the better.

Besides this, my dear wife is in such a terrible state of health, particularly affecting her always very delicate though marvelously strong nerves, that that brings a great tax upon my own. And finally there are extensive repairs that *must* be made to enable us to live through next winter & I naturally have to get plans made, revised, redrawn, considered, re-redrawn, and though my wife attends to all the details & the ideas are wholly hers, still it prevents very largely the continuity of thought requisite for the kind of work which is more particularly mine.

When I get through my work—and often while I am still at it, I fall sound asleep so that I have no odd minutes at all. This has not prevented our talking & thinking a great deal about you at our meals; and I suppose what has set me to writing you this egotistical & complaining utterance is the desire to know about your health & what you are doing in the way of writing and so forth. I hope you will answer this in that way. And believe

me I remain

ever very faithfully yours,

C. S. Peirce

Milford, Pa.

1911, Apr. 17

My dear Lady Welby:

Your post card reached me Good Friday, late in the afternoon. Owing to an appointment with a magistrate, along with two other persons, for Saturday, which occupied the whole day, this is the earliest possible moment at which

I could reply. I am a little surprised that it should take so long a time for the post card to reach me. Although post cards are not here stamped with the date and hour of arrival, yet I have reason to think that no delay took place in the Milford P. O. However, I should not have mentioned this were it not that, if I read a word of your very kind and touching post card as "third," you say that that was your *third* attempt to communicate with me. I have however received nothing from you for a very long time; and therefore the question arises, which Post Office has been in fault. I do not know; but I rather incline to think that if it be either Harrow or Milford, it is the former, since I do not know of any other person named Peirce or Pierce in the vicinity of Milford, where the Post Office people are extra attentive to me, I suppose being under the delusion that I am influential in Washington.

The reasons why I have not written to you are many and physically strong. Indeed they have amounted to absolute necessity. I will mention only a few of them. I am suffering from an early old age, which has been, apparently, the case with all the males of my ancestors; and besides all my later years have been full of worries of almost every description. And this fact has made me desperately anxious to put my logical discoveries into a form in which they may be useful. In the next place, my poor wife and I have been in miserable health for the last few years and particularly since winter before last have been exhausted with more duties than we could severally fulfill and more and more so; and to these difficulties have been added vexations due to other people, continual and cruel. One of our great consolations, dear Lady Welby, has been to remind one another of you.

We have been doing all we could to try to get rid of this estate which has value enough to be a very serious consideration; but now that we no longer entertain and almost all our old friends in this country are dead, the place is nothing but a burden. Just now we are indulging in a definite though not brilliant hope of selling out at a sacrifice, when we shall wish to go abroad or perhaps settle in some French town.

I am just now trying to get a small book written in which I positively prove just what the justification of each of the three types of reasoning really consists in, absolutely refuting the two usual modes of justifying Induction—Mill's & Laplace's, and showing the real nature of Retroduction (which has usually been considered either as not reasoning at all, or as a species of Induction) and from the analysis so proved, I shall show that the essential articles of religious faith have a justification that scientific men have been too apt to pooh-pooh.

I have heard nothing of that volume to which your friends were to contribute. Has it ever appeared? I must not write more today but will do so as soon as I can; & with warmest wishes of good for you from both of us I remain, Dear Lady Welby,

ever truly yours,
C. S. Peirce

Milford, Pa.
1911, May 20

My dear Lady Welby:

I have put off answering your last letter as well as one from Mr. Slaughter, because I could not bear to say it was impossible for me to write for the book, and yet I do not see how I can.

We have been advertising the place for sale; and if it only were sold for half what it might be sold for if we could take our time about it, all difficulty about writing would disappear. But it is so late in the season now that I am in a dreadful state of mind about it. I must sketch my whole situation to you. I don't see any issue to it.

In the first place, my health is like this. I have days when I am in vigorous health of mind and body. But I am extremely emotional, with great self-control; so that anything which affects me has no outlet and simply shakes my whole being, so that I cannot walk across the floor and can hardly hold a pen. The same causes affect my memory so that I cannot think of the words I want to use.

I am not affected by small things; but the difficulties of my situation are not small. In the first place, my poor wife who has not only the highest sense of duty, and far too much energy for her naturally extremely delicate frame, but also a tender solicitude about me and my health, has been sinking in strength and suffering agonizing pain night & day, and I cannot blink the fact that she could not survive another winter in this house. She was constructed to be a princess and she yielded to my wishes & became the wife of a man who ought to have foreseen that it must mean ultimate penury to her.

[May 20, 1911]

. . . That is almost literally our condition now. We cannot afford a servant or to obey the doctor's solemn injunctions about my wife's health. The only thing that I can do is to spend my energy in domestic details. It is what I should be doing at this moment, but that I am utterly broken up by grief so that I should probably fall if I tried to do more than I have done. I, who used to be thoroughly up in the current state of all the principal scientific problems, have not seen a new book or memoir for years. Still, I have in my head a book consisting in, first, a complete proof and somewhat elaborate discussion of just what it is that justifies each kind of sound reasoning.

Second, on that basis I show first how utterly wrong were all the metaphysicians from Descartes to Hume inclusive. I show just how far Kant was right though even when right twisted up in formalism. It is perfectly true that we can never attain a knowledge of things as they are. We can only know their human aspect. But that is all the universe is for us. Reid's position was sounder, except that he seems to think Common Sense is infallible, at least for that human-phenomenal Universe which is all there is for us. This is a great mistake. Common Sense is to be trusted only so far as it sustains critical investigation. Of course I cannot say in short compass exactly what I mean. Moreover not all the judgments of Common Sense are easy to arrive at. I show by what method they must be ascertained; and one important result is that whatever hypothesis we *need* we ought to believe. For example, if a soldier is sure that a certain line of action is the only one that can save him & those he commands, he ought to believe it *will* save him, because that belief will enhance the success or the chances of it. *Useless* doubts are worse than useless. But of course this is a path along which eggs are scattered. It is however mere meaningless pedantry to distinguish such reasoning from accepting a hypothesis because it renders phenomena intelligible. My proof of this must, I am confident, make an impression.

In the third place, I am going on to criticize a number of articles considered essential to religious faith.

There are some propositions favorable to religion which in my opinion are not to be reckoned as matters of *faith* so much as of logical *conviction.*

One of these is that the universe is not governed by immutable law.

The proof of this is surprisingly simple. Namely, I show that if precisely the same consequence always resulted from the same cause, there could be no real progress. Now there is real progress. Every science proves it, and we must believe that the world is governed by a living spirit.

I further show that even if it were true that every physical event were wholly caused by a physical event exclusively, as far as *immediate* action is concerned, nevertheless that would leave room for immaterial beings to act upon matter & the converse.

I show that all the old metaphysicians such as Hume support their skepticism by virtually assuming (when they say, as they perpetually are saying, "But it does not follow," etc.) that the only kind of valid inference is deductive. Now the only justification of Deduction is that its conclusions never assert anything that was not asserted in the Premisses. A perfectly analogous fallacy is involved in supposing the universe governed by immutable law, according to which no element could appear in the effect that was not in the cause. Now I propose to show just what "free will" really consists in and how it acts; and how that renders our con-

duct analogous to the manner in which growth takes place
in plants & animals.

I feel confident the book would make a serious impression much deeper and surer than Bergson's, which I find
quite too vague.[9]

But how is it ever to get written? How am I to find
leisure to write even the article I want so much to contribute to your volume?

For the last three years I have not had sight of a new
book. Evidently I can be of no use except in my family
duties—things which I gladly do under the circumstances
but which it seems ought to get done in some less costly
way.

I can only say that I will write you an article if I possibly can. I desire to please you most earnestly. But I cannot be hopeful about it.

C. S. Peirce

P.S.

Having written this letter in order to make clear how my
not having written (and expressing myself is so little natural to me that my Hibbert Journal article[10] occupied me
exclusively for two months, and after all was not generally
understood; while the writing of it was an expense to me
that weighed upon my conscience,)—as I say I wanted to
explain how my not having written does not argue my not
ardently desiring to say what would, I hope, increase the
general sense of the importance of your message to the
world, and its opportuneness, too. Now when the letter was
written, I feared that, in my eagerness to make what I have
just said evident, the letter might have the air of soliciting
some aid. The word "penury" is probably an exaggeration.
We are able for the present to obtain what is ordinarily
indispensable to sustain life without running into debt. But
there is no doubt that, in my wife's state of health, the hard

[9] *Creative Evolution?* The French edition was published in
1907.—Note by Dr. Lieb.

[10] Peirce's last article for the *Hibbert Journal* was "A Neglected Argument for the Reality of God," reprinted above, pp.
358–379.—Editor's note.

life is killing her *fast*. Therefore it becomes my first desire, as well as my first duty, to work at nothing which does not ameliorate her condition. It is obvious, for example, that it was a wicked thing for me to work two months for fifty dollars, since life could not be sustained at that rate.

I have no doubt my book would make an impression in scientific circles; and every little helps in the development of logical views. You may be sure I feel that strongly. But in my situation it would be my duty to take care of my wife's health, if it put back the clock of progress for longer than it will.

I may however spend a few minutes in explaining a bit more clearly what I *mean* by saying that if the universe were governed by immutable law there could be no progress. In place of the word "progress" I will put a word invented to express what I mean, to wit, *variescence*, I mean such a change as to produce an uncompensated increment in the number of independent elements of a situation. No doubt one might suppose that all the apparent new elements, whenever there is growth or development or evolution of any kind, really were present in all their diversity from the first, though in a form not open to our observation. But what I propose to show is that such gratuitous hypothesis is not logically defensible; but that on the contrary the hypothesis of *variescence* is signally the one that sound logic points out.

Another example of scientific bad logic has been the favor shown to the hypothesis of *telepathy* as explaining a whole lot of easily observed, though infrequent, phenomena. Now telepathy in the sense of a direct action of one embodied spirit on another (which is what it *conveys*, let it be defined as vaguely as it may) is an extremely plausible hypothesis, none is more so, in any field. But the argument against its producing effects capable of being observed more easily than is, e.g., the pressure produced by an incident light-ray is perfectly overwhelming; and it is much more plausible that such effects are due to the action of disembodied spirits. It is true that there are difficulties in supposing that there are any disembodied spirits—and perhaps an *absolutely* unembodied spirit may be impossible. But physics is almost every year—especially the theory of the ether—making finer kinds of matter than that of the 60 odd elements more and more credible. You know Thomson's or Thompson's—I forget the spelling—theory that atoms are vortices in a fluid.[11] Very likely that may be true or some modification of it may be. But if it be true, analogy would suggest that that underlying fluid really consists of separate bodies, and that those atoms of the second class were in their turn vortices of a second class in a second underlying fluid, itself composed of atoms of a third class, and so on, *endlessly*.

Very well, there would be then, not 64 or whatever the number of chemical elements is this afternoon—but an endless series of kinds of plausible matter in which to embody spirits.

Mind, I don't propose to ask anybody to believe seriously in any hypothesis without serious inductive support; but I do say that scientific men—many, I guess most, of them—are in a state of unconscious, or unaware, belief in the *falsity* of such hypotheses, which state of mind is just as illogical as it would be to lean toward believing them. Indeed, it is scientifically much worse, since the latter state of mind, if its substance be false, is bound to get refuted; while the former may go on forever obstructing research into such matters. *Nobody will try new experiments without a leaning to an unsupported hypothesis.* The people who poohpooh such hypotheses make up the class that is most efficient in blocking the wheels of science.

But my dear Lady Welby, I am taking up your time and mine with speculation. Once more good-by for this time. So once more most faithfully (& without misinterpretation I am confident),   C. S. Peirce

1911, May 22

Milford, Pa.
1911, May 25

My dear Lady Welby:
My wife having urged me to it, I think that if you and

[11] J. J. Thomson, "On Bodies Smaller than Atoms." *Popular Science Monthly*, Volume LVIII, August 1901.

the others who are concerned in getting out the famous volume care to wait for what cannot be positively promised, I will do my best to send you in two months—or better say three—the first part of the book I want so much to write. This part deals with the kinds and degrees of assurance that the different kinds of reasoning afford and with the special difficulties that affect that assurance and the means of overcoming them—I mean strictly logical difficulties. For instance, in the theory of numbers, hardly anything can be proved without resort to the principle that whatever is true of a given integer number and which is also true, if of any integer number, then of the next higher one, is true of all integer numbers as high or higher than the given integer number. But *why* should this be true? Some books say it is because, first, of any two different integers one is higher than the other, and second, every integer number has a next higher one. But that is not sufficient, nor would it be made so by adding that every integer is next higher than some other. It is necessary to define the relationship between integers more exactly. If one added that between any two integers there is but a *finite number* of integers, that no doubt is what is wanted; only the word *finite* requires a formal definition. [Of course, you must not talk of a finite number (i.e., an *integer* that is finite) in *defining* an integer.][12] We get that by introducing the abstraction "property" or "predicate." Thus, it suffices to say that if of different integers the lower has a "property" that the higher has not, then there must be an integer as high as *that lower* one, but lower than the higher one, that possesses the property, while the integer next higher than it does not. That illustrates a class of difficulties in mathematics which are overcome by introducing suitable abstractions into definitions. One has in effect defined a "finite series" by means of that word "property" or "predicate." It furnishes a definite *hold* to the mind. That illustrates the kind of considerations that I should notice in my essay on "Assurance through Reasoning."

[12] In manuscript, the bracketed sentence appears in the margin with no insertion mark. Brackets are added.—Note by Dr. Lieb.

I mention it, as enabling you perhaps to decide *pro* or *con* upon whether or not it will be worth waiting for without a positive assurance. This would be the easiest thing for me to write, and therefore presumably the best I could write; and it would be unquestionably very useful. Then I should want to use the essay afterward in my own book which I cannot, however, complete until I can procure a few books, of which the new *Encyclopaedia Britannica* will be first & foremost; for I am so greatly hampered by want of information about the researches since I have been deprived of books, that I feel it won't do for me to appear before the public until I catch up; and that is the reason I take "Assurance through Reasoning" as the only subject on which I can now venture.

. . . I could not venture one step beyond that; and perhaps I am foolhardy to attempt even that. To tell you the plain truth I know I have thought that would be of great use to the world and that nobody is likely for a very long time to reach the same truths; and yet owing to my obscurity and lack of information I had better seek the tomb as quietly as possible.[13]

As for my example about the soldier, don't mistake the point. His confidence may *cause* his success. But that is not what I mean. His confidence is a reason for thinking that he will succeed: it is a sign of that sort of spirit that does succeed. As for me I am long past the military age. I came within an ace of teaching men something to their profit. But certain misfortunes have prevented my keeping up to the times. I will write you the "Assurance from Reasoning" if you desire it, and that will be my last unless by good luck we should sell this estate. It would fetch with patience near forty thousand dollars, and it is ridiculous for us to live in such a place.

Ever very faithfully,
C. S. Peirce

[13] The cancer that afflicted Peirce in his last few years prevented his completing this or any other writing.—Editor's note.

BIBLIOGRAPHICAL NOTE

Chance, Love and Logic: Philosophical Essays by C. S. Peirce, the Founder of Pragmatism, edited with an Introduction by Morris R. Cohen and with a supplementary essay by John Dewey on "The Pragmatism of Peirce" (N.Y.: Harcourt, Brace & Co., 1923; Braziller, 1956).

Collected Papers of Charles Sanders Peirce, edited by C. Hartshorne and P. Weiss. 6 vols. Cambridge, Mass.: Harvard University Press, 1931–35. Two more volumes, with fullest available listing of Peirce's reviews, letters, lectures, etc., are edited by A. W. Burks, and are due to appear in 1958.

Biographical article by Paul Weiss in *Dictionary of American Biography.*

Charles Peirce's Empiricism, by Justus Buchler (N.Y.: Harcourt, Brace & Co., 1939).

An Introduction to Peirce's Philosophy, interpreted as a System, by J. K. Feibleman (N.Y.: Harper & Bros., 1946).

Evolution and the Founders of Pragmatism, by P. P. Wiener (Cambridge, Mass.: Harvard University Press, 1949).

The Thought of C. S. Peirce, by T. A. Goudge (University of Toronto Press, 1950).

Studies in the Philosophy of C. S. Peirce, by 24 contemporary philosophers, edited by P. P. Wiener and F. H. Young (Harvard University Press, 1952).

Peirce and Pragmatism, by W. B. Gallie (Penguin Books, 1952; Dover, 1966).

Charles S. Peirce und der Pragmatismus, by J. von Kempski (Stuttgart and Cologne, 1952).

The Pragmatic Philosophy of C. S. Peirce, by M. Thompson (University of Chicago Press, 1953).

Charles S. Peirce: Essays in the Philosophy of Science, edited with an Introduction by V. Tomas (N.Y.: Liberal Arts Press, 1957).

Aahmes, *Arithmetic*, 233 ff.

Abbot, F. E., x, xv, 192

Abduction, 230, 368–71. See *also* Hypothesis; Retroduction

Abélard, P., 76, 132

Absolute, xx, 60, 68, 155, 179, 202, 349, 351; chance, 48, 142, 172; of space, 156. See *also* Hegel

Abstract, and abstraction, 61, 74, 212–13; 270, 406, 431

Achilles, and tortoise, 34, 38, 405

Acritical inference, 206, 222

Action, xx, 12, 13, 121, 194, 386

Actuality, 217, 292, 358, 393, 406

Aesthetics, xxiii, 270, 337, 401, 415

Agassiz, L., 273, 417

American, culture, ix, x, xvi, 4, 6, 280, 321, 382, 402, 416; education, 330–35; philosophy, xvi, 91, 113

Analogy, and hypothesis, 47, 165

Ancient science, 233–49

Annet, P., 303, 317

Anselm, Saint, 18

Anthropomorphism, 186

Anxiety, 58

Apodictic inference, 43. See *also* Deduction

Apollonius, 246

Apophis, Shepherd King, 233

A *priori*, 11, 15 ff., 85, 92, 106, 132, 172

Aquinas, Saint Thomas, 76–77, 300, 315

Arabs, 79, 111, 258–59, 410

Archimedes, 259

Architecture, scholastic philosophy and Gothic, 77–78; of theories, 142–59, 263

Argelander, F. W. A., 273

Argument, 206, 359, 392 f., 421

Aristotle, 6, 16, 20, 47, 61, 75, 132, 162, 200, 231, 241–42, 245, 292, 340, 368, 399, 408

Aristoxenus, 241–42

Arithmetic, 233 ff., 349, 431

Art, xiv, 5; and religion, 77–78; and science, 136, 154, 263, 282

Aryan language, 410

Association of Ideas, 21, 67 f., 85, 163

Assurance, by reasoning, 431–32

Astrology, 230; Kepler on, 252–53, 256

Astronomy, 14; history of, 132, 157, 230 f., 233 ff., 248–56, 258–59, 273, 290, 335, 350

Atheism, 13, 300

Atoms, 13, 147, 162, 301, 430

Attention, 61–62

Augustine, Saint, 206, 283, 286, 294, 319

Authority, 16, 19, 20, 77; method of, 92 ff., 103 f., 115

Babinet, J., 371

Babylonian science, 229, 233, 248

Bacon, F., 4, 6, 12, 73, 93, 227–28, 315, 369

Bacon, R., 93

Bancroft, G., 416

Bayle, P., 80

Baldwin, J. M., 358, 376

Basque, 410

Being, 60–61, 158, 292, 358. *See also* Ontology

Belief, fixation of, 91–112, 118–19, 189, 207, 306 ff., 378 f., 397–99

Berengarius, of Tours, heretic, 19

Bergson, H., xiii, 230, 428

Berkeley, G., xvi, 21, 35, 63,

68, 73–88, 144, 270, 297, 375, 417
Bernouilli, D., 266, 276
Bernouilli, J., 270, 305
Bernouilli, N., 305
Bible, 77, 111, 233, 293, 304, 318, 397, 400 f., 410
Biology, 272 f., 390. *See also* Evolution
Bode's law, 290 f.
Boethius, A. M. S., 20, 244
Boltzmann, L., 278
Boole, G., xii, xiv, 263, 270, 340
Bordeaux, wines of, 418
Boscovich, R. G., 47
Boyle, R., 146 f., 283
Bradley, F. H., xiii, 106
Brahe, T., 93, 251, 253 ff.
Braithwaite, R. B., xvii
British, culture and philosophy, 7, 75, 76, 144, 282 ff., 291 ff., 332, 402, 417
Brooke, Lord (Greville, F.), 297, 315
Brown, Thomas, of Scottish School, 86
Buchler, J., 433
Büchnerism, 262
Buddhism, 107, 355, 402
Buffon, G. L., 267
Burks, A. W., vii, xvi, 433
Business, and culture, xiv, 12, 77, 237, 241
Butler, Bishop, 283, 286, 319

Cambridge, Mass., xxiii, 4, 375, 410
Carnegie Institution, 287–88
Carnot, S., 231, 266
Carus, P., 142, 199
Categories, 24, 61, 143, 150 ff., 201 f., 216 f., 380, 383 ff. *See also* Firstness; Secondness; Thirdness
Catholics, 39, 76 f., 111, 123 f., 132, 397–99
Causality, xii f., 7, 67, 163, 174 ff., 279
Cayley, A., xv

Cenopythagorean categories, 383
Century Dictionary, xvi, 172, 250, 376, 382
Certainty, 40, 155, 157, 160 ff., 370, 398 f., 402 f.
Chance, lx, xii, xiii, 107, 143, 148, 150, 159–62, 172–79, 201, 257, 262, 279, 372. *See also* Firstness; Diversity; Probability
Chemistry, xxiii, 3, 181, 265, 272 f., 430
Choate, Rufus, 417
Christianity, 5, 8, 9, 10, 12, 107, 209, 246, 259, 304, 315 f., 350, 353 ff., 397–402
Church, xxii, 5, 9, 77, 82, 209, 284, 291, 303 f., 351 ff., 401
Cicero, on law of nature, 282
Cipher. *See* Cryptography
Civilization, xvii, xix; history of, 3–14; religion and science in, 87, 136, 258, 260, 346, 402
Clark University, 331 ff.
Clarke, F. W., 409–10
Classicism, 264
Classification, of sciences, 287, 403
Clausius, R., 95, 266
Clear ideas, 95, 113–36, 205
Cogito, ergo sum, 207, 298
Cognition, 18 ff., 36 ff., 52 ff.
Cohen, M. R., first editor of Peirce, xvii, 433
Colding, A., 266
Columbus, C., 222
Common sense, 11, 86, 101; critical, 101, 204, 214, 426; good, 208. *See also* Scottish School
Community, of inquirers, 17, 69, 83, 88, 241
Comprehension, of terms, 55
Comte, A., x, 82, 137, 139, 271, 345, 349, 361
Conception, 54, 109, 183, 204, 295

Concord School, 15, 345
Conditionals, 216
Confucius, 355
Consciousness, 32, 52, 70–71, 119 f., 205, 379
Conservation of energy, 148, 232, 262, 266
Consistency, 71–72
Constantinople, 410
Constants, in physics, 326
Continuity, xx, 16, 52, 69, 73, 75, 116, 155, 157, 169, 231, 261 f., 276, 301, 405
Cope, J. I., 334
Copernicus, N., 93, 246 f., 251, 259, 351
Correlation of forces, 86
Cosmogony, 158 f., 201 f., 233, 271
Creation, 233, 240, 297
Critique of Pure Reason, Kant's, 7, 25–26, 417
Crookes, W., 147, 268
Crusades, 6, 8, 9, 77
Cryptography, hypotheses in, 44–47, 271
Cudworth, R., 7, 301, 417

Dakota language, 410
Dante, 5
Dark Ages, 8, 236, 249, 258
Darwin, C., x, 86, 94–96, 149, 256–57, 262–63, 268, 276, 363, 372
Davy, H., 268
Deduction, 17, 43 ff., 342, 368–70, 427
Delome, 408
Democracy, 241
Democritus, 6, 162 f.
De Moivre, A., 305–6
Demonstration, 239, 369. See also Proof
De Montford, R., 305
De Morgan, A., xiv, 263, 271
Descartes, R., 6, 17, 39 ff., 47, 68, 75, 113 ff., 132, 283, 298, 426
Determinate, 69, 210, 221

Determinism, 160–79. See Necessity
Dewey, J., xv, xvii, 180, 230
Diagrammatic reasoning, 255
Dirichlet, G. L., 267
Distinct idea, 115, 118
Diversity, 173–77
Doubt, 6, 17, 39 f., 98 f., 118, 189, 207, 427
Dreams, 21, 64; and science, 233
Dualism, 158
Duhem, P., x
Dumas, A., 286
Duration, 24. See Time
Dynamic interpretant, 413–14
Dynamoid object, 406

Economics of research, 232
Education, xvii f., xxiv, 65, 71; science and, 325–42, 381 f.
Effort, 384
Egotism, age of, 13
Egyptian science, and culture, 10, 233 ff., 258, 271, 355
Eighteenth century, 4, 7, 267, 270 ff., 273, 318 f., 427
Electricity, 4, 12, 71, 89, 90, 113, 133, 159, 272, 327
Electrons, 208
Emerson, R. W., 15, 345, 416–17
Emotions, 58–60; as signs, 67
Entropy, 171. See also Thermodynamics
Epicurean, 156, 162, 163
Epinomis, 242
Epistemology, xiii, 15–88, 426
Epping, Father, 237
Erigena, Scotus, 131
Eros, love-god, 240
Ethics, xviii f.; and logic, 190, 199; of suicide, 209; religious, 350, 354; and symbols, 380; of terminology, 394; of intellect, 415
Euclid, 142, 146, 156, 239, 368
European, culture, 76, 258, 321
Evidence, legal, 20; Hume on,

306 f., 309 f.; of immortality, 348
Evolution, of life and thought, x, 95–96, 149–50, 207, 232, 262–63, 268; of laws, 148, 259, 261; progress and, 262; of the history of philosophy, 232, 248, 257, 299, 318; of universe, 156 ff., 201, 277; through self-control, 199
Evolutionary Love, 160, 259, 265
Existential graphs, 213, 389, 408, 411
Experience, 93, 341, 358, 385–86, 408
Experiment, 15, 64, 181, 183, 193–94, 255, 272, 302, 305–6, 326
Explanation, logic of, 279, 296, 298, 367
Expression, thought as, 381

Facts, 405
Faith, 399, 427, 432
Fallacies, 49–50
Fallibilism, xxi, 101, 351, 398, 426
Faraday, W., 266, 272
Fate, xiii, 133
Fay, Melusina (Peirce's first wife), xv
Fechner's law, 308
Feeling, 19, 59–60, 150–51, 159, 176, 223, 389
Feibleman, J. K., 433
Fichte, J. G., 68
Finite numbers, 431
Firstness, 143, 150–51, 158–59, 380–83
Fisch, M. H., 334
Fiske, J., x
Fizeau, A., 132
Force, 126–29, 146, 152, 159, 248
Formalities, Scotus on, 79
Foucault, J., 132
Franklin, B., 71, 267
Fraser, A. C., 34, 74

Freedom, 6, 9, 75, 110, 138, 163
Free will, 8, 162–63, 415, 427–28
Frege, G. W., xii, 340
Frequency theory, xii. See also Probability
French philosophy, 417
Fuller, Margaret, 417

Galilei, G., 6, 93, 145 f., 231, 258, 372 f.
Gallenga (Mariotte), 416
Gallie, W. B., 433
Galois, E., 231
Gassendi, P., 300
Gauss, K. F., 267
General ideas, 66, 69, 73 ff., 152, 197, 210, 276, 295, 301, 379, 420
Generalization, 228–29, 270; inductive, 289–90
Geochemistry, Clarke's, 409–10
Geography, and ancient culture, 258
Geology, 149–50, 273, 409–10
Geometry, and metaphysics, 157; ancient, 238 ff., 259. See also Euclid, non-Euclidean
German, 12, 15, 75, 313 f., 318, 403, 417
Gibbs, J. W., ix, x, xiii
Gilbert de la Porrée, 76
Gilbert, W., 93
Gilman, D. C., vii, xv; Letter of Peirce to, 325–30
God, xvi–xxi, 4, 5, 6, 8, 10, 12, 13, 18, 19, 75, 78, 87, 138, 240, 283, 298, 316, 351, 353, 355, 358–79, 400 f.
Gothic. See Architecture
Grand Logic, of Peirce, 91, 231, 287
Goudge, T., 433
Gravesande, W. J. van's, 47
Gray's Elegy, quoted, 134
Great men, chance and, 262; in science, 265–74, 281

Greek, ix, x, 3, 6, 8, 12, 229–30, 236 ff., 249, 258, 282, 399; etymology of "pragmatism," 183
Green, N. St. John, x, 91–92
Guiding principle, 49, 96–97
Gurney, E., 346

Habit, 62, 95–96, 121; law of, 152, 205–6, 257, 389, 405
Hall, G. S., xv
Hallam, H., 80
Hamilton, W., 18, 171, 210, 417
Hampden, J., 8
Hardy, T., xiii
Harris, W. T., 15
Hartley, D., 86, 144
Hartshorne, C., xvi, 277, 433
Harvard University, vii, x, xv, xvi, xxi; Class Book Entry of Peirce, xxiii–iv; philosophy at, 180, 228, 261, 417
Harvey, W., 93
Hawaiian language, 410
Hegel, G. W. F., xx, 3, 8, 15, 16, 68, 79, 109, 157, 178, 202, 263–64, 271
Helmholtz, H., 85, 266, 272
Henry, Joseph, 266
Herapath, J., 266, 276
Herschel, W., 273
Hertz, H., 271
Hibbert Journal, 358, 428
Hindoos, culture of, 107
History, and values, xix, 3–14; of ideas, 150, 174, 261 ff., 285, 293 f.; of philosophy, 75, 143, 294, 426; of society, 31; sacred and profane, 304; of science, xvii, 136, 225–323
Hobbes, T., 7, 73, 116, 144, 297, 317, 389, 417
Holmes, O. W., Jr., x
Holmes, O. W., Sr., 416
Humanism, xi, xvii, 3–14, 210, 418; F. S. C. Schiller's, 379
Humboldt, F., 13
Hume, D., 7, 63, 68, 73, 86,

270, 426–27; on Miracles and Laws of Nature, 275–322
Husserl, E., xiii
Hutcheson, F., 299
Huygens, Christian, 146
Hypothesis, logic of, 17, 44 f., 47, 69, 165, 230, 256, 277, 283, 289 f., 302, 341, 370, 394, 427, 430

Icons, 368, 391, 407
Idealism, and materialism, 3–88, 153; romantic, 15, 68; Berkeley's, 73–88; objective, 143, 153; absolute, 202; *See also* Hegel; Royce; St. Louis School; Transcendentalists
Ideas, 63, 74–75; How to Make Our Ideas Clear, 95, 113–36, 215; history of, 150, 261–64, 272, 295 f., 299 f.
Ideoscopy, 383–84
Idistical age, 13
Images, 24, 63–64, 205, 395
Imagination, in science, 13, 230, 235, 255, 286
Immediate interpretant, 413–14
Immortality, 8, 75, 138, 345–50
Incognizable. *See* Unknowable
Inconceivable, chance not, 172
Independence, of propositions, 100
Indeterminacy, in cognition, 69; of laws of nature, 148, 210, 221, 427
Indices, 391 f., 408. *See also* Signs
Individualism, xx, 29, 39, 62; and truth, 82, 87–88, 191, 257; in ethics, 333
Induction, 17, 25 f., 44 ff., 62, 69, 74, 160, 165, 271, 290 f., 310 f., 369 ff., 430
Inference, 42 ff.; probable, 165; acritical, 206; three

types of, 230, 425. *See also* Perception; Reasoning

Infinite, 34, 38, 69, 156, 159, 349, 393, 430

Information, 71

Inner light, of reason, 93, 259, 372

Inquiry, science as, 99, 227 ff., 368

Insolubilia, 397

Instinct, 208, 248, 371, 408

Institutions, history of, 150

Instruments, 94, 328

Interpretant, 71, 391 f., 404, 407 f., 412; three kinds of, 403, 413–14

Introspection, 16, 32, 41, 63 f.

Intuition, 15, 18 ff., 25 f., 30–33, 36 f., 41, 52, 64

Jackson, General A., 398–99

Jacobi, C. G. J., 270

Jagalu language, 410

James, Henry, Sr., xxi

James, William, x–xiii, xv, xvi, 91, 180, 186, 267, 345, 375–76

Jamestown, 4

Jannsen, P. J. C., 286

Jastrow, J., 206

Jesus, 8, 12, 304, 316, 318, 355, 401

Jevons, W. S., xiv, 271

Jewish belief in living God, 10, 402

John, Saint, 355

John of Salisbury, 76, 403

Johns Hopkins University, xiv f., 334, 387

Joule, J. P., 266

Journal of Speculative Philosophy, xvi, 15 ff., 39 ff., 203

Justice, xvi, xviii, 321

Kant, I., xxiii, 7, 8, 16, 18, 24–25, 27, 61, 144–45, 183, 208, 213–14, 270, 273, 339 f., 349, 370, 375, 384–85, 420, 422, 426

Kelvin, Lord (Thomson, W.), xv, 266, 273

Kempski, J. von, xvii, 433

Kep(p)ler, J., 93, 106, 230 f., 250–56, 259

King, C., geologist, 149–50

Kirchoff, G., on force, 129

Krönig, A., on heat, 266

Laboratory, minds, xiv, 12, 94, 182, 272, 326 f., 417

Lamarckian evolution, 149–50, 259

Langley, S. P., 273, 275 ff.

Language, is the self, 71; and thought, 235, 266 f., 380 ff., 392, 410; and life, 416, 420

Laplace, P. S., 160, 267–70, 273, 306, 425

Latin grammar, 410

Lavoisier, A. L., 94

Law, evolution of, 143, 146, 148, 160, 175; of nature, 275–322; statistical form of, xiii, 147, 153; civil, 20, 76–77, 238, 395

Leading Principle, 49–50, 97

Legendre, A. M., 349

Legisign, 391

Leibniz, G. W., 7, 47, 113, 116, 340, 378, 389

Leopardi, G., 377

Le Sage, G. L., 47

Letters of Peirce, to Gilman, 325–30; to Langley, 275–322; to Lady Welby, 380–432; to editor of *Science*, 228

Lewis, C. I., xvii

Liberal education, 336–43

Lieb, I. C., xxi, 381

Liebig, J. von, 86

Life, love of, 139; spontaneity, 148; and death, 174; as Expression, 416

Light of nature, 145–46, 259

Linnaeus, C., 185, 273

Lissajous, J. A., 132

Locke, J., 7, 63, 73, 297

Lockyer, N., 274

Logic, ix–xiii, 7, 38 ff., 42 f., 79; of science, 91–136, 158, 171, 200, 213, 249, 262, 270, 281–82, 328–30; of mathematics, 338–41; and liberal education, 336–37; of proof, 393; Whateley's, 401, 408; as ethics of the intellect, 415; definition of, 421

Longfellow, H. W., 416

Love, ix, 12; evolutionary, 160, 259, 265; of life, 138–39; god, 229; reason and, 332; religion of, 355, 398

Lowell, J., 416

Lowell Lectures, history of science, 233, 250, 257

Lucretius, on law of nature, 282

Lully, R., *Ars Magna,* 116

Lyell, C., 273

Mach, E., x, 232. *See also* Positivism

Maestlin, M., 252

Magic, 233, 270

Magyar language, 410

Magnetism, 265, 328

Malebranche, N., 7

Malthus, T. R., 95

Man, faculties claimed for, 15–38, 204; civilized, 87–88; nature of, 13, 71 f., 210; Man's Glassy Essence, 72, 160; as thought-sign, 81

Mangnall, R., *Historical Questions,* 191, 311

Marconi, G., 271

Mars, Kepler on, 250–56

Material quality, 56, 71

Materialism, 10 ff., 13, 86–87, 153, 427

Mathematics, xxiii, 87, 146, 153 ff., 229, 231; ancient, 233–46; and physics, 328; aped by metaphysics, 157; 19th-cent. music and, 263, 269–70; logic of, 330, 338–39, 394

Maxwell, J. C., xiii, 95, 265, 271, 279

Mayer, R., 266

Mead, G. H., xvii

Meaning, xii, 34 ff., 54, 68, 113 ff., 124 f.; pragmatic theory of, 183–87, 194 ff., 204, 375, 380 ff.

Measurement, 155, 169, 326

Mechanical philosophy, of science, xiii, 86, 142, 146, 160, 174, 232, 247, 266; its breakdown, 348–50

Mediaeval thought, 8, 16, 18–20, 39, 73 ff., 79, 82, 93, 265. *See also* Scholasticism

Mellonized idea, 386

Mendeleef, D. I., 232, 265–66, 272

Metaphysical Club, x, 375

Metaphysics, x, 6, 40–41, 60, 74 ff., 98, 105, 122, 135, 140, 193, 232, 271, 300 ff., 426

Metempsychosis, transmigration of souls, 241, 245

Method, scholastic, 40 *(see also* Authority); pragmatic, 91 ff., 113 ff., 182–83, 192; geometrical, 85; of fixing belief, 91–112; of clarifying ideas, 113–36; of reasoning, 294; age of, 336; science as, 350; morals as, 416

Meyer, L., periodic table, 266

Michelangelo, 258

Mill, James, 86, 144, 297

Mill, J. S., 48, 86–87, 171, 239, 263, 271, 297, 420, 422, 425

Miller, Perry, 345

Mind, 74, 84, 150; matter as effete, 153, 176; national, 235; signs and, 359; triadic nature of, 388

Miracles, Hume on, 275–322

Mnesarchus, 240

Modality, 216–23

Monism, neutral, 153

Monist, The, articles of Peirce,

142, 160, 180, 201, 203, 214, 259, 265

Morris, G. S., x

Morals, as method, xviii, 416

Musement, pure play of mind, 360 ff.

Music, xx, 14, 120, 263

N. A. (Neglected Argument), v

Nagel, E., xvii

National mind, English, 76; German, 85; Egyptian, 235; Arabian, 259

Natural selection, 95, 263, 276

Nature, xix, 13, 93, 95, 104; law of, 147, 275–322; light of, 255

Neanthes, 242

Necessitant sign, 405–6

Necessity, 160–79, 215, 221; mechanical, 247; Hume on, 309

Neglected Argument, for God, 358–79, 428

Neugebauer, O., 229

Neutralism, 153

Newcomb, S., 273, 276

Newton, I., 6, 7, 146, 231, 246

Nineteenth century, xiii, 4–14, 158, 232, 247; chief ideas of, 261–64; great men in science of, 265–74

Nomenclature, 184 ff., 394

Nominalism, xii, 64 f., 76, 79, 80, 83, 86–88, 116, 231, 295, 297, 418. See also Ockham

Non-conservative forces, 153

Non-Euclidean space, 156, 231

Nonsense experiments, Darwin on, 256

North American Review, xvi, 73–88, 215

Norton, C., 416

Noumena, 83

Numbers, theory of. See Arithmetic

Objective idealism, xvi, 143, 153

Objectivity, xvi, 64, 84, 108, 197; of possibility, 218, 261; of law, 276, 302; vs. subjectivity, 394–95, 419

Objects, relation to symbols, 421; dynamic, 391

Ockham (Occam), W., 70, 73, 295 ff., 318 f., 389

Ockham's razor, 153, 189, 231

Ontology, 135, 203. See also Being

Operationalism, 113 f., 193 f.

Palmer, E., 410

Papini, G., 376

Pasteur, L., 273

Paul, Saint, on intuition, 18

Peano, G., 340

Pearson, K., x, 137, 275, 332, 395

Peirce, B. (father of C. S.), xiv, 416

Peirce, C. S., life of, vii ff., xi, xv ff., xxiii–iv, 180–83, 265, 268, 275–322, 329, 375, 380 ff., 411, 416–17

Perception, inference in, 20, 65 f.

Peregrinus, P., Letter on the Magnet, 265

Pessimism, xiii

Pheme, 408

Phenomena, 194, 302, 326

Phenomenalism, 83, 84, 87

Phenomenology, 383

Pherecydes, 240

Philosophy, ix, x, 3, 5, 7, 14, 86, 105, 113 ff., 153, 192, 262, 274, 292

Phoenicians, 258

Photometric Researches, by Peirce, xiv

Physics, 13, 126 ff., 132, 138, 146 ff., 181, 246–47, 282, 289; research and teaching in, 325–30

Physiology, 152 f.

Pindar, 92

Plastic nature, 297

Plato, 74–76, 106; and Pythagoreans, 242, 244; idea in, 264, 358; faith in, 399, 407

Play, of musement, 360 ff.; Schiller on, xxiii, 401

Podmore, and psychical research, 346

Poe, E. A., 362

Poetry, and science, 13, 134, 255, 263, 297

Poincaré, H., 275, 279

Poisson, S. D., 306

Political, xx, 8, 101 f., 241, 291, 332, 402, 416

Popular Science Monthly, 91 ff., 113 ff., 204, 230, 276, 281, 332, 375

Positivism, x, 82, 137–41, 192. *See also* Comte; Poincaré

Possibility, 215–23, 240, 404, 406

Postulate, 164, 166, 186

Practical, xx, 88, 96, 124 f., 164, 183, 204 f., 268, 271, 291, 320, 328, 373 ff., 381

Practicism, 183, 381

Pragmaticism, xi, 186–87, 197, 206 f., 375–79, 402

Pragmatism, xi, xix, xx, 91 ff., 124 ff., 183 ff., 230, 375 f., 381

Prayer, efficacy of, 247, 268, 354

Precision, 170, 212

Predesignation, 231, 289 f. *See* Hypothesis; Induction

Prediction, 159, 290 f., 296 f., 302

Prescission, 212 f.

Priestley, J., 86

Principles of Philosophy, Peirce's, 231, 265

Probability, xii–xiv, 43–44, 58, 139, 155, 171, 283, 305 ff.

Proclus, 238

Progress, x, xx, 6–8, 13, 257– 62, 276, 297, 354, 403, 427, 429

Projective geometry, 154, 231

Proof, 239, 293, 349, 368 f., 393, 405

Proposition, 48, 193, 211, 238, 392, 395–96

Protestants, 82, 124. *See also* Reformation

Psellus, *Synopsis*, 47

Psychical Research Society, 345 f.

Psychology, xi, 16, 21 ff., 50, 152, 207, 230, 288, 308

Psychophysics, 23, 288, 308

Ptolemaic system, 233, 251, 350

Pyramids, of Egypt, 234 f., 249

Pythagoras, 239 ff., 246

Qualisign, 391

Quality, 36, 56, 58, 71, 198, 383–84, 393

Quantum mechanics, 142, 147

Ramsey, F. P., xvii

Rankine, M. W. J., 266

Rationalism, 92. *See also* Reason

Rayleigh, J. W. S., 272

Reaction, 143, 151, 158, 385. *See also* Secondness

Real, 69, 70, 74, 77, 80, 107, 114, 197, 219, 358, 379, 419– 20

Realism, 69, 70, 73–88, 197, 215, 418, 420

Reason, 9, 13, 19, 75; and evolution, 199, 261, 274, 282– 83, 300, 332

Reasoning, 13, 16, 93, 206, 249, 255, 370, 425 f.

Reformation, 5, 9, 292

Reichenbach, H., xvii

Reid, T., 18, 208, 426

Relations, 37, 56, 122; as Thirdness, 158; logic of, 214, 261, 387, 396

Relativity, of qualities, 198

Religion, art and, 77–78; philosophy and, 3 f., 10 f., 82, 124, 209, 397; science and, xvi, 137, 241, 247, 345–79; theology and, 7, 77, 104, 397
Renaissance, x, 6 f., 79, 258
Representation, 56, 68. See also Signs
Retroduction, 230, 368, 370–71. See also Hypothesis
Reversible phenomena, 386
Revue Philosophique, 113, 134, 375
Rheme, 392
Rhetoric, 403
Roget's Thesaurus, 410
Romans, 12, 93, 104, 282
Romanticism, literary, 264, 345
Roscellinus, 70
Rowland, H., xv, 325–26
Royce, J., xv, xvi, xxi
Rudolph II, 253–54
Rumford, Count (Thompson, B.), 267
Russell, B., 340, 380, 388–89

St. Louis School, of Hegelians, 15
Salmon, G., 269
Sampling, inductive, 165
Schaff, P., Creeds of Christendom, 400
Schiller, F. S. C., xxi, 186, 230, 379
Schiller, Friedrich, xxi, xxiii, 401
Scholastics, x, 18, 39, 69 ff., 73 ff., 76 f., 93, 231, 292, 300 f., 418 f.; realism, 420. See also Nominalism; Ockham; Scotus
Schopenhauer, A., xiii, 263, 377
Schröder, E., xii, xvii, 214, 340, 387
Science, civilization and, xvii, 3–14; education and, 323–43; philosophy and, xvii, 13, 15, 19, 268; religion and, 345 ff.; definition of, 248 f.;

history of, 36, 227–322; journal, 333
Scottish School, common-sense realists, 86, 208
Scotus, D., 18, 70, 73, 76, 79, 292, 300 f., 418, 420
Search for a Method, Peirce's, xix, xx, 91
Secondness, 143, 150 f., 380, 383 ff., 386
Self-consciousness, 25 ff., 41, 115
Self-evidence, 26, 296. See Intuition
Self-control, logical and ethical, 190, 199, 205, 207, 415
Seme, 408
Semeiotic, 402, 421. See also Signs
Seminary minds, xiv
Sensations, 13, 21 f., 60 f., 151, 261
Sense, 412
Sensationalism, 87
Seventeenth century, x, 3, 4, 7, 93, 246 ff.
Shakespeare, W., 267, 377
Sheffer, H. M., xvii
Significance, 412–13
Significs, xviii, 380 f., 402, 409
Signs, xii, xviii, 15–18, 34 ff., 51 f., 59, 71, 295, 359, 375, 382 f.
Simplicity, 60, 76; of laws of atoms, 147
Simulacra, or icons, 407
Sinsign, 62–63, 391
Skepticism, 7, 8, 13, 139; Hume's, 276, 318, 427
Smith, Adam, on moral sentiments, 86
Smith, W. B., 401
Smithsonian Institution, xvi, 265, 275, 280
Social basis, of ethics, xx, 12, 351. See also Community; Logic
Socrates, 131, 246
Solipsism, 353

Sommelier, Peirce trained as a, 418

Space, 22, 37, 156–57, 176, 223, 248, 420

Speculation, 18. *See also* Musement

Spencer, H., x, 16, 148, 263, 345, 348

Spinoza, B., 7

Spirits, 347, 427, 429

Spiritualism, 232, 347, 427, 429

Spontaneity, and chance, 148, 175, 177

Statistical form of laws, xiii, 147, 153

Steam engine, 4, 12, 231

Stewart, D., 47

Stoics, 163, 246, 355

Stone Age, 248

Story, Judge, 417

Story, W., sculptor, 417

Strauss, D. F., *Life of Jesus*, 8

Subjective, xii, xiii, 30 f., 64, 73, 122, 197, 216, 394, 419–20

Suicide, ethics of, 209

Summum bonum, 199, 274

Sumner, Charles, 417

Syllogism, 42 f., 93, 249, 340

Sylvester, G., xv, 327

Symbols, xii, xx, 207, 368, 391–96, 403–16, 421. *See also* Signs

Symptom, 391

Synechism, ix, 187, 205. *See also* Continuity

Technology, 12, 87–88, 231, 248, 287

Telepathy, 232, 346–47, 429

Tenacity, method of, 92 f., 102 f., 398

Tennyson, A. L., 233

Terminology, 184–85, 409–10, 419–21

Terms, 62–63, 392, 419 f.

Testimony, 312 ff. *See also* Evidence

Thales, 237–39

Theism, 139, 192. *See also* Abbot

Theology, x, 7, 92–93, 104, 291 ff., 354 ff., 376 f., 397–402

Theories, architecture of, 142–59

Thermodynamics, xiii, 171, 266, 276

Thing-in-itself, 16, 82–83. *See also* Unknowable

Thirdness, 143, 158, 380–89

Thompson, M., 433

Thought, 16, 34 ff., 54 ff., 158, 190; a melody, 261; expression as, 381; evolution of, 259; objective reality of, 420

Tillotson, J., 303

Timaeus, of Taormina, 242, 244

Time, 24, 37, 54, 69, 121, 141, 159, 164, 174, 220, 222–23, 292, 385 f.

Token, and type, 391, 406

Tourtalai, J. (Mrs. C. S. Peirce), xv, 281, 284, 288, 411, 426, 428–29, 432

Transcendentalists, 15, 345

Transmigration of souls, 245

Truth, xvi, xviii, 74, 81–83, 93, 100, 108, 111, 114, 134, 189, 199, 233, 274, 369, 378; of religion, 393; as public, 398; formal, 403; objective, 419–20

Tuisical age, 13

Twain, M., xiii

Twentieth century, xiii, 319

Tychism, ix, 277. *See also* Chance

Tyndall, J., 247, 268

Uniformity, of nature, 173–79, 296 f.

Unitarianism, xv

Universals. *See* General ideas

Universes, 358–64, 404

University, defined, 331; aims of, 331–37

Unknowable, 16, 34 f., 41, 68 ff.
U. S. Coast and Geodetic Survey, vii, 232, 325

Vagueness, 209 f., 213 f.
Valentine, Basil, 265
Values, xvii, xix, 87–88, 136, 137–40. *See also* Aesthetic; Ethical; God; Love; Practical; *Summum Bonum*
Variescence, or progress, 429
Veblen, T., ix, xv, xviii
Venn, J., 340
Verifiability. *See* Operationalism
Verification, 170, 193
Vision, inference in, 21, 65, 84 f., 248
Voisin, sommelier of, 418
Voltaire, F. M., 378

Wallace, A. R., 266, 276
Way of Life, 354–55
Ward, L. F., 277
Waterston, 266
Webster, D., 416
Weismann, A., 149, 273

Weiss, P., xvi, 277, 433
Welby, Lady Viola, vii, xviii, 18; Letters of Peirce to, 380–432
Werner, A. G., 273
Whately, R., *Logic,* 401, 408
Whewell, W., 87, 271
Whitehead, A. N., x, 388–89
Whitman, W., xviii
Wilkins, J., *Real Character,* 410
Will to believe, 375–76, 379, 432
William of Champeaux, 76
Wolff, C., 7
Wollaston, W. H., 299
Women, 76, 107, 382
Woolston, T., 283, 303, 317
Words, 403, 421–22
Wright, Chauncey, x

Xenophanes, 245

Young, Thomas, 231, 271

Zeller, E., 239–46
Zulu language, studied by Peirce, 410

CATALOGUE OF DOVER BOOKS

Philosophy, Religion

GUIDE TO PHILOSOPHY, C. E. M. Joad. A modern classic which examines many crucial problems which man has pondered through the ages: Does free will exist? Is there plan in the universe? How do we know and validate our knowledge? Such opposed solutions as subjective idealism and realism, chance and teleology, vitalism and logical positivism, are evaluated and the contributions of the great philosophers from the Greeks to moderns like Russell, Whitehead, and others, are considered in the context of each problem. "The finest introduction," BOSTON TRANSCRIPT. Index. Classified bibliography. 592pp. 5⅜ x 8.
T297 Paperbound $2.00

HISTORY OF ANCIENT PHILOSOPHY, W. Windelband. One of the clearest, most accurate comprehensive surveys of Greek and Roman philosophy. Discusses ancient philosophy in general, intellectual life in Greece in the 7th and 6th centuries B.C., Thales, Anaximander, Anaximenes, Heraclitus, the Eleatics, Empedocles, Anaxagoras, Leucippus, the Pythagoreans, the Sophists, Socrates, Democritus (20 pages), Plato (50 pages), Aristotle (70 pages), the Peripatetics, Stoics, Epicureans, Sceptics, Neo-platonists, Christian Apologists, etc. 2nd German edition translated by H. E. Cushman. xv + 393pp. 5⅜ x 8.
T357 Paperbound $1.85

ILLUSTRATIONS OF THE HISTORY OF MEDIEVAL THOUGHT AND LEARNING, R. L. Poole. Basic analysis of the thought and lives of the leading philosophers and ecclesiastics from the 8th to the 14th century—Abailard, Ockham, Wycliffe, Marsiglio of Padua, and many other great thinkers who carried the torch of Western culture and learning through the "Dark Ages": political, religious, and metaphysical views. Long a standard work for scholars and one of the best introductions to medieval thought for beginners. Index. 10 Appendices. xiii + 327pp. 5⅜ x 8.
T674 Paperbound $2.00

PHILOSOPHY AND CIVILIZATION IN THE MIDDLE AGES, M. de Wulf. This semi-popular survey covers aspects of medieval intellectual life such as religion, philosophy, science, the arts, etc. It also covers feudalism vs. Catholicism, rise of the universities, mendicant orders, monastic centers, and similar topics. Unabridged. Bibliography. Index. viii + 320pp. 5⅜ x 8.
T284 Paperbound $1.85

AN INTRODUCTION TO SCHOLASTIC PHILOSOPHY, Prof. M. de Wulf. Formerly entitled SCHOLASTICISM OLD AND NEW, this volume examines the central scholastic tradition from St. Anselm, Albertus Magnus, Thomas Aquinas, up to Suarez in the 17th century. The relation of scholasticism to ancient and medieval philosophy and science in general is clear and easily followed. The second part of the book considers the modern revival of scholasticism, the Louvain position, relations with Kantianism and Positivism. Unabridged. xvi + 271pp. 5⅜ x 8.
T296 Clothbound $3.50
T283 Paperbound $1.75

A HISTORY OF MODERN PHILOSOPHY, H. Höffding. An exceptionally clear and detailed coverage of western philosophy from the Renaissance to the end of the 19th century. Major and minor men such as Pomponazzi, Bodin, Boehme, Telesius, Bruno, Copernicus, da Vinci, Kepler, Galileo, Bacon, Descartes, Hobbes, Spinoza, Leibniz, Wolff, Locke, Newton, Berkeley, Hume, Erasmus, Montesquieu, Voltaire, Diderot, Rousseau, Lessing, Kant, Herder, Fichte, Schelling, Hegel, Schopenhauer, Comte, Mill, Darwin, Spencer, Hartmann, Lange, and many others, are discussed in terms of theory of knowledge, logic, cosmology, and psychology. Index. 2 volumes, total of 1159pp. 5⅜ x 8.
T117 Vol. 1, Paperbound $2.25
T118 Vol. 2, Paperbound $2.25

ARISTOTLE, A. E. Taylor. A brilliant, searching non-technical account of Aristotle and his thought written by a foremost Platonist. It covers the life and works of Aristotle; classification of the sciences; logic; first philosophy; matter and form; causes; motion and eternity; God; physics; metaphysics; and similar topics. Bibliography. New Index compiled for this edition. 128pp. 5⅜ x 8.
T280 Paperbound $1.00

THE SYSTEM OF THOMAS AQUINAS, M. de Wulf. Leading Neo-Thomist, one of founders of University of Louvain, gives concise exposition to central doctrines of Aquinas, as a means toward determining his value to modern philosophy, religion. Formerly "Medieval Philosophy Illustrated from the System of Thomas Aquinas." Trans. by E. Messenger. Introduction. 151pp. 5⅜ x 8.
T568 Paperbound $1.25

LEIBNIZ, H. W. Carr. Most stimulating middle-level coverage of basic philosophical thought of Leibniz. Easily understood discussion, analysis of major works: "Theodicy," "Principles of Nature and Grace," "Monadology"; Leibniz's influence; intellectual growth; correspondence; disputes with Bayle, Malebranche, Newton; importance of his thought today, with reinterpretation in modern terminology. "Power and mastery," London Times. Bibliography. Index. 226pp. 5⅜ x 8.
T624 Paperbound $1.35

THE SENSE OF BEAUTY, G. Santayana. A revelation of the beauty of language as well as an important philosophic treatise, this work studies the "why, when, and how beauty appears, what conditions an object must fulfill to be beautiful, what elements of our nature make us sensible of beauty, and what the relation is between the constitution of the object and the excitement of our susceptibility." "It is doubtful if a better treatment of the subject has since been published," PEABODY JOURNAL. Index. ix + 275pp. 5⅜ x 8.
T238 Paperbound **$1.00**

PROBLEMS OF ETHICS, Moritz Schlick. The renowned leader of the "Vienna Circle" applies the logical positivist approach to a wide variety of ethical problems: the source and means of attaining knowledge, the formal and material characteristics of the good, moral norms and principles, absolute vs. relative values, free will and responsibility, comparative importance of pleasure and suffering as ethical values, etc. Disarmingly simple and straightforward despite complexity of subject. First English translation, authorized by author before his death, of a thirty-year old classic. Translated and with an introduction by David Rynin. Index. Foreword by Prof. George P. Adams. xxi + 209pp. 5⅜ x 8. T946 Paperbound **$1.60**

AN INTRODUCTION TO EXISTENTIALISM, Robert G. Olson. A new and indispensable guide to one of the major thought systems of our century, the movement that is central to the thinking of some of the most creative figures of the past hundred years. Stresses Heidegger and Sartre, with careful and objective examination of the existentialist position, values—freedom of choice, individual dignity, personal love, creative effort—and answers to the eternal questions of the human condition. Scholarly, unbiased, analytic, unlike most studies of this difficult subject, Prof. Olson's book is aimed at the student of philosophy as well as at the reader with no formal training who is looking for an absorbing, accessible, and thorough introduction to the basic texts. Index. xv + 221pp. 5⅜ x 8½. T55 Paperbound **$1.65**

SYMBOLIC LOGIC, C. I. Lewis and C. H. Langford. Since first publication in 1932, this has been among most frequently cited works on symbolic logic. Still one of the best introductions both for beginners and for mathematicians, philosophers. First part covers basic topics which easily lend themselves to beginning study. Second part is rigorous, thorough development of logistic method, examination of some of most difficult and abstract aspects of symbolic logic, including modal logic, logical paradoxes, many-valued logic, with Prof. Lewis' own contributions. 2nd revised (corrected) edition. 3 appendixes, one new to this edition. 524pp. 5⅜ x 8. S170 Paperbound **$2.00**

WHITEHEAD'S PHILOSOPHY OF CIVILIZATION, A. H. Johnson. A leading authority on Alfred North Whitehead synthesizes the great philosopher's thought on civilization, scattered throughout various writings, into unified whole. Analysis of Whitehead's general definition of civilization, his reflections on history and influences on its development, his religion, including his analysis of Christianity, concept of solitariness as first requirement of personal religion, and so on. Other chapters cover views on minority groups, society, civil liberties, education. Also critical comments on Whitehead's philosophy. Written with general reader in mind. A perceptive introduction to important area of the thought of a leading philosopher of our century. Revised index and bibliography. xii + 211pp. 5⅜ x 8½.
T996 Paperbound **$1.50**

WHITEHEAD'S THEORY OF REALITY, A. H. Johnson. Introductory outline of Whitehead's theory of actual entities, the heart of his philosophy of reality, followed by his views on nature of God, philosophy of mind, theory of value (truth, beauty, goodness and their opposites), analyses of other philosophers, attitude toward science. A perspicacious lucid introduction by author of dissertation on Whitehead, written under the subject's supervision at Harvard. Good basic view for beginning students of philosophy and for those who are simply interested in important contemporary ideas. Revised index and bibliography. xiii + 267pp. 5⅜ x 8½.
T989 Paperbound **$1.50**

MIND AND THE WORLD-ORDER, C. I. Lewis. Building upon the work of Peirce, James, and Dewey, Professor Lewis outlines a theory of knowledge in terms of "conceptual pragmatism." Dividing truth into abstract mathematical certainty and empirical truth, the author demonstrates that the traditional understanding of the a priori must be abandoned. Detailed analyses of philosophy, metaphysics, method, the "given" in experience, knowledge of objects, nature of the a priori, experience and order, and many others. Appendices. xiv + 446pp. 5⅜ x 8. T359 Paperbound **$2.25**

SCEPTICISM AND ANIMAL FAITH, G. Santayana. To eliminate difficulties in the traditional theory of knowledge, Santayana distinguishes between the independent existence of objects and the essence our mind attributes to them. Scepticism is thereby established as a form of belief, and animal faith is shown to be a necessary condition of knowledge. Belief, classical idealism, intuition, memory, symbols, literary psychology, and much more, discussed with unusual clarity and depth. Index. xii + 314pp. 5⅜ x 8.
T235 Clothbound **$3.50**
T236 Paperbound **$1.75**

LANGUAGE AND MYTH, E. Cassirer. Analyzing the non-rational thought processes which go to make up culture, Cassirer demonstrates that beneath both language and myth there lies a dominant unconscious "grammar" of experience whose categories and canons are not those of logical thought. His analyses of seemingly diverse phenomena such as Indian metaphysics, the Melanesian "mana," the Naturphilosophie of Schelling, modern poetry, etc., are profound without being pedantic. Introduction and translation by Susanne Langer. Index. x + 103pp. 5⅜ x 8. T51 Paperbound **$1.25**

CATALOGUE OF DOVER BOOKS

AN ESSAY CONCERNING HUMAN UNDERSTANDING, John Locke. Edited by A. C. Fraser. Unabridged reprinting of definitive edition; only complete edition of "Essay" in print. Marginal analyses of almost every paragraph; hundreds of footnotes; authoritative 140-page biographical, critical, historical prolegomena. Indexes. 1170pp. 5⅜ x 8.
T530 Vol. 1 (Books 1, 2) Paperbound **$2.50**
T531 Vol. 2 (Books 3, 4) Paperbound **$2.50**
2 volume set **$5.00**

THE PHILOSOPHY OF HISTORY, G. W. F. Hegel. One of the great classics of western thought which reveals Hegel's basic principle: that history is not chance but a rational process, the realization of the Spirit of Freedom. Ranges from the oriental cultures of subjective thought to the classical subjective cultures, to the modern absolute synthesis where spiritual and secular may be reconciled. Translation and introduction by J. Sibree. Introduction by C. Hegel. Special introduction for this edition by Prof. Carl Friedrich. xxxix + 447pp. 5⅜ x 8.
T112 Paperbound **$2.25**

THE PHILOSOPHY OF HEGEL, W. T. Stace. The first detailed analysis of Hegel's thought in English, this is especially valuable since so many of Hegel's works are out of print. Dr. Stace examines Hegel's debt to Greek idealists and the 18th century and then proceeds to a careful description and analysis of Hegel's first principles, categories, reason, dialectic method, his logic, philosophy of nature and spirit, etc. Index. Special 14 x 20 chart of Hegelian system. x + 526pp. 5⅜ x 8.
T254 Paperbound **$2.45**

THE WILL TO BELIEVE and HUMAN IMMORTALITY, W. James. Two complete books bound as one. THE WILL TO BELIEVE discusses the interrelations of belief, will, and intellect in man; chance vs. determinism, free will vs. determinism, free will vs. fate, pluralism vs. monism; the philosophies of Hegel and Spencer, and more. HUMAN IMMORTALITY examines the question of survival after death and develops an unusual and powerful argument for immortality. Two prefaces. Index. Total of 429pp. 5⅜ x 8.
T291 Paperbound **$2.00**

THE WORLD AND THE INDIVIDUAL, Josiah Royce. Only major effort by an American philosopher to interpret nature of things in systematic, comprehensive manner. Royce's formulation of an absolute voluntarism remains one of the original and profound solutions to the problems involved. Part One, Four Historical Conceptions of Being, inquires into first principles, true meaning and place of individuality. Part Two, Nature, Man, and the Moral Order, is application of first principles to problems concerning religion, evil, moral order. Introduction by J. E. Smith, Yale Univ. Index. 1070pp. 5⅜ x 8.
T561 Vol. 1 Paperbound **$2.75**
T562 Vol. 2 Paperbound **$2.75**
Two volume set **$5.50**

THE PHILOSOPHICAL WRITINGS OF PEIRCE, edited by J. Buchler. This book (formerly THE PHILOSOPHY OF PEIRCE) is a carefully integrated exposition of Peirce's complete system composed of selections from his own work. Symbolic logic, scientific method, theory of signs, pragmatism, epistemology, chance, cosmology, ethics, and many other topics are treated by one of the greatest philosophers of modern times. This is the only inexpensive compilation of his key ideas. xvi + 386pp. 5⅜ x 8.
T217 Paperbound **$2.00**

EXPERIENCE AND NATURE, John Dewey. An enlarged, revised edition of the Paul Carus lectures which Dewey delivered in 1925. It covers Dewey's basic formulation of the problem of knowledge, with a full discussion of other systems, and a detailing of his own concepts of the relationship of external world, mind, and knowledge. Starts with a thorough examination of the philosophical method; examines the interrelationship of experience and nature; analyzes experience on basis of empirical naturalism, the formulation of law, role of language and social factors in knowledge; etc. Dewey's treatment of central problems in philosophy is profound but extremely easy to follow. ix + 448pp. 5⅜ x 8.
T471 Paperbound **$2.00**

THE PHILOSOPHICAL WORKS OF DESCARTES. The definitive English edition of all the major philosophical works and letters of René Descartes. All of his revolutionary insights, from his famous "Cogito ergo sum" to his detailed account of contemporary science and his astonishingly fruitful concept that all phenomena of the universe (except mind) could be reduced to clear laws by the use of mathematics. An excellent source for the thought of men like Hobbes, Arnauld, Gassendi, etc., who were Descarte's contemporaries. Translated by E. S. Haldane and G. Ross. Introductory notes. Index. Total of 842pp. 5⅜ x 8.
T71 Vol. 1, Paperbound **$2.00**
T72 Vol. 2, Paperbound **$2.00**

THE CHIEF WORKS OF SPINOZA. An unabridged reprint of the famous Bohn edition containing all of Spinoza's most important works: Vol. I: The Theologico-Political Treatise and the Political Treatise. Vol. II: On The Improvement Of Understanding, The Ethics, Selected Letters. Profound and enduring ideas on God, the universe, pantheism, society, religion, the state, democracy, the mind, emotions, freedom and the nature of man, which influenced Goethe, Hegel, Schelling, Coleridge, Whitehead, and many others. Introduction. 2 volumes. 826pp. 5⅜ x 8.
T249 Vol. I, Paperbound **$1.50**
T250 Vol. II, Paperbound **$1.50**

CATALOGUE OF DOVER BOOKS

THE ANALYSIS OF MATTER, Bertrand Russell. A classic which has retained its importance in understanding the relation between modern physical theory and human perception. Logical analysis of physics, prerelativity physics, causality, scientific inference, Weyl's theory, tensors, invariants and physical interpretations, periodicity, and much more is treated with Russell's usual brilliance. "Masterly piece of clear thinking and clear writing," NATION AND ATHENAEUM. "Most thorough treatment of the subject," THE NATION. Introduction. Index. 8 figures. viii + 408pp. 5⅜ x 8.   S231 Paperbound **$1.95**

CONCEPTUAL THINKING (A LOGICAL INQUIRY), S. Körner. Discusses origin, use of general concepts on which language is based, and the light they shed on basic philosophical questions. Rigorously examines how different concepts are related; how they are linked to experience; problems in the field of contact between exact logical, mathematical, and scientific concepts, and the inexactness of everyday experience (studied at length). This work elaborates many new approaches to the traditional problems of philosophy—epistemology, value theories, metaphysics, aesthetics, morality. "Rare originality . . . brings a new rigour into philosophical argument," Philosophical Quarterly. New corrected second edition. Index. vii + 301pp. 5⅜ x 8.   T516 Paperbound **$1.75**

INTRODUCTION TO SYMBOLIC LOGIC, S. Langer. No special knowledge of math required — probably the clearest book ever written on symbolic logic, suitable for the layman, general scientist, and philosopher. You start with simple symbols and advance to a knowledge of the Boole-Schroeder and Russell-Whitehead systems. Forms, logical structure, classes, the calculus of propositions, logic of the syllogism, etc., are all covered. "One of the clearest and simplest introductions," MATHEMATICS GAZETTE. Second enlarged, revised edition. 368pp. 5⅜ x 8.   S164 Paperbound **$1.85**

LANGUAGE, TRUTH AND LOGIC, A. J. Ayer. A clear, careful analysis of the basic ideas of Logical Positivism. Building on the work of Schlick, Russell, Carnap, and the Viennese School, Mr. Ayer develops a detailed exposition of the nature of philosophy, science, and metaphysics; the Self and the World; logic and common sense, and other philosophic concepts. An aid to clarity of thought as well as the first full-length development of Logical Positivism in English. Introduction by Bertrand Russell. Index. 160pp. 5⅜ x 8.   T10 Paperbound **$1.25**

ESSAYS IN EXPERIMENTAL LOGIC, J. Dewey. Based upon the theory that knowledge implies a judgment which in turn implies an inquiry, these papers consider the inquiry stage in terms of: the relationship of thought and subject matter, antecedents of thought, data and meanings. 3 papers examine Bertrand Russell's thought, while 2 others discuss pragmatism and a final essay presents a new theory of the logic of values. Index. viii + 444pp. 5⅜ x 8.   T73 Paperbound **$2.25**

TRAGIC SENSE OF LIFE, M. de Unamuno. The acknowledged masterpiece of one of Spain's most influential thinkers. Between the despair at the inevitable death of man and all his works and the desire for something better, Unamuno finds that "saving incertitude" that alone can console us. This dynamic appraisal of man's faith in God and in himself has been called "a masterpiece" by the ENCYCLOPAEDIA BRITANNICA. xxx + 332pp. 5⅜ x 8.   T257 Paperbound **$2.00**

HISTORY OF DOGMA, A. Harnack. Adolph Harnack, who died in 1930, was perhaps the greatest Church historian of all time. In this epoch-making history, which has never been surpassed in comprehensiveness and wealth of learning, he traces the development of the authoritative Christian doctrinal system from its first crystallization in the 4th century down through the Reformation, including also a brief survey of the later developments through the Infallibility decree of 1870. He reveals the enormous influence of Greek thought on the early Fathers, and discusses such topics as the Apologists, the great councils, Manichaeism, the historical position of Augustine, the medieval opposition to indulgences, the rise of Protestantism, the relations of Luther's doctrines with modern tendencies of thought, and much more. "Monumental work; still the most valuable history of dogma . . . luminous analysis of the problems . . . abounds in suggestion and stimulus and can be neglected by no one who desires to understand the history of thought in this most important field," Dutcher's Guide to Historical Literature. Translated by Neil Buchanan. Index. Unabridged reprint in 4 volumes. Vol I: Beginnings to the Gnostics and Marcion. Vol II & III: 2nd century to the 4th century Fathers. Vol IV & V: 4th century Councils to the Carlovingian Renaissance. Vol VI & VII: Period of Clugny (c. 1000) to the Reformation, and after. Total of cii + 2407pp. 5⅜ x 8.

T904 Vol I	Paperbound	**$2.50**
T905 Vol II & III	Paperbound	**$2.75**
T906 Vol IV & V	Paperbound	**$2.75**
T907 Vol VI & VII	Paperbound	**$2.75**
	The set	**$10.75**

THE GUIDE FOR THE PERPLEXED, Maimonides. One of the great philosophical works of all time and a necessity for everyone interested in the philosophy of the Middle Ages in the Jewish, Christian, and Moslem traditions. Maimonides develops a common meeting-point for the Old Testament and the Aristotelian thought which pervaded the medieval world. His ideas and methods predate such scholastics as Aquinas and Scotus and throw light on the entire problem of philosophy or science vs. religion. 2nd revised edition. Complete unabridged Friedländer translation. 55 page introduction to Maimonides's life, period, etc., with an important summary of the GUIDE. Index. lix + 414pp. 5⅜ x 8.   T351 Paperbound **$2.00**

Psychology

YOGA: A SCIENTIFIC EVALUATION, Kovoor T. Behanan. A complete reprinting of the book that for the first time gave Western readers a sane, scientific explanation and analysis of yoga. The author draws on controlled laboratory experiments and personal records of a year as a disciple of a yoga, to investigate yoga psychology, concepts of knowledge, physiology, "supernatural" phenomena, and the ability to tap the deepest human powers. In this study under the auspices of Yale University Institute of Human Relations, the strictest principles of physiological and psychological inquiry are followed throughout. Foreword by W. A. Miles, Yale University. 17 photographs. Glossary. Index. xx + 270pp. 5⅜ x 8. T505 Paperbound **$2.00**

CONDITIONED REFLEXES: AN INVESTIGATION OF THE PHYSIOLOGICAL ACTIVITIES OF THE CEREBRAL CORTEX, I. P. Pavlov. Full, authorized translation of Pavlov's own survey of his work in experimental psychology reviews entire course of experiments, summarizes conclusions, outlines psychological system based on famous "conditioned reflex" concept. Details of technical means used in experiments, observations on formation of conditioned reflexes, function of cerebral hemispheres, results of damage, nature of sleep, typology of nervous system, significance of experiments for human psychology. Trans. by Dr. G. V. Anrep, Cambridge Univ. 235-item bibliography. 18 figures. 445pp. 5⅜ x 8. S614 Paperbound **$2.35**

EXPLANATION OF HUMAN BEHAVIOUR, F. V. Smith. A major intermediate-level introduction to and criticism of 8 complete systems of the psychology of human behavior, with unusual emphasis on theory of investigation and methodology. Part I is an illuminating analysis of the problems involved in the explanation of observed phenomena, and the differing viewpoints on the nature of causality. Parts II and III are a closely detailed survey of the systems of McDougall, Gordon Allport, Lewin, the Gestalt group, Freud, Watson, Hull, and Tolman. Biographical notes. Bibliography of over 800 items. 2 Indexes. 38 figures. xii + 460pp. 5½ x 8¾. T253 Clothbound **$6.00**

SEX IN PSYCHO-ANALYSIS (formerly CONTRIBUTIONS TO PSYCHO-ANALYSIS), S. Ferenczi. Written by an associate of Freud, this volume presents countless insights on such topics as impotence, transference, analysis and children, dreams, symbols, obscene words, masturbation and male homosexuality, paranoia and psycho-analysis, the sense of reality, hypnotism and therapy, and many others. Also includes full text of THE DEVELOPMENT OF PSYCHO-ANALYSIS by Ferenczi and Otto Rank. Two books bound as one. Total of 406pp. 5⅜ x 8. T324 Paperbound **$1.85**

BEYOND PSYCHOLOGY, Otto Rank. One of Rank's most mature contributions, focussing on the irrational basis of human behavior as a basic fact of our lives. The psychoanalytic techniques of myth analysis trace to their source the ultimates of human existence: fear of death, personality, the social organization, the need for love and creativity, etc. Dr. Rank finds them stemming from a common irrational source, man's fear of final destruction. A seminal work in modern psychology, this work sheds light on areas ranging from the concept of immortal soul to the sources of state power. 291pp. 5⅜ x 8. T485 Paperbound **$2.00**

ILLUSIONS AND DELUSIONS OF THE SUPERNATURAL AND THE OCCULT, D. H. Rawcliffe. Holds up to rational examination hundreds of persistent delusions including crystal gazing, automatic writing, table turning, mediumistic trances, mental healing, stigmata, lycanthropy, live burial, the Indian Rope Trick, spiritualism, dowsing, telepathy, clairvoyance, ghosts, ESP, etc. The author explains and exposes the mental and physical deceptions involved, making this not only an exposé of supernatural phenomena, but a valuable exposition of characteristic types of abnormal psychology. Originally titled "The Psychology of the Occult." 14 illustrations. Index. 551pp. 5⅜ x 8. T503 Paperbound **$2.00**

THE PRINCIPLES OF PSYCHOLOGY, William James. The full long-course, unabridged, of one of the great classics of Western literature and science. Wonderfully lucid descriptions of human mental activity, the stream of thought, consciousness, time perception, memory, imagination, emotions, reason, abnormal phenomena, and similar topics. Original contributions are integrated with the work of such men as Berkeley, Binet, Mills, Darwin, Hume, Kant, Royce, Schopenhauer, Spinoza, Locke, Descartes, Galton, Wundt, Lotze, Herbart, Fechner, and scores of others. All contrasting interpretations of mental phenomena are examined in detail — introspective analysis, philosophical interpretation, and experimental research. "A classic," JOURNAL OF CONSULTING PSYCHOLOGY. "The main lines are as valid as ever," PSYCHO-ANALYTICAL QUARTERLY. "Standard reading . . . a classic of interpretation," PSYCHIATRIC QUARTERLY. 94 illustrations. 1408pp. 2 volumes. 5⅜ x 8. Vol. 1, T381 Paperbound **$2.50** / Vol. 2, T382 Paperbound **$2.50**

THE DYNAMICS OF THERAPY IN A CONTROLLED RELATIONSHIP, Jessie Taft. One of the most important works in literature of child psychology, out of print for 25 years. Outstanding disciple of Rank describes all aspects of relationship or Rankian therapy through concise, simple elucidation of theory underlying her actual contacts with two seven-year olds. Therapists, social caseworkers, psychologists, counselors, and laymen who work with children will all find this important work an invaluable summation of method, theory of child psychology. xix + 296pp. 5⅜ x 8. T325 Paperbound **$1.75**

Teach Yourself

These British books are the most effective series of home study books on the market! With no outside help they will teach you as much as is necessary to have a good background in each subject, in many cases offering as much material as a similar high school or college course. They are carefully planned, written by foremost British educators, and amply provided with test questions and problems for you to check your progress; the mathematics books are especially rich in examples and problems. Do not confuse them with skimpy outlines or ordinary school texts or vague generalized popularizations; each book is complete in itself, full without being overdetailed, and designed to give you an easily-acquired branch of knowledge.

TEACH YOURSELF ALGEBRA, P. Abbott. The equivalent of a thorough high school course, up through logarithms. 52 illus. 307pp. 4¼ x 7. T680 Clothbound **$2.00**

TEACH YOURSELF GEOMETRY, P. Abbott. Plane and solid geometry, covering about a year of plane and six months of solid. 268 illus. 344pp. 4½ x 7. T681 Clothbound **$2.00**

TEACH YOURSELF TRIGONOMETRY, P. Abbott. Background of algebra and geometry will enable you to get equivalent of elementary college course. Tables. 102 illus. 204pp. 4½ x 7. T682 Clothbound **$2.00**

TEACH YOURSELF THE CALCULUS, P. Abbott. With algebra and trigonometry you will be able to acquire a good working knowledge of elementary integral calculus and differential calculus. Excellent supplement to any course textbook. 380pp. 4¼ x 7. T683 Clothbound **$2.00**

TEACH YOURSELF THE SLIDE RULE, B. Snodgrass. Basic principles clearly explained, with many applications in engineering, business, general figuring, will enable you to pick up very useful skill. 10 illus. 207pp. 4¼ x 7. T684 Clothbound **$2.00**

TEACH YOURSELF MECHANICS, P. Abbott. Equivalent of part course on elementary college level, with lever, parallelogram of force, friction, laws of motion, gases, etc. Fine introduction before more advanced course. 163 illus. 271pp. 4½ x 7. T685 Clothbound **$2.00**

TEACH YOURSELF ELECTRICITY, C. W. Wilman. Current, resistance, voltage, Ohm's law, circuits, generators, motors, transformers, etc. Non-mathematical as much as possible. 115 illus. 184pp. 4¼ x 7. T230 Clothbound **$2.00**

TEACH YOURSELF HEAT ENGINES E. DeVille. Steam and internal combustion engines; non-mathematical introduction for student, for layman wishing background, refresher for advanced student. 76 illus. 217pp. 4¼ x 7. T237 Clothbound **$2.00**

TEACH YOURSELF TO PLAY THE PIANO, King Palmer. Companion and supplement to lessons or self study. Handy reference, too. Nature of instrument, elementary musical theory, technique of playing, interpretation, etc. 60 illus. 144pp. 4¼ x 7. T959 Clothbound **$2.00**

TEACH YOURSELF HERALDRY AND GENEALOGY, L. G. Pine. Modern work, avoiding romantic and overpopular misconceptions. Editor of new Burke presents detailed information and commentary down to present. Best general survey. 50 illus. glossary; 129pp. 4¼ x 7. T962 Clothbound **$2.00**

TEACH YOURSELF HANDWRITING, John L. Dumpleton. Basic Chancery cursive style is popular and easy to learn. Many diagrams. 114 illus. 192pp. 4¼ x 7. T960 Clothbound **$2.00**

TEACH YOURSELF CARD GAMES FOR TWO, Kenneth Konstam. Many first-rate games, including old favorites like cribbage and gin and canasta as well as new lesser-known games. Extremely interesting for cards enthusiast. 60 illus. 150pp. 4¼ x 7. T963 Clothbound **$2.00**

TEACH YOURSELF GUIDEBOOK TO THE DRAMA, Luis Vargas. Clear, rapid survey of changing fashions and forms from Aeschylus to Tennessee Williams, in all major European traditions. Plot summaries, critical comments, etc. Equivalent of a college drama course; fine cultural background 224pp. 4¼ x 7. T961 Clothbound **$2.00**

TEACH YOURSELF THE ORGAN, Francis Routh. Excellent compendium of background material for everyone interested in organ music, whether as listener or player. 27 musical illus. 158pp. 4¼ x 7. T977 Clothbound **$2.00**

TEACH YOURSELF TO STUDY SCULPTURE, William Gaunt. Noted British cultural historian surveys culture from Greeks, primitive world, to moderns. Equivalent of college survey course. 23 figures, 40 photos. 158pp. 4¼ x 7. T976 Clothbound **$2.00**

History of Science and Mathematics

THE STUDY OF THE HISTORY OF MATHEMATICS, THE STUDY OF THE HISTORY OF SCIENCE, G. Sarton. Two books bound as one. Each volume contains a long introduction to the methods and philosophy of each of these historical fields, covering the skills and sympathies of the historian, concepts of history of science, psychology of idea-creation, and the purpose of history of science. Prof. Sarton also provides more than 80 pages of classified bibliography. Complete and unabridged. Indexed. 10 illustrations. 188pp. 5⅜ x 8.   T240 Paperbound **$1.25**

A HISTORY OF PHYSICS, Florian Cajori, Ph.D. First written in 1899, thoroughly revised in 1929, this is still best entry into antecedents of modern theories. Precise non-mathematical discussion of ideas, theories, techniques, apparatus of each period from Greeks to 1920's, analyzing within each period basic topics of matter, mechanics, light, electricity and magnetism, sound, atomic theory, etc. Stress on modern developments, from early 19th century to present. Written with critical eye on historical development, significance. Provides most of needed historical background for student of physics. Reprint of second (1929) edition. Index. Bibliography in footnotes. 16 figures. xv + 424pp. 5⅜ x 8.   T970 Paperbound **$2.00**

A HISTORY OF ASTRONOMY FROM THALES TO KEPLER, J. L. E. Dreyer. Formerly titled A HISTORY OF PLANETARY SYSTEMS FROM THALES TO KEPLER. This is the only work in English which provides a detailed history of man's cosmological views from prehistoric times up through the Renaissance. It covers Egypt, Babylonia, early Greece, Alexandria, the Middle Ages, Copernicus, Tycho Brahe, Kepler, and many others. Epicycles and other complex theories of positional astronomy are explained in terms nearly everyone will find clear and easy to understand. "Standard reference on Greek astronomy and the Copernican revolution," SKY AND TELE-SCOPE. Bibliography. 21 diagrams. Index. xvii + 430pp. 5⅜ x 8.   S79 Paperbound **$2.25**

A SHORT HISTORY OF ASTRONOMY, A. Berry. A popular standard work for over 50 years, this thorough and accurate volume covers the science from primitive times to the end of the 19th century. After the Greeks and Middle Ages, individual chapters analyze Copernicus, Brahe, Galileo, Kepler, and Newton, and the mixed reception of their startling discoveries. Post-Newtonian achievements are then discussed in unusual detail: Halley, Bradley, Lagrange, Laplace, Herschel, Bessel, etc. 2 indexes. 104 illustrations, 9 portraits. xxxi + 440pp. 5⅜ x 8.   T210 Paperbound **$2.00**

PIONEERS OF SCIENCE, Sir Oliver Lodge. An authoritative, yet elementary history of science by a leading scientist and expositor. Concentrating on individuals—Copernicus, Brahe, Kepler, Galileo, Descartes, Newton, Laplace, Herschel, Lord Kelvin, and other scientists—the author presents their discoveries in historical order, adding biographical material on each man and full, specific explanations of their achievements. The full, clear discussions of the accomplishments of post-Newtonian astronomers are features seldom found in other books on the subject. Index. 120 illustrations. xv + 404pp. 5⅜ x 8.   T716 Paperbound **$1.65**

THE BIRTH AND DEVELOPMENT OF THE GEOLOGICAL SCIENCES, F. D. Adams. The most complete and thorough history of the earth sciences in print. Geological thought from earliest recorded times to the end of the 19th century—covers over 300 early thinkers and systems: fossils and hypothetical explanations of them, vulcanists vs. neptunists, figured stones and paleontology, generation of stones, and similar topics. 91 illustrations, including medieval, renaissance woodcuts, etc. 632 footnotes and bibliographic notes. Index. 511pp. 5⅜ x 8.   T5 Paperbound **$2.25**

THE STORY OF ALCHEMY AND EARLY CHEMISTRY, J. M. Stillman. "Add the blood of a red-haired man"—a recipe typical of the many quoted in this authoritative and readable history of the strange beliefs and practices of the alchemists. Concise studies of every leading figure in alchemy and early chemistry through Lavoisier, in this curious epic of superstition and true science, constructed from scores of rare and difficult Greek, Latin, German, and French texts. Foreword by S. W. Young. 246-item bibliography. Index. xiii + 566pp. 5⅜ x 8.   S628 Paperbound **$2.45**

HISTORY OF MATHEMATICS, D. E. Smith. Most comprehensive non-technical history of math in English. Discusses the lives and works of over a thousand major and minor figures, from Euclid to Descartes, Gauss, and Riemann. Vol. I: A chronological examination, from primitive concepts through Egypt, Babylonia, Greece, the Orient, Rome, the Middle Ages, the Renaissance, and up to 1900. Vol. 2: The development of ideas in specific fields and problems, up through elementary calculus. Two volumes, total of 510 illustrations, 1355pp. 5⅜ x 8. Set boxed in attractive container.   T429,430 Paperbound the set **$5.00**

A CONCISE HISTORY OF MATHEMATICS, D. Struik. A lucid, easily followed history of mathematical ideas and techniques from the Ancient Near East up to modern times. Requires no mathematics but will serve as an excellent introduction to mathematical concepts and great mathematicians through the method of historical development. 60 illustrations including Egyptian papyri, Greek mss., portraits of 31 eminent mathematicians. Bibliography. xix + 299pp. 5⅜ x 8. T255 Paperbound **$1.75**

A SHORT ACCOUNT OF THE HISTORY OF MATHEMATICS, W. W. Rouse Ball. Last previous edition (1908) hailed by mathematicians and laymen for lucid overview of math as living science, for understandable presentation of individual contributions of great mathematicians. Treats lives, discoveries of every important school and figure from Egypt, Phoenicia to late nineteenth century. Greek schools of Ionia, Cyzicus, Alexandria, Byzantium, Pythagoras; primitive arithmetic; Middle Ages and Renaissance, including European and Asiatic contributions; modern math of Descartes, Pascal, Wallis, Huygens, Newton, Euler, Lambert, Laplace, scores more. More emphasis on historical development, exposition of ideas than other books on subject. Non-technical, readable text can be followed with no more preparation than high-school algebra. Index. 544pp. 5⅜ x 8. S630 Paperbound **$2.00**

ON MATHEMATICS AND MATHEMATICIANS, R. E. Moritz. A ten year labor of love by the discerning and discriminating Prof. Moritz, this collection has rarely been equalled in its ability to convey the full sense of mathematics and the personalities of great mathematicians. A collection of anecdotes, aphorisms, reminiscences, philosophies, definitions, speculations, biographical insights, etc., by great mathematicians and writers: Descartes, Mill, De Morgan, Locke, Berkeley, Kant, Coleridge, Whitehead, Sylvester, Klein, and many others. Also, glimpses into the lives of mathematical giants from Archimedes to Euler, Gauss, and Weierstrass. To mathematicians, a superb book for browsing; to writers and teachers, an unequalled source of quotation; to the layman, an exciting revelation of the fullness of mathematics. Extensive cross index. 410pp. 5⅜ x 8. T489 Paperbound **$1.95**

SIR ISAAC NEWTON: A BIOGRAPHY, Louis Trenchard More. Standard, definitive biography of Newton, covering every phase of his life and career in its presentation of the renowned scientific genius as a living man. Objective, critical analysis of his character as well as a careful survey of his manifold accomplishments in many areas of science, and in theology, history, politics, finance. Text includes letters by Newton and acquaintances, many other papers, some translated from Latin to English by the author. Scientists, teachers of science will especially be interested in this book, which will appeal to all readers concerned with history of ideas, development of science. Republication of original (1934) edition. 1 full-page plate. Index. xii + 675pp. 5⅜ x 8½. S79 Paperbound **$2.50**

GUIDE TO THE LITERATURE OF MATHEMATICS AND PHYSICS, N. G. Parke III. Over 5000 entries included under approximately 120 major subject headings, of selected most important books, monographs, periodicals, articles in English, plus important works in German, French, Italian, Spanish, Russian (many recently available works). Covers every branch of physics, math, related engineering. Includes author, title, edition, publisher, place, date, number of volumes, number of pages. A 40-page introduction on the basic problems of research and study provides useful information on the organization and use of libraries, the psychology of learning, etc. This reference work will save you hours of time. 2nd revised edition. Indices of authors, subjects. 464pp. 5⅜ x 8. S447 Paperbound **$2.49**

Prices subject to change without notice.

Dover publishes books on art, music, philosophy, literature, languages, history, social sciences, psychology, handcrafts, orientalia, puzzles and entertainments, chess, pets and gardens, books explaining science, intermediate and higher mathematics, mathematical physics, engineering, biological sciences, earth sciences, classics of science, etc. Write to:

Dept. catrr.
Dover Publications, Inc.
180 Varick Street, N.Y. 14, N.Y.